TRULY HUMAN

Indigeneity and Indigenous Resurgence on Formosa

T0355624

The Sediq and Truku Indigenous peoples on the mountainous island of Formosa – today called Taiwan – say that their ancestors emerged in the beginning of time from Pusu Qhuni, a tree-covered boulder in the highlands. Living in the mountain forests, they observed the sacred law of Gaya, seeking equilibrium with other humans, the spirits, animals, and plants. They developed a politics in which each community preserved its autonomy and sharing was valued more highly than personal accumulation of goods or power. These lifeworlds were shattered by colonialism, capitalist development, and cultural imperialism in the twentieth century.

Based on two decades of ethnographic field research, *Truly Human* portrays these peoples' lifeworlds, teachings, political struggles for recognition, and relations with non-human animals. Taking seriously their ontological claims that Gaya offers moral guidance to all humans, Scott E. Simon reflects on what this particular form of Indigenous resurgence reveals about human rights, sovereignty, and the good of all kind. *Truly Human* contributes to a decolonizing anthropology at a time when all humans need Indigenous land-based teachings more than ever.

(Anthropological Horizons)

SCOTT E. SIMON is a professor in the School of Sociological and Anthropological Studies at the University of Ottawa.

ANTHROPOLOGICAL HORIZONS

Editor: Michael Lambek, University of Toronto

This series, begun in 1991, focuses on theoretically informed ethnographic works addressing issues of mind and body, knowledge and power, equality and inequality, the individual and the collective. Interdisciplinary in its perspective, the series makes a unique contribution in several other academic disciplines: women's studies, history, philosophy, psychology, political science, and sociology.

For a list of the books published in this series, see page 363.

Truly Human

*Indigeneity and Indigenous
Resurgence on Formosa*

SCOTT E. SIMON

UNIVERSITY OF TORONTO PRESS
Toronto Buffalo London

© University of Toronto Press 2023
Toronto Buffalo London
utorontopress.com
Printed and bound by CPI Group (UK) Ltd, Croydon, CR0 4YY

ISBN 978-1-4875-4733-2 (cloth)   ISBN 978-1-4875-4601-4 (EPUB)
ISBN 978-1-4875-4586-4 (paper)   ISBN 978-1-4875-4954-1 (PDF)

Anthropological Horizons

Library and Archives Canada Cataloguing in Publication

Title: Truly human : indigeneity and indigenous resurgence on Formosa /
    Scott E. Simon.
Names: Simon, Scott, 1965–, author.
Description: Includes bibliographical references and index.
Identifiers: Canadiana (print) 20220484864 | Canadiana (ebook)
    20220484937 | ISBN 9781487547332 (hardcover) |
    ISBN 9781487545864 (softover) | ISBN 9781487546014 (EPUB) |
    ISBN 9781487549541 (PDF)
Subjects: LCSH: Truku (Taiwan people) | LCSH: Taiwan aborigines. |
    LCSH: Ethnology – Taiwan.
Classification: LCC DS799.43.T66 S56 2023 | DDC 951.249/0049925 – dc23

We wish to acknowledge the land on which the University of Toronto
Press operates. This land is the traditional territory of the Wendat, the
Anishnaabeg, the Haudenosaunee, the Métis, and the Mississaugas of the
Credit First Nation.

This book has been published with the help of a grant from the Federation
for the Humanities and Social Sciences, through the Awards to Scholarly
Publications Program, using funds provided by the Social Sciences and
Humanities Research Council of Canada.

University of Toronto Press acknowledges the financial support of the
Government of Canada, the Canada Council for the Arts, and the Ontario Arts
Council, an agency of the Government of Ontario, for its publishing activities.

Canada Council
for the Arts
Conseil des Arts
du Canada

ONTARIO ARTS COUNCIL
CONSEIL DES ARTS DE L'ONTARIO
an Ontario government agency
un organisme du gouvernement de l'Ontario

Funded by the   Financé par le
Government   gouvernement
of Canada   du Canada

This book is dedicated in loving memory of

Yudaw Pisaw 田信德 *(1925–2015)*
Tadaw Mowna 黃明源 *(1929–2018)*
Rabay Rubing 簡金美 *(1932–2022)*
Igung Shiban 田春綢 *(1943–2022)*
Kuhon Sibal 田貴芳 *(1946–2020)*
Dakis Pawan 郭明正 *(1954–2021)*
And the younger lupung *(friends) who also crossed the Rainbow Bridge,*
much too soon.
Mhuway namu balay!

These aboriginal inhabitants held the island to be theirs by the right of centuries of possession; and when the Chinese came they were regarded as intruders, who would not respect native rights.

– Canadian missionary George Leslie Mackay (1895) 2005, 268

The land is our blood. The mountain forest is our home. Only with hunters do we have land. Only with hunters do we have wild animals.

– Tera Yudaw (Truku) at the United Nations (2007)

Contents

Maps, Illustrations, and Tables

Maps

Illustrations

Tables

Note on Orthography and Pronunciation

Chinese is rendered in the Hanyu pinyin widely used in international sinology, with the exception of most personal names and words that are customarily rendered in Wade-Giles, for example, "Taipei" instead of "Taibei," "Kaohsiung" instead of "Gaoxiong." The result is the idiosyncratic mixture that reflects what one sees in Taiwan. Revised Hepburn is used for Japanese.

Language materials are being developed for Seediq (Tgdaya), Sediq (Toda), and Sejiq (Truku) in Nantou, as well as for Truku as spoken in Hualien. Although the research for this book was done in Nantou and Hualien, and with Tgdaya and Truku speakers, most of the research was done with Hualien Truku speakers. For the sake of consistency, words are rendered in Hualien Truku unless otherwise indicated.

Vowels

English comparisons are approximate.

a, as in "f<u>a</u>ther"
e, as in "l<u>a</u>ke"
i, as in "s<u>ee</u>"; or sometimes, after *h* and *q*, *é* as in "ob<u>ey</u>"
o, as in "t<u>o</u>tal"
u, as in "m<u>oo</u>n"
aw, as in "<u>ow</u>l"
ay, as in "<u>ai</u>sle"
ey, as in "ob<u>ey</u>"
ow, as in "l<u>ow</u>"

Consonants

Most consonants are similar to English, with the following exceptions:

c, as in "ca<u>ts</u>" but without aspiration; but as in "gel" before *i* and *y*
g, as in "girl" but with very strong friction
h, has a very strong aspiration, voiced glottal fricative, as in "a<u>h</u>a"
k, pronounced without aspiration, but not as hard as *g*
j, as in "ju<u>dge</u>"
l, voiced alveolar lateral fricative is one of the most difficult sounds, made by putting the tongue between one's teeth and pronouncing *l*, while pushing air through both sides of the tongue
q, voiceless uvular stop, like the Arabic *q*
r, vibratory alveolar, flap *r*, as in "ci<u>t</u>y" (American accent)
s, as in ve<u>ss</u>el with more emphasis; but as "<u>sh</u>eep" before *i*
t, pronounced without aspiration, but not as hard as *d*
x, like the German *ch*, as in "doch"
ng, nasal like si<u>ng</u>ing
', glottal stop

Multiple consonants are pronounced with a very short schwa (ə) between them. For example, Truku is pronounced *Tᵊruku*, and *mgaya* is pronounced *mᵊgaya*.

Exchange rate: New Taiwanese dollar (NT$), average of NT$23 to one CAD$ from 2017–20.

Preface and Acknowledgments

The initial inspiration for this book was sparked by a conversation with an elder shopkeeper in Gluban, a rice farming village in central Taiwan. It was my third year of research on indigeneity and development in Taiwan. At the time, local leaders were lobbying their government for legal recognition as an Indigenous group and had decorated the roads across the township proclaiming their national identity. Frustrated by being classified as part of a larger group known as the Atayal, they imagined a confederation of villages who spoke the closely related languages or dialects of Truku, Tgdaya, and Toda. Because all three of those languages in the Tgdaya village of Gluban used a very similar term, *seediq*, to mean "human," they proposed that the new Indigenous nation would carry the name Seediq. The shopkeeper suddenly said to me: "Have you seen all those flags along the side of the road with the word 'Seediq' printed all over them? Those politicians are hoping to make new positions for themselves by calling us Seediq. Seediq is not an appropriate term for an ethnic name that is meant to categorize and divide people. That is too narrow-minded. It just means human being."

Pointing his index finger in my chest, he said: "You, too, are seediq." He reminded me in Chinese that I may be a foreigner, but I am also human. As if to drive the point in deeper, he repeated in Seediq: "*Isu uri seediq o.*"

Those words lit a fire in my heart. After all, I was trained as an anthropologist. I had been taught to classify humans into discrete cultures and to believe that the sociolinguistic differences between them are the most salient ways of understanding ways of being in the world. He was telling me something different. He was telling me that, even though we came from opposite sides of the planet, we were united by our common belonging to an ontological category called seediq, which he repeated means human. In the immediate context, the important point was that a small group of political leaders were misguided to reserve this word to label a group of maybe ten thousand people, somehow implying that everyone else was less than human. He even portrayed their political agenda as a moral failure. I left his shop wondering what it would be like to reflect upon what it means to be human, rather than what it means to live culturally as Atayal or Seediq or Truku, or even Taiwanese or Chinese or whatnot. I also realized that his understanding of seediq as a universal ontological category had its own social and historical trajectory that overlaps with, but does not have the same ontological connotations as the English "human" or the Chinese *ren* 人. I would spend years trying to reconcile this teaching, which I cannot ignore because it comes from a respected Indigenous elder, with my own support for Indigenous rights movements, including the right of his community to join with others and seek legal state recognition as a Seediq Nation (Simon 2008).

This conversation was even more unsettling to me because it happened in Gluban, which, as this book will show, lies at the very centre of what it means to be "Indigenous" in Taiwan. Assuming that Indigenous and non-indigenous were the most relevant ontological categories, I was researching what development means to the Indigenous peoples of Taiwan. I expected to find widespread and open resistance to development projects, with Indigenous peoples "in the way" of development (Blaser, Feit, and McRae 2004). Although I did find resistance, especially localized protests against mines, national parks, and the criminalization of hunting, in everyday life, I was just as likely to encounter people content to make a living as mine or national park employees. No matter what political opinions they held, they were all motivated to send their children to school in Chinese so that they could succeed in school and earn a living in modern society.

Over nearly two decades of research, I encountered a great variety of people in Taiwan with Indigenous identity. I met construction workers and mining engineers, day labourers and people who seem to get by with no work at all, grade school teachers and university professors, people who make a solid income as members of bureaucracies of indigeneity as well as others who obtained high positions as talented, well-connected individuals. I met entrepreneurs who opened humble general stores, others who sell Amway products, and some with larger scale projects that take them well beyond Taiwan. I met some who deplored the loss of their traditional hunting traditions due to the imposition of national parks on their forests, and others who, seemingly with no regret, cut down forests to make way for tea or cabbage plantations. I met others who seem to have left this all behind, even one woman who made a career in Belgium singing Italian opera. I studied with the people who, during my research, came to inhabit political identities of Truku and Sediq in contemporary Taiwan. Although they collectively number around 44,000 people, they are as diverse in their way of experiencing development as are the other 23 million people in Taiwan, or as in our own societies. In order to do field research with them, and in order to write a book about them, I had to make decisions about the people with whom I interact and the stories I tell. I had my biases.

Like some of these people, especially those who would be labelled in more Marxian approaches as working class or lumpenproletariat, I found myself attracted to the mountains and forests that bordered their villages in central and eastern Taiwan. Over the years, the people who know those mountains the most intimately were generous with their time, with their knowledge, and with their meat. They offered to teach me a world very different from the world of universities, bureaucracies, and corporations, a world that attracts many of their brethren and with which they have certainly identified me, an anthropology professor from a Canadian university. When hunters and trappers took me up the mountain paths, teaching me about deer, birds, ferns much bigger than me, and ultimately about such things as sacred law and ritual, they challenged me intellectually. They took me away from the Marxian political economy that I loved so much, mentoring me in such topics as ethno-ornithology as well as in more typical anthropological preoccupations such as ritual. As the years passed, I slowly realized that they were sharing with me their lifeworlds and ontologies, their ways of perceiving not only development but also their political situation in general. Industrial development and globalization on one side, an affirmation of ancestral spirits and animal life on the other, all experienced through various relations with other humans and in a particular way of being universally human, are all part of the same story. Learning about the forest provides new ways of understanding mines and factories. Even without open protest, the people who highly value the forests and their inhabitants affirm life projects that still get in the way of development.

I began writing this book in a very special and unexpected place – at the Institut für Ethnologie at the University of Heidelberg, Germany. It was, as one would expect from a 630-year-old institution, an unparalleled intellectual experience. For four months as a visiting professor in 2016, my thinking and writing were inspired by serendipitous findings in the library and stimulating conversations with Professor Guido Sprenger, as well as his colleagues and students. I nearly finished the book in 2017–18 at another special place, the National Museum for

Ethnology in Osaka, Japan. There I had the pleasure of working with Professor Nobayashi Atsushi on "The Material Ecology of Human-Animal Relations in Japan and Taiwan." This work got me started on my new project on human-animal relations in the western Pacific and gave me time to finish this book in what is one of the most intellectually nourishing places available to an anthropologist. I did further revisions in the summers of 2020 and 2021, when the global COVID-19 pandemic confined me to my home on unceded Algonquin territory in Quebec, nestled between *Te-nagàdino-zìbi* (Gatineau River) and Gatineau Park. I began to realize that Sediq-Truku people had also taught me a different way of perceiving the place where I came from.

Of course, between periods of fieldwork and periods of retreat and writing, I lived in Canada during a time of Indigenous resurgence. In December 2013, as the Indigenous movement Idle No More brought protests to the streets across Canada, Chief Theresa Spence of Attawapiskat began a hunger strike on Victoria Island in the middle of the Ottawa River. When the news became international, the Indigenous leaders of Taiwan's tiny First Nations Party of Taiwan wrote a letter of support in Chinese and sent it to me so that I could translate it into English and deliver it to Chief Spence. I was myself getting closer to Algonquin people, fully aware that I was living and working on unceded territory of that nation. I attended activities of Kitigan Zibi elder *Comis* (Grandfather) William Commanda (1913–2011) when he held the international "Circle of All Nations" gatherings in front of his home. I also participated in activities run by his protégé Comis Dominique Rankin and *Kokum* (Grandmother) Marie-Josée Tardif, who founded the Kina8at (meaning "together" organization) to promote First Nations cultural reconnection and reconciliation with everyone. Recollecting my experience with the Seediq, I was moved by the way in which Dominique repeatedly taught everyone that the word *anicinape* means "human" and that "you should not forget to be anicinape." He also reminds me that the Indigenous nations of Turtle Island are related to those of Asia and the Pacific Islands (Rankin and Tardif 2020, 29). As in Taiwan, I cannot ignore the words of an Indigenous elder who shares these teachings with honest and good intention. In fact, everyone who shares teachings with me knows that I am a teacher and a writer, so I have the responsibility of passing down the understandings that I learn from them in an honest and respectful manner. This responsibility makes what I teach and write into my personal journey of learning, combining mind and heart knowledge in what Algonquin scholar Lynn Gehl taught me is called my *debwewin* in Algonquin (Gehl 2014, 8).

One thing I have learned from Algonquin teachers is that it is proper protocol to begin with a self-introduction. I was born in Fort Wayne, Indiana (or Kekionga, land of the Miami Nation), but had a cross-border childhood. My father claimed German ancestry and, when I queried him and my grandfather about genealogy, they both told me that "the Simons were once Jewish," leaving me wondering if they were proud of having Jewish roots or of having become Christian. My mother's parents had moved to Fort Wayne from Toronto for work reasons, the happenstance that allowed my mother to meet my father and me to be born. I thus grew up with annual visits across the Ambassador Bridge from Detroit to Windsor so that we could visit relatives across southern Ontario and as far as Toronto. My Canadian grandmother encouraged me to study at McGill, which I did for graduate school, and I decided to spend my adult life in Canada. Only after my grandmother passed away and left me her Bible collection, did I read through some old documents and discover a family connection with Indigenous Taiwan. Her parents, themselves newly arrived from England, were members of the Bonar Presbyterian Church in Toronto and helped raise funds for missionary efforts in the Japanese colony of Formosa (the name for Taiwan at the time). In Chinese, my relationship with Indigenous Formosa is thus an intergenerational *yuanfen* 緣分 (destiny). It is also no coincidence that I established the most intimate rapport in Taiwan with people much like my father: church-going, working-class men who enjoy walking in the forest, watching the animals, and certainly drinking a good beer while eating a venison steak. These are also people who prioritize common sense and direct experience with the world. My parents Dan and Angela Simon did not live to see the publication of this book, but I am thankful that they made me into the person who could embrace the life I found in Taiwan and thus do research so successfully there. They prepared me well for that journey.

Like all books, this one leaves the author with many intellectual and other debts. Over the course of this journey, I have made many friends in international academia and in the villages in Taiwan where I did my field research. By now, the academic conferences in anthropology and Taiwan studies are too numerous to recount with any degree of accuracy, but these and many individual invitations to speak at universities in Taiwan, Japan, North America, and Europe have all shaped my ways of thinking about anthropology and humanity. The reflections that led to this book have been nourished in academic conversations with Guido Sprenger, Nobayashi Atsushi, Michael Stainton, Linda Arrigo, Ishigaki Naoki, Mohacsi Gergely, Awi Mona, Kuan Da-wei, Futuru Tsai, Kui Kairisir, Chiang Bien, Haisul Palalavi, Ye Shu-ling, Agilasay Pakawyan, Lin Ching-Hsiu, Lo

Yung-ching, Aaron Valdis Gauss, Frédéric Laugrand, Bernard Saladin d'Anglure, Françoise Morin, Natacha Gagné, Daffyd Fell, Paul Servais, Astrid Lipinsky, Arthur Miller, Irène Bellier, Jérôme Soldani, Stéphane Corcuff, Myron Cohen, Murray Rubinstein, Anru Lee, Marc Moskowitz, Andrew Morris, Melissa Brown, Chen Shu-Juo, Kharis Templeman, Scott Harrison, Michael Hathaway, Noah Theriault, Oona Paredes, Francesca Merlan, Jean Michaud, D.J. Hatfield, Colin Scott, Charles Menzies, Mario Blaser, Sylvie Poirier, Gregory Forth, William Hipwell, Julie Laplante, Hsieh Shih-Chung, Wang Mei-hsia, Michael Hsiao Hsin-Huang, Chang Mau-kuei, Wang Fu-chang, Frank Muyard, Paul Jobin, Liu Pi-Chen, Huang Shu-min, Yu Shuenn-Der, Syaman Lamuran, Darren Byler, David Jaclin, André Laliberté, Alexis Calvé-Genest, and Karine Coen-Sanchez, among many others. My colleagues at the uOttawa Human Rights Research and Education Centre, including John Packer and Errol Mendes (who was with me when I discussed hunting rights at Peking University), kept me focused on human rights. Paul Barclay kept my Taiwan ethnology rooted in Japanese history. Michael Rudolph challenged me to question the category of Indigenous, and Charles Stafford introduced me to cognitive anthropology. Paul Barclay, Julie Laplante, Charles Stafford, Toulouse-Antonin Roy, and Jenhao Randolph Cheng have generously provided feedback on chapters, and Darryl Sterk, Awi Mona, and Kerim Friedman on the entire book, as have anonymous peer reviewers at the University of Toronto Press. Awi even read and commented on the book twice. Amy Pei-jung Lee and Apay Tang helped me with the Truku spelling and phonetics. Ciwang Teyra and Skaya Siku also provided useful feedback. Frédéric Laugrand invited me to present the entire book in a five-day seminar at the University of Louvain in November 2021, a real luxury for an author, in the midst of a global pandemic. Liao Hsiungming made the map, and Biluan in Puli created the beautiful multispecies illustrations between the chapters.

In Taiwan, the College of Indigenous Studies at National Dong Hwa University has become a second home to me because of Pasuya'e Poiconu, Masegseg Zengror Gadu, Janubark Kujayau, Apay Tang, Jolan Hsieh, Awi Mona, the regretted Chi Chun-Chieh, Joyce Yeh, Amy Pei-Jung Lee, Kerim Friedman, Yang Cheng-hsien, and Chen Yifong, among others. In Taiwan, I have stayed in the homes of Kuhon Sibal and Rabay Teymu, Kujiang Weili, Yuli Taki, Yaya Howat, Isaw Tatao and Qoro Domiyu, Loking Yudaw, Hayu Yudaw and Bubie Fely Ching, Jiru Yudaw and Umat Sudu, Watan Diro and Emi Hweymin, and Takun Walis and Dumun Bihao, enjoying life with their families. I have benefited greatly from discussions with local intellectuals of all stripes, including some of these people as well as Kumu Tapas, Jiro Haruq, Dakis Pawan, Tera Yudaw, Walis Pawan, Igung Shiban, and Deng Shian-yang. Yudaw Pisaw gave me my first Truku lessons, and Rabay Rubing gave me the Truku name Walis. Tibusungu 'e Vayayana and Isak Aso provided different perspectives as they welcomed me into their Indigenous circles in Taipei. I thank them heartily, as well as the hundreds of other people who have so kindly invited me into their homes and shared with me their lives in Gluban, Bsngan, Skadang and Xoxos, Ciyakang, Buarung, Alang Toda, and Sadu. Aeles Lrawbalrate (Lily) provided me an occasional retreat down in Rukai territory.

In Canada, I have remained rooted because of mentors and friends such as Dominique Rankin, the late Elder William Commanda, Romola Vasantha Thumbadoo, Lynn Gehl, Ed File, and Donna Loft. Like the shopkeeper quoted earlier, they made me think with my heart about what it means to be human and what it means to be Indigenous. My husband, D. Kai Ma, tolerated my long absences from home and encouraged me to continue my research and writing, even at the darkest moments. I would not be who I am today, and this book would never have seen the light of day, without any of them. We are all related.

The research for this book has been funded by the Social Sciences and Humanities Research Council of Canada, the University of Ottawa, the Chiang Ching-kuo Foundation for International Scholarly Exchange, the Republic of China Ministry of Education, the National Museum of Ethnology in Osaka, and the Ontario/Baden-Wuerttemberg Exchange Program. My colleagues at the University of Ottawa made it possible for me to leave frequently for field research and always return home to a hearty welcome and an enriching environment for creative thought. Finally, I would like to thank Michael Lambek, Jodi Lewchuk, Mary Lui, and Carolyn Zapf at the University of Toronto Press for shepherding this book through the entire publication process.

TRULY HUMAN

Rooted in Formosa

In the beginning, the Earth was empty and deserted, with not a single human habitant. In the centre of what we now call the Central Mountain Chain, a giant boulder rose towards the sky, every morning absorbing the first beams of the sun rising from the east. Exposed to the sun, to the moon, and to storms of all the seasons, the surface of the boulder was smooth and shone brilliantly in the sunshine. Suddenly one day, as the first ray of sun hit the rock, there was a resounding thunder and the rock split in two. Three people, two men and one woman, stepped out from the fissure. They were disoriented but curious about their new environment. One of the men was terrified by the mountains with their high cliffs, the tangled mass of jungle, and the deep lakes. He turned around immediately and returned inside the rock. The woman and the man tried to convince him to come back out, but suddenly there was another rumbling sound. The hole in the rock closed, and he disappeared forever. The woman and the man stayed on Earth, where they became the ancestors of all the humans.[1]

This story is the legend of Pusu Qhuni, a giant boulder rising emergent from the forests in Nantou. The name Pusi means "root," and Qhuni means "tree," so it means "root of the tree."[2] The tree grew out of the stone, and the fissure opened just at the root of the tree. The tree is no longer there. According to oral tradition, it fell away in a landslide, exposing the rock. One Presbyterian minister told me this place was the true site of the Garden of Eden. In both present-day Nantou and Hualien, some people say it is the origin of humanity. Others, especially in the politics of recognition, say it is the origin of the Seejiq/Sediq/Seediq people only (Kuo 2011, 35). The relationship between the boulder and certain Indigenous confederations seems to have a long history, as Japanese anthropologists identified Pusu Qhuni with the

Sədeq, which includes today's Truku and Sediq peoples.[3] Other Atayalic groups apparently emerged from other large stone features, and other Indigenous groups also had their sacred sites in the mountains (Utsurikawa, Mabuchi, and Miyamoto 1935, 10).

Pusu Qhuni is one of the world's sacred sites. Hunters dare not catch prey there or make jokes, but they may approach it respectfully and rest in a cave at its base (Chien 2002, 23–4). There are many taboos against behaviours around Pusu Qhuni, such as not pointing to it, not laughing or making jokes within its sight, not hunting in the vicinity, and not washing in the nearby waters. In its presence, people use euphemisms to describe features in the environment, for example, calling the sun a "woven basket" and the stars "sand" (Kuo 2012, 99–102). Traditionally, women were not allowed to enter the forests around it (Kuo 2012, 266). Because it is difficult to access and requires at least five days of walking through dense jungle with no trails, very few people go there anymore. In 2002, an expedition of Indigenous leaders to Pusu Qhuni organized by the Ren'ai Township Office ended abruptly when one member got alpine hypothermia and had to be rescued by helicopter (Kuo 2011, 49). Because Pusu Qhuni is their common point of origin, Hualien Truku people have also made pilgrimages to it (Kuo 2012, 263).

Pusu Qhuni is a place that few people know from direct experience but rather from stories and legends. Truku hunter and elder Lowsi Rakaw (Huang Chang-hsing), who served as chair of the "Association of Promotion for Truku Name Rectification" (Wang 2008, 14), deplored how Christians in the 1950s tried to tame its powers by placing crosses there, only to have their community devastated by a decade of natural disasters as ancestral retribution (Huang 2000, 68–9). In recent years, Pusu Qhuni and other sacred mountain sites have also been trampled upon by non-Indigenous leisure hikers, which elders see as the cause of recent disasters such as typhoons, landslides, and earthquakes (76).

Pusu Qhuni itself is rich in ontological significance, a source of knowledge and philosophy, as well as a physical emanation of *Gaya*. Gaya in both Truku and Tgdaya (*waya* in Toda) is usually glossed as "ancestral law" or "sacred law," which it is, but it also used by native speakers as a translation for "culture." Kaji Cihung defines Gaya as "the rules for mutual interaction between people and the spirits, people and their social environment, and people and the natural environment" (Kaji 2011, 34). It can also be called "cultural ontology" (Sterk 2020, 7). Every Indigenous nation on the planet has an equivalent, the unextinguishable legal and ontological basis of living on a given territory. For the Algonquin, the equivalent is *Ginawaydaganuk*, which can be loosely translated as "the interconnection of all things" (McDermott and Wilson 2010, 205). This kind of moral code that ensures the wellness of all beings is so essential that the lack of such concerns in modern consumerist society puts our very existence at risk (Gehl 2017, 22). In this spirit, I begin this book with Pusu Qhuni in order to root it in a Formosan ontology, one that is shared between the peoples who in Taiwan's modern politics of recognition have chosen for themselves the collective names of Seejiq/Sediq/Seediq and Truku. Not only is Pusu Qhuni an inappropriate marker of difference between "East Sədeq" (Truku) and "West Sədeq" (Wang 2008, 15); shared reverence to it is a sign of their historical unity. It is thus a symbol of their shared political ontology (a concept to be discussed later), a way of focusing on the relationships between them rather than on the conflicts and different ethnic names that resulted from their incorporation into the nation-state system.

If we were to use Google Earth to look at Pusu Qhuni and then zoom out, we would see an immense territory of towering mountains, high cliffs, dense jungles, and lakes as part of a verdant island rising from the waters of the western Pacific. Pusu Qhuni is in the middle of the island. Although Portuguese explorers couldn't see Pusu Qhuni from their ships, they looked at the island in awe and baptized it "Ihla Formosa," or beautiful island. In 1624, the Dutch were the first Europeans to drop anchor in those waters in order to set up a small trading post. Tayouan, originally the name of a group of people living on the southwest coast near what is now Tainan, became the name of that area to the Dutch. The Dutch and the Chinese used several different versions of the name, but finally settled on Taiwan and started using it for the entire island. The people of Pusu Qhuni, deep in the mountains, would not be interpolated by "Taiwan" or come under any state jurisdiction until nearly three centuries later. Their first experience with state-centric governmentality happened under Japanese tutelage, only as recently as the early twentieth century and within the memory of some of the people I encountered. That gives them very unique perspectives on indigeneity, as well as on Formosa's place in the world.

Starting with Pusu Qhuni, a giant rock surrounded by thick forests and high mountains, is a good way to consider the way we, human or otherwise, perceive the island itself. It is a place where some lives emerge through birth, take their first uneasy steps in the forest, and gradually come to an understanding of other beings around them. Most of those lives are other than human, like a Reeve's muntjac, a small deer born in the undergrowth that can take its first steps shortly after birth. Some humans may leave their home villages, a backpack filled with provisions and a rifle in their hands, making a difficult journey across the mountain and through dense jungle in search of muntjacs

and other game animals. Recognizing Pusu Qhuni as a place of potentially dangerous spiritual power, some humans approach it with great
reverence and awe. This book is based on research with them. The hope
is to decolonize the way in which we do ethnography, putting local,
Indigenous ontologies at the heart of the reflection and writing. That
means not dismissing any part of those ontologies or reducing them to
"beliefs." I take seriously the claims that some people made to me that
all humans originated from Pusu Qhuni and that Gaya is open to all.
That hope does not absolve me of the professional responsibility to also
engage with anthropological theoretical concerns, but it does require
me to open those theoretical discussions to greater dialogue with Indigenous ways of living in the world.

When I write about that tangled meshwork of lives radiating outward
from Pusu Qhuni, I must be careful and respectful about the choice
of words that I use to refer to the land and the people who construct
their human lives upon it, especially if I am referring to political and
national units that label bundles of relations between people, which
may be contested. There is no Sədeq word for the entire island. For this
reason, I use "Formosa" to refer to the island and think that "Formosan"
is appropriate as an adjective to refer collectively to the original inhabitants who were there before the subsequent waves of colonialism. I
reserve "Taiwan" to refer to the multicultural society that has emerged
there since the Dutch arrived in 1624 and brought in the first settlers
from Fujian, in Southeast China. The Republic of China (ROC), a state
founded in China in 1911, arrived on Formosa in 1945 and transformed
Taiwan. The ROC is only the most recent in a "succession of colonialisms" (Dirlik 2018, 8), as I will explore in detail in the chapter 1.

My Entanglements with Taiwan

Like the three people who emerged from Pusu Qhuni, I can only see one
small part of Formosa at a time. Only in my imagination can I perceive
it as an island, or even as Taiwan or the Republic of China. I have done
fieldwork on Formosa and in Taiwan since 1996, a fateful year when,
trying to influence the results of the presidential elections, the Chinese
military shot empty missiles into the waters off the ports of Keelung
and Kaohsiung. Since then, Taiwan has become my second home. For
my PhD research, I worked in Tainan with leather tanners from 1996 to
1998. I taught English at Wenzao University in Kaohsiung from 1998 to
1999. I did postdoctoral research from 1999 to 2001 at the Institute of
Sociology, Academia Sinica, focusing on women entrepreneurs in Taipei. During this time, my initial anthropological agenda of studying

"Chinese culture" was challenged by research participants who insisted they were not Chinese. I soon met people who said they were neither Chinese nor Taiwanese. In 2001, while I was teaching anthropology part-time at the National Dong Hwa University in Hualien, Truku activist Igung Shiban invited me to write about her community's struggle against mining (Simon 2002) and to do field research in her community. Her friendship changed my life and my way of doing anthropology. She brought me into Indigenous studies.

Igung's invitation brought me to the Truku, and the people I met guided my research moving forward. Her brothers Kuhon and Kimi introduced me to the Sediq and patiently taught me how they could have the same parents as their sister but a different Indigenous identity.[4] On both sides of the mountains, people helped me select the field sites and research topics, and even taught me research methods. Most of all, they encouraged me to learn from direct experience, saying that I must live with and like them to understand their lives. They shared their lives with me, knowing that I would be writing and teaching about them, because they want an international readership to know about their way of living and their experience with colonialism. This kind of study, combining knowledge from the mind and heart, is most at home in the current era of decolonization and indigenization of research. These methods of learning from experience, consulting experts, learning from traditional stories, embracing my subjectivity rather than seeking to be highly analytical and objective, and using personal introspection to arrive at my own truth – all of which I learned from Indigenous people on Formosa – is very similar to Indigenous Anishinaabe methods of knowing (Gehl 2017, 8).

If I were to try to articulate this project with an established conversation in international anthropology, I think these methods are most compatible with what is now called phenomenology. Phenomenology invites us to understand culture, not as a pre-existing entity or an explanatory force but as an understanding that emerges from and is improvised within lived experience (Laplante and Sacrini 2016, 12). While in the field, the idea is to bracket, at least temporarily, such cerebral concerns as representations, discourses, symbols, and culture in order to become more aware of the corporal dimensions of the body moving through space. The hope is that we can learn something profound and meaningful from the vertigo of following a hunter along the edge of a cliff, the sore muscles gained from spreading fertilizer on tea plantations, the sweat and itchy skin from harvesting rice, the ecstasy of speaking in tongues in church, and the pungent flavour of lightly boiled flying squirrel intestines, but also from the release of sitting down in a cold mountain stream with friends and enjoying a six-pack of beer at the end of a day. Focusing on the bodily experience in places allows for greater receptivity to place-based ethics, grounded normativity, and other notions of *what* exists in the world (ontology). It means refusing to take the position of the rational expert who can define the borders of culture and then seek to understand Atayal, Seediq, or Truku culture. I was taught the risks of such traditional anthropological assumptions by listening to people arguing among brothers and sisters about whether they are Atayal, Seediq, or Truku. Instead, they invited me to think of them as humans (*seejiq*) in embodied contexts, where they might be contemplating a swallow's nest in the eaves of a grocery store or marching angrily in the street at a protest for hunting rights.

Writing With and About Indigenous Peoples

The politics of writing about Indigenous peoples has come under increasing scrutiny in anthropology, not least with the influence of postmodern, post-structural, and postcolonial currents since the 1980s. James Clifford explored how an American court's essentializing notions of culture as stable and rooted stymied Mashpee Indian claims to recognition (Clifford 1988, 338). He argued instead for a study of identity "not as a boundary to be maintained but as a nexus of relations and transactions actively engaging a subject" (344). Clifford and Marcus argued very clearly that "cultural analysis is always enmeshed in global movements of difference and power" (Clifford and Marcus 1986, 22). In my own engagement with Clifford's approach, while reflecting upon my collaboration with Igung, I expressed hope that anthropologists could draw attention to and widen support for Indigenous political struggles rather than merely cataloguing cultural differences (Simon 2009).

Mohawk anthropologist Audra Simpson, from whom I have been learning ever since we attended graduate school together at McGill University in Montreal, warns more forcefully against the tendencies of anthropology to fetishize cultural difference and authenticity. She says that anthropologists working with the Iroquois have tended to overlook social history and mainstream political processes, thus missing the bulk of Iroquois experience. The anthropological focus on "culture" rather than on the ongoing land dispossession that shapes Indigenous lives means that "Indigenous elimination holds hands with disciplinary formation" (Simpson 2014, 67). As we begin to indigenize and decolonize anthropology in both Taiwan and Canada, settler colonialism has become a new productive analytic focus. By living and working with Formosan Indigenous people, I have learned that the ongoing colonial situation is one reality that constantly hangs over their lives. That colonial situation simultaneously fragments their communities, as social classes crystallize and political factions rise and fall, while also uniting them in the face of land dispossession and discrimination.

Although I will explore more of the specific details about Taiwan, its Indigenous nations, and ethnic relations in the chapters to follow, I explain my use of the word "Indigenous" here. The use of the term "Indigenous" points to the historical fact that Indigenous peoples with their own legal-political ontologies and institutions have been challenged by the arrival of settler populations on their territories, an ongoing dispossession of land and a denial of sovereignty. Capitalization of the term risks reifying Indigenous (or Aboriginal) as if we were writing about a single ethnic group, thus obscuring differences between, for example, the Mohawk and the Algonquin, or the Truku and the Amis, a danger which Mohawk philosopher Taiaiake Alfred warned against as another form of assimilation to state hegemony (Alfred 2005, 23). But, in English, the term "indigenous" has many meanings. As an interesting illustration, if one were to search for "Taiwan indigenous" on an internet search engine, it would also turn up the development of "indigenous submarines" and the spread of "indigenous COVID cases." Capitalization makes it possible to distinguish in writing whether the author is writing about the political goals of colonized peoples or about anyone and anything else that just happens to be local or native to a place. Capitalization is not an issue in Chinese, which uses characters rather than phonetic symbols and already has two different words to express the two meanings that merge in one English word.

In Taiwan, Indigenous activists chose their own Chinese vocabulary and eventually got the government to accept it, even in the revisions to the Constitution of the Republic of China in the 1990s. Their own chosen vocabulary of *yuanzhumin* 原住民 refers to "Indigenous people" and *yuanzhu minzu* 原住民族 to "Indigenous peoples." They were intentionally creating a place for themselves in the international framework of indigeneity that led to the United Nations Declaration on the Rights of Indigenous Peoples (UNDRIP). They choose the Chinese name after diplomatic exchanges with First Nations of Canada, most notably with Mohawk leader Donna Loft when she was training social activists with the Urban-Rural Mission. This Chinese term is thus a product of a long-standing international process of Indigenous diplomacy (Henderson 2008). To the chagrin of Formosan Indigenous activists, the People's Republic of China have imposed on the UN system another word, *tuzhu* 土著, which, because it begins with the character for soil, has pejorative connotations of primitiveness. Of course, each Formosan Indigenous nation has its own words for "Indigenous." In one possible gloss, many people translate yuanzhu-min 原住民 back into Sediq languages as *Sediq balay*, which means "truly human" and also means a brave warrior or morally upright person. That inspired the title of this book, and I discuss it in depth in chapter 5. But for now, we can return to the mountains of Formosa.

The annual "plum rains" are in full force in the late spring of 2013 as I settle into my new field site of Alang Buarung, a Truku language village in the central mountains of Nantou County. From the running track where I do my morning exercises in front of the primary school, I can look across the valley to Nenggao Mountain (Dgiyaq Silung), which at this time of the year is often covered in mist and clouds. This sojourn is by no means my first in an Indigenous village in Taiwan. In fact, I have been doing research with Truku speakers for nearly a decade already, including nearly two years of residence in similar villages in coastal Hualien County. As I look eastward, I recall that just across that peak are the rainforests of Hualien, the coastal plains, and then the vast expanse of the Pacific Ocean. I think about the stories I have heard about the nomadic Truku people, who centuries ago made their way along the mountain river streams to settle in Hualien. From this vantage point, I understand very well why Truku elders called the territory that corresponds roughly to Nantou *Mqribaq* (behind the mountains) and coastal Hualien *Nklaan hidao* (where the sun rises). This naming describes well their historical itinerary through the mountains from west to east. Truku elders told me that their people once crossed the mountains and saw the reflection of the sun on the ocean in the distance for the first time, blinking their eyes because of the pain of the bright new sight. I reflect on those words every morning as the clouds over the mountains take on a pinkish hue and a new day begins. My goal is to understand the mountainous territory that the Truku of both Hualien and Nantou consider to be their ancestral homeland.

Most Taiwanese people, if they think about Indigenous people at all, consider the Truku as one of sixteen Indigenous "tribes" in their multicultural country, unaware of the contentious local politics that clouded the legal recognition of that group by the state. As a political anthropologist, I am very aware of those debates, since my most intensive period of field research coincided with a tense period from 2004, when the Truku broke away from the Atayal, to 2008, when the Sediq gained legal recognition independent of both the Atayal and the

Truku. During those years, I walked with Truku nationalists as they made their first demands for self-government and with Sediq nationalists as they rejected Truku identity and lobbied for recognition of their own political identity. Sediq nationalists, in a political confederation they call 3S3T, move between three spellings for the word "human" to unite a group that combines speakers of Truku (Seejiq), Toda (Sediq), and Tgdaya (Seediq). Spelling is less confusing in Chinese, because all three groups agree about which Chinese characters to use.

Moving between two Truku villages in Hualien and one Seediq (Tgdaya) village in Nantou during my 2012–13 fieldwork, I spent most of my days during this period with ordinary people, day labourers, farmhands, hunters, and others who had little to do with Taiwan's Indigenous rights movements but who embodied deep knowledge of their language and life practices. Few of them were directly engaged in the political debates of legal recognition or, as it is called in Chinese, "name rectification," but most of them complied when asked by township officials to change the ethnic classification on their household registration files to Truku in Hualien or to Sediq in Nantou. In February 2022, from a total Indigenous population of 581,134 individuals, some 33,246 had registered as Truku and 10,812 as Sediq.[5] I take these statistics with a grain of salt. Having spent time walking with so many different people, I know that these identities are not embraced in the same way by all. Some people have one Truku and one Toda parent, or even one non-Indigenous parent, and struggle with questions of identity. Some people affirm Truku or Sediq identity wholeheartedly, even as a form of oppositional identity politics, whereas others identify more as citizens of the Republic of China. Some even consciously try to pass as non-Indigenous. When I was teaching anthropology in Taiwan, one student even told me that she had never dared to tell other students she is Indigenous until she took my class and learned to take pride in that identity. Statistical classifications may appear to be mutually exclusive, but in daily life they are not.

Ethnic Labels, State Legibility, and Dispossession of Sovereignty

These Indigenous identities and population statistics are part of the strategies of governance that James Scott called legibility: "a state's attempt to make society legible, to arrange the population in ways that simplified the classic state functions of taxation, conscription, and prevention of rebellion" (Scott 1998, 2). These categories date to the first half of the twentieth century, when Formosa came under Japanese administration (1895–1945). Before then, the Qing Dynasty classified the island's original inhabitants as either *shoufan* 熟番 (cooked savages), who accepted Qing political rule, or *shengfan* 生番 (raw savages), who did not.[6] The Qing, at least until the last two decades of their rule, seemed content to leave the latter groups in a state of effective political autonomy in the mountain regions. As Dakis Pawan reminds us, the practices of classifying people and giving them collective ethnic names began for them only in the Japanese period (Kuo 2012, 96).

After 1895, as the Japanese military advanced across the island pacifying one group after another, anthropologists followed in their wake, looking for linguistic and cultural commonalities to determine which of the dispersed groups could be placed together in governable centres of calculation (Barclay 2007). They classified them into nine territorially based tribes as part of a colonial-type governance that made Formosa and its peoples legible to Japanese military and forestry planners. Robert Tierney probably overstated the point when he argued that "bounded territories and ethnic borders existed in the mind of the ethnographers *alone*" (Tierney 2010, 85, emphasis added). The Japanese were showing respect in the cases where they used the word for "human" as an ethnonym, for example, Atayal or Bunun. They classified Sedeq as one of three Atayal dialects. In transforming those words into ethnonyms, the Japanese grouped together smaller units who had never imagined themselves as belonging to one coherent group. Only some of them had experience of forming higher level political confederations with other groups. Those ethnonyms reflected cultural and linguistic commonalties perceived by ethnographers and administrators, rather than any form of Formosan political organization. They sometimes grouped together groups who were locked in long-standing hostile feuds. These ethnic classifications also made the boundaries look less permeable than they were in daily life. It took generations for the Formosan people themselves to identify with those classifications and to imagine the maps as their national territories. That process, however, as this book will show, is still incomplete and, in some places, resisted.

Based on those colonial classifications, Taiwan's Indigenous peoples are classified into territorially based political groupings called *zu* 族, a word translated as "tribe" in English versions of Republic of China state law and in most English-language publications. For anthropologists, "tribe" may seem like a relic of earlier eras, when notions of bands, tribes, and chiefdoms were used to classify supposedly primitive stages in political evolution. The Japanese government, even as they gradually transformed Chinese settlers into Japanese imperial subjects with legal rights, treated the island's native peoples as wards of the state. The word "tribe," as a marker of biopolitics, is useful in historical works exploring the colonial state–Indigenous relationship. It is still useful to indicate the arbitrariness of state-made legal categories, as opposed to movements of self-determination, as long as Indigenous peoples are treated as populations to be governed by positivist state law. Even Taiwan's Indigenous social activists rarely dare affirm their communities as self-defined nations whose legal traditions can co-constitute a post-colonial, independent Taiwanese law based on ontological parity. Many Truku and Sediq nationalist leaders alike now seem to accept the contemporary legal definition of "tribe" in law, as it holds out the promise of political autonomy under the jurisdiction of the Republic of China. There are reasons to question these liberal politics of recognition (see chapter 1), and that is a major theme of this book. But let's begin with a look at the Indigenous Peoples Basic Law, legislation passed in 2005.

Article Two of the Indigenous Peoples Basic Law leads to some confusion if one relies on the English translation, so I will explain both the English and Chinese versions here. The Basic Law first defines "Indigenous peoples," in the English translation, as

> the traditional peoples who have inhibited [sic] in Taiwan and are subject to the state's jurisdiction, including Amis tribe, Atayal tribe, Paiwan tribe, Bunun tribe, Puyuma tribe, Rukai tribe, Tsou tribe, Saisiyat tribe, Yami tribe, Tsao tribe, Kavalan tribe, Taroko tribe and any other tribes who regard themselves as indigenous peoples and obtain the approval of the central indigenous authority upon application. (ROC Ministry of Justice [2005] 2018)

Here the word "tribe" is used to describe the sixteen currently recognized Indigenous peoples, which have become confederations of what were in most cases formerly autarkic communities. As map 1 on page 28 shows, state authorities represent these confederations in terms of imagined spatial regions. This representation gets confusing when, after defining Indigenous person and Indigenous peoples' regions that belong to those sixteen "tribes," there is the legal definition of "tribe" as "a group of indigenous persons who form a community by living together in specific areas of the indigenous peoples' regions and following the traditional norms with the approval of the central indigenous authority" (ROC Ministry of Justice [2005] 2018).[7] There are at least 746 "tribes" by this definition. Another definition is "Indigenous land," which is classified as "traditional territories" (*chuantong lingyu* 傳統領域) or "reservation land" (*baoliudi* 保留地). This terminology is only slightly less confusing in the Chinese original, where "tribe 1.0" is zu 族, which means an "ethnic minority" or "ethnic nationality" in a sense very similar to the Stalinist definition used in China. The Chinese original for "tribe 2.0" is *buluo* 部落, which might be better translated as "community" but is uncannily similar to the use of "band" in Canada's Indian Act. In any case, defining them as "traditional" peoples who are subject to the state's "central indigenous authority" is far from recognizing them as sovereign peoples or nations. In a legalistic sleight of hand, the ROC re-affirms the control of state institutions over populations and both traditional territories and reservation land in a law that holds out the promise of political autonomy and self-determination.

One Sediq nationalist who openly questions this terminology in Chinese is Watan Diro, a Presbyterian minister who has encountered Indigenous First Nations in Canada. Since at least the year 2000, he has referred instead to the Sediq Nation (*guo* 國) in his church sermons and political speeches.[8] The idea may be gaining productive traction. In the summer of 2019, one of his compatriots referred to the mountain pass of *Renzhiguan* 人止關 (literally the barrier where people stop) to me as "the national gate of the Seediq." In the nineteenth century, this pass was the boundary line between what the reigning Chinese Qing Dynasty considered to be the civilization under their jurisdiction and the savagery beyond the pale. No Han (Chinese) settlers were permitted upstream of that mountain pass, and no "savages" were permitted downstream. Nowadays, a commemorative plaque marks the spot, where the Sediq also fought off the invading Japanese in 1902 (Takun 2012, 281). Driving past it is part of the embodied experience in which people live their identity as Sediq. This cliff and the plaque are part of what we can actually see with our eyes, as we begin to think about Sediq, Taiwan, or China.

Roads and Communities in Contemporary Taiwan

Until the twentieth century, Formosa's rough mountainous terrain, as in the Southeast Asian massif that James Scott calls Zomia, provided the same kind of "friction" to keep Chinese and other states at bay (Scott 2009, 43). Formosan mountain peoples, the ancestors of today's Indigenous peoples, maintained a high degree of autonomy as societies "against the state" (Clastres 1974) until the Japanese imposed modern forms of capitalist extraction on their lands. The Japanese built the initial road infrastructure so that troops, with horses and cannons, could enter the mountains and subdue the people who lived there. The peoples of Pusu Qhuni, due to their rough terrain, were the last Indigenous peoples on the island to experience the dispossession of their lands and self-determining authority that Marx labelled as "primitive accumulation" (Coulthard 2014, 7). They remember with grief the destruction of their mountain homes by the Japanese military, and still take children to view their family ruins in the forests. Their lives have changed greatly. Until the twentieth century, they could rarely venture beyond their own territories for fear of violence from neighbouring peoples. Now they travel freely throughout Taiwan and beyond.

Due to the modern infrastructure of paved roads, a network of mountain roads criss-crossing Nantou and Hualien are now part of peoples' daily itineraries, whether they are taking the bus down to school, driving a pickup truck loaded with cabbages down to market, or driving up to the villages to promote a favoured political project or a candidate in an election. The narrow, paved roads snake through the mountains, often with barely enough space for one vehicle. Forests, managed by the Forestry Bureau, the Taroko National Park, or even the Veterans Affairs Council, are interrupted by broad swatches of farms and orchards. Sometimes the terrain is so steep that the roads seem to hang precariously from the sides of cliffs. Traces of landslides are visible on the faces of the mountains, and road signs indicate the danger of falling rocks. In the rainy season, drivers sometimes must navigate carefully around rocks strewn across their paths, but at most for a couple days because the township road maintenance crews are amazingly efficient. Daily travellers on these roads, themselves part of local government efficiency, are the garbage truck drivers, who make daily passes through each lane playing Beethoven's "Für Elise" while residents emerge from their houses with garbage bags and neatly sorted recyclables. These township jobs are considered by locals to be very lucrative forms of employment. Due to the relatively slower travel time, the mountains still provide some friction compared to the heavily urbanized west coast, but Taiwan's Indigenous people no longer enjoy the isolation or autonomy that only some of the most elderly people in the communities still recall. If anything, the state is omnipresent in their lives. For much of the drive from Nantou to Hualien, one passes through Truku territory that is occupied by and labelled as the Taroko National Park. One is constantly reminded of the reality of settler colonialism.

At the nodes of these roads are small residential clusters, where people live in the proximity of their own relatives and other clans. In the Truku language, the word *alang* is used to refer to these hamlets or communities, and in ROC law (as discussed earlier), they are called buluo 部落. In daily interactions, it is somewhat like the German *Heimat*, as alang carries similar connotations of home, village, community, land, and tradition. It is relevant that even young people who do not speak Sediq languages will use alang instead of the Mandarin term. That usage indicates that the term is very important and difficult or impossible to translate.[9] Usually, several alang are grouped together in the artificial boundaries of administrative villages, but everyone knows the name of their own alang and has some idea of the historical trajectory that brought their people from places deeper in the mountains to the current locations. When telling the stories of these forced displacements, the people of nearly every alang refer to the Japanese period, saying that the Japanese military moved them down the mountains and closer to the roads so that they would be easier to control. I think of each village with its adjacent territory as a "zone of refuge" or "shatter zone" (Scott 2009, 7) to which people have been resettled, in most cases against their will, but where they still maintain a certain degree of autonomy and social cohesion. Attention to detailed local histories (Masaw 1977, 1978) shows that each village is a forced amalgamation of previous settlements, but that even alang formation is a flexible process that happens when people construct Heimat within the constraints of colonial surveillance. Most importantly, alang is a highly flexible, partly kin-based, territorial organization with clearly defined membership and is the basic unit of sovereignty in Gaya. Takun Walis remind us that the alang is the core value of Gaya, as a group that protected its territory by any means necessary (Takun 2012, 277).

In governance regimes rooted in Japanese administrative practices, the houses and agricultural lands used by Indigenous people are classified as Indigenous reserve land (*yuanzhumin baoliudi* 原住民保留地). Since usufruct rights (rights to use) over these lands can, since the 1960s, only be legally bought and sold between people with legal Indigenous identity, this system ensures a certain degree of segregation between Indigenous and non-Indigenous people. Since land disputes are negotiated at the township offices, township politics grasp the attention of local people more closely than national elections or even relations between Taiwan and China. The absence of the character zu 族 (people) in the legal term for reserve land reflects the political reality that the land is administered by the ROC state and used by Indigenous individuals rather than managed or owned by any Indigenous self-governing body. The mountain Indigenous people are very aware that they still governed over 50 per cent of the island as recently as 1895, but that they are now restricted to reserve land that amounts to about 7.1 per cent. Seediq politician and thinker (as well as former Catholic priest) Walis Beilin argued that land reform broke Gaya because land became a tool for capital accumulation (Walis 2009, 33).

Indigenous activists would like very much to change this situation by creating Indigenous autonomous regions that would manage reserve land but also bring back to their direct control the state-run forests (called "traditional territories" in the Basic Law). They are emboldened by the Basic Law, as this law holds out the promise of legal autonomy and other Indigenous rights covered by the United Nations Declaration on the Rights of Indigenous Peoples. They also know that, despite Indigenous rights being promised in the ROC Constitution and relevant laws, the implementation of those laws will require years of political struggle and negotiation. As I finish this book in early 2022, not a single Indigenous autonomous zone has been established as promised in that legislation.

Truku and Sediq: Indigenous Ethnicity in the Era of Recognition

The name Truku reflects the origins of one group of people spanning Nantou and Hualien. In local folk etymology, the word "Truku" was formed by blending the word *tru-* (three) and *-ruku* (mountain plateau) to refer to a series of three relatively flat areas in the Nantou highlands. "Truku Truwan," the full name given to this area, means the original "homeland of the Truku" (Kaji 2011, 17; Tera 2003, 17).[10] Kim noticed "Seejiq Truku" literally means "mountain people" (Kim 1980, 183). The winding road in front of Buarung's primary school can take me upward towards Truku Truwan, one of the flat plateaux being Alang Sadu, which, because of the high-altitude climate, has become important for tea and cabbage production in the contemporary political economy. One of the primary school administrators from Alang Toda, strategically placed right between the two Truku villages, even took the trouble of showing me the three mountain peaks that are the historical homelands of the Truku, Toda, and Tgdaya peoples. Truku speakers in both the highlands of Nantou and the foothills of Hualien refer to themselves in their own language as "Seejiq Truku," which means the "people of Truku." In the past, Nantou elders used a plant metaphor to describe the relationship between the closely related people of these two places. The people in Nantou called themselves *cina sari* (old taro) and referred to their eastward relatives as *bqan sari* (taro sprouts) for those who have spread outward from the original source.

Truku speakers, especially in Alang Buarung, are in a somewhat liminal position. In the identity politics of the early twenty-first century, as Taiwan was seeking its own non-Chinese identity on the international stage, the country's Indigenous people were offered the right to determine their own legal classifications in a process called "name rectification" (*zhengming* 正名). In Nantou and Hualien, local elites had long hoped to break away from the Atayal, which they all saw as part of the

Japanese colonial legacy, and create their own legal identities based on local understandings of histories, languages, and cultures. In Hualien, where Truku speakers are in the absolute majority, people eventually took on an identity as Truku, naming themselves after their ancestral homeland in Nantou (Hara 2003). Some people contested the new ethnic classifications, saying that the term "Sediq," even as pronounced differently in Truku, Toda, and Tgdaya inflections, equally means "human being" in all three topolects and is thus more inclusive of those related peoples who came to Hualien from other nearby places in Nantou. In Nantou, where there is demographic parity between the speakers of the three dialects, the ethnonym Sediq became official (Hara 2004). Nantou Indigenous activists take care to spell out the word in all three dialects, as it is Sediq in Toda, Seejiq in Truku, and Seediq in Tgdaya. These three variants are all rendered in exactly the same way in Chinese characters 賽德克 (Saideke). In Buarung, most people speak the Truku language, but since they are in Nantou, most of them have agreed to register their ethnic identity at the local household registration bureau as Saideke. Ambivalent identities can have advantages, at least for some local elites. Indigenous legislator Kung Wen-chi (Chinese Nationalist Party, KMT), who hails from Buarung, is notorious for self-identifying as Truku, Sediq, and Atayal, depending on the audience he is addressing. His Indigenous name is Yosi Takun. He is best known in Buarung for only making the journey up the mountains at election time. I got to know him as our paths crossed teaching English at the same university after we both returned to Taiwan with newly minted PhDs in our hands. I frequently encountered him as I did the research for this book, for example, in the protest and hearing about hunting rights discussed in chapter 2.

In the spring of 2013, I have come to Buarung to study Truku relations with birds. This morning, after my brief run in the chilly rain, I am grateful to accept a seat on the tattered leather sofa in front of Pisaw's general store.[11] The other men are drinking beer, but I need my morning caffeine and take a can of "Mr. Brown's Coffee" instead. Pisaw's veranda is adorned with cages, each one containing a songbird from the nearby forests. As Pisaw tells me their names in Truku, he explains that he has found abandoned fledglings in the forest and is raising them to maturity before he will free them in their original habitat. He pretends to be a bird rescuer, and I pretend to believe him. He encourages me to sit back and look up. In the eaves of the veranda, glued to the plaster ceiling, is the

Figure 0.1. Swallows nesting in Buarung. Swallows, like all creatures, dwell in the affordances of other lives.

Source: Photograph by Scott E. Simon.

mud and straw nest of swallows (*klaway*). The men seem to enjoy watching while the adults fly out of the nest, the young ones poke their crying heads into the open, and the parents return to feed them insects (figure 0.1). Pisaw says that the same swallows return every year, taking shelter in his human home, which then becomes a swallow refuge as they lay eggs and raise a family. He leaves the nest in its place and awaits their return every year with the plum rains. He encourages me to take photos of both the caged birds and the swallows. "Humans can also learn from birds," he tells me.[12] If there are many swallows flying around, for example, it is a sign that it will soon rain. I am amazed at the way in which swallows find shelter in a human-built home and at how Pisaw accepts them proudly as part of his human life. Ignoring ethnic politics for the moment, he uses the word "Seejiq" to mean human being, as opposed to birds (*qduda*) and other life forms.

For years, I have sought refuge, food, companionship, and conversation in the miniscule grocery stores, breakfast shops, and restaurants that dot the landscape of Indigenous Taiwan. Quite useful for the curious anthropologist, they are important places where ordinary people meet, relax, and debate the political issues that shape their lives. In both Hualien and Nantou, ordinary people mocked the name rectification process, saying it is just a way for local elites to gain access to government posts and state funding for their pet projects. Even in the Sediq strongholds of Nantou, one of the store owners told me: "When the Japanese ethnographers asked us who we are, we said 'Sediq.' We did not mean the name of an ethnic group, since we did not have ethnic groups back then. We meant that we were human as opposed to being dogs or boars or deer." As I explained in the preface, the words of this local elder stuck in my heart and became the inspiration for this book. Explaining his opposition to the proposed ethnic name, he continued to explain: "Seediq is not an appropriate term for an ethnic name that is meant to categorize and divide people … That word means human being. You may be a foreigner, but you are also human. *Isu uri seediq o.*"

Most of all, through what Darren Byler (2021) calls "anticolonial friendship," I have struggled to understand and empathize with the various lifeworlds I encountered in these villages. What does it mean to be human for the Truku nationalists, the Sediq politicians, the tea pickers, the cabbage farmers, the quarry workers, the Presbyterian elders, the hunter arrested for "poaching" in the Taroko National Park? How can the existential quandaries of ordinary people reveal what it means to be human? What does being human, even being *truly human*, say to the emergent discourse of indigeneity in Taiwan and around the world, as well as to the possibility of Indigenous resurgence? In the meandering ways of ethnography, I weave together reflections on the legacy of Marx, anthropological notions of culture, and the contemporary worldings made possible by indigeneity and Indigenous resurgence.

Wrestling with the Legacy of Marx

Research with Indigenous communities made me question some of my most treasured assumptions. From graduate school through mid-career, when I did this fieldwork, I self-identified as a Marxist. I was initially interested in Taiwan because the success of its development model seemed to be an important anomaly in a world capitalist system designed to extract resources from the periphery and enrich the capitalist core. I came to view Taiwan's subcontracting industrial system, which thrived due to privileged access to US markets, through the framework of America's Cold War against communism. In my book about this industrial model, I wrote about how entrepreneurs manufacture consent and avoid overt class struggle by hiring a strategic mix of migrant workers and local middle-aged women (Simon 2005, 93–116). Since I assumed that workers' physical engagement in the labour process contributed to their perceptions of the world, one of my main research methods was working on the production line of a leather tanning factory. Ever since then, my field research has always been characterized by working alongside my research partners whenever possible.

While still living in Taiwan, I chose to do research on the island's Indigenous peoples, whom I saw as an ethnic group deprived of most of their historical land base and forced into proletarian existence. I was particularly interested in Asia Cement on Truku territory. I hoped to find a strong resistance to capitalism, but instead found myself in the predicament of Marx who, in *The Eighteenth Brumaire*, wrote about how French peasants lacked self-identity or class consciousness because of their context in which the French state used a series of measures to appease smallholders (Marx [1852] 2010). I found among Asia Cement workers no desire to reach out in working-class solidarity to migrant workers, non-Indigenous workers, or even to Amis workers (the nearby coastal Indigenous group). There was a strong local identity within each alang and widespread affirmation of being yuanzhumin 原主民, even as people were suspicious of new institutions that claimed to represent them. Managers at Asia Cement had done their own research about the importance of the alang and had intentionally spread out the most lucrative positions so that each alang would have Asia Cement employees, dressed in uniform before and after going to work, who would speak on their behalf. Most strikingly, people resented Asia Cement not for exploiting their labour but for stealing their land. Again, Asia Cement understands local priorities. People also told me that they prefer Asia Cement to the Taroko National Park. The reason is that Asia Cement occupies only a small fraction of Truku land and tolerates local people hunting on the rest. The Taroko National Park, on the other hand, claims nearly exclusive jurisdiction, and conservation officers sometimes arrest hunters.

Although Marxism has been a powerful explanatory model in the social sciences, exploring Indigenous lifeworlds reveals some of its limitations. The Marxist classics had little to say about Indigenous peoples for the simple reason that the modern legal category had not yet been invented. Instead, Marx and Engels used the peoples we now think of as Indigenous to stand in for an early stage in the evolution towards capitalism and eventually socialism. In *The Origin of the Family, Private Property and the State*, Engels portrayed the Iroquois as a primitive society. Even as his descriptions show admiration for their political and economic structures, he thought that this "very undeveloped state of production" was possible only with a sparse population scattered across a wide area. He consigned them to the past, saying that "the power of these natural and spontaneous communities had to be broken, and it was" (Engels [1902] 2021, 119).

Glen Coulthard criticizes this *temporal framing*, as Marx himself attributed primitive accumulation to the distant past rather than as a persistent process of dispossession (Coulthard 2014, 9). Coulthard also disapproved of Marx's normative developmentalism, which posited as inevitable that all peoples would be drawn into the capitalist mode of production (10). Before my fieldwork, I had myself assumed that part of the problem was that Truku Indigenous workers were not given permanent full-time jobs, as promised, in the Asia Cement mine and factory (Simon 2002). When I did fieldwork in that community, I found myself dealing with people who prefer temporary jobs or day labour to full-time employment or entrepreneurship because it provides them with an income without interfering with their hunting and other activities (Simon 2010b, 73). Coulthard's third criticism of Marx is that Marx tells a story only of violent dispossession, whereas Canada shows that dispossession can also happen through ostensibly peaceful liberal and multicultural practices (Coulthard 2014, 15). This fact should serve as a warning for studying Taiwan as well.

An additional issue I have with Marx was his idea of an Asiatic mode of production or Oriental despotism, which in *Capital* he described as the "key to the riddle of the *unchangeability* of Asiatic societies" (quoted in Lefort 1978, 632, emphasis added). This assumption of not just Marxism, but of Western understandings of history, was disproven by none other than Andre Gunder Frank, who demonstrated that both China and India had the necessary elements of a capitalist economy long before the West (Frank 1998). Marx himself should have known better when he wrote the first volume of *Capital* in 1867. For already over a century, Qing Dynasty China had been just as expansionist and imperialist as the European powers, having expanded into Xinjiang (new frontier), Tibet, Mongolia, and Taiwan, dispossessing the original inhabitants in practices no less genocidal than what happened in North America. There was nothing "unchangeable" about the Qing Dynasty, which was, in Marx's time, better conceptualized as a dynamic "conquest regime" (Rawski 1996).

None of this history implies giving up the explanatory power of Marxism. Instead, I think it is better to follow the footsteps of Coulthard, as well as those of Cedric Robinson who, in his concept of "racial capitalism," explored the way in which racism was intrinsic to the global system of capitalism. He thought that Marxism's internationalism was insufficiently global, as Marx failed to see non-Western struggles as anything other than pre-modern, underdeveloped, or peripheral (Robinson 2020, xvii). This book takes on this task, with a look at primitive accumulation or dispossession as an ongoing process on Indigenous Formosa, as well as at racialization and Indigenous resurgence, in a part of the world usually considered removed from such concerns.

Grappling with the Legacy of "Culture"

Ever since postmodernism entered the mainstream of North American anthropology in the 1980s, with Clifford (discussed earlier) as only one example, the entire discipline has sought more dynamic ways of understanding cultural difference. In the United States, the anthropology of Taiwan during the Cold War developed as scholars denied access to the People's Republic of China turned instead to Taiwan as a laboratory of Chinese culture. The subfield of sinological anthropology, especially as practised in Taiwan, has proven to be remarkably resilient to postmodern critiques of culture. Twenty-five years after *Writing Culture*, to give just one example, Avron Boretz combined fieldwork with gangsters in Taitung (Taiwan) with readings of Ming Dynasty martial arts knowledge in a poetics of Chinese nationalism, and even compared contemporary drinking practices to those of China's Zhou Dynasty three thousand years ago (Boretz 2011, 177). Considering that Taitung is the homeland of Amis, Paiwan, Pinuyumayan, and Rukai Indigenous nations, this reading is akin to seeking cultural commonalities between French speakers in Quebec and first century Gauls, without considering the colonial context, mentioning the presence of Indigenous peoples, or recognizing the newcomers as settlers. In fact, few people would consider calling Quebeckers "French" just because they speak French. Basing their arguments on Edward Said's (1979) *Orientalism*, Stephen O. Murray and Keelung Hong have repeatedly rebuked anthropologists for "looking through Taiwan to see China," which includes overlooking the existence of Indigenous Formosans (Hong and Murray 2005; Murray and Hong 1994). Stated bluntly, treating Taiwan as merely a variation of China naturalizes a non-Western colonialism that is no less violent or genocidal than that of North America. A postmodern critique, such as that by Michel-Rolph Trouillot, should encourage us to avoid futile searches for common ahistorical essences, as we gain greater knowledge of nations, states, "tribes," or even modernity and globalization, if we study them instead as sets of relations and processes (Trouillot 2003, 5).

Again, we can take our cues from Indigenous scholars and political philosophy as we negotiate this terrain. Essentializing culture can become a form of hegemony, and anthropologists are complicit when, for example, they reduce Taiwan to a manifestation of some ancient Chinese culture. At the same time, however, attacks on all essential-ist claims-making can undermine actions of Indigenous peoples when they appeal to "culture" and "tradition" as part of their national lib-eration struggles. The key is that culture is a discursive formation, in a Foucauldian sense, that legitimizes certain ways of thinking and speak-ing while limiting other possibilities. Coulthard thus admonishes us to distinguish carefully between discourses, including cultural ones, that naturalize repression and those that naturalize resistance (Coulthard 2014, 103). Mohawk anthropologist Audra Simpson, writing about her own community, even engages in ethnographic "refusal" when she decides to focus neither on cultural themes like traplines nor on socio-logical fetishes like poverty, but describes instead a community that includes the *New York Post*, a pet cemetery, and a variety of vehicles from Cadillacs to Volkswagens (Simpson 2014, 6). In the case of Tai-wan, I would say that state-led discourses that essentialize all people on Formosa as being somehow Chinese or depict Indigenous cultures as merely colourful tiles in a multicultural mosaic of liberal Taiwan are hegemonic. When Sediq and Truku affirm their own cultural specificity, even to create distinctions from one another, this act can be a form of Indigenous resurgence. Anthropologists should be aware of those dis-tinctions. What is important is that culture is not a *thing*; it is a *discursive formation* and way of worlding that arises in social relations as people stake out positionality relative to others.

Indigeneity, Indigenous Resurgence, and Human Rights

In addition to "culture," the central concept of "Indigenous" risks rei-fication and essentialization. Anthropologists seem to have been taken by surprise when Indigenous peoples emerged in international organi-zations as autonomous political actors. Ever since Adam Kuper's initial liberal critique in which he denigrated the Indigenous rights move-ment as a new form of primitivism (Kuper 2003), anthropologists have been able to build careers on deconstructing this international political movement. Because of my work with hunters and trappers, I concur with Lucas Bessire, who argues that multiculturalist indigeneity further marginalizes the poor (Bessire 2014). But I am uncomfortable with the way in which, just as Indigenous peoples gain a voice in international politics, some non-Indigenous anthropologists or sociologists take it upon themselves to criticize and deconstruct the movement. In the most egregious cases, they dismiss the Indigenous rights movement as the self-serving actions of Indigenous elites. In chapter 1, I will discuss how those critiques play out in the study of Taiwanese indigeneity.

I take more seriously the critiques of Indigenous scholars and allies who deconstruct not the Indigenous rights movement but rather the institutions of state-centric indigeneity. Audra Simpson gets directly to the point when she argues that the fixation in politics of recognition on cultural difference occludes Indigenous sovereignty (Simpson 2014, 20). She borrows from the work of Elizabeth Povinelli, who observed in Australia that rights initiatives in courts and legislatures are more about advancing state law than accepting Indigenous peoples and their laws as ontological equals (Povinelli 2002, 185). Mario Blaser argued that rights of Indigenous peoples are limited by reducing differences to culture (Blaser 2009a, 891). Coulthard reasons that state-sponsored recognition and reconciliation is "still *colonial* insofar as it remains structurally committed to the dispossession of Indigenous peoples of our lands and self-determining authority" (Coulthard 2014, 151, emphasis in the original). I think it is important to consider both legalistic indigeneity, the state-centric legal framework that puts limits on Indigenous sovereignty through politics of recognition, and the emerging Indigenous resurgence that is happening in Taiwan and around the world. It is important to recognize and appreciate the efforts of Indigenous individuals who may be committed over the course of a lifetime to *both* projects, even seeing the institutions of indigeneity as providing the necessary opening for more radical Indigenous politics. They are not necessarily mutually exclusive choices for individuals over the course of a lifetime. Just as with class and culture, both indigeneity and Indigenous resurgence are discursive formations to which people refer in their worlding projects, or lifeworlds. The challenge for the political philosopher may be to discern which discourses are hegemonic and which are liberating. For the ethnographer, life is more than discourse, and what seems mutually exclusive in language may be very fluid in actual practice.

One of the main proponents of phenomenological anthropology has his own approach to indigeneity. In an essay originally presented at the National Museum of Ethnology, Osaka, British anthropologist Tim Ingold took on the issue of indigenous peoples (not capitalized in his essay, and thus not in these two paragraphs) being defined in the United Nations and related organizations according to *descent* from the people who originally lived on those lands prior to the colonial encounter. He even dared to ask the politically incorrect question of whether it is reasonable to withhold indigenous status from persons who are born and raised in a country and have lifelong familiarity with it just because their ancestors came from somewhere else (Ingold 2000, 132). In a broad survey of the anthropological literature, he contrasts the Western arboreal model of genealogy, which extracts people from their surroundings, to a non-Western rhizomatic model of relations based on peoples' relations to the land and its other inhabitants. He concludes that "the categorial opposition of indigenous and non-indigenous populations, conceived respectively as the descendants of natives and settlers, is itself a construction of colonialism" (Ingold 2000, 151).

Frankly, I was furious when I first read Ingold's essay. Ingold seemed to imply that those people who do not have lifetime familiarity with a country are somehow less indigenous than those who do, regardless of descent and genealogy. Reflecting on the reality of Sediq and Truku youth, who are estranged from the mountain forests and may even be more comfortable in urban areas, I saw Ingold's approach as disrespectful of their political movement. I even found it cruel how he seemed to reproach people for having left the land, after they had suffered and continue to suffer the dispossession from their own territories by forces beyond their control. He seemed to set aside politics and ignore realities of settler colonialism and inequalities in power. This essay could easily be read as an example of unexamined white privilege. Eventually, I realized that Ingold's essay illustrates the difference between the capitalized Indigenous – which is a political identity, a way of affirming a desired new relationship between Indigenous peoples and the state – and a non-capitalized indigenous, which means something else. The former is central to the spirit of our times and is addressed in this book. Ingold was pointing to something else, however, which may also emerge from between the lines of this book.

Culture and Indigenous are important parts of our modern ontology because they contribute to our understanding of a particular kind of human rights. Evolving international and national frameworks, including the United Nations Declaration on the Rights of Indigenous Peoples and Taiwan's Basic Law on Indigenous Peoples, are all part of an increased recognition of "Indigenous rights." These new legal instruments promise to defend Indigenous peoples against claims to their territories by outsiders, or at least to uphold the principle of free, prior, informed consent, while facilitating profit sharing as resources are developed on their lands. As Mario Blaser pointed out, these rights are limitations because they reduce Indigenous worlds to cultures and force Indigenous peoples and lands to fit into the modern world (Blaser 2009a, 891). They merely redistribute rights, but do not even consider Indigenous peoples as fully equal nations who might be able to help us re-imagine the way nations relate to one another and to other lives on this planet.

Maps and State-Centric Legibility

The notion of mapping cultures as discrete units is part of state strategies to render populations visible and subject to policy. In fact, maps may even historically precede the political units and forms of territoriality they draw into being, making claims to sovereignty (Branch 2014). An example of a cartographic way of understanding culture can be seen in the maps of Indigenous "tribes" produced by the Council of Indigenous Peoples in Taiwan and widely distributed on the internet (map 1). The idea represented in the maps is that each tribe possesses its own distinct language, culture, and traditional territory, and that all of these can be meaningfully represented in maps. Let's look at one of the maps of Indigenous Taiwan produced by the government. I repeat that this language of "tribe" is that of the Republic of China as part of their governmentality of populations. My goal is to unsettle that hegemonic discursive formation, not to naturalize it.

This map in no way represents the way in which people move across real physical territory. The map shows the Truku as a sliver on the east coast and the Sediq as a fragment in the centre, separated from each other by a large swath of Atayal territory. This map does not conform to the political knowledge that the Truku are the majority in Hsiulin and Wanrong Townships of coastal Hualien and that the Sediq are the majority in Ren'ai Township of central Nantou, nor that there are important dissenters in both townships. It does not show that these ethnonyms were imposed on people, even as they sometimes conflict with how people view themselves and their families. The most striking dissonance with lived experience is that this map does not depict the fact that these townships and territories are adjacent to one another, as they are on the ground. Since Hsiulin Township claims to represent Truku territoriality and Ren'ai Township Sediq territoriality, one can stand on the border, which is marked by a sign on the cross-mountain highway, with one foot in each township. This situation is not solely a by-product of poor map-making. Such maps, along with a vocabulary of tribalism, reveal a lack of concern for Truku and Sediq political claims to restore their traditional territory, and these maps reduce Truku and Sediq political status. They also reflect an ontology of territoriality and exclusivity, rather than one of relationality and sharing.

Maps do not capture the sense of movement through space. A map cannot capture the narrow winding roads along steep cliffs, ferns larger than humans, and conifers reaching to the sky, let alone the sense of vertigo one experiences while looking down into limestone caverns carved by the rivers below or the adjustments of the ears and lungs to

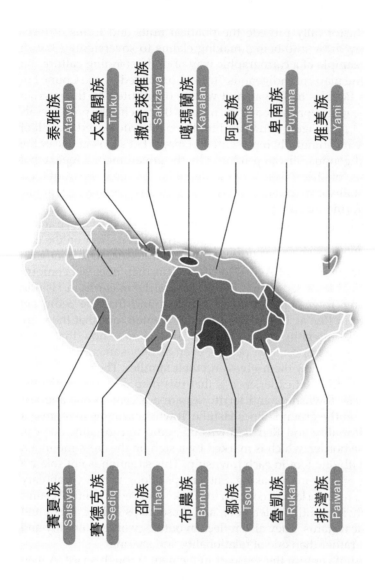

泰雅族 Atayal
大魯閣族 Truku
撒奇萊雅族 Sakizaya
噶瑪蘭族 Kavalan
阿美族 Amis
卑南族 Puyuma
雅美族 Yami

賽夏族 Saisiyat
賽德克族 Sediq
邵族 Thao
布農族 Bunun
鄒族 Tsou
魯凱族 Rukai
排灣族 Paiwan

Map 1. Map of Taiwan Indigenous "tribes." Modern maps, based on Cartesian rationality, illustrate peoples in terms of exclusive spatial territory.

Source: Courtesy of the Republic of China Council of Indigenous Peoples.

changes in altitude while driving. Maps cannot capture the feeling of a Truku-speaking woman returning from coastal Hualien to her natal village high up in the mountains of Nantou, where she will speak the same dialect in both places even though her husband in Hualien identifies as Truku and her brothers in Nantou as Sediq. They cannot convey the memories of a mountain goat caught on a certain cliff or those of a grandfather recounting around a campfire the warfare that his clan once had against the Toda clans who lived in that valley in a particular settlement long destroyed and accessible only by navigating the waters and rocks by foot along one stream. These lived experiences are betrayed by any attempt to represent them, whether by making maps, writing books, or telling stories.

Japanese anthropologist Tōichi Mabuchi (1909–88), early observer of Taiwanese Indigenous life, tried to move beyond this limitation by thinking of geography as lived experience rather than as cartography. Working in Taiwan, which was part of Japan at that time, he divided the natural knowledge of the mountain peoples into concentric circles: the "life sphere" of direct contact in daily life, the "observation and hearsay" sphere known through commerce and travel, and the "legend sphere" of oral history (Mabuchi 1974, 179–82). The life sphere, based on perception that arises from farming, hunting, and living in the forest, is that of daily life experience. Much of it is not spoken at all, but merely lived. The observation and hearsay sphere also emerges from direct experience, from more sporadic encounters, as in long-distance trade or headhunting expeditions or in conversations with those who have just returned to the village. The legend sphere refers to the rich oral traditions, with knowledge of such things as the first human beings who emerged from a rock in the centre of Formosa or the origins of human greed. Nowadays, this sphere would include the stories that the elders tell about their youth when Formosa was under Japanese administration. Looking at how people construct their lives by moving on paths through these spheres will make it possible to study, not necessarily discrete cultures, by how people grow into knowledge "in their movement along a way of life" (Ingold 2011, 162).

The phenomenological concept of the lifeworld (*Lebenswelt*) was first popularized by Husserl, but expresses an idea very common in Indigenous thought: knowledge comes from lived experience. I used this concept in my very first book (Simon 2003b) as a way of bypassing the essentializing dimensions of culture and getting instead to the embodied experiences of individuals. I root it in ideas of the human individual as organism. It is about the constellation of ideas, passions, and projects that animate human existence, in which individuals may orient themselves to various cultural ideas but without reducing themselves to one identity or necessarily allowing themselves to be restrained by notions of reified cultures. This approach opens to different kinds of relationality, not only between humans but with non-human lives as well. In the words of Ingold, organisms and persons are "knots in a tissue of knots, whose constituent strands, as they become tied up with other strands, in other knots, comprise the meshwork" (Ingold 2011, 70).

Lifeworlds are an important component of what Mario Blaser and Marisol de la Cadena call "Political Ontology" (capitalized in the original), which assumes "divergent worldings constantly coming about through negotiations, enmeshments, crossings, and interruptions" (Blaser and de la Cadena 2018, 6). This concept also assumes that people come to an understanding of their worlds through embodied experience. Political ontology, however, takes that insight further by recognizing the political nature of those movements and relations, and by paying attention to conflicts. Phenomenological anthropology is not sufficient for understanding colonial situations, including indigeneity. For that, we need much greater attention to politics and inequality between human groups. Marxist insights are still important, but so are insights from the most remote places in the mountain forests.

This Book: Gaya as Ethical Becoming

If I were to choose one Indigenous concept to sum up where this book is going, it would be Gaya. At least as much as to any of the anthropologists and Indigenous scholars discussed in this chapter, I am indebted to the Indigenous people in Taiwan who nourished my thoughts and reflections in both their conversations and their written work. One example is Seediq intellectual Takun Walis, who has nourished me intellectually more than my anthropological predecessors like Boas and Lévi-Strauss, not only because I have read his written work. He also hosted me in his home for six months in 2007, and I spent time with him on every subsequent annual trip to Taiwan. Takun wrote:

> Before the Japanese occupied the Musha district in 1903, our people followed our own Gaya. By revering Heaven and Earth, worshipping the ancestral spirits, and cherishing a conviction in symbiotic coexistence with Nature, we were living a carefree, nomadic life without government institutions. For thousands of years without interruption, the life-stage ceremonies, life rites and customs, ethical relations, and traditional names and other norms within Gaya made it possible for the fate of our people to continue and the destiny of our people to develop. (Takun 2002, 5)

The people recognize great local diversity in Gaya as a result of geographical separation in different mountain valleys but also because of the practices of different clans and ritual groups. This diversity is where Gaya differs from anthropological concepts of culture. Rather than trying to understand the mentality of a people, it accounts for local histories of wayfaring that lead to local idiosyncrasies. Nonetheless, there are core moral precepts in Gaya, which make it appear more like law than as a theory of mental representations. The most important ones are political egalitarianism, sharing with others (economic egalitarianism), protecting one's family and the territory of the community (alang), and sexual fidelity. Older people say that young people in the past would sleep naked with a member of the opposite sex to test their ability to abstain from sexual contact before marriage. Kaji Cihung, local scholar and primary school teacher in Bsngan (Hualien), draws attention to rituals that are expressions of Gaya: *powda* (sacrifices), *smapuh* (traditional healing), *mkan hadur* (feeding heads), *maduq* (hunting), and *tminun* (weaving; Kaji 2011, 33). Takun Walis, cited by Dakis, thought of Gaya as a more comprehensive historical emanation from Pusu Qhuni, the rules for coexisting with nature, and modes of reconciliation, contracting peace after conflicts in rituals of burying stones and even creating new confederations (Kuo 2012, 263). I encountered elders who claim that Gaya is a universal concept, with implications for all humans, even if the high mountain people apparently master it better than others. Many of them contrasted the morality of their Gaya to the supposed money-oriented greed of the Taiwanese. At its most fundamental level, Gaya is the natural order of the world, and life and action in agreement with that order (Kim 1980, 181). Gaya is simultaneously a product of wayfaring, a moral compass in human lifeworlds, and an understanding of interpersonal and interspecific relations in the meshwork of life. Only those who uphold Gaya fully are truly human – Seejiq balay!

An Overview of the Chapters

The bulk of this book is a series of five essays. The goal is to show how I came to understand lifeworlds as the paths of my wayfaring intersected with those of other people over years of field research. The book is thus not a sustained analytic engagement with concepts or with theories created by people far away from this meshwork of life. When I evoke theories, it is because they are part of the baggage that I was carrying on the journey and because what I learned from the encounters may have implications for future anthropological research. The book is mostly written around anecdotes and conversations but occasionally around written work, as my life temporarily entwined with those of others and we communicated about that situation. When I describe my itineraries, I hope that this open and transparent style of ethnography is relevant to younger anthropologists just beginning their own paths. I am sharing, in addition to the intellectual learnings, my "heart knowledge," as I reflect upon what Sediq, Truku, and some Indigenous people in Canada have taught me about being human. Especially in the conclusion, I bring these lessons into dialogue with what I have learned from Indigenous scholars and elders in Canada. I am not the first person to bring together Indigenous perspectives from Taiwan and Canada. In fact, as mentioned earlier, Indigenous people in Taiwan chose their new collective name in Chinese, yuanzhu minzu 原住民族, at least partly after dialogue with a trusted Mohawk friend.

I construct each chapter around a discussion of a Sediq-Truku concept, bringing in anthropological debates only secondarily, because I share Zoe Todd's concern that certain trends in Western scholarship entrench the prestige of European philosophy while eliding the contribution of Indigenous thinkers (Todd 2016). This chapter has already introduced some Sediq vocabulary, and even if it may seem repetitive, it is worth reviewing the three crucial concepts that inform all the chapters to come. Gaya, often translated as "sacred law" or "ancestral law," is a Truku and Tgdaya word that can also be translated as "culture" or "mode of life." It animates various projects that we can study effectively as competing political ontologies. Some people, but not all, imagine Gaya as a universal teaching applicable to all humans. Alang, often translated as "community," is a flexible grouping of people, usually formed around a nuclear clan or kin group, which holds moral claims on its members and exercises sovereignty over territory. Subgroups are also called alang, and they may form confederations with other alang, which is what led to the three identities of Truku, Tgdaya, and Toda even before the Japanese arrived. Seejiq (Truku), Seediq (Tgdaya), or Sediq (Toda), often translated as "human," can also mean "someone" or "person." One can refer, for example, to Seejiq Kanada (Canadian person). Some people, but not all, support making it into the name of an ethnic group in multicultural state categories, and some, but not all, affirm it as the name of an Indigenous nation. With the adjective *balay*, which makes it "truly human," Seejiq balay is a morally upstanding member of his or her alang. Some people, but not all, use Seejiq balay to mean "Indigenous people."

With those concepts in mind, chapter 1 is an introduction to Taiwan and its Indigenous peoples. The ethnography begins in chapter 2, in which I explore the animal world. Truku people began teaching me their language and way of life in my first days of field research with animals and their names. *Samat* is the word that the Truku use for the animals of the forest, as opposed to *tnbgan*, animals of the village.[13] This differentiation is important because of the centrality of hunting in Indigenous lifeworlds. In chapter 3, I explore the meaning of *mgaya*, the historical ritual of "headhunting" that is often evoked by ordinary people in somewhat surprising ways. Obviously, I cannot go back in time and personally experience headhunting. Instead, I rely on Japanese colonial-era documentation but reflect on what it means to discuss and re-enact headhunting today. In chapter 4, I look beyond the living to the world of *utux*, the spirits, in a chapter that explores both the reality of the dead and the nature of religion. In chapter 5, looking at *lnglungan* (the heart, not as anatomical organ but rather as a way of thinking similar to that discussed earlier), I examine the search for social justice through social movements and politics. Like tnbgan, lnglungan has the locative suffix -an, indicating that the heart is the place of thinking and wisdom. Finally, in chapter 6, I get to the tminun, weaving. This chapter is partly a tribute to women, as weaving was considered to be women's contribution to their families, while men focused on hunting. But tminun also refers to the weaving of stories and thus of social memory. In this chapter, I explore memories of the 1914 Taroko Battle and the 1930 Musha Uprising, when local communities defended Gaya in armed resistance against the Japanese. This chapter is also my opportunity to engage in a sustained way with Sediq and Truku thinkers – especially the work of retired policeman Kuhon Siban in Hualien and feminist Presbyterian theologian Kumu Tapas in Nantou – as they reflect upon their local histories and contemporary political status. The conclusion is a final reflection on indigeneity and Indigenous resurgence.

The illustrations are also very important. Photos illustrate the themes of each chapter but are also part of the methodology. They are intended to draw attention towards the physical presence of human and non-human actors in the meshwork of life so that readers may see the world from which the political practices of indigeneity and Indigenous resurgence both emerge. Interspersed between each essay is an illustration of a non-human actor in the story. I added these illustrations as a wink of recognition to the studies in anthropology beyond the human and new materialism that inspired the discipline and my own thoughts as I was doing the research and writing the book. The choice of illustrator was part of the collaborative ethnography. Kumu Tapas introduced me to illustrator Biluan in Puli. Biluan does not have legal Indigenous identity, but adopted the name Biluan in order to make visible the presence of the yet-to-be recognized Kaxabu and Pazeh *pingpuzu* 平埔族 (see page 49) in the Puli Basin. Although I gave Biluan the names of five non-human actors to draw, I did not give her precise instructions as if she were an employee. Instead, I encouraged her to express her own creativity as she used those images to represent the reality of that mountain world to outsiders. The pingpuzu have historically been mediators between the mountain peoples and the outside world, and this form of collaboration is an extension of that historical process. She also drew the cover illustration.

It is now time to return to Pusu Qhuni and even dare to think of it as the origin of all humanity. In a way, every morning we awaken with a choice that is not unlike that which our ancestors faced when they first emerged from that giant rock-tree in the woods. One of the men looked out into the world with wonder because of its richness, not least because of the presence of so many birds, animals, and plants. The other, fearful of a world that was full of disease, death, and danger, returned into Pusu Qhuni and never emerged again. Only the woman did not hesitate about becoming truly human. Today, we can still look down from the mountains to a world that is full of beautiful human and non-human lives. Nowadays, it is also a world full of highways, pipelines, mines, tea plantations, pollution, colonial dispossession, wars, violence, pandemic, and death. Do we turn away from it? Or do we seek a way to move through it ethically, following our hearts and obeying Gaya? In this era of climate change, environmental destruction, and rumours of war, we must all reflect on these questions if we wish to attain true reconciliation among related humans and beyond. This book contains some lessons that I learned from Sediq, Truku, and others on Formosa as people shared with an anthropologist what they want to share with the world. I hope it is a way for others to learn about Taiwan and its Indigenous peoples but also a way to reflect on larger issues.

Chapter One

Introducing Taiwan and Its Indigenous Peoples

Taiwan is no bigger than a ball of mud. We gain nothing by possessing it, and it would be no loss if we did not acquire it.

– Kangxi Emperor, 27 November 1683
(quoted in Teng 2004, 34)

Most introductions to Taiwan begin with some statement about it being an island of approximately 36,000 square kilometres, which would make it slightly larger than Belgium, Maryland, or Vancouver Island and roughly the size of Algonquin territory on the Ottawa River watershed. Just like the map discussed earlier, this notion of space is strictly Cartesian. It takes the perspective of statecraft.[1] Maps are political claims, which is why some maps of Taiwan colour it as part of China, whereas other maps separate it from China. Measurements of space are important for state legibility. Military planners, for example, may try to estimate how many troops and artillery would be needed to occupy the island. Such quantifications are also useful to Taiwanese diplomats in foreign capitals like Ottawa trying to justify why their host governments should take them as seriously as they do that of, say, Belgium. Such measurements, however, do not capture life as it is lived by any of those who create a dwelling for themselves in their own particular circumstances. Not a single person on the island of Formosa lives their life on a space of 36,000 square kilometres; in fact, most of the mountainous terrain is inaccessible to humans. Instead, people stake out livings by carving rice paddies in the earth, setting up food stands in urban alleys, or strategically setting a snare where a muntjac is likely to descend a densely covered slope on the way to find water. Ingold thus writes against space as a form of logical inversion that, akin to notions of culture, overlooks life as it is experienced (Ingold 2011, 145).

From the perspective of mountain-dwelling people, places in the mountains are more important than anything that happens in space. Neither cabbage farmers nor hunters need to know that Taiwan has 165 mountains surpassing 3,000 metres, but they know exactly where they can grow plants, install water pipes, or find flying squirrels. Most mountain dwellers even prefer leaving the windy, stony summits to the intrepid hikers who like to collect photos of all the peaks they have conquered. From lived experience, it is less important to quantify that 54.5 to 58.5 per cent of Taiwan is covered by forests (Liu, Lin, and Kuo 2002) than to show how peoples' lifeworlds are shaped by the relationships they have with trees, ferns, and mushrooms, as well as with birds, game animals, and snakes. It is also important to note that there is no longer a single Truku or Sediq community in which people live full-time in the forest. They do not inhabit the Amazon or a remote forested island in the Philippines. Their lifeworlds are thus also shaped, if not more so, by landscapes of irrigated crops, paved roads connecting villages, railroads taking them off to schools and military service, construction sites and factories, and even flights on aeroplanes leaving Taiwan. They live in a meshwork that includes the organic inhabitants of the world as well as the physical manifestations of statecraft. Their wayfarings include paths through the forest but also meeting rooms in the township office and church services. Although this book will discuss life in all these contexts, I begin in the heart of Truku migrations, an area now known as the Taroko National Park. The people there called themselves Truku, and since the Japanese could not pronounce that word, they called that geographical area Taroko.

The Taroko National Park, which occupies Truku traditional territory, is an exercise in Cartesian surveying and state legibility. Most Truku, whether they feel threatened by conservation officers or empowered by the lure of employment at visitor centres, know about Taiwan's eight national parks, even if they have only a vague idea that these parks cover 8.64 per cent of Taiwan's land mass. For park administrators, it is important to know that the Taroko National Park covers 92,000 hectares from tropical rainforest to snow-capped peaks up to 3,705 metres. Most of these forests overlap directly with Indigenous hunting territories or even Indigenous reserve lands. Cartesian maps see land as detached from human lives, whereas relational perspectives see the deep connections between humans and the land. For these reasons, Truku protesters advocating for hunting rights in the Taroko National Park have used the motto "The land is our blood; the mountain forests are our home." It is also why one woman there, while expressing her feeling of alienation towards the Indigenous rights movement, said to me: "I would rather be called 'mountain people' than 'Indigenous.' At least it is a description of where I live." The land occupied by the Taroko National Park, in the centre of the Truku territory, thus simultaneously hosts Truku traditional territory, a state claim to sovereignty, a dwelling place for its inhabitants (human and non-human), and an arena for conflicting political ontologies.

A Brief Political History of Formosan Indigenous Peoples

For Formosan Indigenous peoples, modern history is defined by the arrival of colonial powers, dispossession, and genocide. The difficulty of understanding the pre-colonial history of Formosa's Indigenous peoples is that they had no written language and thus kept no written record of their activities in ancient times. Archaeologists demonstrate that Formosa has been inhabited for at least 6,000 years by Austronesian peoples. They are related linguistically and genetically to the peoples who, most likely radiating outward from Formosa, peopled the islands of the Pacific and Indian Oceans (Bellwood, Fox, and Tryon 1995). Archaeological evidence shows that Neolithic migrants from Formosa settled Luzon around 4,000 years ago, bringing with them nephrite jade from what is now Fengtian, Hualien. Green nephrite from this source was used to make two specific kinds of ear pendants, which were distributed around the coasts of the South China Sea until about AD 400 (Hung et al. 2007).

The Formosan peoples, unlike the people on smaller "offshore" islands in the Taiwan Strait also governed by the Republic of China (Taiwan), knew nothing of the various state forms that have characterized Chinese history for the past three millennia. Instead, the different Formosan peoples developed their own political organizations in ways as diverse as the institutions that emerged across Oceania. Taiwanese anthropologist Wei Hwei-Lin classified pre-colonial polities according to political authority as (1) patrilineal, "quasi-horde" societies (e.g., the Atayal), (2) composite tribal societies with patriclans, (3) matrilinear societies with age ranks, and (4) dominion-based societies with "noble" ranks and local defence societies (Wei 1965). Huang Ying-kuei classified the Paiwan, Rukai, Tsou, Amis, and Puyuma as chief (type A) societies; the Bunun, Atayal, and Yami as Big Man (type B) societies; and the Saisiyat as an intermediate type (Huang 1986). Both approaches characterize the Atayal, and by extension the Sejiq, as egalitarian Big Man groups (Huang 1986). These societies against the state, to borrow the vocabulary of Pierre Clastres (1974, cited earlier), stand in stark contrast to the bureaucratic state system of imperial China that waxed and

Table 1.1. Waves of colonialism on Formosa

Colonizers	Years	Impact on Indigenous lifeworlds
Spain (N Formosa)	1624–41	Trading post and mission
Dutch East India Company (SW Formosa)	1624–62	Trading post; negotiated treaties with plains peoples; made SW Formosa safe for Chinese settlement
Tungning Kingdom (Ming loyalists)	1662–83	Expanded Chinese settlement on SW Formosa by violent means
Qing Dynasty (Manchurians)	1683–1895	Expanded Chinese settlement to nearly half of the island (in the western plains); created distinctions between "raw savages" and "cooked savages" as they brought groups under Qing political jurisdiction
Japan	1895–1945	Military conquest of the entire island; created reserves and tribal councils on the American frontier model for the "raw savages," who became "Formosan peoples" (*Takasago minzoku* 高砂民族) after 1930
Republic of China (martial law era)	1945–87	Policies of integration created a political elite dependent on the ruling Chinese Nationalist Party (KMT) as "mountain compatriots"
Republic of China (post–martial law)	1987–present	Growth of Indigenous social movement; official policies of multicultural indigeneity regarding *yuanzhu minzu* 原住民族 (Indigenous peoples), the first time the Indigenous people got to create a collective name for themselves as political actors

Sources: Various, summarizes this chapter.

waned over millennia on just the other side of the Taiwan Strait, and even on the adjacent archipelago of the Pescadores, for about one millennium. Their way of life was disrupted by subsequent waves of colonialism, which from their perspective continues unabated to this day (table 1.1).

The first Formosan groups to encounter state administration were the peoples of southwestern Formosa, now known mostly as Siraya. The Dutch, rather than the Chinese, first brought state forms to Formosa when the Dutch East India Company established a colony near what is now Tainan from 1624 to 1662. The Dutch strategy, like what they pursued at the same time with the Iroquois in Manhattan (Hauptman and Knapp 1977), was to fight with some local groups to gain access to land, establish alliances with others, and ultimately negotiate treaties that defined their joint sovereignty. In Dutch Formosa, these political alliances were solemnized in the rituals of the *landdag* (literally "land day"), in which the Dutch governor met with representatives of the peaceful communities, selected representatives from each one to serve as leader, and presented them with symbols of authority such as an orange flag, a black robe, and a rattan staff embellished with a silver head and the company insignia (Andrade 2008, 186). Maybe, if we could go back in time to live with those people, we would find that those emergent leaders saw themselves as doing their best to preserve the autonomy of their peoples in the face of new threats. We might also find that others in their midst found them to be collaborators out for their own personal benefit. They may have even laughed at the flags and robes, just as people laugh at the pretentions of self-proclaimed elites today.

The lasting heritage of the Dutch is that they brought the first perma-nent Chinese settlement to Taiwan. As the Dutch expanded their influ-ence over territory and needed labour for sugar plantations and other enterprises, they opened the island to Chinese settlement. From Indig-enous perspectives, the Chinese on Taiwan are settlers in the same sense as the English and the French are in North America. The Dutch were expelled in 1662 by Chinese rebel Koxinga (Cheng Cheng-kung), who claimed for himself the mantle of the Ming Dynasty, which had just been conquered by the Manchurian Qing. The brief rule of Koxinga and his son was ended by defeat to the Qing navy in 1683. During the subse-quent Qing rule on part of Formosa (1683–1895), Chinese settlers fought fierce battles with the aboriginal peoples, ultimately gaining control of the cultivable western plains of Taiwan (Shepherd 1993). The plains aborigines were supposedly assimilated into Chinese society through intermarriage and identity change, even as many of their rituals and social practices persisted and were relabelled as Chinese (Brown 2004).

The Qing period, during which Han Chinese settlers colonized the western plains of Formosa and brought it under Qing domination, set the discursive foundations for categorizing the island's inhabitants into "plains" and "mountain" aboriginal peoples. The Qing classified the former as "cooked savages" (*shoufan* 熟番) and the latter as "raw sav-ages" (*shengfan* 生番). Although the usage of these terms has a long his-tory in China, historian Emma Teng traces the first usage in Taiwan to the 1717 Gazetteer of Zhuluo County, which made a distinction between cooked savages, who pay taxes, and raw savages, "those who had not yet submitted to civilization" (Teng 2004, 125). The two groups could be visibly distinguished because people in the subdued communities shaved their heads and wore the long queue required of Han Chinese under Manchurian jurisdiction, whereas people in the autonomous mountain communities kept long hair. Beginning in 1722, the Qing court implemented an aboriginal boundary policy to keep Chinese settlers out of the mountains, a practice that by the mid-nineteenth century led the Japanese and Western powers to doubt Qing jurisdiction over aboriginal territories (Chang 2008).

For much of this history, Taiwan's native peoples have been treated as less than human. Near the end of the nineteenth century, as conflict intensified between Chinese settler villages and native peoples, the Chinese openly sold "savage flesh" in the markets along with pork (Davidson 1903, 255). When challenged about these cannibalistic practices, the Chinese would simply "smile and say the savages are not men but a species of large monkey" (Takekoshi [1907] 1996, 228). I didn't believe these colonial reports until an elderly Taiwanese man recalled to me that his grandfather told him that human flesh was once sold openly in the markets in Puli.

Most Qing governments did not see it as a priority to take the mountain areas. If anything, the mountains served the early Qing as a "hedgerow" for China that provided a natural barrier against outside enemies (Tung 2001, 60). This situation changed after the 1871 Mudanshe Incident, when shipwrecked sailors from the Ryukyus (now Okinawa) were murdered on the Hengchun Peninsula. The Qing refused to take responsibility, saying that land beyond the "Savage Boundary" was not under their jurisdiction. After Japan retaliated with a punitive expedition, the Qing realized the need to declare sovereignty over the entire island (Teng 2004, 209–10). The Qing began a new policy of "Opening the Mountains and Pacifying the Savages," but they lost many of the initial battles and never managed to subdue the fiercest warrior peoples of the interior (Linck-Kesting 1979).

After defeat in the Sino-Japanese War, the Qing ceded Formosa and the Pescadores to Japan in the 1895 Treaty of Shimonoseki. Since the Qing had never really governed the half of Formosa that remained under the control of the original inhabitants, Japan found itself endowed with the onerous task of "pacifying" the shengfan 生番. In the north, where Atayalic groups provided the most entrenched resistance, the Japanese military used scorched earth campaigns. From 1903 to 1915, they gradually encircled entire areas of the mountains with electrified guard lines, cutting off each group from trade relations with others and from access to hunting grounds. One by one, each group surrendered to the Japanese and, in formal ceremonies, became Japanese imperial subjects (or so thought the Japanese). Military operations lasted until 1914, when the Truku in Hualien surrendered after three months of fierce resistance. The Japanese thought of this surrender as *kijun* 帰順 (submission), which they translated as *snegul* in the dictionaries prepared for police officers assigned to those areas. For the people, however, snegul simply meant a temporary agreement to "follow" the Japanese, as this verb is also used in the sense of following a skilled hunter through the forest. The people did not perceive these rituals as political submission or a transfer of sovereignty to Japan.[2] There were still sporadic moments of resistance, including a notable uprising in Paran (called Musha by the Japanese) by Tgdaya groups in 1930. I will return to memories of these military events in chapter 6.

The high mountain groups had the most intimate relations with the forests. The Atayalic groups, which included those now known as Sediq and Truku, were portrayed by Japanese historian and statesmen Yosaburo Takekoshi as follows:

> They live mostly in mountain recesses, are extremely ferocious and attach great importance to head-hunting. This group is more uncivilized than any of the others. They are divided into many small tribes, the members of which are like one family, under the patriarchal rule of the chieftain. (Takekoshi [1907] 1996, 219)

The Japanese, however, wanted access to the forest resources, the most valuable of which was camphor. Camphor, which had traditionally been used as an insect repellent and medicine, became used to manufacture celluloid plastics, smokeless gunpowder, and photographic or cinematic film (needed in large quantities due to the rise of the global film industry). Takekoshi deplored the fact that half of Taiwan was still under the exclusive control of "savages," preventing the Japanese from exploiting resources of timber and minerals to be found in the mountain forests.

Japanese administrators were still not ready to accept the native peoples as truly human. Takekoshi was surely thinking metaphorically when he wrote that "the savages can run like deer and climb like monkeys, sometimes springing up into trees for refuge when closely pursued, and sometimes covering the ground in long leaps or skilfully hiding themselves in the bushes" (Takekoshi [1907] 1996, 217). Nonetheless, there were debates in Japan about whether Formosan native peoples, characterized by their lack of government and supposedly savage acts of headhunting, possessed the legal personality possessed by civilized human beings. Taiwan governor-general advisor Mochiji Rokusaburō opined that "sociologically speaking, they are indeed human beings, but looked at from the viewpoint of international law, they resemble animals" (quoted in Barclay 2018, 28). Even as Japanese administrators recognized land title for Chinese settlers, such arguments undergirded the *terra nullius* policy towards native lands by which Japan unilaterally declared all forests on Formosa to be imperial property. Knowing this history gives new meaning to peoples' assertions that they are humans (*seejiq*) as opposed to being animals (*samat*). It is as if their parents passed down the memories of these debates and as if they think that claiming humanity is still the most fundamental way of asserting rights. This thinking is why Dakis Pawan concluded one of his books about the Musha Uprising by saying that the rebellion was a "human rights action." Because the Japanese treated them like animals, stealing their territory and using forced labour as if they were driving cattle or horses, the Seediq had no choice but to rebel in order to reclaim their own humanity and the rights that come with that ontological status (Kuo 2012, 274–5).

Japanese practices of governance over Taiwan's non-Han populations changed only near the end of Japanese rule. For the first decades, the Japanese governed their areas with military force and punitive biopolitics. In contrast, by the mid-1910s, they were already ruling the lowland Han populations with disciplinary modalities of governance, using institutions of public health, schools, markets, and so on to create subject-citizens (Barclay 2018, 29). The violent repression of 1930, after what the Japanese depicted as an uprising called the "Musha Incident" (*Musha jiken* 霧社事件), proved the failure of Japan's aboriginal policies and practices. In 1935, supposedly on orders of the emperor himself (Yamaguchi 1999, 32), the Japanese began to collectively refer to Taiwan's non-Han peoples as *Takasago minzoku* 高砂民族 (literally "high sands peoples," from an ancient Japanese word for Formosa). The goal of this new administrative rationality, which deepened after 1939 with policies of *Kōminka* (imperialization 皇民化), was a new type of subject formation, creating political subjects who were willing to die for the emperor (Ching 2001). The separate forms of governance for Han and non-Han populations created what Barclay calls a "second-order geobody" (Barclay 2018, 33). It created the path dependence for today's politics of both indigeneity and Indigenous resurgence.

The Japanese period continues to hold a deep influence on Indigenous societies. Historian Paul Barclay called this system, in which Han Taiwanese of Chinese descent were endowed with private property and educated to become Japanese citizens whereas native peoples were restricted to reserve lands and treated as wards of the state, "bifurcated sovereignty" (Barclay 2018, 17). Indigenous leaders now use the ethnographic maps of the Japanese period to imagine the limits of their traditional territories. Because of the primary school education given to all native children during the time, the elderly people (when I began my project) all spoke Japanese. The men of that generation were often proud of having been conscripted into the Japanese military, and people in their communities praised them for their "Japanese spirit" of courage and honesty. And when anthropologists come around asking questions about traditional culture, people still refer to Japanese-era ethnographies to give authoritative answers.

After the Japanese defeat in the Second World War, Taiwan was transferred to the Republic of China. From 1947 to 1987, the Chinese Republican government ruled Taiwan under martial law. The incoming government maintained many of the policies created by the Japanese. They kept the forests under state control but revised reserve land regulations to permit individuals to register title to land under their direct cultivation and to permit sale of usufruct rights among Indigenous individuals. At the same time, they sought to modernize the mountain people by forcing them to learn Mandarin Chinese, involving them in agricultural extension projects and economic development schemes, while encouraging them to make lifestyle changes such as adopting the use of chopsticks. The Chinese Nationalist Party (KMT) cultivated a local political elite, maintaining "mountain compatriots" as a distinct legal category important for land policy and electoral politics. The positions of mountain township magistrates and quotas for provincial legislators were reserved for Indigenous people, who voted on a separate electoral list. Outsiders had to apply for a "mountain permit" to visit Indigenous communities, which made them like "countries within a country" (Takun 2012, 278). As a result, Taiwan evolved from bifurcated sovereignty to bifurcated citizenship, all in the name of "local autonomy" and "democracy." From an Indigenous perspective, however, the incoming government seemed to be little more than a second wave of colonialism (Chiu 2000).

Table 1.2 illustrates the changes made by the Republic of China (ROC), in what I call the period of integration. Clearly, the relationship started out with mistrust because the Indigenous people spoke Japanese, had a reputation for violent rebellion, and the men were returning from the frontlines where they had served as Japanese soldiers. Under martial law, it was advantageous for Indigenous communities to adopt a "Chinese" identity, but they were able to negotiate certain political and economic status even in a period marked by a politics of assimilation. It is worth noting that there was never an equivalent of Canada's residential schools and "sixties scoop" that removed Indigenous children from their families and communities with the intention to destroy their languages and ways of life. The ROC tried to "modernize" them,

Table 1.2. Landmarks of indigeneity, 1945–83 (period of integration)

Year(s)	Event(s)
1945	Japanese defeat in Second World War (15 August)
1945–7	Japanese police and teachers replaced with Chinese equivalents; Indigenous men return from Japanese military service; community leaders start thinking about relations with new state
1946	Japanese-era reserves reorganized as thirty mountain townships and 162 villages with the stated goal of "autonomy" and quotas on elected positions
Early 1947	"February 28" Taiwanese movement against ROC corruption and brutality is crushed by ROC forces; Tsou youth participate in Chiayi uprising; Indigenous leaders propose the creation of an Indigenous autonomous region
1947	The ROC adopts a terminology of "mountain compatriots" for Indigenous people; Indigenous administration becomes the responsibility of the Taiwan Province Bureau of Civil Administration
1949	First Indigenous representative (Atayal) elected to the Taiwan Provincial Assembly
1951	Quota established in the provincial assembly for two mountain and one plains representative
1952	New legislation leads to registration of tribal lands, a movement to improve the lives of mountain compatriots, obligatory Mandarin language instruction, and so forth
1954	Execution of Uyongu Yata'uyungana (Tsou), Losing Watan (Atayal), and four other Indigenous leaders (17 April)
1956	The provincial government establishes employment programs for mountain compatriots; changes to land registration regulations permit non-Indigenous people to apply for land use in mountain townships
1958	Land surveys in mountain areas are completed
1962	ROC signs International Labour Organization Indigenous and Tribal Populations Convention 107
1964	Changes to land registration regulations promise usufruct rights to all mountain compatriots
1966	Townships require mountain compatriots to register agricultural land under cultivation with townships to gain recognition of usufruct rights; ROC signs the International Convention on the Elimination of All Forms of Racial Discrimination
1982	Mountain compatriots start having to pay taxes

Note: ROC = Republic of China.
Sources: Dawley (2015); Harrison (2001); Simon and Awi (2013); Yang (2021).

but kept their identities and protected their modern political rights in a "dual track democracy" (Pao and Davies 2021, 165).

For many people, as they reported to me in nearly all villages, the most traumatic period was the 1966 land reform. All Indigenous people were given the opportunity to register with the township government the location of the land they farmed so that farmers could receive title with usufruct rights. The township government placed the written claim on a bulletin board in front of the township office so that people with competing claims to the same land could contest the initial registration if it were fraudulent. Some township employees, who knew which land was targeted for leasing to mines or industrial parks, falsely registered land in their name or names of relatives, judging that the actual farmers were illiterate and unlikely to read the notice on the bulletin board. After the registration period was over, some people were suddenly evicted from the land they had cleared, and other families became wealthy by leasing out those tracts of land. Resentment towards their own village elites was still very much alive forty to fifty years later when I did my fieldwork.

During the rapid economic growth and industrialization of the 1970s, Indigenous people streamed into the cities in search of work. They found themselves with new problems, such as labour market discrimination and human trafficking for prostitution (Rudolph 1993). They also established new social networks, as people from different regions were now all speaking Mandarin and meeting in the same urban churches. In the 1980s, these urban Indigenous people, based in the Presbyterian Church as well as among university student groups, launched the Indigenous rights movement with ties to international Indigenous groups (Allio 1998b; Rudolph 2003). The first Indigenous non-governmental organization (NGO), the Alliance of Taiwan Aborigines (ATA), was founded in Taipei in December 1984. The first demands of the Indigenous rights movements were to "return our land" and "return our names." The latter was a wide process of "name rectification" in which the mountain compatriots demanded recognition as Indigenous peoples (*yuanzhu minzu* 原住民族), local groups claimed the right to define their own ethnonyms, and individuals pressed to use their own native names as opposed to state-imposed Chinese names on legal documents. The ATA has even brought international attention to Taiwanese Indigenous issues by showing up at Indigenous events at the United Nations in Geneva and New York.

Table 1.3 illustrates the changes made after the 1987 lifting of martial law in what I call the period of recognition. Responding to the demands of the Indigenous social movement, as expressed through street protests and publications by Indigenous leaders, the state created a Council of Indigenous Peoples, incorporated Indigenous rights in the Constitution

Table 1.3. Landmarks of indigeneity, 1983–2021 (period of recognition)

Year	Event(s)
1983	Establishment of Indigenous magazine *Gaoshan Qing* 高山青
1984	Creation of the Alliance of Taiwan Aborigines (ATA; 29 December)
1987	End of martial law (15 July)
1991	The ATA participates for the first time in the UN Working Group on Indigenous Populations
1991	Quota established for six "mountain compatriot" seats in the Legislative Yuan
1994	Inclusion of "Indigenous people" (*yuanzhumin* 原住民) in the Additional Articles of the Constitution
1996	Creation of the cabinet-level Council of Indigenous Peoples (CIP)
1997	Igung Shiban speaks to the UN Working Group on Indigenous Populations; inclusion of "Indigenous peoples" (*yuanzhu minzu* 原住民族) in the Additional Articles of the Constitution
1998	Education Act for Indigenous Peoples
1999	DPP presidential candidate Chen Shui-bian signs a "New Partnership Agreement" with Indigenous activists, including Igung Shiban (Truku) and Watan Diro (Sediq)
2001	Status Act for Indigenous Peoples; Indigenous Peoples Employment Protection Act; legal recognition of the Thao
2002	Legal recognition of the Kavalan; CIP begins Indigenous traditional territory surveys; declaration of twenty-five plains Indigenous townships (with funding for cultural projects)
2004	Legal recognition of the Truku (14 January); discussions at the CIP on how to incorporate Indigenous rights into a Constitution of Taiwan
2005	Indigenous Peoples Basic Law; as number of legislative seats is halved, the Indigenous quota is reduced from eight to six; 1 August designated as "Indigenous Peoples Day"
2007	Legal recognition of the Sakizaya
2008	Legal recognition of the Sediq (23 April)
2014	Legal recognition of the Hla'alua and Kanakanavu
2016	Newly elected DPP President Tsai Ing-wen apologizes to Indigenous peoples for four centuries of colonialism and creates the Presidential Office Indigenous Historical Justice and Transitional Justice Committee
2017	Indigenous Languages Development Act; Regulations for the Delineation of Indigenous Traditional Territory provoke protests because they exclude private land
2021	Constitutional court upholds laws that restrict Indigenous hunting

Notes: ATA = Alliance of Taiwan Aborigines; CIP = Council of Indigenous Peoples; DPP = Democratic Progressive Party.
Sources: Kuan (2021); Simon (2012b, 2016); ROC Ministry of Justice (2022).

(Van Bekhoven 2019), and made substantial legal reform. The Democratic Progressive Party (DPP), consistent with its own political ontology based on sovereignty and local identities, made most of the legal and political changes when they held the presidency (2000–8 and 2016–present). Most of those changes were cultural or developmentalist. The DPP failed to recognize Indigenous sovereignty when it came to the test in legislation about the delineation of traditional territory and Indigenous hunting issues.

There have been remarkable continuities in Indigenous governmentality in Taiwan. The Japanese period saw a shift from military force and punitive biopolitics to more disciplinary modalities of subject formation. The Republic of China, while promising democracy, began with policies of forced assimilation under martial law while still governing Indigenous people under a separate set of legal institutions. This practice has hence transformed into a celebration of multiculturalism, in which Indigenous people are encouraged to identify with territorially based "tribes," while obfuscating the possibility of Indigenous sovereignty. Ideas of radical discontinuity, creating the need for governance through a separated second-order geobody, remain in place until today. To borrow James Scott's vocabulary about statecraft, all of this legal structure means an increase in the legibility of Indigenous populations. Yet, as one looks at official statistics of Indigenous populations, an interesting resistance to legibility becomes visible. If the number of people who refused to declare one specific Indigenous identity were considered to be a political unit, they would be Taiwan's ninth largest Indigenous nation by population (table 1.4). Again, all of these units are "tribes" when they remain as state-based categories. These ways of establishing legal identities are still based on colonial assumptions and poorly reflect Indigenous worldviews (Van Bekhoven 2016). They become nations only when the people themselves use these categories, or create new ones, in political projects of their own.

This brief historical overview is my attempt to summarize the context in which some seejiq (human beings), while affirming identities as Indigenous, make homes for themselves in contemporary Taiwan. The wayfaring trajectories of different individuals, families, and communities have taken them in different directions. There are families who cooperated with the Japanese, politicians and political entrepreneurs deeply related to the KMT networks, and others who seek change through social movements and oppositional politics. There are those who have sought livelihoods in the cities, encountered discrimination in the workplace, and chosen to return home for a simpler life. There are some who have never left the townships of their birth, and others who are very much at home flying to meetings at the United Nations or to

Table 1.4. Registered Indigenous "tribes,"
February 2022, ranked by population

Tribe	Population
Amis	216,964
Paiwan	104,652
Atayal	93,831
Bunun	60,646
Truku	33,246
Pinuyumayan	14,943
Rukai	13,607
Sediq	10,812
Undeclared	9,841
Saisiyat	6,820
Tsou	6,703
Yami	4,804
Kavalan	1,558
Sakizaya	1,013
Thao	829
Hla'alua	445
Kanakanavu	390
Total	**581,134**

Source: ROC Council of Indigenous
Peoples (2022).

international workshops with First Nations in Canada. There are some who embrace the politics of Taiwanese indigeneity, some who are positioning themselves to benefit from the arrival of the People's Republic of China, and others who would rather just go hunting. I try to do justice in writing about the diversity of people I have met while wayfaring in villages that get identified politically as Truku or Sediq. In spite of the differences between them, I find that there are common themes that unite them, and I will highlight those in the chapters of this book.

A Sociological Portrait of Taiwan's Indigenous Populations

A sociological portrait of Taiwan's Indigenous populations puts this book into perspective. To begin, there is the issue of residence. Taiwan's Indigenous communities are classified into "mountain" and "plains" townships and districts. These two legal categories do not correspond to the historical distinctions between "raw" and "cooked," as the inhabitants of all of them are descended from the "raw" groups that had become Takasago minzoku 高砂民族 during the Japanese period. The main differences are twofold. First, the inhabitants of mountain townships do not have private title to their land. They have usufruct rights, rights to use reserve land that is state property managed by township governments, but may own the buildings constructed on the land. Only Indigenous people are permitted to buy and sell usufruct rights and property in those areas. Although some non-Indigenous individuals find ways around the restrictions to gain access to land, this law contributes to a form of residential segregation. Most residents in these communities (see later in this chapter for details on each village) are Indigenous. In the plains townships and districts, landowners have fee-simple title to land, which can be bought and sold on the real estate market, resulting in residential patterns that have more mixture with non-Indigenous people. Mountain townships account for less than one-third (30.43 per cent) of Taiwan's Indigenous population fifteen years of age and up. Of the rest, 24.6 per cent live in plains jurisdictions, and 44.97 per cent live in non-Indigenous cities and towns (ROC Council of Indigenous Peoples 2021, viii). Of course, as in Canada, these legal categories and differential land regimes confine some Indigenous people to reserves, while erasing the memory of their presence everywhere else. We should not forget that *all* of Formosa was once under exclusive Indigenous control and that Taiwan (like Canada) emerged from a history of genocide and erasure.

It is important to note which groups are *excluded* from this definition of Indigenous. The plains groups, roughly corresponding to the descendants of those classified as "cooked savages" by the Qing and early Japanese rulers, now call themselves *pingpuzu* 平埔族. As political circumstances changed over history, they were sometimes clearly marked as Other, such as during the Qing when the pingpuzu did not bind their feet but the more prestigious Han Taiwanese did. At other times, as during the ROC martial law period, it was more advantageous to blend in as Han Chinese (Brown 2004). They now seek recognition as Indigenous peoples (Hsieh 2006), the largest and most politically active being the Siraya of Tainan. Like the Métis in Canada, they are said to have assimilated but have in fact struggled to keep alive their autonomous life practices and languages. Unlike in Canada, they remain unrecognized by the central state (although the Tainan local government recognizes the Siraya). The already recognized Indigenous groups tend to oppose pingpuzu political demands, fearful that they could dilute the budgets and other resources dedicated to Indigenous projects. Household registration statistics were collected on pingpuzu status until the end of the Japanese period, which means that Taiwanese people can easily verify if their grandparents or great-grandparents had pingpuzu status before 1945. No population statistics are kept on the number of pingpuzu today. They are not included in official statistics of Indigenous peoples and do not have the special political and economic rights of Indigenous peoples, such as a quota of legislators. I have done no research in their communities.

Economic and social indicators suggest certain gaps in the well-being of Indigenous populations, compared to the general population of Taiwan. The *2017 Economic Status Survey of Indigenous Peoples in Taiwan*, compiled by the ROC Council of Indigenous Peoples (2018a), provides some important information.[3] In 2017, the average annual income of an Indigenous household was NT$727,683 (equivalent to CAD$31,638), a growth of 10 per cent over 2014. This amount was 63 per cent of the average of all households in Taiwan, compared to 61 per cent in 2014. In the same year, the poverty rate was 4.82 per cent for Indigenous households and 5.6 per cent for Indigenous individuals, compared to 1.65 per cent for non-Indigenous households and 1.35 per cent for all households. A useful way to compare economic status is to compare the percentage of families in different percentile groups of disposable income. The two lowest income groups account for 65.97 per cent of Indigenous households and 70.85 per cent of Indigenous households living in mountain townships (ROC Council of Indigenous Peoples 2018a, 31–2). Interestingly, Taiwan also calculates the Gini coefficient, an index between 0 and 1, in which higher numbers reveal higher inequality. The Gini coefficient for Indigenous households was 0.420, compared to 0.337 for all households (ROC Council of Indigenous Peoples 2018a, xxiii–xxiv). These data already indicate that Indigenous households are relatively poor and, interestingly, have higher inequality between them, compared to the general population.

Employment statistics, revealed in the annual *Employment Status Survey of Indigenous Peoples*, are also interesting (ROC Council of Indigenous Peoples 2018b). In 2017, Taiwan's Indigenous labour force participation rate was 60.82 per cent, and the unemployment rate was 4.02 per cent, compared to a labour participation rate of 58.83 per cent and an unemployment rate of 3.76 per cent in the general population. In terms of occupation, the most common were service and sales workers (23 per cent), craft-related workers (18.18 per cent), machine operators and assembly workers (15.12 per cent), and low-skilled and manual workers (14.48 per cent). Those working in the last three categories of manual labour account for approximately 50 per cent of Indigenous workers, compared to 30.96 per cent of the general population (ROC Council of Indigenous Peoples 2018b, xv–xvi, 60). For men, the most common occupation was in construction (26.06 per cent; ROC Council of Indigenous Peoples 2018b, 73). Due to the system of subcontracting and flexible labour, these jobs are often hired and paid daily. For women, the most common occupations were in manufacturing (17.75 per cent; ROC Council of Indigenous Peoples 2018b, 264). When asked if they encounter discrimination in the workplace because they are Indigenous, 4.69 per cent said yes, down from 10.69 per cent in the 2002 survey. Older workers over forty are more likely to report discrimination, as well as those with less education and lower wages (ROC Council of Indigenous Peoples 2018b, 224–5). Employment statistics show a concentration of Indigenous people in manual jobs and indicate that those in the most subaltern positions are most likely to perceive racial discrimination.

Indigenous people are also likely to have less education. The percentage of Indigenous people with only primary school or lower in 2017 was 18.07 per cent, compared to 12.82 per cent in the general population. Schooling for Indigenous people ended with middle school for 18.65 per cent and high school for 39.36 per cent, compared to 12.08 per cent and 30.56 per cent, respectively, in the general population. At 6.58 per cent and 17.34 per cent, respectively, Indigenous people are less likely to attend vocational school or university and above, which is attained by 11.23 per cent and 33.32 per cent in the total population (ROC Council of Indigenous Peoples 2018b, 54).

Health outcomes also show disparity. In 2017, Indigenous people had an average life expectancy of 67.9 years for men and 76.6 years for women, much lower than the average 77.3 years for men and 83.7 years for women (ROC Council of Indigenous Peoples 2020, 32). The leading causes of death for both Indigenous and non-Indigenous people are malignant cancer and heart disease (excluding high blood pressure). The main differences are that the third cause of death for Indigenous people is liver cirrhosis and other liver diseases, which is the tenth cause of death for non-Indigenous people. Indigenous people are five times more likely than non-Indigenous people to die of liver problems. They are nearly twice as likely to die of accidents and injuries (mostly traffic accidents), and that is the fifth most common cause of death among Indigenous people. For non-Indigenous people, accidents and injuries rank sixth (ROC Council of Indigenous Peoples 2020, 45). Health outcomes for youth (ages 15–44) are especially disconcerting. The leading two causes of death are accidents and injuries, followed by liver diseases, with suicide as the fifth (15 per 100,000 deaths; ROC Council of Indigenous Peoples 2020, 66). Overall, the crude suicide rate is 16.7 per 100,000 deaths (ROC Council of Indigenous Peoples 2020, 75).

These sociological trends lend credence to the idea that Taiwan's Indigenous people are oppressed, compared to Han Taiwanese, in all five "faces" of oppression, to use the typology developed by Iris Young. They endure *exploitation*, even the "superexploitation" of racialized groups (Young [1990] 2011, 51), because of a segmented labour market that keeps large numbers of Indigenous workers in manual jobs, often with precarious labour conditions. High labour force participation and low unemployment rates suggest that they are not as subject to *marginalization* as, say, what Iris Young perceived as the dangerous predicament of American Indians on reservations (53). They certainly experience *powerlessness*. Unlike Young, who looks at decision-making power in the workplace, Indigenous people feel powerless when they are excluded from their forests and subject to criminalization of hunting practices. It is a different kind of powerlessness, but it is nonetheless a painful lived experience of disempowerment. They also suffer the oppression of *systematic violence*, especially if we consider conservation officers ejecting them from their hunting grounds but also discrimination in the workplace or harassment, being called pejorative names. Most of all, however, they live with *cultural imperialism* because the dominant group stigmatizes them with stereotypes as a cultural Other marked as primitive, while rendering their own cultural perspectives invisible. The dominant group projects their own experience as representing humanity, which the Othered group is constructed as lacking (59). This way of thinking is the heart of Indigenous peoples' oppression, as oppressive power mediates who gets to express their realities, or ontologies (Gehl 2017, 44). Borrowing explicitly from phenomenological philosopher Martin Heidegger, Young examines these five dimensions of oppression as "thrownness," since people find themselves to be members of groups that they experience as having always been that way (Young [1990] 2011, 46).

It is useful to compare the situation of Indigenous peoples in Taiwan to that of Canada (table 1.5). Employment and Social Development Canada in 2017 boasted that it had reached Canada's lowest poverty rate in history at 9.5 per cent (Government of Canada 2019a). In that year, Canada had a Gini coefficient of 0.439 (Statistics Canada 2021a). Canadian urban Indigenous populations had a poverty rate of 25 per cent and a food insecurity rate of 38 per cent (Arriagada, Hahmann, and O'Donnell 2020). In 2017, Canada's Indigenous population had a labour force participation rate of 63.4 per cent, compared to the total population of 65.2 per cent, and an unemployment rate of 11.4 per cent, compared to 6.4 per cent in the total population (Statistics Canada 2021b). For 2016 education rates, the Assembly of First Nations used

Table 1.5. Measuring Indigenous rights in Taiwan and Canada, 2016–17

	Taiwan		Canada	
Statistic	Indigenous	Total	Indigenous	Total
Poverty rate (%)	4.82	1.65	25	9.5
Unemployment (%)	4.02	3.76	11.4	6.4
University attainment (%)	17.34	33.32	15 (on reserve) 23 (off reserve)	45
Male life expectancy (years)	67.9	77.3	73–4	79
Female life expectancy (years)	76.6	83.7	78–80	83

Sources: Various, see discussion in this chapter.

census data to show that 15 per cent of First Nations people living on reserve and 23 per cent of those off reserve had a university certificate or degree, compared to 45 per cent of those with non-Aboriginal identity (Assembly of First Nations 2018). In Canada, Métis and First Nations in 2017 had an estimated life expectancy of 73 to 74 years for men and 78 to 80 years for women, compared to 79 years for men and 83 years for women in the total Canadian population (Statistics Canada 2017). Canada has a very serious epidemic of Indigenous suicide. A 2019 study by Statistics Canada estimated the suicide rate at 24.3 per 100,000, and nearly twice that on the reserve. The suicide rates for First Nations and Métis adults are twice as high as those for non-Indigenous people (Kumar and Tjepkema 2019). Indigenous people in Taiwan may be oppressed relative to non-Indigenous people around them, but when we try to quantify that oppression, it pales in comparison to Canada's human rights crisis.

On the surface at least, this sociological snapshot makes it appear as if Indigenous Formosans are better off than First Nations in Canada. Focusing on such issues as labour market participation, unemployment, and education levels, however, is based on an ideology of developmentalism and undergirds what Amis intellectual Isak Afo calls "welfare colonialism" (Isak 2016, 196–7). The problem is that state control, up to and including today's multicultural Republic of China, has appropriated Indigenous land, dispossessed Indigenous peoples, and obscured Indigenous sovereignty. Having never ceded that inherent sovereignty, Formosan Indigenous nations must now assert it, especially if Taiwan is to survive increasing US-China competition in the region (Namoh and Lee 2016; Liu 2021).[4] In Canada, by contrast, I would argue that the (still colonial) Indian Act affords First Nations some opportunity to exercise limited sovereignty through band councils and other institutions that were meant to control them.

Most of the disagreements in Formosan Indigenous communities are not about the reality of Indigenous sovereignty. Sediq and Truku people agree that Gaya and alang pre-existed the state and continue to exist, holding sway on individuals and establishing an unchanged claim to sovereignty. There is thus strong consensus that they are Indigenous in a very meaningful way, even among people who have very little understanding of the UN Declaration on the Rights of Indigenous Peoples or domestic and international law. The disagreements are about what form sovereignty should take as Indigenous nations emerge and seek a new relationship with the state. Some leaders look to Canada, with its band councils and royal commissions, as a model (Xianfa Yuanzhuminzu Zhengce Zhixian Tuidong Xiaozu 2005). Ordinary people are not involved in those discussions but still enact sovereignty in other ways.

In both Taiwan and Canada, the ongoing trauma of colonialism, which includes displacements, forced cultural and linguistic assimilation, prohibition of traditional practices, and discrimination, is the root of many problems. Truku social work scholar Ciwang Teyra argues that high alcohol use, which explains rates of liver disease and accidents being higher in Indigenous than in non-Indigenous populations, is a stress-coping strategy for dealing with these issues (Ciwang and Hsieh 2023). Indeed, when I brought up the issue of Indigenous suicide in Canada with Seediq people, one person said: "Can't you see that we are also committing suicide? It is just that we do it gradually, by drinking until we die." Ciwang and Hsieh argue that Truku people can overcome these traumas through hunting practices that connect people with their ancestors and allow them to visit the sites of historical traumatic events and massacres. Canadian experience supports this argument, as communities with stronger cultural community and political projects of self-determination have much lower suicide rates (Chandler and Lalonde 1998). The difficulty, however, is that hunting, arguably the most important cultural activity for the Truku, is illegal in Taiwan's national parks, which occupy much of Truku land (Ortega-Williams et al. 2021, 231). Walis Beilin, writing about his own attempts as an Indigenous legislator to legalize Indigenous hunting, attributes subsequent failed attempts to the legal restraints of the ROC system and to discrimination against Indigenous peoples by the overwhelming majority who control the law-making process (Walis 2009, 69). One of the main questions that needs to be answered is how much do policies of multiculturalism and indigeneity, as well as movements of Indigenous resurgence led by Indigenous peoples themselves, contribute to resolution of trauma and an end to oppression.

In this book, I have decided not to focus on the dimensions of oppression related to quantifiable inequality for several reasons. First, a focus on misery frames people as victims, suggesting that they lack agency and need to be saved by the state or other outsiders. Second, this focus carries assumptions of developmentalism, implying that everyone seeks full employment in the formal economy and desires higher education in state schools. Either way, it defines Indigenous people by what they lack in comparison to the "mainstream" society. Third, by most counts, Indigenous people in Taiwan are in a better situation than those in Canada, which suggests that Canadian scholars would be better off seeking change at home. But I think that even Iris Young misunderstood Indigenous dilemmas by focusing on developmentalist criteria and trying to fit Indigenous peoples into the same model of oppression as urban minorities. This approach led her to downplay the main issue that Indigenous sovereignty is actively denied by colonial forces. Indigenous peoples are not marginalized because they live on reservations; Indigenous peoples living on reserve are protecting the final outposts of sovereignty. Therefore, even as I recognize the existence of cultural imperialism, I focus on Indigenous political ontologies that play out in both state institutions of indigeneity and Indigenous-led political and cultural resurgence. There is more to Indigenous lifeworlds than oppression.

Critiques of Taiwan's Multicultural Indigeneity

In the introduction, I made a distinction between, on one hand, the state-based discourses and practices of indigeneity and, on the other hand, the relational, land-based discourses of Indigenous resurgence. I was inspired by Indigenous scholars, notably Taiaiake Alfred, Glen Coulthard, and Audra Simpson. In this chapter, I focus even more clearly on Taiwan.

There is already a body of literature about scepticism and outright refusal of indigeneity in Asia. Alpa Shah, for example, wrote about Indigenous politics in Jharkhand, India, as a new form of hegemony by the same local elites (Shah 2010). Tania Li explored the paradox of Indonesian farmers of an ethnic minority who lost land because they embraced capitalist modes of production but have seen little need to affirm Indigenous identity (Li 2014). In most parts of Asia, where dense populations have centuries of history of migration, displacement, and absorption, states have often refused arguments that any group has distinct rights based on first occupancy as "we-are-all-indigenous." The People's Republic of China (PRC) argues that the 1949 Revolution liberated everyone from colonial domination and, without admitting the reasons, points out that no Chinese groups claim recognition at the United Nations (Niezen 2003, 73). On the ground, China attempts to assimilate any group that might claim Indigenous identity based on prior settlement (Miller 2003, 185). China's counterfactual insistence that Taiwan is an integral part of the PRC is the main reason why Taiwan's Indigenous peoples get few hearings at United Nations Indigenous meetings. Although they participated in the early years of UN Indigenous discussions, China has in recent years succeeded in removing all ROC (Taiwan) passport holders from UN premises, thus limiting Taiwanese participation to "side events." China's marginalization of Taiwan on the international stage thus contributes to the oppression of Taiwan's Indigenous peoples (Simon 2020b).

It is surely no coincidence that the three Asian countries that officially recognize Indigenous peoples on their territories – Taiwan, Japan, and the Philippines – share three common features. First is geography, because they are all composed of islands. In Japan, the peoples with claims to indigeneity are the Ainu of Hokkaido and other islands, and the Okinawans. In all three cases, they meet the "saltwater test" of being colonized by peoples coming from across water, if only from the next island. Second is a temporal aspect, as the peoples identified as Indigenous are on lands colonized by ethnic others in the nineteenth century or later. This feature is important because, unlike places where peoples have mixed for centuries, both colonizer and colonized peoples interpreted their new situation through nineteenth-century assumptions. Third is the geopolitical dimension, as all have strong American influence (direct control in the case of the Philippines from 1898 to 1941) on their policies towards those peoples since the 1870s, especially since Japan employed US advisors to deal with both Hokkaido and Formosa. Tania Li defines Indigenous self-identification as a "positioning which draws upon historically sedimented practices, landscapes and repertoires of meaning, and emerges through particular patterns of engagement and struggle" (Li 2000, 151). Nineteenth-century geopolitics, and the role of a rising United States in East Asia, led to shared practices of frontier governmentality on that long archipelago of islands. Due to Taiwan's long history of "bifurcated sovereignty," there is full consensus among Indigenous people on Formosa that the island is inhabited by Indigenous peoples and descendants of settlers. Sometimes they claim to be "the only real Taiwanese." This situation is very different from that on the Asian continent and even in much of island Southeast Asia, where there is scepticism towards or even denial of indigeneity.

In the contemporary era of UN-driven Indigenous rights and state-sponsored multiculturalism, some scholars in Taiwan study the paradoxical situation where local elites make competing expressions of indigeneity while some outspoken village folks remain cynical about their motivations. Taiwanese anthropologist Hsieh Shih-Chung (1992) was the first to draw attention to the phenomenon of indigeneity and elite formation, but I first encountered this argument through the works of Michael Rudolph, who did research with the Truku and Amis of Hualien. Examining Taiwan's Indigenous social movement since nearly its inception, Rudolph explores the situation in which common people seem alienated from the Indigenous social movement that speaks in their names. Coming from outside of anthropology, Rudolph's primary theoretical inspiration is political scientist Paul Brass (1991), who argued that "ethnic self-consciousness, ethnically-based demands, and ethnic conflict can occur only if there is some conflict between indigenous and external elites and authorities or between indigenous elites" (quoted in Rudolph 2004, 241, lower-case "indigenous" in the original) Anthropologist Ku Kun-hui similarly argued that public recognition of Indigenous peoples was used to separate Taiwan from Chinese identity but has not led to equal treatment or the new partnership relationship proclaimed by Taiwanese politicians in electoral statements (Ku 2005). Sociologist Chi Chun-Chieh and his graduate student Chin Hsang-Te accused Truku elites of land grabbing and internal colonialism in tribal mapping exercises (Chi and Chin 2012). I was initially furious about these arguments, seeing them akin to Adam Kuper's notorious refutation of anthropological engagement with Indigenous rights (Kuper 2003) or the argument of Canadian political scientist Thomas Flanagan, who decried aboriginal rights as an orthodoxy that merely empowers a small elite of activists (Flanagan 2000).

As the years passed, however, I had to admit that these authors make important points and acknowledge that their arguments seem to be confirmed by what I have written in my own field notes. Rudolph gives an example well known in Taiwan, contrasting the views of ordinary people who see traditional facial tattoos as a historical stigma versus the tattoo photography webpage run by Kimi Sibal, who works at Asia Cement (Rudolph 2004, 248–9; figure 1.1). He thus portrays Kimi as one of those Indigenous elites who profit from indigeneity. Probably the most internationally known member of his community, Kimi expresses Atayal/Sediq/Truku pride by exhibiting photos of tattooed elders around the world, even contributing to ethnological and world

Figure 1.1. Asia Cement quarry, Hualien. Asia Cement is an important employer of Indigenous workers.

Source: Photograph by Scott E. Simon.

art exhibitions in Toronto, Montreal, and Paris. I know Kimi quite well. In fact, I have helped him draft English-language speeches to deliver to foreign audiences.

Kimi's conflict with his sister Igung, who first brought me to the community, seems at first glance to be the best proof of Rudolph's argument. Whereas Kimi has financed his pet projects with Asia Cement funding and sought political power through KMT networks, his sister Igung led a social movement against mining (figure 1.2), was one of the first leaders to lobby for Truku recognition, and ran unsuccessfully for a township political position on the ticket of the opposition DPP. Kimi's wife even ensured that Igung would lose the election by running herself as the KMT candidate, thus guaranteeing that votes in their very large extended family (one of the largest clans in the village) would be split by competing family loyalties. Igung even reported in her testimony to the United Nations that Asia Cement had provided funding so that her opponent could purchase votes with prices of up to NT$10,000 (Igung 1997).Whereas Igung represented the Truku in 1999 when DPP presidential candidate Chen Shui-bian promised a "new partnership" with Indigenous peoples, Kimi was an outspoken opponent in Hualien of

Figure 1.2. Indigenous and environmental politics. Igung speaks at an anti-mining protest during the Taroko National Park's annual marathon, Hualien, 13 December 2014.

Source: Photograph by Scott E. Simon.

Truku recognition and an advocate of his community joining the Sediq. Those political tensions were very acute and public during my first ten years of fieldwork.

Since my perspectives were initially rooted in the same Canadian Presbyterian networks that supported Igung and the oppositional movement, it was psychologically difficult for me at first to see either the moral legitimacy of Kimi's work or the value of Rudolph's analysis. This difficulty shows the strength of social networks in shaping our perceptions of the world, including my own. Strolling into the lanes behind Kimi's house, however, I met people who described the machinations of his family over generations as colonial collaboration. With strong moral conviction, they depicted *both* Igung and Kimi to me as political actors manipulated by external political forces. Over years of fieldwork, I have watched as ordinary people laugh at elites who try to get them to rally around flags – regardless of whether those flags are the tricolour

Chinese Republican flag, the green flag of Taiwan Independence, or a variety of flags representing variant imaginaries of Indigenous self-determination. As an anthropologist, my task was to try to empathize with the lifeworlds of Igung, Kimi, and their more subaltern kin. I tried very hard to avoid assumptions from the beginning that one faction was good and the other had sold out to evil.

During my field research, people criticized Kimi for his relationship with the KMT and Igung for her relationship with the DPP. As I write this, Kimi has publicly joined forces with the DPP, even representing the Sediq people as a member of the Presidential Office Indigenous Historical Justice and Transitional Justice Committee founded by President Tsai Ing-wen (DPP). He presents himself in all these activities with different political parties as a selfless advocate of Indigenous interests, shrugging off all local criticism. From his perspective, he is like an ambassador to a foreign state, who must continue to maintain cordial relations even if the government changes. When people around him say he just gravitates to whichever party seems able to provide him with financial advantages, they contest his desire to be their ambassador.

To some, the vocabulary of "ordinary people" may seem dangerous because it has been appropriated by right-wing populist forces in both North America and Europe. Here, I draw from Hsieh and Rudolph, who wrote long before contemporary political considerations. The issue in Taiwan anthropology is how to translate a common word from Mandarin Chinese to English. Most people in the villages refer to themselves, in contrast to local elites, as *laobaixing* 老百姓 in Chinese. This word, which literally means the "old one-hundred surnames," is entirely a Chinese concept, since the Chinese have had surnames and strong lineage organizations for at least centuries, whereas the Indigenous peoples did not. This word historically captured the contrast between officials assigned to localities by the central government and the many local families who have long lived in a locality. By contrast, people nowadays refer to would-be elites in Chinese as *zhengke* 政客, a word for "politician," which literally means "guest of politics." This word has negative connotations that these individuals are in fact opportunist and dependent on political relations with higher-ups.

It is relevant that people use Chinese terms for these concepts, yet somewhat ironic to say "old one-hundred surnames" because there are no surnames in Atayalic kinship terminology. Names of Atayalic people are their personal names followed by the name of a parent, usually the father. Kimi Sibal, therefore, means that Kimi is the son of Sibal. Sibal would in turn use the name, for example, Sibal Yagao, which means that

Sibal is the son of Yagao. In pre-colonial times, therefore, the very term laobaixing 老百姓 would have been meaningless to them.

The fact that people use the Chinese terms for both elites and common people reveals that these hierarchies and forms of personal accumulation are novelties derived from external political systems. The alternative, which people evoke when they say that collaboration with external powers violates Gaya (see chapter 5), is to think through the ethics of being human (seejiq). *Seejiq balay*, real people, are not dependent politicians but rather those who can exercise leadership because of proven ability and skill. People thus say of Kimi (and others like him): "He is not a Seejiq balay. He is nothing but a zhengke." They say the same thing about his sister.

The examples of Kimi and Igung seem, on the surface, to support Rudolph's approach. Even though they are brother and sister, born of the same parents, Kimi was one of the main proponents of the creation of the Sediq Nation and Igung of establishing the Truku Nation. Already, some people are writing about Sediq culture or Truku culture, and some anthropologists (e.g., Wang 2006) have bypassed local conflicts by studying them in cultural anthropology under the umbrella concept of Atayal culture. Yet, I think that approaches based on constructionism fail to understand Indigenous lifeworlds. I agree entirely with Leanne Betasamoke Simpson, who says that social movement theory fails to understand Indigenous resistance because it is based on Western worldviews, ignores Indigenous political theory, overlooks centuries of resistance to colonialism, and takes the state for granted (Simpson 2011, 16). In every village where I did research, people brought their colonial situation to my attention and demonstrated a strong identity with their own alang. There were disagreements about which larger confederation (Sediq or Truku) they should join, and people expressed strong feelings about how certain local elites interact with the state or other external actors. Nobody debates about the importance of Gaya, but like any legal system, Gaya provides room for divergent interpretations and even open disagreement. Indeed, Gaya assumes that each alang is autarkic and that each individual has to make his or her own ethical decisions. The principle of non-interference is intrinsic to non-hierarchical ways of being and non-authoritarian leadership (Simpson 2011, 18).

Indigenous Resurgence on Formosa

Western theories of nationalism or social movements are equally insufficient for understanding Indigenous political resurgence. The main problem is that they are based on Western notions about social relations.

They assume that the goal is to unite atomized individuals into a territorial state or other territorial unit through a shared culture. Taiaiake Alfred directly addresses Paul Brass (1991) and Benedict Anderson (1983) when he says that these theories are all based on a selective memory about European historical nation-building and apply it as a global standard (Alfred 1995, 9). These approaches lack the necessary depth to incorporate the experiences and perspectives of political communities reacting to statist political and cultural hegemony. Most importantly, "in considering the development of their nations, Native peoples do not take the present internal-colonial system as their reference point" (7). What they do take as their reference point is their own sovereignty, based on their own political and legal history and philosophy, which continues to be assaulted and denied by colonial state forms of power. This frame of reference is why Glen Coulthard prefers the term "mode of life" (Coulthard 2014, 65) to combine the ideas of "mode of production" and culture. In anthropology, these contemporary Indigenous concerns are well taken up as political ontology, which examines the politics of world-shaping and focuses on conflicts between ontologies (Blaser 2009a). Attention to political ontology is what allows us to make a distinction between indigeneity, which is based on modern ontologies derived from Western experience, and Indigenous resurgence, which is based on Indigenous modes of life. Indigeneity attempts to integrate Indigenous peoples into multicultural polities, whereas Indigenous resurgence affirms the ontological reality of unceded Indigenous sovereignty. It also proposes non-Western, non-statist approaches to sovereignty.

Indigenous resurgence in Taiwan can be seen in the works of university-based scholars across the disciplines, local scholars, film-making, literature, and other arts. Much of the Indigenous political thought has come from the Presbyterian Yu Shan Theological Seminary, where Rector Pusin Tali has long promoted Indigenous self-government. Explaining the Atayal title *Klahang Nanaq Yasa Pqyanux Qnxan Tayal*, Pusin Tali pointed out that self-government is not a matter of government policy but of the experience of each community (*buluo* 部落) governing itself for the centuries (Pusin 2008, 11). Considering the centrality of the community (alang; see the preceding chapter) to the Atayalic groups (which include Sediq and Truku), it is not surprising that the alang is at the centre of those preoccupations. Seediq (Tgdaya) intellectual Dakis Pawan explains that the alang is simultaneously community, home, region, and nation. Within a village, there may be several alang, and there can also be a confederation of groups faced with natural disaster or a common enemy (Kuo 2011, 60–2). Seejiq (Truku) Shen Ming-ren (Pawan Tanah), who interprets the contemporary meaning of ancient myths, affirms Gaya as the "good life" (*malu kndsan*; Shen 1998, 27), thus making it a route to the future. Gaya, the law, ontology, and mode of life that holds together these communities, is thus not the quest for some unitary state or even culture to which individuals relate. It is rather reproduced continually at the level of the alang. It is an ethical guide and ritual framework for mutual relations between Heaven (spirits), Earth (with its non-human inhabitants), and Humans (Shen 1998, 27).[5] Gaya is furthermore the basis of sovereignty, but it is a sovereignty that resides in those mutual relations rather than in abstract notions like states.

Anthropologists have begun studying these dynamics only recently. Nearly two decades after Fred Chiu called for a decolonization of anthropology (Chiu 2000), Tomonori Sugimoto criticized anthropologists for complicity with a new indigeneity that prolongs settler colonialism through pageants of repentance and recognition (Sugimoto 2018, 2019). Kerim Friedman similarly argues that multicultural education and local community revitalization policies turn the quest for local authenticity into a new hegemony (Friedman 2018). At the same time, John Christopher Upton, in a study of Taiwan's Indigenous hearing rooms, has described several initiatives in which Indigenous groups have simply asserted and implemented sovereignty on their own terms without waiting for state recognition. Even in the state-dominated courts, Indigenous people took the opportunity to remind non-Indigenous actors that this land is not their land (Upton 2020, 25; 2021). D.J.W. Hatfield demonstrated how Amis people in Taiwan use ritual dances and festivals as acts of "sovereign assertion" (Hatfield 2020). It is reassuring to see this new generation of anthropologists stop using the state as our point of reference and look more closely at assertions of Indigenous sovereignty in everyday life. It is also insufficient to merely catalogue cultural difference in a multicultural state. Rather, it requires a decolonial framework of grounding our own research and moral reflections in Gaya. In an attempt to do this grounding, I weave throughout this book conversations with Truku and Sediq, as well as with Indigenous thinkers from what we call Canada. My attempts are surely incomplete, and I know that Sediq scholars are simultaneously working on their own writings, but at least it is a beginning. I think that the next step of decolonization is to recognize that each field-based study in anthropology, including this one, produces the heart knowledge of each anthropologist.

Arrival in the Village: Overview of Research and Methods

Indigenous people in Taiwan, because they are so often approached by researchers, professors, and students from Taiwan, Japan, and elsewhere, are very familiar with anthropology. Their first impulse is to take a visiting anthropologist to the oldest people in the community to ask about what life was like in the Japanese period, assuming that the anthropologist wishes to study culture or tradition and that this way of studying culture is somehow the most authentic. When an anthropologist takes up residence in the village and begins to cultivate friendships, however, people are more likely to say that true knowledge comes only from experience. They insist that it is important to actually walk on the mountain paths, to taste the wild meat, and to sweat from labour.

My journey in Indigenous studies began with Taiwan's Indigenous religious and intellectual leaders. In the summer of 2002, I participated in the Urban-Rural Mission, the training camp for social activists run by the Presbyterian Church from which Igung had graduated (discussed in chapter 4). In the summer of 2004, I joined a series of meetings with Indigenous scholars at the Council of Indigenous Peoples in Taipei about how to incorporate Indigenous rights into a new Constitution of Taiwan, should Taiwan achieve legal independence from the Republic of China. Because Taiwan has never been a part of the People's Republic of China, there is no need to declare independence from that state. But even though there is overlap between Taiwan and the areas under the effective jurisdiction of the Republic of China, Taiwanese people debate about whether or not they should seek independence from the latter. Independence would extricate them from the legacies of the Chinese Civil War, including debates on "one China," and set them on a new path towards decolonization. The Presbyterian Church of Taiwan is historically one of the main proponents of this political position in Taiwan. They highlight the notion that the Republic of China was an external imposition and insist on the right of self-determination.

Looking for international inspiration, participants in the 2004 meetings read Canada's *Report of the Royal Commission on Aboriginal Peoples* and discussed the works of political philosophers such as Will Kymlicka, Charles Taylor, James Tully, and Iris Young. They discussed such possibilities as guaranteeing a place for an Indigenous vice-president or creating an Indigenous chamber of Parliament, but the discussion was all about the place of Indigenous peoples in a modern state. The proceedings, published in Taiwan (Xianfa Yuanzhuminzu Zhengce Zhixian Tuidong Xiaozu 2005), remain a precious documentation about the relationship between Taiwanese independence forces and the Indigenous social movement. The lasting influence on me was the notion that I can productively bring Indigenous Formosan political philosophy into dialogue with First Nations philosophy from Canada.

My research itinerary has always followed the suggested paths of local research partners. From 2004 to 2007, I conducted a total of eighteen months of fieldwork with the Truku in Hualien and in a Seediq community in Nantou. I began my work in Igung's natal village of Bsngan. She introduced me to her brothers, and her younger brother Kuhon became an important research partner and friend. In 2004, 2005, and for two months in 2006, I rented a house across the street from the Ciwang Presbyterian Church and focused my attention on development-related conflicts in that village. In 2004, local elites had convinced the government to recognize them as Truku rather than as a subgroup of the Atayal. They campaigned further for the creation of a Truku Autonomous Region, which they hoped would be recognized by the state as an equal nation-to-nation relationship. In 2006, following the suggestions of some of these people, I spent an additional six months in the village of Ciyakang, renting a home from a Presbyterian minister and his brother, a township politician involved on the autonomy project. In 2007, following the advice of yet other people in Bsngan, I went to the Tgdaya village of Gluban in Nantou for six months, where I was able to study development conflicts, as well as the political demands for recognition as Seediq. I lived with economist and Seediq nationalist intellectual Takun Walis, who in daily conversations taught me much about the ongoing colonial situation and Gaya.

Although the first research project was concluded in 2007, I had developed strong friendships with some people and visited them in annual summer visits, up to the summer of 2020, when I sheltered in Taiwan from the COVID-19 pandemic that was spreading nearly everywhere else. In 2012 and 2013, with funding from the Chiang Ching-Kuo Foundation, I conducted six months of research on human-bird relations in the villages of Bsngan and in the Seediq (but Truku dialect) village of Buarung in the highlands of Nantou. I have visited them annually ever since, three times with students on an international field research course. As technology has transformed all our lives, I remain in daily contact with many of these people via Facebook, including some of those ordinary people with only precarious employment at best. They have become an intimate and ongoing part of my personal life in a way that was never possible for earlier generations of anthropologists. Some of them have even visited me in Canada.

Although I did conduct formal interviews in all these villages and used ethno-ecological methods of free-listing and pile sorting in the latter project, my main research method was always the anticolonial friendship of hanging out with people and sharing their lives as much as possible. I spent time with the relatively more educated village elites and learned quite a bit about their political projects. But, since the elites are often very busy and even absent from their villages, I spent even more time with the "ordinary people," some who live precariously between day labour and unemployment, and others who have more regular working-class jobs. These were the people who incorporated me into farm work teams, took me hunting, fishing, and trapping, and shared their lives with me through shared meals and drinking. I also regularly attended church services, probably amusing or annoying people by visiting Presbyterian, Roman Catholic, and True Jesus denominations. People made me very aware of their colonial situation and of the limits of racial capitalism. In Ciyakang in 2006, we read and discussed a Chinese translation of Fanon's *Wretched of the Earth*, which people told me also reflects their contemporary situation. With some people who have studied English, we even read Alfred Talalake's *Wasàse*. In no place did I imagine people as objects of my research; rather, I engaged with people as intellectual partners and friends.

In addition to these research methods, I also refer to the ethnographic literature from Taiwan's Japanese period. At the time, these survey anthropologists were in many ways the intermediaries between Indigenous people and Taipei-based bureaucracies, part of what historian Paul Barclay called "centres of calculation" (Barclay 2007). These began under the leadership of Gotō Shinpei, head of civilian affairs in Taiwan from 1898 to 1906. Chief among his contribution was the creation of the Taiwan Governor-General Office Provisional Taiwan Committee on the Investigation of Taiwan Old Customs, which published work on Taiwanese legal issues, as well as, most importantly for my research, a series of reports on Indigenous peoples. These reports, which have been translated into Chinese by Academia Sinica, are used by Taiwanese anthropologists but also by Indigenous people themselves, as they seek to understand their cultures at the time of colonial contact. Of course, I have also been an avid reader of the excellent anthropological studies done by contemporary Taiwanese anthropologists and of the books written by Indigenous thinkers themselves.

A Note on Language Use

As with Indigenous nations in many parts of the world, linguistic survival is a serious issue in Taiwan. When I first began visiting these communities in 2000, I was impressed that I could still find people in their thirties and forties who spoke the language, and I appreciated the fervour with which the Presbyterian Church kept the language alive with a Bible translation, as well as hymns, sermons, and prayers in Truku. As I write these words, I am alarmed that it is now difficult to find speakers younger than fifty. Linguistic survival is one of the main goals of the College of Indigenous Studies at National Dong Hwa University in Hualien, with Truku language instruction dependent on the work of Dr. Apay Ai-yu Tang as well as linguist Amy Pei-Jung Lee. Providence University in Taichung even offers an MA in Sediq studies, run by the Sediq themselves. There are also government-sponsored language initiatives in schools, with textbooks in Truku, Tgdaya, and Toda variants, and different pedagogical materials developed in Hualien (only Truku) and Nantou (all three). So far, language revitalization initiatives seem to be failing in a context of systemic racism. Parents, who were taught in school that Indigenous lifeways are primitive, often refuse to teach their children Indigenous languages because they perceive Mandarin and English to be more useful on the job market. The problem seems to be that, unlike the Māori of Aotearoa (New Zealand) or the Gaelic speakers of Scotland, cultural imperialism still denigrates Indigenous lifeways (McNaught 2021)

In this situation, I made efforts to learn the language, seeking language tutoring at the Presbyterian churches and sitting in on primary school language classes. Although I attained basic listening comprehension and conversational skills, I was already fluent in Mandarin from the beginning, which made it convenient for everyone to simply use Mandarin for most conversations. I also conversed with older people in Japanese. Secular public and township or village meetings, which were important in my studies of Indigenous politics, were mostly in Mandarin. People tended to speak their own language when they went into the mountains, which made hunting an important vector for intergenerational language transmission. When people want to emphasize important parts of their lifeworlds, bracketing them off as different from the Han Taiwanese around them, they explain them in their own terms. When I did research, everyone called me Walis, a Truku name given to me by Truku shaman Rabay Rubing during my first period of fieldwork. She said I reminded her of Walis Watan, her classmate in the Japanese era who loved to read.

Brief Summary of the Villages and Their Wayfaring Pathways

The wayfaring paths of Taiwan's Indigenous peoples have long been of interest to anthropologists. In 1935, the Institute of Ethnology at Taihoku Imperial University (now National Taiwan University) published the authoritative *Formosan Native Tribes: A Genealogical and Classificatory Study* (Utsurikawa, Mabuchi, and Miyamoto 1935), which has now been translated into Chinese, edited, and republished by the Council of Indigenous Peoples and the Southern Materials Centre (Yang 2012). This anthropological study was led by Utsurikawa Nenozō, the chair of the institute who had obtained his PhD in anthropology from Harvard under Roland B. Dixon; an assistant professor Miyamoto Nobuhiro; and Mabuchi Tōichi, who was employed as a part-time researcher. This study, funded by private donations from the Kamikaya Foundation established by a retired governor-general, was large-scale interview-based, and genealogical research done from 1929 to 1932 (Shimizu 1999, 135). The first volume of the treatise uses geography, oral history, and mythology to justify the classification of hundreds of small communities into nine Indigenous tribes. The second volume, labelled "data," gives detailed genealogical charts of all of the Indigenous communities. The Atayal are subdivided into the linguistic categories of Səqoleq, Tsəʔoleʔ, and Sədeq, with the latter further classified as Tək-Daya (Pulevao), Taroko (Toroko), and Toda (Tausa, Tausai). This study is thus the foundation for the current division of peoples into dialects of Tgdaya, Toda, and Truku.

The second volume is interesting because, rather than merely presenting colour-coded maps of ethnic territories, the authors recreate the paths of specific groups through mountain passes and along river streams over about four centuries prior to Japanese colonial administration, with policies of forced resettlement in the plains and sedentarization. This work is obviously the beginning of Mabuchi's spherical approach to geographical knowledge. Map 2 is the map of the Atayal wayfarings. On this map, the migrations of the Səqoleq peoples are marked in blue, and the Tsəʔoleʔ in red. These two groups, which occupy most of the territory mapped here, are now known as the Atayal. They are the first two groups explained in the legend, with the ethnonyms represented in both Japanese and Latin phonetic scripts. The lines in black, the arrows on the lower part of the map pointing eastwards towards the sea, indicate the migrations of the Sədeq peoples. The different dialects are clearly marked by different kinds of lines, and the six names the peoples use for themselves are indicated in the map's legend. With no regard to dialect, the Sədeq of Nantou are now classified as Sediq and those of Hualien as Truku. Although this map is difficult to read, the topographical map showing rivers gives a better indication of the terrain than most political maps. The map illustrates how the different dialects and languages, including ethnonyms,

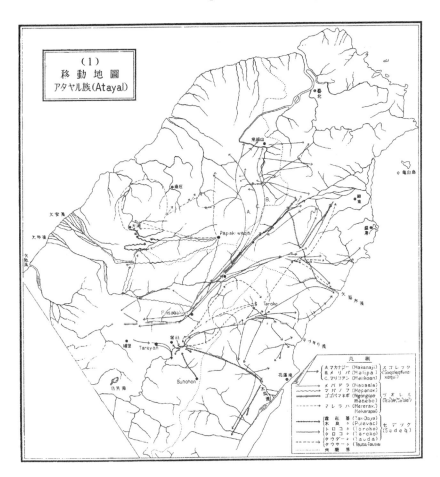

Map 2. Map of Atayal(ic) migrations. This map traces the historical migrations of the Atayalic peoples prior to the Japanese colonial resettlements.

Source: Utsurikawa, Mabuchi, and Miyamoto (1935, 97).

emerged as people inhabited different watersheds. Social identities were formed as peoples moved together through the forests and along the rivers.

Although this map is as much a colonial construction as was map 1 (page 28), there is an important distinction. Map 1 used polygons to mark peoples, as if they expressed an ontology in which exclusive territories contain peoples and cultures. Such maps, which we are accustomed to seeing due to the Westphalian state maps we use, give territoriality priority over relationality. This migration map, based on oral interviews, uses lines to mark the pathways that different peoples have followed over time. This perspective assumes that the pathways of different peoples may cross one another. It is consistent with the view that different groups of people used the same places in history and may even use the same areas of the mountains at different times of the year for different purposes. In each of the villages where I did research, people could tell me very precisely where their families originated in the mountains, how they came into relationships with other groups, and what was the nature of that relationship. In an ontology that prioritizes relationality, they have long negotiated use of territory, burying stones as signs of peace agreements and establishing stone boundaries between territories. Because they describe these human relations orally, in this book I also privilege narrative rather than more mapping to describe those relations and the political realities that are formed from them.

I have conducted research in the following villages (see map 3). A brief introduction to each village will gave an overview of the socio-historical context of how each place became a home to different people, as well as information on the location where I did my research.

Nantou Villages

Alang Buarung (Lushan Buluo 廬山部落)

This is a high mountain village (1,391 metres above sea level) on the road between Ren'ai Township of Nantou and Hualien, above the Zhuoshui and Mhebu Rivers. Buarung, the Indigenous name now used for this village, was the name used by the Tgdaya people who lived there when they were interviewed for *Formosan Native Tribes* in 1929 (Yang 2012, 74). They were called "Musha savages" by the Japanese, *Tgdaya* (high mountain people) by other Indigenous groups, and called themselves *Seediq balay* (real people). In 1930, Buarung was one of six Tgdaya alang, from the twelve who were part of a wider confederation, who participated in the uprising in Paran (Musha Incident). Buarung's population was 192 before this conflict. Only 41 people survived the subsequent military reprisals and the 1931 retaliatory massacre called the Second Musha Incident, in which Toda and Truku people attacked and killed Tgdaya people held in detention centres, supposedly under military protection. They were sent to Gluban. Buarung's land was given to the

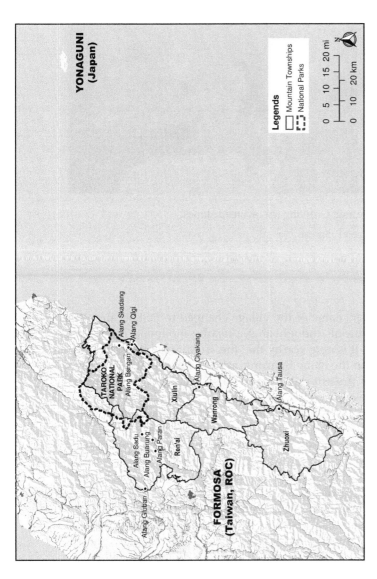

Map 3. Map of field sites. This map shows as points the field sites and the location of some of the other communities (alang) mentioned in this book, and as polygons the areas claimed by the Taroko National Park and five township governments. This map is intentionally decentred to show the proximity of Formosa to Yonaguni, as geography inevitably has led Taiwan to be as entangled with Japan as it is with China over history. On a clear day, one can see the mountains inhabited by Atayal and Truku peoples from Yonaguni.

Source: Map by Liao Hsiungming. Data source for the shaded relief map copyright © 2023 Esri, HERE, Garmin, FAO, NOAA, USGS. Used by permission under license.

Figure 1.3. Alang Buarung. Growing tea on steep slopes.

Source: Photograph by Scott E. Simon.

Truku people, and the name of the village changed to Fuji because the Japanese military officials thought that a nearby mountain resembled Japan's Mount Fuji. It is noteworthy that the Truku inhabitants eventually decided to retain the name Buarung, which shows that it is a place name. The Truku of present-day Buarung also use the term to refer to the people who moved from there to Gluban. This naming contrasts to the practice in Alang Snuwil (meaning "cherry"), who adopted a Toda translation of the post-Musha Japanese name for the village rather than retaining the former name of Gungu after the people who previously lived there.[6]

The village is very much a part of modern Taiwan. After the Second World War, it was renamed Lushan, but incorporated administratively as Jingying Village in 1967. Household registration statistics for April 2018 showed a population of 853, including 713 Indigenous people (83.6 per cent). The majority language is Truku, and they are politically part of the Sediq. I conducted three months of research on ethno-ornithology in Buarung in 2013. Nowadays, many of the mountains around the village are cleared of forests. People own or work on tea plantations and cabbage farms (figure 1.3). The nearby area also hosts a burgeoning tourist industry, including Qingjing Farm, a high mountain resort full of European-style architecture that includes the highest elevation Starbucks in Taiwan.

Alang Gluban (Qingliu Buluo 清流部落)

The location of this lowland village (415 metres above sea level) in the Beigang River Valley of Ren'ai Township seems like an anomaly for "high mountain" people, but the location itself is a potent reminder of the tragedy of Japanese rule. This village, surrounded by rapidly flowing rivers, is called Kawanakashima 川中島 in Japanese, meaning "island in the middle of the river." The 298 survivors of the Musha repression, from the six Tgdaya alang that rebelled against Japanese rule, were placed here under strict military surveillance on 6 May 1931. The Japanese taught them paddy rice farming, which subsequently became an important part of their social identity (figure 1.4). After the Second World War, the village was agglomerated with upstream Naka-hara, home of Sediq refugees from Japanese dam construction during the 1930s, and Maibara, an Atayal community, as part of the administrative village of Huzhu. In April 2018, Huzhu Village had a total population of 1,371, including 1,253 Indigenous people (91.4 per cent). The majority language is Tgdaya, and they are politically part of the Sediq. I conducted six months of research in 2007 on development and resistance in Gluban, which has about 500 residents. For the wealthier families, Gluban is a proud farming community, but there are also a good number of landless people who work as day labourers in agriculture or in construction as far away as Taichung. When I visit Gluban, people still call me Walis Takun because I lived in the home (*sapah*) of Takun Walis.

The historical wayfaring from Nantou to Hualien basically followed three watersheds from the central mountains to the Pacific Ocean. Truku anthropologist Masaw Mowna recounts two stories about the first migration. In the first story, an ancestor named Awi left Alang Sadu (Truku Truwan) high in the mountains and walked towards the east. Finding that game was plentiful, he set up a hunting lodge in Tpdu, now called T'ien-hsiang. Shortly thereafter, his wife imagined that he had died and moved in with another man. More than a month later, Awi returned home loaded with meat. When he found his wife with another man, he killed them both in anger. He married his wife's younger sister, and they departed to live in Hualien, with others following afterwards. In the second story, an unnamed family from Alang Sadu walked east and found that the forests were full of game animals. One day, the whole family went out to hunt. Discovering that they had forgotten to

Figure 1.4. Alang Gluban. Farmers celebrate the annual rice harvest.

Source: Photograph by Scott E. Simon.

bring their fire flint, they sent their son back home to fetch it. When he did not come back within half a day, they went to look for him. Finding blood on the ground near their hunting lodge, they knew their son had been killed. They followed footprints through the forest, which brought them to a clearing where people were dancing and singing around their son's head. Full of anger, they went back to Alang Sadu, gathered their forces, and returned to avenge the boy's death. They killed the enemies and celebrated with a ceremony of song and dance around the heads. After that event, some of the people returned to Alang Sadu, and others spread throughout the mountains to the east. Because of what had happened to the boy, they had no trust in outsiders and began a practice of headhunting (Masaw 1977, 72).

Hualien Villages

Alang Bsngan (Fushih Cun 富世村)

Alang Bsngan, although local people commonly refer to their village in this way, is very much a misnomer. Most people use Bsngan, interchangeably with the Chinese Fushih, to refer to the settlements along the highway between the place where the Liwu River flows into the Pacific Ocean in the north and Asia Cement in the south. In fact, Hsiulin Township's Fushih Village, with an area of 600 square kilometres reaching up to the Nantou border in the mountains, is Taiwan's largest village in area. Fushih is actually an accretion of different alang who have been moved to those lowlands since 1904, including Truku and Toda people. In 2017, as people in Fushih debated how to best follow government instructions to create a local "band council," opponents of a broader Fushih Band Council argued that this proposal obscures the fact that people identify instead with five distinct alang: Ayo, Rocing, Bsngan, Kele, and Minle. This list of five alang is itself a simplification reflecting new identities formed over decades of intermarriage, friendship, and conflict resolution. In 1978, Masaw Mowna, who reconstructed a very detailed history of Truku migration and settlement in Hualien, documented that Bsngan was actually an amalgamation of ten distinct alang and Kele a fusion of fifteen (Masaw 1978, 146–7).

Over the years, I have worked most closely with three Bsngan communities. The first is Bsngan proper, the community formed around the Ciwang Presbyterian Church, which began as people were moved down the Liwu River beginning in 1917. The second is Qlgi (Kele in Chinese), directly across from Asia Cement and organized around the True Jesus Church, which was founded in 1927 with the first migrants brought down the mountain from the original Qlgi by Umao Yakau (Walis and Yu 2002, 124). Kele maintains a very strong identity separate from Bsngan because of this origin, the presence of a large Toda group in their midst, and their distinct religious identity as members of the True Jesus Church. The third is Minle, but more precisely Alang Skadang. Minle is the residential area in the floodplains that was created in 1979 when the hamlets of Skadang (also known in Chinese as Datong) and Xoxos (in Chinese, Dali) were forced to relocate to make way for the creation of the Taroko National Park. Skadang, which means "molar," refers to the memory that the earliest settlers in their mountain hamlet (at 1,128 metres above sea level) found a human tooth when they were digging to build the new settlement. They gather around the Skadang Presbyterian Church, whereas the people of Xoxos gather in the Taroko Presbyterian Church about 200 metres away. Household registration statistics for April 2018 show that Fushih Village had a population of 2,237, including 1,916 Indigenous people (85.7 per cent). The majority language is Truku, and most people have registered membership as Truku. The contemporary legal classification of Truku was created largely due to the efforts of activists based at the Ciwang Presbyterian Church, but there was outspoken opposition led by elites in Kele who identify as Sediq. Skadang, Xoxos, and Qlgi all confusingly refer to both places in the mountains and their new neighbourhoods in Bsngan because they are all names of groups of people as well as place names.

Bsngan is the village with which I relate the most intimately. I did my longest periods of field research in Bsngan for four months in 2005, two months in 2006, and three months in 2012, but I am a frequent visitor. In 2015, 2017, and 2019, I even took University of Ottawa students on field trips to Kele and mountaintop Skadang, which is now becoming a centre for ecotourism. Bsngan has a healthy economy due to the presence of the Asia Cement Company, the Taroko National Park, and increasing tourism. In the first two years, I followed the advice of a Taiwanese anthropologist who suggested I not live with a political family because people would associate me with them and other factions in the village would ostracize me. In subsequent trips, however, I lived in Kele with Kuhon Siban, the retired policeman who was brother of Kimi and Igueng. Over time, people in Kele came to call me Walis Kuhon. After he passed away in 2020, his sons invited me to sit with them in the family section at his funeral. This village and this family gave me a sense of home. When my own parents passed away in 2012, they helped me manage my grief.

Alang Ciyakang (Xilin Buluo 西林部落)

Nestled east of the foothills and south of the Shoufeng River in Wanrong Township of Hualien County, this village (around 200 metres above sea level) was Tgdaya hunting territory until Truku Qrao Wadan set up a hunting lodge and drove out the Tgdaya. He followed the Shoufeng River downstream and established a settlement he called Bonkul, meaning "fertile soil." After fighting against the Japanese in 1914, his group hid in the mountains but was forced to return to this location by the river in 1915. Between 1918 and 1929, other alang were moved here by the Japanese, where they established Ciyakang, meaning "a cavern," one kilometre to the east of that first settlement. So, Ciyakang is unambiguously a place name. The modern village was established in 1930, divided into three residential areas. Over the decades, with intermarriage and changes in land holdings, they no longer identify with the old alang and have established an identity as Ciyakang (Walis and Yu 2002, 134–5). Household registration statistics for April 2018 showed a population of 1,326, including 1,283 Indigenous people (96.8 per cent). The majority language is Truku, and they belong politically to the Truku. I conducted six months of research in Ciyakang in 2006. When I was there, farmers were complaining about the low prices they were getting for their corn and peanut crops. The nearby tourist resort was an important source of employment, as were construction sites in Hualien.

The historical wayfarings of entire communities down the mountains are still very important today, but more as social and political identity than as contemporary lifestyle. The people of all these villages, including those who can look out their window to view the Pacific Ocean, identify resolutely as mountain people. Politically, they are all classified as "mountain Indigenous people" as opposed to "plains Indigenous people." This classification means that they vote from separate voting lists, as there is a quota in the Legislative Yuan for three mountain Indigenous representatives and three plains Indigenous representatives. It also means that they live in the mountain townships, in which the township magistrate by law must be Indigenous, and that they have access to Indigenous reserve land. From a phenomenological perspective, "mountain" identity corresponds best with the embodied experience of the hunters and trappers who stake out hunting territories in the adjacent mountain forests. They all know the origins of their families in mountain communities, even if the forced displacements happened a century ago. Sometimes they take their children on hikes up the mountains to see where their grandparents and great-grandparents lived, in what has become the most successful form of political mobilization (Yang 2015). From what I could observe during field research, people have a strong distaste for the sea. Although people frequently offered to take me up the mountains, nobody ever took me to the beach. And when I asked people for names of birds, even those who lived near the ocean listed exclusively mountain birds rather than shore birds. People were horrified in 2005 when the Canadian graduate student who accompanied me went off on his own initiative and swam in the ocean. In contrast to what we would have experienced in nearby Amis communities, the sea is simply not a part of their lifeworlds. These observations echo what Korean anthropologist Kim Kwang-ok observed among the Truku, when people told him that mountains are for the "true man" and the sea is for the "worthless" (Kim 1980, 172). Instead, they refer to enchanted mountain forests inhabited by myriad animal lives. It is thus fitting that I begin the ethnography with animals.

ETHNOGRAPHIC REFLECTIONS

Sakus (camphor) 樟腦樹

Figure 2.1. Camphor (*Cinnamomum camphora*), a giant tree with a height up to 30 metres, grows scattered in the forest; it is useful for many manufactured products, including celluloid for cinematic and photographic film. Because camphor cannot be grown on plantations, it drew Chinese workers and Japanese military officers deep into the forests, where the camphor was distilled before transport. This manufacturing process, shaped by the tree and the terrain, made camphor stills into easy targets for Indigenous warriors protecting their territories. American consul James Davidson wrote: "The Camphor question is in reality the savage question inasmuch as the success or failure of the industry is dependent upon the position occupied by the savages" (Davidson 1903, 398).

Source: Illustration by Biluan.

Chapter Two

Samat (Forest Animals)

The capture of forest animals (*samat*), or hunting (*maduk*), is the core of *Gaya*, and because of that, it is the most prominent Indigenous rights issue in contemporary Taiwan. Contrary to what many urban people may think, hunting is not primarily about killing animals. Hunting is important for the intergenerational transmission of lifeworlds, as hunting provides a rare context in which Sədeq men transmit bodily skills and the ethics of Gaya to their sons in their own languages. Hunting is a relationship with deceased ancestors, whom hunters invoke in rituals surrounding the hunt and remember while traversing the pathways of the forest. Discussion of hunting also casts light on other issues such as the right to self-government, use of traditional territories, and free, prior informed consent when outsiders wish to use hunting territories for other purposes. It is the core of Sədeq sociality and an activity that takes them well beyond the human.

Attention to hunting, especially when we move from the forest to the worlds of police officers, judges, or bureaucrats and politicians holding out promises of "co-management," reveals the nature of conflicts at the heart of both indigeneity and Indigenous resurgence. In the first instance, there are the relations and negotiations between the entities that compose a lifeworld or ontology. For the Sədeq, these are the relations between men hunting in the same place, between hunters from different communities as they define the boundaries of hunting territories, between hunters and their families or communities as they share meat, between hunters and the animals of the forest, and between hunters and spiritual beings. That is the world that most hunters and trappers wanted to share with me. Only secondarily do different peoples come into contact, and negotiations and conflicts arise as people fight to sustain their own ontologies. Although there were also conflicts in the past, the colonial situation creates new kinds of conflicts and gives different meanings to them. This area is the field of political ontology, which not coincidentally Mario Blaser first developed while studying a sustainable hunting program created for the Yshiro people of Paraguay under the supervision of the National Parks Direction (Blaser 2009b). It is where institutions of indigeneity are created and become contested, as state actors and local leaders alike try to seize agency and ordinary people judge what is happening. It is also a place for Indigenous resurgence. Indigenous people remind us constantly that these conflicts happen in a context of colonialism and political inequality.

The writing of this book, which happened over the years from 2016 to 2022, coincided with the progress of an important Indigenous rights case in Taiwan at both the beginning and the end of the writing. In July 2013, Talum Suqluman, a fifty-four-year-old Bunun man, went hunting to obtain meat for his elderly mother, bringing back a Formosan serow (similar to a mountain goat, *Capricornis swinhoei*) and a Reeve's muntjac (a small deer, *Muntiacus reevesi*). He was arrested and charged first with violating the Controlling Guns, Ammunition and Knives Act, which grants Indigenous hunters an exemption to possess and use hunting rifles provided they are "home-made," "traditional," and duly registered with local authorities. This time, Talum used a handcrafted 12-gauge rifle with a mounted scope and five bullets, which he claimed to have found by the river. The local judges determined that he had violated the law because he had not made his own gun, it had been modified beyond the traditional form, and differing from the guns of other men in the community, did not conform to the Indigenous "culture" that is protected by law. He was also charged under the Wildlife Conservation Act, which forbids hunting of protected or endangered species, including serows and muntjacs. Moreover, the Wildlife Conservation Act permits Indigenous people to hunt for certain "cultural" reasons, usually ceremonial and ritual activities, for which Indigenous groups must obtain advance permission. He had not applied for permission in advance. He was fined NT$700,000, which (as we saw in chapter 1) is nearly the average household income for Indigenous families. He was sentenced to three years and two months for the firearms violation and seven months for the wildlife charges, which the judge reduced to three years and six months.

Talum was defended by the Taitung Legal Aid Foundation. His lawyers argued that subsistence hunting is an integral part of Bunun culture, that the legal home-made guns are dangerous to the hunters, and that regulations about species and advance application are unreasonable because hunters receive prey from the ancestors and cannot know in advance what will happen. His appeal was rejected, and he was scheduled to return to prison on 15 December 2015. He refused to go. A Truku friend assisting the Legal Aid Foundation asked me to raise international awareness of the issue, prompting me to write a blog and launch an online petition (Simon 2015b). As a result of both domestic and international attention to the case, the prosecutor-general decided to send the issue to the Constitutional Court, and Talum was allowed to stay at home in the meantime. The final decision, which came down only after I finished this book, will be discussed at the end of this chapter. I need to first unpack the ontological relations in the lives of hunters and explore what recent debates in anthropology can contribute to understanding these conflicts.

The Turning Point in My Fieldwork

One of the turning points in my understanding of hunting was on the morning of 16 April 2007, when I attended a demonstration and public hearing on hunting at the visitors' centre of the Taroko National Park (described in Simon 2012b, 113–16; 2013). Early in the morning, I accompanied Tera Yudaw, a retired school principal who was one of the most active proponents of creating a Taroko Indigenous Autonomous Zone, to the airport to pick up Chinese Nationalist Party (KMT) legislator Dr. Kung Wen-chi. On the way from the airport to the park, they decided that protesters would chant three slogans: "Indigenous people want human rights; Indigenous people want subsistence; Indigenous people want respect." I asked Dr. Kung if they also want land. He responded with silence.

The immediate conflict that sparked the protest was that two older men had gone hunting in the Taroko National Park. On their way home, with flying squirrels in their backpacks, they were accosted by park police officers, who shone lights directly in their eyes. One of the hunters fled in fear, falling down a cliff. The other hunter was afraid to speak out against the police. The two Truku leaders had organized the protest (figure 2.2) after hearing rumours that local men were planning to storm the police station and, in a revival of headhunting, take an officer's head in retaliation. They hoped to defuse potential conflict. When we arrived at the park, the police had already prepared paddy wagons in case they had to haul off large numbers of protesters. Both sides, the police and the Truku, seemed wary of potential violence. Even the protest organizers felt the need to explicitly instruct the hunters not to bring guns to the demonstration. The protest lasted less than fifteen minutes before everyone headed for a public hearing in the auditorium of the park's visitors' centre.

Figure 2.2. Hunters' protest. KMT Indigenous legislator Kung Wen-chi leads an action on hunting rights, 2007.

Source: Photograph by Scott E. Simon.

The hearing unfolded peacefully, but both sides were unyielding. At the request of the Taroko National Park authorities, the Truku did not prepare demonstration banners or signs, which could attract the attention of tourists. After about thirty people showed up in the parking lot, they chanted the three slogans perfunctorily and quietly entered the auditorium under police escort. Kung, Tera, and one hunter sat at a table on the stage. The police, park administrators, and a representative from the Ministry of the Interior sat in the front row. Community members spread out across the auditorium. Kung framed the issue as a human rights problem, adding: "We are merely subsisting on our own land." Tera took the microphone and summarized the colonial history, from the Qing Dynasty, which never ruled the mountain interior, through the Japanese period, to the National Park Law that justified the police action, which he characterized as unacceptable violence. The first hunter to testify switched rapidly between Truku and broken Mandarin. Speaking directly to the dignitaries in the front row, he said in Chinese: "You will never stop us. Hunting is part of our culture, our life, the spirit of the Truku. Do you want another Taroko Incident? Do you want another Wushe Incident? The police should not force us. We are prepared to use our own lives to protect our land." He concluded his words by saying: "We Indigenous people have always lived here. You are all guests." As the microphone was passed through the auditorium, community members testified about having been harassed and fined by the police for carrying weapons, collecting wild plants, or cooking. They recounted being injured in police attacks, and even those who still own land within the park boundaries reported being warned from visiting the mountains too frequently.

The written petition was a bold statement of sovereignty. Kung's office, three Presbyterian congregations, and four Truku non-governmental organizations (NGOs) made three demands. The first was an apology, to be given with a guarantee that such behaviour would never happen again. The second specified that, if any police officer again violates their human rights, the captain and the offending officers should be immediately deported from Truku territory. The third demanded the government revise all relevant legislation in accordance with the Indigenous Peoples' Basic Law. The petition declared that the Truku affirm their land and cultural sovereignty over the traditional territory of their own ancestors. In elegant Chinese, it said that the police had "reversed the order of guest and host."

At first, the authorities resisted. The representative from the Ministry of the Interior characterized the problem as a poor "service attitude" and promised that they would reflect on their practices and "ways of speaking." The local police captain said that they must enforce the law, especially if tourists report hearing gunshots. As people started to get angry, they called out: "We are killing squirrels, not people!" and "We are the masters of this land!" Finally, Tera seized the microphone, looked directly at the police captain, and said: "I can't accept what you just said. Just apologize!" The officer bowed his head and said he was sorry. Dr. Kung concluded by suggesting that the police simply refrain from enforcing laws against hunting until the Legislative Yuan had done their job of revising legislation to permit Indigenous hunting for cultural and subsistence reasons, as stipulated in the Basic Law.

The idiom of sovereignty, expressed in Chinese at this event, is revealing. The Chinese term for sovereignty, *zhuquan* 主權, literally means "host power." Jeffrey Martin, in his study of police on Taiwan, traced the origin of this term to the 1864 translation of Wheaton's *Elements of International Law* by an American missionary commissioned by the Qing Ministry of Rites (Martin 2019, 149, fn2). Chinese dyadic relations are defined in terms of host (*zhuren* 主人) and guest (*keren* 客人), expressing a relationship of subject (*zhuti* 主體, literally "host body") and object (*keti* 客體, "guest body"). Police in Taiwan, who may often find themselves in a position of weakness vis-à-vis locals, are instructed to try to "seize agency" (*bawo zhuti* 把握主體; Martin 2019, 58). This directive explains why the police responded first by reflecting on their impolite ways of speaking. The police attempt to seize agency, however, was consistently repudiated by the Truku people present, who repeatedly insisted that they were the hosts and the state officials were merely passing guests. These are strong ontological claims that resonate across Taiwan, where "the cosmic principle of popular sovereignty really is the living foundation of Taiwan's political worldhood" (Martin 2019, 139). Dr. Kung tried to frame the issue as one of human rights that can be solved by the Legislative Yuan. Everyone else present, however, asserted that they had never ceded their sovereignty and that their land was illegitimately occupied by the state. Their evocations of the "Taroko Incident" and the "Wushe Incident" (the Chinese name for the Musha Incident), as well as threats to revive headhunting, were ways of saying that they are prepared to use violence if provoked too far. They do not agree with the notion that the state has the only legitimate monopoly on the use of force. It is telling that they all discussed these issues in a Chinese idiom, but that is certainly because they were communicating in Mandarin with state officials. This marginalization of their language and ontologies is part of cultural imperialism.

In the days before and after the protest, I discussed the issue with people in the village. Some people were upset that they had not been invited to the protest and did not even know it had happened. Some people expressed criticism of Dr. Kung, or the Presbyterian Church, or the way in which the event was dominated by people with political agendas. One hunter from a neighbouring village accused the two older hunters of being notorious poachers who sell bushmeat on the black market in a flagrant "massacre" of animals. But everyone was in agreement that the Taroko National Park was constructed on unceded Indigenous territory and that the local hunters know more about animals and how to hunt sustainably than anyone from the Ministry of the Interior, the National Park, or police stations.[1]

When hunters subsequently encouraged me to help them document their lifeworlds and perspectives on forests and the lives in them, I struggled to find appropriate methods and writing strategies. In this chapter, I thus stay as close as possible to Truku and Sediq worlds. I begin where my Indigenous interlocutors almost always begin: with a description of the contemporary political context in which their perspectives are marginalized and their practices criminalized. This background is an appropriate place to think about my entry into the worlds of hunters. I then, inspired by Anishinabek scholars John Borrows (2010) and Leanne Simpson (2011), show how Sediq/Truku law (Gaya) and human-animal ethical relations are storied forms of knowledge. I only then come back to the anthropological debates, discuss hunting as a form of apprenticeship, and explore how hunting is an expression of Gaya. I also bring in more traditional forms of ethnobiology, which, looking for a way to validate Indigenous knowledge about the mountain forests of Taiwan, I learned during an intensive five-day course on research methods at the Duke Marine Lab in North Carolina in the summer of 2011. I used those methods, rooted in more traditional ethnobiological concerns such as folk taxonomy, during my ethno-ornithology project with Truku people in 2012 and 2013. That led to new research on how Truku people classify the living world. What the Truku and Sediq hunters tell me about politics remains important. I thus come back to their concerns to conclude the chapter.

The Political and Social Context of Hunting

For hunters and trappers, the core problem is that their subsistence activities have been criminalized and stigmatized by the non-Indigenous majority. After two decades of lobbying for hunting rights, Taiwan's Indigenous activists finally convinced the Legislature in 2005 to pass the Basic Law on Indigenous Peoples. Article 19 recognized in principle that Indigenous people have rights, as "not-for-profit activities," to hunt wild animals, collect wild plants and fungi, or extract minerals, rocks, and soils, but only "for traditional culture, ritual, or self-consumption" (ROC Ministry of Justice [2005] 2018). This law has not yet been fully implemented, because legislators have been slow to revise the relevant laws, including one that forbids hunting in national parks. Human rights activists, and legislators like Dr. Kung, have assumed that the Basic Law is secondary only to the Constitution and that all other laws must be interpreted and revised according to the principles laid out within it.

Since the project of revising all other laws to permit Indigenous hunting remains incomplete, hunters were still arrested and charged with violations of weapons, poaching, and national park laws during the entire period of this research. Revisions to firearms laws permitted Indigenous men to craft their own muzzle-loading rifles, but they had to use ball bearings or lead pellets rather than real bullets. They could be charged with a crime if they, like Talum Suqluman, used technologically more advanced weapons or rifles acquired elsewhere. Hunters noted to me in frustration that their front-loading muskets are less advanced than the firearms the Dutch brought to Taiwan in 1624 (see Lin 2016) and that they can cause serious injuries to the hunter. This ruling basically means that men are allowed to hunt – but only on the condition that they use unsafe rifles. Hunters also say that more modern rifles would allow them to kill the animals more swiftly and with less pain, arguing that Gaya says they should consider the suffering of the animal. Cultural reasons are often narrowly interpreted by enforcement officers to permit activities organized by NGOs, sometimes even with a tourist audience in mind. In those cases, organizers apply to local authorities in advance to take a specified species of animal on a specified date in a specified location. Such interpretations give little or no leeway for cultural reasons important to individual hunters, such as to provide meat to prospective in-laws or to obey the directives given by a deceased ancestor in a dream. Subsistence reasons were usually ignored, probably because only the poorest families rely on game for protein. It is completely illegal to hunt in a national park or to use traps of any kind, even though trapping is the most common hunting practice among older men. It is illegal to hunt threatened and endangered species. These restrictions mean all but a narrow scope of hunting practices are criminalized, if not completely illegal. During the time that I did this research, hunters could only hope that police and conservation officers would be kind and turn a blind eye to their activities. In Nantou, people told me that local compromises permitting most hunting are the norm.

The hunters do not give state restrictions precedence over other considerations. Despite the criminalization of hunting, or perhaps because they feel a need to resist the regime, they boast that "the forest is our refrigerator." Most importantly to them, they consider hunting to be the sole sign of real manhood (*snaw balay*, meaning "real men"), just as weaving is a symbol of womanhood. Traditionally, women were not allowed to even touch hunting equipment, and men were not supposed to touch looms or other weaving tools. In 1985, at a workshop concluding a research project on human rights among Taiwan's Indigenous peoples, Seejiq Truku anthropologist and politician Masaw Mowna pointed out that even men who have migrated to urban areas expect to hunt when they return home on weekends. He argued that externally imposed hunting restrictions constitute a violation of their human rights (Chinese Human Rights Association 1987, 313). Indigenous hunters maintain that state laws on hunting conflict with Gaya and are ultimately subordinate to Gaya. Every time they shoot a flying squirrel or lay a trap in the forest, they resist a state-centric legal system that many perceive as a colonial imposition. This context of cultural imperialism makes hunting a very sensitive area of inquiry for anthropologists, as people are simultaneously proud of their way of life and wary of telling outsiders about what can be marked as illegal behaviour. Hunting is one area in which it is beneficial to be a foreign researcher. Whereas many Taiwanese people describe hunting as repugnant and are amazed that people "still" hunt, as if hunting were a primitive stage of cultural evolution, many North Americans find hunting to be a normal and highly valued part of rural life. In Taiwan, the animal rights movement is influenced by Buddhist notions that the taking of even one single animal life is fundamentally wrong.

Although I had never hunted in my life, encounters with hunters provoked childhood memories of my father hunting with his friends and of my grandmother's freezer that seemed always stocked with venison. I was the first generation of my family to not hunt, and I imagined it was a lifestyle I had left behind by acquiring university education and an urban lifestyle. Nonetheless, my recollections of the men in my childhood sparked in me a curiosity that led me to accept invitations to accompany older men as they inspected their traps, follow young men as they shot squirrels, or hike the forests as people showed me their past and present hunting territories. I was surprised to find myself quickly at ease with people who reminded me of my own relatives. Eventually, I returned to Canada and acquired a Quebec trapping license, much to the delight of my friends in Taiwan. They were also quite excited when I gave them hunting and trapping magazines from Canada, quite envious of the hunting technology and the apparent ease of hunting large animals. All of this helped me to establish rapport with hunters and trappers.

Humans and Others in Mythical Time

The Seejiq and Truku have a rich oral tradition of myths about animals, many of which are moral tales intended to convey lessons about Gaya. During the colonial period (1895–1945), Japanese ethnographers carefully documented the oral teachings they could gather. Post-war Korean anthropologist Kim Kwang-ok (1980) further analysed those that he collected during his field research in the 1970s, as have Shen Ming-ren (1998) and many other Indigenous scholars. I have also heard many of these stories told as parts of church sermons or as conversations around the hearth in the evenings, which shows that the oral traditions are still a vital part of life in the twenty-first century. Two related stories, which I heard frequently in the villages where I did field research, are about the origins of hunting and of agriculture. Most important is the moral lesson against greed, as they remind people not to take more than they need. The stories are as follows:

Hunting

In ancient times, people did not hunt. Instead, they simply called the name of the animal they wanted. The animal, whether a boar, muntjac, or sambar deer, would emerge from the forest and approach the person. The person would take a single strand of hair from the animal and place it in a bamboo container. When he or she later opened the container, it would be full of meat. Once, a woman became greedy. She called a boar, who came to her, and cut off his ear, thinking this would procure even more meat. The boar screamed in pain and ran back to the forest, where he told the other animals what happened. Ever since, animals have been afraid of humans, and men have had to endure hunting as a dangerous ordeal. (Rimuy 2002, 41–70)

Farming

In ancient times, people did not farm. Instead, they wore an earring made from a bamboo stem, which they used to store millet grains. They could carry four to five grains of millet at a time, but it was enough to eat for a week. If they put one grain of millet into a pot, it would turn into enough cooked millet for one and a half days. You were not supposed to wash the grains. If you did, it would cause a typhoon. Once, somebody wanted to cook more than the portion that was needed. When she opened the cooking pot, the millet had turned into hundreds of sparrows. From then on, people have had to farm and spend their time chasing birds away from their crops. The lesson is that you should not be lazy or greedy and want more than you have. (Field notes, 16 May 2015)

These two stories reveal ways in which people view the immediate surroundings of forest and garden. The explicit meaning is that human greed caused a fall from an original condition of harmony with other beings, leading to the situation in which people must risk their lives and work hard to hunt and farm. The stories set up several dualities, the kind that French anthropologist Claude Lévi-Strauss thought was the basis of human thought, such as the contrast between hunting (maduk) and planting (mhuma) or working the earth (psakur). Hunting is a male preoccupation, whereas mmiyak (the mountain work of collecting firewood or plants to eat, nowadays household chores) is female work. This duality is parallel to other contrasting pairs in the Truku language

Table 2.1. Logical binaries in Truku mythology and descriptions of human life

Mountain forest	Settlement
Mountain forests (*dgiyaq*)	Settlement (*alang*)
Forest animals (*samat*)	Settlement animals (*tnbgan*)
Hunting (*maduk*)	Farming (*mhuma, psakur*)
Men (*snaw*)	Women (*kuyuh* in Hualien, *qrijil* in Nantou)
Hunting (*maduk*)	Gathering (*mmimak*)

Note: Spelling is according to online Truku dictionary (see glossary).
Sources: Fieldwork; Pecoraro (1977).

(table 2.1), most notably that of the forested mountains or hunting territory (*dgiyaq*) versus settlement (*alang*) and of forest animals (samat) versus the animals of the settlements (*tnbgan*), but also between men (*snaw*) and women (*kuyuh, qrijil*). These stories also set up human life as being in relationship with two different categories of beings. On the one hand are the animals to be hunted – samat – and on the other hand are the plants to be cultivated – most especially millet.

When these stories are told in the context of church sermons given by Truku ministers, they provide a foundation for the discussion of ethics and morality. They emphasize that humans must observe certain norms of conduct; otherwise, there will be immediate repercussions in the physical world. This teaching is true about human greed but, interestingly in this version of the story, with the idea that human mishandling of a plant may cause typhoons. Tyhoons are a natural concern on Formosa, where annual typhoons threaten the safety of human settlements and crops. In both stories, the moral is that one should never take more than one needs. Finally, there is a gender dimension, as the greed of a woman is what made it necessary for men to hunt.[2]

Classifying and Understanding the Living World

In the summer of 2010, as I prepared to conduct an ethnobiological study with Truku people in Hualien, I first met with a small group of people who are locally identified as experts in either Truku language or hunting. These were a Presbyterian minister, two hunters, and Kuhon, a retired policeman who devotes a great deal of his time to cultural and historical research. When I asked them how the Truku understand the natural world, they quickly came to a consensus around several points. First, living things are collectively called *mneudus*, a word based on the root *udus* meaning "life."[3] These are further divided into the two categories of "things that move" (*lmglug*) for animals and "things that don't move" (*ini klgug*) for plants. As I noted the spellings provided by the minister, I was immediately struck by how closely the category lmglug resembled the English notion of animal, which, based on the Latin *anima*, also refers to things that move.

As the conversation moved forward, one of the hunters divided the plants into *qhuni* (tree) and *spriq* (which he translated into Chinese as *cao* 草, grass), but I was more interested in the animals. The hunters made a distinction between the animals of the forest (samat) and the animals of the settlement (tnbgan), which seems to resemble a classification of "wild" versus "domestic," even though close observation of human-animal interactions suggests that the concept of "domestication" fails to accurately explain the relationships hunters have with dogs or pigs (Simon 2015c; figure 2.3). The pastor said that there are living things that "fly in the sky" (*mneudus skaya kalat*), those that "crawl on the ground" (*mneudus mkarang dxgal*), and those that "live in the waters" (*mneudus ska qsiya*). Picking up on the animals of the sky, one of the hunters said that birds are called *qbhni* and that there are also insects (*kuwi*). The pastor added that qbhni is not restricted exclusively to birds, since hunters who return with only small game such as flying squirrels will say that they got *qbhni nanak* (only small critters). Although the pastor translated those that crawl on the ground into Chinese as *pachong lei* 爬蟲類, which in Chinese means "reptiles," even though he listed some amphibians among his examples, the hunters seemed most interested in snakes (*quyu*) as the most important in this category. Interestingly, they gave cockroaches and geckos as examples of *kuwi*, while placing lizards along with snakes as "animals that crawl on the ground."

I only later realized that the pastor had opened the conversation with the vocabulary of the biblical book of Genesis. Interestingly, the hunters all found it difficult to fit their observations of phenomenal reality to those categories. Insects, which are not even mentioned in Genesis, are a residual category that arbitrarily includes both geckos and cockroaches, as well as those non-birds that also fly in the air such as butterflies, mosquitos, and flies. These are everywhere exceptions because they are not as evident to human perception as are vertebrates (Atran 1990, 6). Snakes, in addition to being prominent in Genesis, are important in the lives of hunters who, by spending so much time in the forest and at night, sometimes get bitten by venomous snakes. They must be able to identify snakes as a matter of survival. This conversation revealed an important dynamic that is one of the main themes of this book. Sejiq Truku ontologies, even the way in which they

Figure 2.3. A hunter's dog. A dog is a hunter's most important partner, not part of any taxonomic scheme.

Source: Photograph by Scott E. Simon.

think about what exists in the world around them, are a bricolage of Truku linguistic transmission, experiences in the forest, and Christian interpretations.

When asked how to say "nature" in Truku (as a translation of the Chinese *daziran* 大自然), people spontaneously said dgiyaq. But when asked to explain dgiyaq, most people would point to the mountains and say it means the mountain forests. On this day, one hunter concurred with the minister when he suggested it would be better to translate daziran as *babaw dxgal*, which literally means "on the (whole) earth." When asked to translate "culture" (from the Chinese *wenhua* 文化), people spontaneously said Gaya. The different semantic fields of these terms show that they do not place nature and culture in opposition, as has been the case in Western philosophical traditions. There is an opposition between mountain and settlement, but no idea that humans are excluded in any way from the mountains. On the contrary, hunters forge pathways through the forest and constantly move between the two social realms. In pre-colonial times, moreover, people cleared the forests to make way for settlements and horticulture. They made a dwelling for themselves in the forests. Mountains and settlement were thus intimately linked until very recently. Gaya, even though it is used as a translation for culture, is in no way separate from the living world; Gaya is, rather, the moral guide for humans who live within it.

French anthropologist Philippe Descola, taking up the mantle of Lévi-Strauss, argues that "nature" and "culture" as opposed ontological categories is a product of Western philosophy (Descola 2011). In Taiwan, this ontological category has become hegemonic and is the justification since the 1930s for creating national parks on the territories of Indigenous peoples with little or no consideration for their needs. The use of the concept clearly dates to Japanese colonialism. In the nineteenth century, as European science was being translated into Asian languages and Darwinism gained popularity in Meiji-era Japan, Japanese naturalists translated "nature" as *shizen* 自然, a word that came into common Japanese usage only in the 1890s (Thomas 2001, 7). The Japanese were the first to bring that notion to Taiwan.

Literally meaning "that which comes into being from itself," shizen is a borrowed term from Europe. The English word "nature," like that of "nation," is derived from the Latin *natura*, derived from *natus*, or "birth." The Latin *natura*, meaning the "course of things, natural character, the universe," implies a flowering or growth from innate powers. The prefix "dai-" meaning "large" makes a distinction between the smaller "nature" of objects and persons (shizen 自然) and the larger nature of the external environment (*daishizen* 大自然). Later, when I was training with a Japanese mountain ascetic (*yamabushi* 山伏) in Japan, he told me that the Meiji was the epoch when the Japanese started to believe in a distinction between culture and nature. Before this time, the Japanese saw themselves as part of nature.

This Meiji-era Japanese word, like many other words of modernity, was soon accepted into Chinese usage as well, with the pronunciation daziran. Due to this colonial past, the dominant view in Taiwan, like in the West, is that nature is somehow separate from urban life and culture. Throughout the Japanese period, Japanese naturalists, using research questions and methods from the West, visited the island's Indigenous communities as they searched the mountains for samples of plants, birds, and animals. This naturalist approach, now reinforced because Taiwan's leading biologists and forestry experts study in the United States, is the hegemonic ontology of Taiwan's national parks. This way of thinking remains very different from that of the people who have the most intimate relations with other beings in the island's forests.

Learning to Hunt

Descola argued that hunting, as an example of a practical cognitive schema, takes a long time to master because of the quantity of disparate items of knowledge that must be organized in order to successfully bring back game (Descola [2005] 2013, 100). This necessary apprenticeship is perhaps why Sediq and Truku men have traditionally taught boys how to hunt by practising on birds or rodents for years and why the first hunt of larger game is an important coming-of-age ritual. Young men hunt by shooting flying squirrels, whereas older men tend to focus on trapping. Parents often begin by taking their children on hikes into the mountain forests to experience the sites where their ancestors once lived, farmed, and hunted. This practice is surely important, because walking on the steep mountain terrain requires the acquisition of rapid motor reflexes to keep balance, avoid tripping over roots, and gain the confidence necessary to walk along the side of a precipitous cliff without freezing in horror.

In one of my first expeditions into the forests, a hunter (and one of the interlocutors in the conversation mentioned earlier) whom I shall call Ichiro, took me and a Taiwanese student to his hunting lodge in the mountain forests.[4] On this trip early in my mountain experiences, I was dependent on his supporting hands to make my way up and down steep paths, as well as across precipices and the skeletons of decrepit bridges. My sore legs after the six-hour hike bore testament to the fact that my muscles had not yet learned to walk in the mountains. As we walked through the forest, Ichiro was able to point out the same kind of information that he might show to his son.

Much of this teaching is what Ingold would call the intergenerational transmission of perceptual skills, as it is done through guidance and personal embodied experience rather than through the oral transmission of knowledge. Ichiro pointed out the cliffs where a *mirit* (Formosan serow), a kind of mountain goat, is likely to be found. He also indicated that the goats could identify hunters and defend themselves by butting hunters off the cliffs to their deaths. He revealed traces of animals around us that I had never noticed and found almost magical at first, simply because I had never been taught to perceive such things. These included traces of animal scat from which he could immediately identify the animal, indentations in the grass that show that the small deer known as a *pada* (Formosan Reeves muntjac) has slept there recently (figure 2.4), or paths in the forest carved by *bowyak* (wild boar, *Sus scrofa*). He identified the calls of muntjacs in the valleys, but also those of various birds, including the *sisil* (grey-cheeked fulvetta,

Figure 2.4. Muntjac. A hunter asked me to photograph a muntjac he had trapped and was carrying in his woven basket.

Source: Photograph by Scott E. Simon.

Alcippe morrisonia), which, as we will see later, can indicate the success or failure of a hunt.[5]

At one point, Ichiro stopped to identify a pungent odour, which he said smelled like cobras. He recalled historical events, including the site of battles with the Japanese and the place where his father fell to his death. Walking through the forest is thus an intense sensorial experience, overlaid with the knowledge of individual experience and the memory of a specific community. Reading these signs is the culmination of a learning process on how to obtain and interpret information from sensory perceptions. Even without experience, I could identify an unpleasant smell in the forest, but I lacked the knowledge needed to associate it with a particular animal. It took an experienced mentor, one with sufficient experience of facing off venomous snakes, to point out the danger of cobras at that spot. I asked Ichiro why he is so concerned about cobras, because in my experience snakes usually notice humans and slither away into the underbrush ahead of us. Unlike other snakes, he explained, cobras may attack to protect their territory. After we arrived at Ichiro's hunting lodge, the student and I helped him move logs as we had promised and then settled in.

On the second evening, Ichiro asked us to sleep in a neighbour's bamboo shelter while he hunted by night with two other men. In the morning, he showed up with four dead flying squirrels and a live serow. He first told us a story about the two men. He said that they had started to complain about the weight of carrying the squirrels, even though Gaya prohibits hunters from complaining while hunting. As a result, the next squirrel they shot fell into a ravine and its body mysteriously disappeared. The ancestral spirits, or *utux*, express displeasure with hunters sometimes by causing the prey to mysteriously disappear after being killed. That is usually a sign that the hunters should atone for a misdeed and return home as quickly as possible.

Ichiro showed us how he had shot the serow, which already had an injured leg from having been caught in a trap, in the back of the head. The small lead pellet he used for a bullet had merely grazed its head, but it fell unconscious long enough for them to ties its legs and put it in a canvas bag to bring back. Although Ichiro had agreed with the two men that they would share any meat equally, he wanted to keep the serow for his in-laws and thus gave them each NT$1,000 for their fair share. Still, the hunt was not yet over. Hunting is much more than killing an animal. It is a long social process that begins with the selection of hunting partners, tools, and the location and timing of the hunt. It ends with the selective sharing and eating of the meat. It is an emotionally salient process that contributes to the identity construction of the hunter – in this case as being a real man in the immediate social circle and being Indigenous in a wider society that stigmatizes these very same practices.

After breakfast, we loaded our goods to return to the village. Realizing that I had a choice between carrying down thirty kilograms of supplies in a backpack or the thirty-kilogram serow in its canvas bag, I offered to take the animal. Wanting to help, I argued that conservation officers are unlikely to suspect a pale, spectacled foreigner of carrying an animal. What I did not realize was that it was already difficult to negotiate the steep descent, which was made even more challenging by a live animal that occasionally squirmed and shifted positions. About a third of the way back down, we exchanged loads. Nonetheless, Ichiro said that I had done some of the work, and that labour made me part of the hunting party, just like the two men who received cash rather than meat. He said that Gaya does not permit any individual person to boast about his ability or to take credit for the hunt. It was a collective effort and must be recognized as such.

After we arrived at the foot of the mountain, we loaded the serow and our bags into the back of Ichiro's pickup truck and drove to his father-in-law's urban apartment. For Ichiro, hunting is part of an important and long-standing social relationship, as men often hunt with their fathers-in-law as preferred hunting partners and are expected to provide in-laws with game.

Ichiro, his father-in-law, the student, and I prepared to kill the serow in the laundry room, the practical considerations being that the tile floor and the drain in the floor would make it easier to clean up afterwards. Ichiro told us that forest animals, unlike raised pigs, face death bravely and do not cry in protest. Thinking of the many ethnographic descriptions I have read about Indigenous hunting practices in North America, I stroked the serow on the forehead and said in Chinese: "Thank you for giving up your life for us." Ichiro simply glared at me and said: "You are crazy!" Ichiro first shaved the serow's throat. His father-in-law deftly struck his knife deep through the serow's throat, twisting it to puncture the heart. The animal did not cry at all, just as Ichiro had predicted. It continued to struggle, however, even as Ichiro squeezed the blood from its neck into a bucket, into which he also emptied the contents of several bottles of rice wine.

After the animal finally died, it was slowly transformed into meat as Ichiro burned off the fur and the men cut the flesh up into pieces that could be cooked. The whole family got involved with this process, making a soup with some of the innards, boiling the small intestine, baking the ribs, and stir-frying some of the choice meat. They placed the raw liver and stomach, sliced into small pieces like sashimi, on a plate to be served with salt. Ichiro's father-in-law cut a slit in the gall bladder, dripping the verdant green bile with rice wine into crystal port glasses. He described it as a fortifying drink to strengthen a man's sexual drive and emphasized that only men are permitted to drink the bile. The Truku word for the organ, *pahung*, means "courage," which is one of the main characters of a real man, *snaw balay*.[6]

Cooking may be central to transforming the animal self into an object to be eaten, but people intentionally consume parts of the animals raw, especially the livers and the blood mixed with rice wine, saying that it allows the human to absorb the vitality of the animal. In the case of male flying squirrels, the young men eat the penis and genitals raw in order to increase their sexual energy. Eating parts of the animal raw, explicitly saying that we are absorbing its strength, maintains awareness of the animal as a living self, even while, in death, it is transformed into a fundamental part of our lives. Linking it to male sexuality makes the point that the death of these animals contributes not only to individual lives but also to the fertility and continued existence of the community. This idea is important. It means they recognize that male virility comes from the forest.

We ate the meal as a feast, with copious servings of sorghum wine, quickly forgetting that the meat in front of us was once a living creature and that I had even spoken to it. We were certainly proud of ourselves for having brought back so much meat to the women, but Ichiro's father-in-law drew attention to the wider political context of our hunt. In the past, he lamented, they would bring back the animal openly, with loud calls of joy, to share the meat with their neighbours. Nowadays, they must conceal the animal in a canvas bag, kill it secretly in their home, and share the meat only with the immediate family and most intimate friends. An activity that was once a public source of social pride for men has been transformed into a clandestine act savoured only within the confines of home. Most of the practices of hunting, however, are firmly anchored in the concept of Gaya, as we could see in the ways in which Ichiro upheld his promises to the other hunters, shared the credit for hunting with those who had helped carry the animal, and shared the meat in an appropriate manner. As Ingold reminded us, hunting is always a total process in social life (Ingold 1988, 209).

Hunting as a Moral and Legal System

Hunting is an important part of an ethical and moral human life, even as details about the ethical norms of Gaya vary between communities or families. Many people describe hunting as an integral part of a righteous life, saying that in the past men needed to learn to hunt and women needed to learn to weave in order to obtain the right to a facial tattoo, which was necessary to become a full adult since only people with facial tattoos could find a spouse and get married. Finally, after a person's death, each person will have to cross the Rainbow Bridge or spirit bridge (Hakaw Utux), at the top of which is a giant crab. The person will have to wash their hands. If their hands bleed, it means that they have been industrious workers all their lives, either as hunters or as weavers. They may then cross the bridge into the land of the ancestors. If their hands do not bleed, it means they have been lazy all their lives. In that case, they will be pushed off the bridge to be consumed by crabs.

In this framework, successful hunting is a sign of moral righteousness. In Hualien, Truku people describe it in terms of a certain "spirit," which they call *bhring* (Huang 2000, 57). This moral righteousness, and power, of the hunter involves a mixture of innate ability, knowledge of the environment, and the ability to provide for others. Hunters must uphold Gaya, which means sharing with others but also carrying out the correct rituals. The ethics of hunting can be categorized as sets of ethical responsibilities to four different types of others: living people in one's own community, ancestors, living people in other communities, and the animals of the forest.

Ethical Responsibilities to the Living Members of One's Own Community

Hunters most frequently refer to sharing as a central part of Gaya. This concept is not at all surprising to anthropologists, especially since practices of sharing meat in hunter-gatherer societies have been very important in our understanding of altruism in human communities. But there are three kinds of sharing: sharing of meat, sharing of knowledge, and sharing of land.

Sharing meat is one of the most important dimensions of hunting (Nadasdy 2003, 67). A Truku metaphor for people who eat alone is *qowlit* (rats), the implication being that they are stingy and thus immoral. Although there seem to be no formal rules about sharing, it is an important part of social relations and is expected to be part of an ongoing reciprocal relationship of some kind. Meat is shared outward from the hunter in concentric circles. First, as the hunting story illustrated, hunters are expected to share meat with all members of a hunting party. Second, hunters share with their immediate family. The relationship between a man and his in-laws is forged through meat sharing, as he is expected to provide meat to the parents of his prospective wife as part of the prelude to marriage negotiations. If successful, this practice also creates a lifelong bond between the young man and his father-in-law. Third, all members of the alang can legitimately make claims on meat if they see their kin cooking and eating, which can happen regularly, since many people like to cook and eat in front of their homes. This custom creates some awkward situations in contemporary society, as one woman exemplified by complaining to me about her uncle. Poorer people sometimes develop the habit of visiting clan members at mealtimes, which puts a financial strain on their kin who feed their own families on working-class wages that nowadays includes purchasing condiments and rice as well as game meat. Finally, people quite proudly share game meat with friends and colleagues from work, but only when they trust them not to notify the authorities. The now clandestine meat market, with exchange of meat for money from outsiders, lies just outside of these circles of sharing.

Another kind of sharing, knowledge and power, is less explicitly articulated. Fathers teach their young sons to hunt, and older men also share experience and hunting territory with their sons-in-law. Men of the same generation will hunt together, nowadays even occasionally with friends from other communities. Men will also seek the advice of knowledgeable elders. Some hunters carry with them a small leather bag, called a *lubuy*, which can be used to enhance their *bhring*. They place animal parts, such as a boar's tusk or the small horn of a muntjac, in this bag to enhance their hunting luck. In order to be effective, they must obtain these body parts from more experienced hunters. One young man described it to me as "like getting married," because it is necessary to cultivate a relationship with the older hunter, who may even request the sacrifice of a chicken or pig before sharing the animal parts.

There is also the question of dividing up the use of territory. The general principle is that hunting territories are exclusive to the alang. In contemporary Taiwan, there is keen awareness of where each group hunts, even as the forests are claimed by the Forestry Division of the Council of Agricultural Affairs or by national parks under the administration of the Ministry of the Interior. Within each hunting territory, members of the group can freely shoot and catch flying squirrels, birds, and other small animals, but adult men consider none of that to be "real" hunting. Trappers negotiate with one another about where to establish traplines, but once a trapper has carved out a path through the jungle vegetation, the trapline is for his exclusive use to catch larger game, although trappers freely let others use the path for other reasons. Some well-established hunters, such as Ichiro, can also establish areas in which they regularly hunt large game. Establishing an area also involves the labour of maintaining paths, and some hunters even nourish certain fruit- or nut-bearing trees that are known to attract animals. Within a community hunting territory, individuals may have overlapping hunting rights. Within a community, hunters have the ethical responsibility to share territory and to respect the labour of others. In 2012, I spent two weeks up in the mountains with an elderly trapper and found that Truku institutions and rules about hunting are very much alive and effective, even where hunting is forbidden (Simon 2023). The hunters who taught me all of this knowledge by showing me their traplines and territories were making a very important point. Park administrators and even some scholars who research hunting rights assume that hunters simply roam the forests in search of animals. In fact, demarcating a hunting territory, altering the distribution of plants, and making paths is all labour intensive, and that labour is the basis of property rights.

In addition, hunters refer to taboos (*psaniq*). Traditionally, they avoid sexual contact with women before hunting and are not permitted to hunt during certain moments in the life cycles of their families, such as when their wives are pregnant or when they are in mourning (Huang 2000). They are especially not permitted to commit adultery before hunting. If they violate these principles of Gaya, especially about adultery, they are likely to have an accident while hunting or simply return empty-handed.

Ethical Responsibilities to the Ancestors

There are responsibilities to the ancestors as well. When hunters enter the forest, they sometimes begin the hunt with ritual oblations of rice wine, cigarettes, or betel nuts. Trappers used to leave behind the tail of the animal caught in the first trap, and only later created new rituals of leaving oblations. Some Christians may replace all of this ritual with a simple prayer. When hunting, the hunters avoid areas of the forest where they know that ancestors are buried. The ancestors may communicate to them in dreams, telling them to hunt on a certain day or in a certain place, or reminding them to check their traps. One hunter told me that he always speaks to the ancestors when he sets traps for large animals. They do not believe that a special deity or animal master provides them with game.

Hunting is successful only within a proper relationship between the living and the deceased. There is a strong sense that people must maintain the proper rituals of domestic pig sacrifices to the ancestors in order to sustain hunting success (Simon 2015c). There is also a sense that people should not break the relationship with their ancestors by abandoning the land. People say that families who sold their land to make way for the Taroko National Park were subsequently punished by a spate of fatal traffic accidents. It is thus an ethical imperative that some people must stay on the land and continue to hunt. This idea puts people in a double bind. As citizens, they do not wish to violate state law. Real people (*sejiq balay*), however, must above all respect the law passed on to them from their ancestors.

Ethical Responsibilities to Other Communities

From the preceding discussion, we can see that hunting is a social relationship that involves the sharing of meat, knowledge, and territory within a bounded community. Ritual components of hunting, ranging from abstention from sex in the days immediately preceding the hunt to ancestor rituals, reinforce these social relations in the lives of individuals through repetition and habit. There are fewer explicit norms and practices regarding other communities. There is no obligation to share meat with strangers, for example, and meat is usually sold rather than given to outsiders.

The primary responsibility towards other communities is to respect their hunting territories, with the correlate that one must protect the hunting territory of one's own group from others. When discussing Gaya, hunters say that they must not enter the territory of an adjacent group, even when chasing an animal that flees into that territory. If a trapped animal flees into another territory with the trap on its leg, the hunter may pursue it and will retrieve his trap, but he will share the meat with the other hunter. In the past, as the hunters point out, they would enforce their territorial claims through practices of headhunting, a practice so important to local lifeworlds that it will be discussed in a chapter of its own.

Even today, hunters enforce the boundaries of their hunting territories. Therefore, in 2015, Truku hunters asked by authorities of the Taroko National Park to simply hunt outside of the park boundaries could not comply. Those groups who have long hunted in the territory later labelled as a park may not simply start hunting on territories belonging to others. To give another example, a Truku man, who had moved from Hualien to Nantou to lead a church congregation, liked to snorkel and fish in the rivers in his spare time. He avoided Indigenous territories because he knew that he would be driven away from their areas and risked unnecessary conflict. Instead, he chose areas populated by Hakka (Chinese), as he knew they would tolerate the presence of outsiders in their rivers. One could say that the establishment of bounded hunting territories with enforcement mechanisms is an important institution for the conservation of natural resources. It is only part of the way in which people discuss Gaya about forest animals. Animals are not "resources." They are lives. They are not distant lives, located out in "nature" to be preserved. They are entangled in human lives in ways that are regulated by the law of Gaya.

Ethical Responsibilities to Forest Animals

Huang Chang-hsing (Lowsi Rakaw) published a treatise on "Eastern Seejiq" hunting culture. He argued that traditional rules regarding the behaviour of hunters before, during, and after the hunt, especially rules delimiting hunting territories and seasons, all constitute a conservation ethic of "respecting nature, sustainable use" (Huang 2000, 19). In a similar vein, hunters told me that they prefer to hunt in the winter, although only a few people said that it is done to avoid the spring when animals

Table 2.2. Words spoken when using a trap

Words spoken	English translation
Kana gndax haran heidaw	All of you that come from the place where the sun rises
Kana gndax uqiyan heidaw	All of you that come from the place where the sun sets
Kana gndax bnqilan ujilung	All of you that come from around the ocean
Bukung namu ka Yuma	You are all leaders
Klngi mudu hini	You will pass by here
Kana ka lgnux, bowyaq, milit…	All of you sambar deer, wild boars, mountain goats, and so forth

Note: Spelling as provided by the speaker.
Source: Fieldwork, 2013.

are likely to be pregnant or caring for young animals. Others merely said that meat spoils more easily in the summer heat; in fact, I observed people who hunt all year round. I sometimes observed these customs more in the breach, as when two hunters cooked a muntjac embryo but the mother refused to join the meal, saying that catching a pregnant animal is a violation of Gaya. Apparently, there was once the notion of sacred grounds, where all hunting is forbidden, which would have the effect of giving animals a permanent safe place for reproduction. People said that they never venture far into the mountains to hunt, which also preserves entire swathes of forest as safe habitat for the animals. They say they only hunt animals when their numbers have increased to the point where they must move down the mountains closer to human habitation.

One person, in Buarung, asked me to write down the proper words to be used when setting a trap (table 2.2; the spelling here is his). These words show respect to the animals.

A trapper can recite the names of all the animals except for the bear. If one calls the bear's name, she might think she is being called and come out of the forest. That would be dangerous to the trapper, because bears can kill humans. Hunters and trappers thus avoid even saying the name of the bear. Instead, they use the euphemism *bungu qhuni*, meaning "rough roots at the base of a tree," which are hard and strong like a bear. This custom is an interesting variation on traditional knowledge because, although only one person told me about this practice, it implies that animals can still be called out of the forest by a skilled hunter.

The *kumay* (Formosan black bear, *Ursus thibetanus formosanus*) is of particular interest. Most people told me that it is taboo (psaniq) to kill a bear, which is the most powerful animal in the forest, even saying that killing a bear is punished by death in the family. One man and his brother, however, insisted that this notion is mere "superstition," pointing out that their grandfather and uncle are the only people in their village who have ever hunted bears, and they never suffered from negative consequences. Other people, however, pointed to the same family, saying that these men's father was killed in a traffic accident and two of their siblings were born with serious birth defects as punishment for having killed a bear.

The people I met lack the elaborate symbolic systems about mammals or speculation about animal souls that is so prominent in the ethnography of native peoples in the Americas. They do not thank the animals for giving up themselves to the hunters or talk about hunting as a relation of trust between humans and animals. Instead, they thank the ancestors for providing success in hunting. They even think of animals as inferior to humans in many ways, because of their cruelty, immorality, or cowardice. People do not believe that animals have souls that survive death (Kim 1980, 183). Nonetheless, they perceive animals to be selves, as can be seen in discussions about when and where they can be killed. This idea can also be seen in the stories they spin about individual animals, such as the wild boar that turned on the hunter or the aged flying squirrel in one village that people called "PhD" in jest because he has so successfully learned to avoid hunters for years. The fact that they love talking about animals and that animal names are among the first words they teach children and foreign anthropologists is further indication that they perceive forest animals as part of their community of beings. If a child falls ill, people may even change his or her name to that of an animal (or plant) in order to affirm the child's dependence on the natural world (Shen 1998, 78). Despite the diversity among hunters, this practice is all part of an ethic in which they should not take more than they need and must hunt carefully to ensure that future generations will still be able to hunt. Their awareness of these issues nourishes their certainty that the Indigenous peoples are the best stewards of the animals on Formosa. Animals are, moreover, important figures in legend and art. The most elaborate symbolic speculations are about birds.

People and Birds

Across Nantou and Hualien, the Sədeq have a very elaborate avian folklore (Simon 2015a, 2018), like many other peoples of Southeast Asia and Oceania (Feld 1982; Forth 2004; Le Roux and Sellato 2006). They have a wealth of practical knowledge about bird behaviour, habitat, and reproduction based on generations of accumulated observations in the mountain forests. Echoing Lévi-Strauss's intuition that birds are "metaphorical human beings" (Lévi-Strauss 1966, 207), the Sədeq use rich metaphors to describe both human and bird behaviour. For example, they refer to a person who boasts vainly about what he can do yet fails to fulfil his promises as a *swiraw* (whistling thrush, *Myophonus insularis*). For months I asked people why, yet nobody could explain. Finally, one hunter told me that this bird is often found near mountain streams. When hunters are up in the mountains and hungry, they sometimes shoot at or trap birds and eat them. This bird appears to have substantial flesh, but once the feathers have been removed, there is in fact very little meat on the bones. In this case, a person can be like a bird. Taking a metaphor in the other sense, people point out the aggressive nature of the *psidul* (black drongo, *Dicrurus macrocercus*), which can be observed attacking large raptors that would otherwise eat smaller birds and even poultry. One elder said it is the police officer of birds, because it can protect the others. In this case, a bird can be like a person.

One small songbird emerges with particular symbolic importance. When asked about birds, and sometimes when asking "What is Gaya?," people often evoke the sisil, even as the final source of Gaya (Shen 1998, 95). I was initially very confused when I asked an elder about Gaya, and he replied by saying by saying: "Let me tell you about a small bird in the forest." This reply is because Gaya is not an orderly list of prohibitions. Instead, it is a comprehensive way of life that includes relations with non-human beings. The sisil, usually identified as the grey-cheeked fulvetta (*Alcippe morrisonia*), is a small (12–14 centimetres long), grey passerine with a white eye ring. It was first identified with Linnaean classifications by Japanese naturalist and ethnographer Kano Tadao (Simon 2020a, 78; Kano 1934). Because these birds often appear in mixed-species feeding flocks (Chen and Hsieh 2002), people call them all sisil or, noting the morphological differences between birds within the flocks, "friends of the sisil." This way of naming them has caused enormous confusion among both scholars and local people who try to identify the sisil with a precise Linnaean species but get different answers from different people when asking them to identify the bird in field guides. The *Alcippe morrisonia* is thus the prototypical sisil, even as that category of birdness also extends to socially related kinds. This bird has furthermore become a symbol of both Sediq and Truku nationalisms, as could be seen in 2007, for example, when Sediq nationalists in Nantou collectively swore an oath as "people of the Sisil" in one of the many local events meant to promote the newly proposed ethnic identity. This bird likewise appears several times as an ethnic symbol in the 2011 Taiwanese film *Warriors of the Rainbow: Seediq Bale* about the 1930 uprising against the Japanese (see chapter 6). Gaya thus includes a privileged relationship between some people and some birds. There are reasons why the sisil is appropriate as a symbol for these peoples, which I will explore in greater depth later.

The sisil is evoked due to its role in hunting and is usually understood in anthropology as part of a wider set of practices of ornithomancy, or divination by watching the behaviour of birds (Takoshima 2015; Yamada 2014). Kaji says that hunters listen to their dreams at night (*spian skeeman*) and to the sisil by day (Kaji 2011, 13). What people told me was generally consistent with what their elders told anthropologist Kim Kwang-ok two generations ago or the anthropologists of the Japanese period. People say that, as they walk up the narrow mountain paths, they watch carefully the behaviour of birds. Although there is some variation in what people report, the overarching principle is that if the sisil birds congregate on the right side of the path, or if they emerge from the right, it is an auspicious sign. My informants tended to tell me that sisil birds gathering on the left side means that the hunt will fail. People told Kim that continuous calls on either side can be auspicious (Kim 1980, 196). It is inauspicious if the bird cries behind a man, which means an enemy is approaching. Worst of all is when the birds fly back and forth across the path of the hunters in an agitated manner. This behaviour means that something unfortunate, such as an accident or illness, has happened at home and that the hunters should return immediately. Like hunting itself, divination skills are acquired through experience, which means that it is usually done by an elder in a hunting expedition (196). In the case of the sisil, the presence of a particular bird, probably due to unique characteristics of its behaviour (Simon 2018), became associated with hunting success. The sisil was so important to the identity of the Seediq as a hunting people that it finally became their nationalist symbol.

The type of phenomenal experience available to hunters has changed due to the legal context that criminalizes many hunting practices. Most importantly, the criminalization of hunting means that people are forced to hunt at night, when the hunters are less likely to be seen by hikers and conservation officers but when the diurnal bird is absent.[7] Instead, contemporary hunters are more likely to discuss owls, which they can classify carefully into different kinds. In the case of owls, however, the owls watch human behaviour more than humans watch owls. Owls are best known for suddenly swooping in and snatching a flying squirrel just as a hunter, armed with a headlamp and a rifle, has shot it.

Observation of such phenomenal events gets transformed into more symbolic kinds of knowledge; for example, experienced hunters tell stories about young men who foolishly mistake the sound of an owl for that of ghosts in the forest. Kim's informants told him about owls that predicted grave misfortune when they flew into peoples' houses (Kim 1980, 195).

There are many reasons to observe birds. I was told, for example, that owls predict the sex of unborn children by landing in the village near a pregnant woman and hooting. A high-pitched "awk" means a girl, and a low-pitched "hoo" means a boy. Some older women insist that the owls were more accurate than ultrasound testing. In Hualien, I was told that if the *hghug*, a black bird with red feathers on its legs, landed on a roof-top and called out at dusk, somebody in that house would surely die.[8] Other birds were used to tell the time of day or predict weather events, but people say these practices have been replaced with wristwatches and weather forecasts. One older woman told me that the birds can no longer tell time accurately because they are confused by the effects of climate change. When I asked people if birds have souls (utux), some older people told me that sisils, as well as raptors, owls, and crows, have souls. Others warned me that their ancestors once believed in such superstitions, but that it is a sin for Christians to even talk about them. While doing field research on birds, I got the impression that people are losing empirical knowledge of birds because they spend less time in the forests, and losing symbolic knowledge of birds because those forms of knowledge are being replaced with others. The forest birds are decreasingly part of their life spheres, and their legend sphere is increasingly filled with other imaginaries. This trend leads me to the final discussion of how people think about, even classify, non-human animals.

A Foray into Ethnobiology

The ethnobiological methods and analysis used in this section are controversial in anthropology, as some postmodern anthropologists perceive the use of Western taxonomies as a hegemonic practice that does not adequately represent the oral traditions of non-state societies involved in acephalous politics (Sillitoe 2002). Ethnobiology also has writing conventions that may be unfamiliar to many readers, such as writing the names of cognitive domains (linguistic categories) in all-caps, and many anthropologists are uncomfortable with quantifying Indigenous knowledge. Even the use of Latin names when writing about animals, useful as it is for helping Western readers understand what we are writing about, is rejected by some anthropologists. In the process of fieldwork, I have myself come to privilege the oral traditions and the politics of Indigenous resurgence. Nonetheless, at the beginning of my journey with hunters, ethnobiological methods were as important to me as the walking sticks that I first used to stabilize myself on mountain treks but eventually discarded. I include in this chapter the results of this research, which was done collectively with Truku and Tkedaya people, because it illustrates a part of my sojourning, and was a good enough way to begin learning about human-animal relations.

In 2010, I conducted a pilot study using free-listing in one Truku village in Hualien and one Tkedaya village in Nantou. In 2012 and 2013, I conducted six months of ethno-ornithological research in two Truku-dialect villages. In addition to longer interviews, field excursions into the forest, and participant observation in daily life, I did free-listing exercises with ordinary people in the villages. Like Anna Tsing, who used the same research method in Indonesia (Tsing 2005, 163), I found that people tended to enjoy the exercise. The technique is deceptively simple, as one invites people to simply give a list of all the animals they know in a particular domain. Almost always, this exercise led to more elaborate conversations about the animals, their likely locations in the forest, their habits, and a wealth of personal stories about encounters with them. In 2010, I then analysed the lists with the software Anthropac, which allows one to quantify the frequency in which items appear on lists and the priority that people give those items, to measure the saliency of the items in an index called Smith's S (Quinlan 2005). Since I was exploring the cognitive domains of SAMAT and QBHNI, I was able to establish lists of forest animals (table 2.3) and birds (table 2.4) known in those communities in order of salience.[9] I give the top ten in each list here. As is the custom in ethnobiology, the local names are in all-caps.

From these two tables, several interesting phenomena can be observed. First, the names of the animals are spelled slightly differently in the two villages due to linguistic differences between Truku and Tgdaya. Second, and this finding is important for understanding human-animal relations, the Smith's S for mammals tends to be much higher than that for birds. It means that more people mentioned the same animals, which makes sense because there are fewer mammal kinds than bird kinds. It also indicates higher consensus about which animals to place higher on their lists, which probably indicates food preferences. On both mammal lists, the top four are animals that are commonly hunted and eaten. On both bird lists, the top three include the Mikado pheasant and the bamboo partridge, the two most hunted and eaten birds. Crows evoked strong emotions of repugnance. When crows came up in the free-listing, people reported that crows eat corpses, and if eaten by a desperate hunter, they taste like rusty

Table 2.3. The top ten free-listed forest animals

Local name	English name	Smith's S
Hualien, Truku (*Samat*)		
PADA	Formosan muntjac	0.801
MILIT	Formosan serow	0.765
BOYAQ	Formosan wild boar	0.734
LAPIT	Formosan flying squirrel	0.504
LONGAI	Formosan macaque	0.364
LGBUX	Formosan gem-faced civit	0.362
LQNUX	Formosan sambar	0.321
QEULIT	Rat	0.302
KUMAI	Formosan black bear	0.294
BALIT	Small Chinese civet	0.270
Nantou, Tgedaya (*Samac*)		
BOYAK	Formosan wild boar	0.820
PADA	Formosan muntjac	0.725
MIRIC	Formosan serow	0.547
RABIC	Formosan flying squirrel	0.415
RGEBUX	Formosan gem-faced civit	0.359
RUNGE	Formosan macaque	0.353
RQENUX	Formosan sambar	0.255
QOLIC	Rat	0.218
SUME	Formosan black bear	0.198
ALUNG	Chinese pangolin	0.169

Note: Spellings standardized in a focus group with village informants.
Source: Fieldwork.

Table 2.4. The top ten free-listed birds

Local name	English name	Smith's S
Hualien, Truku (*Qbhni*)		
LAQUNG	Mikado pheasant	0.464
TKUREH	Bamboo partridge	0.363
JIYAQUNG	Jungle crow	0.353
BURUT	Sparrow or brown bullfinch	0.347
RHO	Hawk	0.310
PURUNG	Owl	0.294
PSIMA	Shrike	0.262
KJIRAW	Eagle	0.238

(Continued)

Table 2.4. Continued

Local name	English name	Smith's S
SIPIL	Black bulbul	0.207
MLMUR	Barred buttonquail	0.152
Nantou, Tgedaya (*Qduda*)		
URAQAN	Mikado pheasant	0.540
TYAQUN	Jungle crow	0.494
TKUREH	Bamboo partridge	0.459
QDIRAW	Eagle	0.398
PUAH	Green pigeon	0.317
BYUCUH	Spotted-necked dove	0.224
RAMAN	Taiwan hill partridge	0.223
RHUG	Hawk	0.220
BRAGO	Taiwan barbet	0.202
TUKUNG	Owl	0.183

Note: Spellings standardized in a focus group with village informants.
Source: Fieldwork.

iron. In some ways, a crow is a competing predator because, like hawks, eagles, and owls, it might steal from hunters' traps. In mountainous Nantou, people have more knowledge about doves and partridges, simply because there are more of them there and the differences are highly visible and audible. The different kinds of owls, known only to experienced hunters, came up very low on the list, and only in Nantou.

It is striking to note that very few people gave me information about animals that would be terminal level species in a Linnaean taxonomy. Instead, they referred to what would in that system belong at the genus or even family level. In most cases, it was because there is only one species from each genus in their surroundings and thus no need for further classification. Nobody confuses a muntjac with a sambar, even though they are both in the Cervidae family and thus both kinds of "deer." The muntjac live in a wider mountain range, are small animals about the size of a dog, can often be seen or heard as isolated individuals, and are easily caught in traps. The sambars live much higher in the mountains, are large animals, can sometimes be seen in small herds, and are usually hunted with a rifle. There is thus the idea of distinct kinds of animals within the larger category of SAMAT, even in the absence of explicit taxonomic vocabulary about families, genus, or species. Catholic priest Ferdinando Pecoraro translated the word *kndsan* as "nature, kind, own quality," giving the serow as his example (Pecoraro 1977, 106), yet this idea that each distinct kind of animal has its own nature or essence is not precisely the same concept as that of species in zoology. It does not matter to anyone that the muntjacs on Formosa represent only one of twelve muntjac species recognized worldwide by biologists. Nor does it occur to hunters that they need to consider both muntjacs and sambars as being related in any way, although lumping together two kinds of deer is intuitively more apparent than grouping them both together with serows and wild boars as an "order" of Artiodactyla because they all have an even number of toes. These Linnaean taxonomic categories are clearly extended analogies that emerge from a particular history (Atran 1990) rather than a part of phenomenal experience.

When there is local diversity of animal types, people are quick to point out the differences. In the case of flying squirrels, for example, most people simply call them all LAPIT (now standardized as *rapit*). A smaller number of people listed all three local kinds: the white-faced flying squirrel (LAPIT BAXGAI, white-faced flying squirrel, *Petaurista alborufus lena*), the red-faced flying squirrel (LAPIT BANAX, Formosan giant flying squirrel, *Petaurista philippensis*), and the "other little one" (LBNAWI, Formosan hairy-footed flying squirrel, *Belomys pearonii*). People prefer to eat the white-faced flying squirrel and do not hunt the small hairy-footed flying squirrel at all. It is interesting that they name the animals, followed by a descriptive adjective, just as in the Latin, referring simply to white and red flying squirrels for the two important kinds. Since the white-faced flying squirrel is listed by the government as endangered, and the Formosan giant flying squirrel is common enough that conservation officers take no interest in it, hunters joke about how they identify the kind of squirrel from a distance at night: "We shoot it down from the tree and then look at the face." In fact, the hunters know exactly which kind is likely to be found in which part of the forest, which is why they can almost always return with the tastier and more highly prized white-faced ones. Some people were able to distinguish between over ten different kinds of rats and mice, saying that they learned these names from their fathers as they learned to hunt by practising on rodents. These experts do produce taxonomic schemes that correspond well to the Linnaean system.

The important point is that kinds of animals are not first classified in grand schemes and then looked for in the forest. They are first known and only then classified subsequently as discreet kinds because people encounter them as animals with morphological differences that live in different places and can be observed over the year through different phases of the animal's reproductive cycle. People have different kinds of relationships with different kinds of animals, and that is what they think of when they are asked by anthropologists to list the animals they know. These types of animals may not fit the narrow definition of species as elaborated by systematic zoology or, more recently, by genetics. They do, however, meet the criteria of species as defined by Ernst Mayr: "a reproductive community of populations ... that occupies a specific niche in nature" (quoted in Atran 1990, 70).

A final example will suffice to illustrate how the classification of animal kinds is rooted in phenomenal experience. In Nantou, people use the word *psima* to refer to the Japanese white-eye (*Zosterops japonicus*). In coastal Hualien, people wait in the autumn months for the arrival of the long-tailed shrike (*Lanius schach*), which they describe as a migratory bird that gets blown in annually by the typhoons and which they call psima. They used to catch these birds in bamboo traps, roast them, and sell them openly on the roadsides, not least to eager Taiwanese tourists. Now that laws against trapping birds are strictly enforced, with no exceptions for Indigenous people, only a handful of people trap and sell these birds clandestinely. They say that the high fat content of the bird makes it a very special annual treat. The Internet Bird Collection may say that shrikes come in three genera, thirty-one species, and ninety-nine taxa. To bird hunters in Hualien, however, the only important psima is the one that can be caught, cooked, and eaten. This phenomenal experience with shrikes is a very different from that of the ornithologist in a natural history cabinet in Europe who makes a career from collecting and distinguishing between different "species" from around the world and fitting them into evolutionary theory.

The following photos, the first being of a shrike caught in a trap (figure 2.5) and the other of shrikes on display in the Natural History Museum in Vienna (figure 2.6), illustrate the differences in phenomenal experience. The hunter knows only one kind of shrike and is interested primarily in eating it, but is also aware that the strong beak of this bird that kills and eats snakes can also cause serious injury to his hand. The ornithologist knows many kinds of shrikes and is motivated to display and classify them correctly in order to advance a scientific career. There is less of a direct relationship with the bird, as there is no need to struggle with it and kill it (even the specimens are usually taken by other professionals) or any possibility of eating it. Hunters and naturalists first interact with animals in different ways before they can elaborate different kinds of symbolic systems to explain what they have seen and experienced.

These knowledge systems are all subject to historical change, as change in people's lives means that they encounter different animals in different contexts. A historical example of this phenomenon can be found in the lives of the people who migrated from Nantou to

Figure 2.5. Truku relations with shrikes. A hunter has trapped a shrike to eat.

Source: Photograph by Scott E. Simon.

Hualien, encountering different birds. They took the word psima with them, merely transferring it from one kind of bird to another. Similarly, English speakers moving from Britain to America brought the word "robin" but used it for another kind of bird. The Hualien people's knowledge of birds and other animals is not reduced to lists of taxa. Far more important to them are their experiences with animals in the forest, the challenges of the hunt, and the symbolic use of birds and animals in myths told across generations. They package these forms of knowledge together to describe their way of living in the forest, which is why they can claim the hunt and the sisil as markers of their ethnic identities in contemporary Taiwan.

The people with whom I did this research encouraged me to seek direct encounters with the animals. One of my closest friends, Kuhon, encouraged me to take up bird photography and even took me to Hualien to purchase a professional camera. When I was inquiring about the sisil, one woman elder, Yaya, advised me: "If you want to understand the sisil, you

Figure 2.6. Shrikes in natural history. Shrikes from around the world, Natural History Museum, Vienna.

Source: Photograph by Scott E. Simon.

have to sit quietly in the forest and watch the birds for yourself." When she invited me to spend two weeks in her mountain cottage, watching the sisil that came to eat from her fruit trees every afternoon at 3 pm, she taught me a new methodology that I came to call ethno-ethology (Simon 2018, 151). I am reminded of Ingold's notion that "one gets to know the forest, and the plants and animals that dwell therein, in just the same way that one becomes familiar with other people, by spending time with them, investing in one's relations with them the same qualities of care, feeling and attention" (Ingold 2000, 47). Over time, I have been surprised at how well this method works, even with birds and other wild animals.

Throughout my research, people did not hesitate to put me in my place. When we did the free-listing exercises, some people listed the different kinds of squirrels. The Formosan striped squirrel (*Tamiops maritinus*), a small striped squirrel, resembles a North American chipmunk very much. Like a chipmunk, it scurries back and forth in the undergrowth, collecting and storing food. Telling me the Truku name of this small animal was *tuku*, one person said: "This animal is very stupid, always running around with no purpose, just like some person who keeps running around asking the same question of many different people." Half in jest, he was making a judgment about the value of my ethnobiological methods, but the fact that he could do so by referring to an animal underlies what Lévi-Strauss proposed about the place of animals in human societies. Animals are good to eat. Animals are good to think. Animals are partners in world-building. And animals provide convenient ways for describing and classifying human behaviour.

Discussion

In this chapter, I have explored human-animal relations in the lives of Seejiq hunters. They refer to the animals of the forest as samat and explain how they, as hunters, relate to animals in ways regulated by the ancestral laws of Gaya. They express anxiety about the legal framework that has criminalized most hunting and trapping activities, and show concern that young people are losing contact with the forest beings. They describe this separation with the forest as being the most violent and painful lived experience of colonialism. They are thus aware that the state, along with other institutions like church and school, has wrenched them from a treasured meshwork of other living things. Yet, they fight back. Like elsewhere in Taiwan (Yang 2015), they regularly take their own youth as well as visitors on hikes on traditional territory, as this form of embodied knowledge becomes integral to the Indigenous land rights movement.

By walking with hunters, listening to and observing birds with them, and learning about the forest animals, I came to realize that people interact with certain animals with an understanding that these other creatures are also perceptual, cognitive beings. This way of thinking, in fact, is the only way in which humans can predict the behaviour of other animals, making it possible for them to successfully trap or hunt animals for food. Hunters are aware that different animals live in different parts of the forest. They thus look for serows along particular cliffs and intentionally hunt flying squirrels known to live in one area while avoiding others. They attribute intentionality to these animals, whether the animals be serows and boars that identify and may kill hunters or merely small birds with strong beaks that know how to protect themselves. They know that different kinds of animals have different ways of being, as they can point out the lonely muntjac calling out for a partner during mating season but also a troop of macaque monkeys who look and act in very human-like ways.

Sədeq hunters led me to the animals, both literally and as an intellectual project. As I brought those stories into anthropology, I was able to bring them into conversation with diverse and even conflicting anthropological theories in over a decade of conference presentations and academic publications. But the hunters always brought me back to their reality and why they shared those worlds with me. They have a way of living with the other than human, and they regulate those relations with the ontological premises of Gaya. Most importantly, they live in a colonial situation subject to police violence on their own lands and to cultural imperialism that stigmatizes their hunting practices as primitive. This situation is certainly because Taiwan has adopted the kind of modern civic public that, in the words of Iris Young, excludes "others associated with nature and the body" (Young [1990] 2011, 108). In a form of Indigenous resurgence, hunters and trappers have shared with me practices (and meat) that they know to be illegal according to state law. They want me to bring those lifeworlds to an international readership in a respectful way that also protects their privacy. Their goal is to share the lessons of Gaya.

It is important to render visible the ontological differences, not only the differences between these hunters and the West (the task of most Western anthropology) but also the conflicts of political ontology between them and the Republic of China state. When hunters talk about *dgiyaq*, they do not mean a "nature" that is separate from culture. Their Gaya is a meshwork of respectful living together with game animals (samat), birds (*qbhni*), and even spirits (utux). They contrast their ways to the state-centric institutions that have destroyed forests through clear-cutting and high-altitude agriculture, but more recently through ecotourism and trekking. If I had gone to Taiwan between 1956 and 1975, I would not have even been permitted to enter the mountains with them, but during that time commercial timber production was destroying forest habitat more thoroughly than during the Japanese period (Wang 2021, 226). Since 1991, when the environmental movement successfully convinced the Forestry Bureau to ban logging (Huang and Chen 2020, 68), the forests have grown back, and animal populations have returned. This context has permitted hunters and trappers to launch their own form of Indigenous resurgence.[10]

As people shouted out during the 2007 hearings on hunting and police violence that I attended, the main issue is sovereignty. Although they used Chinese idioms of sovereignty in that meeting, they have their own understandings of sovereignty, which emerged in all the conversations I had with people about animals and hunting. Claiming the heritage of Pusu Qhuni is itself a declaration of sovereignty, as it is a way of saying that they were here – and hunting – from the very beginning of time. Darryl Sterk asked Walis Pering, who served as legislator from 1992 to 2004 and subsequently as chair of the Council of Indigenous Peoples from 2005 to 2007, how to say sovereignty in Seediq. Walis immediately came up with *tndheren*, formed of *tn-*, "of" or "belonging to," and *dheran*, "earth/world." This word suggests that Seediq sovereignty is based on possession but is even more based on belonging (Sterk 2019).[11] The Truku word for earth is *dxgal*, which is the land from which lives emerge. The Seediq would thus affirm sovereignty by highlighting how they belong to the forests full of animals and birds, the sisil emerging as the symbol of that relationship. That relationship with the forest, the hunters remind me, is a fundamental part of what it means to be *Seediq balae*! – truly human. Many people fear that, if hunting were to cease as a way of life, there would also be no more truly Indigenous people on Formosa.

For this reason, Indigenous rights activists were disappointed by what happened to Talum Suqluman. On 7 May 2021, Taiwan' Constitutional Court ruled on his case in Interpretation 803. Activists had hoped that it would be a decisive legal case, like Australia's 1992 Mabo decision or Canada's 1997 Delgamuukw case, both of which confirmed Indigenous land title and inherent sovereignty. Instead, the court did not even consider Taiwan's own 2005 Basic Law, and narrowly focused on whether the laws under which Talum had been sentenced are consistent with constitutional principles of clarity and proportionality. The court upheld the firearms legislation under which Talum was charged, but declared that a clearer definition of "self-made" weapons is needed in the subordinate regulations. The court also upheld the wildlife laws, as Indigenous "culture" does not justify hunting endangered and protected species.

The court, however, determined that regulations requiring hunters to register in advance the species and number of animals caught are too inflexible and limit Indigenous cultural rights (Simon 2021a). Chief Justice Hsu Tzong-li was cited in the *New York Times*, saying that "the Constitution recognizes both the protection of Indigenous peoples' right to practice their hunting culture and the protection of the environment and ecology. Both fundamental values are equally important" (Chien and Qin 2021, A10). President Tsai Ing-wen granted Talum pardon, the first pardon of her tenure. These moves all reveal the main ontological conflict. State leaders of the Republic of China (ROC) on Taiwan claim sovereignty (host power) and the resulting ability to distribute rights among its citizens, as if they are hosts distributing tea and cakes to guests. The Indigenous people claim that they have always belonged to the mountain forests and that the ROC state is just the most recent group of uninvited outsiders. This conflict is between a liberal state that promises redistribution of justice against oppressed peoples who dream of a radical change in the system itself. Hunters pointed out to me that Talum's pardon did nothing to help the many other hunters in jail and with criminal records, nor will it prevent others from being charged for the same actions in the future.

Since 2016, when Dr. Tsai Ing-wen of the Democratic Progressive Party (DPP) was first elected president, the ROC has made important progress in state-led indigeneity. One of President Tsai's first acts was to apologize to Indigenous peoples for 400 years of colonization. She subsequently established the Presidential Office Indigenous Historical Justice and Transitional Justice Committee. Taiwan has also developed an innovative system of Indigenous hearing chambers in the courts to listen to Indigenous perspectives, which have been used widely in cases related to hunting (Upton 2020, 2021). The Forestry Bureau started exploring a new system in which Indigenous villages can self-manage hunting lands under wildlife monitoring schemes (Wang 2021, 235). The Truku established a Truku Hunters' Association, with the power to issue hunting licences to be recognized on Forestry Bureau lands. Even the Taroko National Park has signalled intent to create co-management regimes. All these initiatives, as well-intentioned as they may be, are state-centric forms of indigeneity. They do not recognize Indigenous sovereignty, and even though these institutions engage with Indigenous lifeworlds on a more equal basis, they are not fully grounded in Indigenous ontologies. This state-centric focus means that they are likely to become new areas for conflicts of political ontology.

Sisil (oracle bird) 占卜鳥

Figure 3.1. The grey-cheeked fulvetta (*Alcippe morrisonia*) is a small bird (12 to 14 centimetres) with white masking around its eyes. Found in dense shrub up to 2,500 metres in mountain forests, it is commonly the nuclear actor of mixed flocks, especially in the winter. Its calls alert birds and others to the presence of predators. It is the most important bird in divination, a symbol of the Seediq/Sediq/Sejiq and Truku. Catholic priest Ferdinando Pecoraro wrote that the *sisil* is "the privileged partner of Truku ornithomancy, indicator of fortune and misfortune, in every activity that involves movement or an expedition" (Pecoraro 1977, 254).

Source: Illustration by Biluan.

Chapter Three

Mgaya (Headhunting)

Mgaya, one of the words used to describe the ritual complex called "head-hunting" in English, is no longer practised and thus can no longer be directly experienced through participant observation. Even the very old people recall at best the fear they felt as children walking past skull racks at night or, worse, being asked to feed the skulls. In the past, headhunting may have been a violent way of dealing with the existential challenges posed by other humans from beyond the pale of the horizon. It is now a symbol that may be rejected as ethnic stereotyping or embraced in post-modern identity politics. Yet, the main point of keeping the memories of it alive is expressed in the first and last anecdotes of this chapter. Usually, in a spirit of jest, the people now talk of headhunting as a way of reminding guests: "This is our territory. We could still kill you at any time. You live and thrive here only because of our indulgence." This territorialization of headhunting may very well be a modern reinvention. As much as any overt political activity, however, such expressions affirm the ongoing power of society against the state. It is a strong declaration of sovereignty.

Once, as I was eating and drinking with a group of young men, some-body suddenly placed a choice piece of flying squirrel meat directly in my mouth, saying that feeding me with his own hand was his way of expressing the intimacy of our friendship. Another man took his beer mug and, pressing his cheek and lips against mine, guided me to drink from the same vessel. This gesture, I had already learned, is a common fraternal bonding practice. With obvious delight, another person lit a cigarette and placed it in my mouth. The second person laughed and said: "If you had come here 100 years ago, we would have cut off your head before we did this." He was referring to the ritual in which, after bringing an enemy head to the village, they would pour oblations into the victim's skull in order to welcome him as a friend and transform him into an ancestor. In the days of headhunting, the ritual feeding of the head was called *mkan hadur* (Kaji 2011, 27).

Obviously, the statement about "we" and "you" cannot be taken literally. I was not born 100 years ago, and neither were any of them. They were using the "you" and the "we" to express in extended analogy how people have dealt with outsiders in the past – and in an exercise of daily collective memory. In this case, the young men found it humorous to play with the trope of feeding a live head in much the same way that their grandfathers might have treated a dead head. A further implication is that their once savage group has come a long way in a very short period. After all, they remember hearing stories from relatives about headhunting, just as I recall my elderly relatives talking about Canadian actions in the First World War, which happened at about the same time. And when I did genealogical research, my father and grandfather both told me that the Simons used to be Jewish. We all grow up with the past of our ancestors as fundamental parts of our legend spheres.

Headhunting is the most paradoxical, yet also perhaps the most compelling institution in the history of Formosa, just as it has been in the rest of Oceania. Headhunting has been used by outsiders in a discourse of savagery that marked Formosans as less civilized than the ruling groups from outside the island. During the Japanese period – in postcards, World Expo displays, and publications in both English and Japanese – the Atayalic groups were depicted as the most dangerous headhunters of Formosa (Barclay 2015).

The rulers of Taiwan have manipulated symbols of savage headhunting in ways that displeased the island's Indigenous people, especially during the 1980s social movements. After the Republic of China (ROC) took over Taiwan, school textbooks commemorated Wu Feng, a Confucian merchant said to have sacrificed his own life to convince the Tsou people in the mountains near Chiayi to abandon headhunting. The story, which dates to the early nineteenth century, is that Wu Feng befriended the Tsou, who were addicted to the glory of headhunting and constantly raided Han Chinese communities. The Tsou learned to respect and love Wu Feng because of the magnanimity he showed towards them, but no matter how much he reasoned with them, they refused to give up headhunting. Finally, he came up with a plan. He told them that, if they wished to go headhunting, they should show up at a given place early in the morning where they would see a man in a red cloak. They should take his head, but it would be the last time that they went headhunting. The next day, they went to the appointed place, saw a man covered in a red cloak, and killed him. To their horror, they discovered that they had killed their beloved Wu Feng and, because of their grief, gave up headhunting forever. The Han Taiwanese glorified Wu Feng as a symbol of the civilizing influence of Han Chinese culture. They have commemorated him since the nineteenth century in a temple near Chiayi and, later, through classroom stories and the erection of statues in public places. Until the 1990s, the Chiayi temple and the adjacent Chinese Culture Village were destinations of obligatory school trips. Indigenous people, however, found the story to be racist and a source of shame for their children. As a result, one of the first goals of the Indigenous rights movement was to remove his hagiography from the school curricula (Rudolph 2008, 49). In 1988, graduates of the church-based Urban-Rural Mission took direct action by destroying a Wu Feng statue in Chiayi. When I finally got around to visiting the temple on 1 May 2020, I was delighted to find the temple complex completely empty. The Chinese Culture Centre was abandoned and boarded up. I could only gaze through the iron gates at the dust-covered ticket wickets. The societal rejection of the Wu Feng myth is a success story of the Indigenous rights movement.

Paradoxically, as I noted from my first week of fieldwork in 2005, Seejiq and Truku people take pride in their past as headhunters, talk about headhunting freely, and even re-enact it in contemporary ritual and spectacle. The important difference is that the Wu Feng myth casts the Confucian merchant as the subject-hero and the Formosan peoples as objects of a Chinese civilizing project. In their own stories, the head-hunting warriors are heroic subjects, either resisting colonial projects of outsiders or intentionally adopting new ways of life on their own terms. In the postmodern era of identity politics, headhunting has become a symbol of defiant resistance. Headhunting is historically one of the central institutions in all Formosan groups, but was not practised on nearby Botel Tobago (now Orchid Island). Headhunting must be understood in order to comprehend these societies on their own terms, especially because the evocation of this past is an important part of the present.[1] Seejiq Truku Shen Ming-ren (Pawan Tanah) sees headhunting as part of the glorious Seejiq tradition that needs to be affirmed, especially considering the dominant (cultural imperialist) discourse that labels Indigenous people as backward, poor, drunken, and uncultured (Shen 1998, 141). In an era of Indigenous resurgence, headhunting is the most important source of Indigenous pride (Shen 1998, 222).

In this chapter, I will attempt to do what at first seems impossible: to imagine headhunting from a phenomenological perspective, grasping for an understanding of what it felt like for participants in the ritual and keeping in mind that it was above all a ritual complex. This goal is difficult for very practical reasons. Headhunting has not been practised in any form since the 1930s, which makes it impossible to join a headhunting expedition for participant observation. I thus rely upon ethnographic descriptions and one eyewitness account, that of Japanese Kondō Katsusaburō, who joined a headhunting expedition in 1897 to spy on the Seejiq and wrote about the experience (figure 3.2). I can

Figure 3.2. Japanese soldiers in front of a Truku skull rack. Skull racks like this one were features in every settlement until the Japanese period.

Source: Special Collections & College Archives, Skillman Library, Lafayette College.

also reflect on what people have told me and on my observations of headhunting as spectacle and re-enactment. People often say that they replaced headhunting with hunting for animals, which suggests that it is possible to transfer some insights from one activity to the other, although this analogy must be used parsimoniously. What did head-hunting mean historically to the people now called Seediq and Truku, and what significance does it continue to hold in contemporary Taiwan?

Headhunting as Implementation of Gaya

From Seejiq perspectives, headhunting was and remains essentially related to *Gaya*. Pecoraro glossed Gaya as "custom, rule, tradition, taboo, the *liturgy* of hunting and cutting off heads" (Pecoraro 1977, 70, emphasis in the original). He thus reflects local understandings that Gaya is made reality by the actions of hunting and headhunting. Add-ing the prefix "m," meaning "bringing into being" or "practising," to the stem Gaya makes mgaya, a Truku word for headhunting. Mgaya is thus the implementation of sacred law. Some traditional elders tell me that, strictly speaking, I should add the modifying adjective *balay*, which means "very" or "truly," to refer to this sacred ritual, as mgaya would mean the implementation of just any law.[2] This modifier reveals the admiration that people still hold for this historical practice without, of course, implying that anyone would wish to revive it. Headhunting rituals are religious because they evoke the presence of supernatural beings, whether they be the deceased ancestors who judge the pro-ceedings or the souls from the decapitated dead who in turn become ancestors. This idea is also interesting because, in stark contrast to Han traditions of ancestor worship, it indicates that the Atayalic concept of "ancestor" is not strictly genealogical.

   Linguistic differences reveal distinct worlding practices. The Chinese term for headhunting is *chucao* 出草, which means "emerging from the grass." We will leave the Chinese perspective aside, although it is worth noting that this word has a rather long history (Suzuki 1932, 161). Most of all, it evokes a sense of latent fear and constant threat. The terms mgaya and chucao, more than representing the same act in two dif-ferent languages, express different ontological perspectives and phe-nomenological experiences. The ontological differences are that, for the Indigenous, headhunting was a sacred ritual that emanated from Gaya, whereas for the Chinese, it was an act of random violence and a symbol of savagery. The two words are also different subject positions, with mgaya being that of the warrior and chucao that of the one whose head might be taken. Kado Kimi (Ai Chung-Chih), local Truku scholar and director of general affairs at Mingli Primary School in Hualien, wrote that older people in his community refer to both hunting and head-hunting as *knbuyu*, which is a verbal inflection of *kbuyu*, "grass" (Ai 2010). This interpretation may be influenced by the larger discourse in Mandarin.

Mgaya puts the headhunter in the subject position. In the past, young men in all Formosan groups had to participate in a headhunting expedition in order to be considered adults, to receive a facial tattoo (for Atayalic groups), and to be considered eligible for marriage. There were certainly always young men eager to participate in a headhunting expedition, just as today there are young men aspiring to play hockey, serve in the military, join violent gangs, participate in jihadist movements, or if it gets them the right woman, go to law school. Even within a headhunting expedition, there are different perspectives, which is why Renato Rosaldo, who studied headhunting on neighbouring Luzon in the Philippines, contrasted the adolescent turmoil of young men eager to attain adulthood to the more cautious elder leaders who postpone expeditions until moments like grief drive them to headhunting as a place to carry their anger (Rosaldo 1987, 242–3).

The facial tattoo, given only to men who had participated in a head-hunting expedition, was an important motivation. The Atayalic practices of headhunting are reminiscent of the "societies against the state" described so passionately by Pierre Clastres, who argued that, in certain Amazonian societies, tattoos were a mark of the law on the body of each individual. Clastres was quite unequivocal about what this idea meant: "The mark on the body, equal on all bodies, announces: You should not desire power; you shall not desire submission" (Clastres 1974, 160, free translation by the author).[3] For young warriors, tattoos would imply that each body became a living incarnation of Gaya so that all people would remember their obligations to the law and, because the designs were subject to local variation, to which community they belonged. Women could also earn tattoos if they demonstrated proficiency in weaving. In Truku, *patas* means "tattoos" and is now also used to mean "writing." *Ptasan* means "tattoos" but also "school."

Gaya was once engrained in the face of each individual and thus part of everyday existence, whereas state law, separate from embodied experience, is written in books and becomes the domain of trained specialists. The Japanese prohibition of tattoos is thus a visible manifestation of the imposition of state dominance on a "society against the state." Putting an end to the practice of tattooing was a way of psychologically wrenching people from the meshwork of ancestral souls in the mountain forests. The prohibition was not without its own violence.

Some elderly women described to me in wretched detail the pain they endured when the Japanese police forced them to remove their tattoos. Eighty years later, the scars were still visible on their cheeks. Tattooing is still important to struggles over political identity. Kimi Sibal, who has spent his life photographing and documenting this history of tattoos, likes to propose that all Atayalic peoples (Atayal, Truku, Tgdaya, Toda) and the neighbouring Saisiyat should unite as the Ptasan (tattooed ones) rather than argue about state-recognized ethnic names. This idea goes back to at least Pawan Tanah's work, when he suggested that a better name for the entire pan-Atayalic people would be Ptasan or even the Gaya People (Shen 1998, 20).

Although we will have to unpack these ideas about "egalitarian" societies, and headhunting provides us with a very good way to do so, I note that many contemporary people think through similar philosophical questions of power and domination in much the same way as did Clastres. Many young people refer to headhunting as the way in which their ancestors protected their territories, arguing that it precluded the emergence of state hierarchies now incarnated in the uniformed bodies of conservation officers, policemen, and military officials. I have even met two men who permanently tattooed their faces, albeit without having gone headhunting, both saying that it is an act of resistance against the state as they affirm Truku sovereignty. As we shall see, the link between headhunting and sovereignty was true to some extent, but headhunting was more than a primitive form of warfare or policing. Before these peoples entered state systems in the colonial period, they could not possibly have held ideas about defending territory as carefully delineated spaces on Cartesian maps. What gets omitted in that narrative is that headhunting was part of an emotionally salient ritual.

Seejiq Truku anthropologist Masaw Mowna made a distinction between mgaya and warfare, saying that "ordinary warfare" without ritual was called *muetsipo*, or "shooting to kill" (Masaw 1998, 232). Pecoraro glossed as warfare the word *mtlaqel*, derived from *tlaqel*, for harming someone or being in a bad condition (Pecoraro 1977, 308).[4] In Masaw's interpretation, headhunting is about law, whereas ordinary warfare is about mutual suffering. The most important difference between headhunting and warfare, noted by colonial and postcolonial anthropologists (Kojima [1915] 1996, 258; Yamada 2015, 24), is that, even if soldiers sometimes bring back heads, the defining characteristic of headhunting is that the main goal is to procure a head for ritual purposes. Moreover, I think that Masaw exaggerated by referring to any former practices as warfare. Warfare implies a more complex level of social organization, including coercion so that men must serve and strict orders of command and obedience. Colonial observers record that armed conflict between Indigenous groups involved no well-organized troops, and even though skilled men would inevitably lead the actions of the small hunting groups, there was no equivalent of a general who could coordinate the action of the entire attack (Kojima [1915] 1996, 269). There was no caste or occupation of warriors, as in neighbouring Japan or China, because all men were expected to participate at least once in a headhunting expedition during their lives. Moreover, *muetsipo* (or more accurately *mtsbu*) simply means "shooting" and is the same word used to describe the practice of shooting flying squirrels. Head-hunting expeditions thus more closely resembled violent feuding than organized warfare.

Headhunting is embedded in a symbolic and ritual complex in which warriors return with the head, and only the head, of their victims for subsequent ritual treatment. Janet Hoskins thus defined headhunting as "an organized, coherent form of violence in which the severed head is given a specific ritual meaning and the act of headhunting is conse-crated and commemorated in some form" (Hoskins 1996, 2). It may be seen as one part of an animistic conception of the world in which all (or many) things have souls and in which the skulls are made into fetishes (Yamada 2015, 69). Since Seejiq and Truku myths offer emic explana-tions of why people hunt the heads of other human groups, it makes sense to begin with these interpretations of the practice. These three myths about headhunting also reveal other social dynamics.

A Headhunting Story (I): Origins

Korean anthropologist Kim Kwang-ok carefully documented Truku myths in his PhD thesis, which remains an important source for under-standing traditional Truku and Seejiq cosmology, much of which has been replaced by Christianity and has been forgotten. This story is probably the same one as studied by Masaw Mowna, as presented in the introduction to this book, but with greater detail and better incor-porated into a full Truku cosmology. In ancient times, a chief sent his young son to fetch a fire-making flintstone that he had forgotten to bring with him on a long journey through the forest. The young boy was found murdered, and his family saw from a distance that people were singing and dancing around his head. They sought the advice of their supreme chief Skum Awi, who was living in the ancestral land of Torowan (Truwan). Skum Awi said that the incident was caused by the father's own carelessness, as he had not taken care of his flintstone. As a result, they would have to learn headhunting themselves.

Skum Awi told them to follow the bird *siling*. The bird guided them through the forest. When they arrived near the enemy encampment, the siling told them to wait. After a while, the bird arrived and its beak had turned blood red, a sign that the enemies were sleeping so soundly that they did not feel the bird pecking their cheeks. The bird cried four times and flew to the right. The people went through the forest in the direction from which the bird came, found the sleeping enemies, and attacked. They were able to take four heads before the enemies began to fight back. From then on, they had to take heads in order to enter the land of the ancestors after death (Kim 1980, 155–7).

The depiction of Truku society in this myth is quite interesting. It portrays the Truku as nomadic peoples roaming the forests east of Torowan (Nantou). They met an unnamed enemy group that likewise drifted through the forests. Headhunting existed already among the enemy group, but the Truku had to take up the practice as punishment for one man's neglect to take care of his group's property (the flintstone). The Truku were thus transformed from victims of headhunting to warriors, and each generation was obliged to prove their courage in order to take a place in the promised Paradise. The idea of protecting the property of the group was already present in this myth, even if ideas of territoriality and immovable property were not.

This myth also reveals the close relationship between the Truku headhunters and birds. Kim associates the siling with the *sisil*, the bird used as an oracle in both headhunting and hunting expeditions. The red beak, however, suggests another possibility. People point to the black bulbul (*Hypsipetes leucocephalus*), a noisy bird very common in the forests between Nantou and Hualien, which has the obvious features of stark black feathers and a bright red beak and feet. In fact, in free-listing exercises, the black bulbul was one of the favourite birds, ranking ninth in terms of salience. People call it the *sipil*, with pronunciation very similar to what Kim recorded. They often laugh at the pronunciation, saying it is easy to remember because it sounds like the Mandarin *xibing* 喜餅, the biscuits distributed at Chinese-style weddings. Kim says that the bird is white with a red beak and feet, yet nobody ever described such a bird to me, and no bird fits that description in the area.[5] Neither the black bulbul nor the grey-cheeked fulvetta (sisil) is white. Nowadays, people tell a very different story about the black bulbul. They say that it was sent out to retrieve fire after the Great Flood. It dropped the fire, but its feet and beak turned red. Dakis Pawan tells the story that the black bulbul brought back fire, which turned its feet and beak red, and then left behind the first flint stones so that people could make their own fire (Kuo 2012, 292–3). People also tell a different story about the origin of headhunting, one with more obvious political connotations.

A Headhunting Story (II): Insiders and Outsiders

I have heard many myths, including the following one, first in the context of a Presbyterian sermon. One Sunday morning, the pastor opened his sermon with this story:

> Our population in the mountains grew so rapidly that there was no longer enough game to provide food for everyone. Some people decided to leave the mountain and live in the valley. As a community, they decided that an equal number of people should live on the mountain and in the valley. In order to measure the size of each group, since they didn't know how to count in those days, the people stood together in the two places and shouted loudly. The group on the mountain shouted so loudly that all the leaves fell from the trees, but the sound from the valley was weak. When the mountain people sent some of their own to live in the valley, they discovered that they had been deceived. The valley people had intentionally shouted in low voices in order to get more people. Telling untruths was a violation of Gaya, the sacred ancestral law, so this created enmity between the groups. Henceforth, the mountain people tattooed their faces and went down into the valley on headhunting raids.

The meaning of this myth depends on the context in which it is told. Kojima Yoshimichi interpreted it to explain the enmity between the Atayalic peoples and the people of the plains, whom he understood to be the Han or *pingpuzu* 平埔族 (plains aborigines; Kojima [1915] 1996, 24). The minister, however, used this old and familiar tale to illustrate the danger of creating division within their own people. He wanted to make the point that all people should support his personal political project of creating a Taroko Autonomous Zone. Those who opposed the establishment of an autonomous zone, or Truku name rectification, are like those who violate Gaya. They commit a serious sin by sowing disaccord within the community. He did his best to take the moral high ground and link this legend to a contemporary political agenda.

Kojima's explanation makes more sense from an anthropological perspective. Although the story began with the division of one group, it ended with a distinction between people of the mountains and people of the plains, those who have tattoos and those who do not, those who follow Gaya and those who do not. In Kojima's days, the story explained the long-standing enmity that the Atayalic peoples had towards the

Han and the plains aborigines, who often acted as trading intermediaries between the mountain peoples and the Han. Sometimes, they would also make peace with the Han. Truku local scholar Kado Kimi cited elders in Hualien relating how they intentionally abstained from headhunting against their Han trading partners but instead sought out non-Han enemies (Ai 2015, 7). The overarching theme is that of relationality: some groups were enemies, and others were allies. Even the pastor's version was about relationality, because he and others were debating the limits of a proposed Taroko Autonomous Region at a time when some people in both Nantou and Hualien insisted that they were Sediq or Seediq or Sejiq rather than Taroko or Truku and wanted nothing to do with the project. Both interpretations also declare that headhunting was never random violence. Heads were always taken from enemies in clearly defined communities. The pastor was clearly declaring: "Either you are with us or you are against us." A third myth, this time with a gendered twist, depicts headhunting as a sacred ordeal even suitable for a young woman.

A Headhunting Story (III): A Woman Headhunter

In my very first year of field research, people told me stories about a young woman who went headhunting to prove her virginity, the logic being that the ancestors would only let her come back safely if she were innocent. As Truku language instructors began drafting their own pedagogical materials to teach Truku language, they wrote out the entire myth with a Chinese translation and published it online with assistance from the Ministry of Education. One of the women elders, on my 2017 summer visit, showed me the mimeographed story in both languages, explaining to me the words in Truku.[6] The following is my translation into English, which is based on a comparison of the Truku and Chinese versions:

> Once upon a time, there was a young Truku woman named Sita Duku. In Alang Ebung, there was a young man called Wilang Kurul. Having a crush on Sita Duku, he told people that he had had sex with her. When she heard those rumours, she was very sad. She said: "Who had sex with him? I surely did not!" Because of this, she made a pact with the ancestors and called all of the villagers to come and say farewell. That evening, she prayed to the spirits. After she felt a good premonition, she took a hunting knife and went headhunting [the Truku word is *mdkrang, krang* being the onomatopoeia for a bowl or object falling to the ground and breaking]. Before she left, she said: "If I am guilty as charged, I will not return."

Going off headhunting, she arrived at the enemy's village by evening and watched their coming and going. After a while, someone left to defecate. Sita Duku unsheathed her knife and chopped off his head: "Tak!" When the people heard it, they cried out: "The enemy! The enemy!" She hid silently behind a tree trunk as the entire village grabbed their fire torches and ran out into the forest in pursuit. She seized her knife and ran away. There were bamboo traps everywhere, and she hurt her foot, but she kept running. When she got to the river, she first threw the bloody knife to the other side before crossing. This way she could prove that she had really taken the head of an enemy. The next morning, she emerged with the knife exclaiming: "Wuy! Wuy! Tai! Tai! I have taken the head of the enemy!" When the people heard, they cried: "It really is Sita Duku!" Everyone went out to greet her and found that she had become even more beautiful than before. When Wiling Kurul found out that Sita Duku had returned, he felt ashamed because he had hurt her by spreading untrue rumours.

This story is interesting on many levels. First, it is noteworthy that it is told at all, and in a public forum. Indigenous activists may have protested the Wu Feng story, but this story shows that the issue was not the discussion of headhunting in general. The problem was how the story was told. Whereas the Wu Feng story depicted the Indigenous peoples as savages and the Han as a civilizing force, with headhunting as a symbol of bloodthirstiness, this story told from a Truku perspective shows headhunting as an expression of Gaya. In this case, the ancestors could use Sita Duku's success and safe return as proof of her innocence. There is an important gender component, as the story violates expectations that headhunting is invariably a male occupation. Because Sita Duku was a woman, however, it sufficed for her to return with a bloody knife, whereas a man would be expected to bring back the head.[7]

The printed story, the only one of the three narratives that I have been able to study in a Truku version, is also of interest because it captures Truku ways of storytelling. Certain Truku sounds, in fact, are simply not translated into Chinese: Krang! Tak! Wuy! Tai! "Krang" becomes a word in Truku because the teller added the prefix *md-*; the onomatopoeia becomes a verb for Sita Duku's desired action of creating the sound of a head falling. This word is impossible to express in English or Chinese, so it just becomes going headhunting (chucao 出草). "Tak!" – surely expressed each time with a hand gesture – conveys the sound of a neck being severed. To Truku listeners, and probably even to non-Truku people learning in situ, "Tak" is not a word and thus needs no translation. In itself, it is the sound of the knife chopping through flesh.

We can visualize it as a knife slicing through the neck of a chicken or of a human, the sound of the head abruptly detaching from the body. Tak! "Wuy" is the sound of triumphant return, translated here rather inadequately as the Chinese exclamation *wei* 喂, which is also used to answer the telephone. This sound is familiar to Truku singers, as they use it in song and dance performances that portray the triumph of headhunting or returning from the hunt with a dead boar on one's back. "Tai" is translated as "look at me," but it is again a preverbal exclamation of joy, with which Sita Duku proclaims her now undeniable innocence. Through headhunting, she re-established her relationship with her *alang*.

Relationality and Headhunting

Relationality is an important context for headhunting. Tōichi Mabuchi, who did field research in Taiwan from 1931 to 1932, studied Atayal and Sedeq (his spelling) use of territory. In 1931, the two groups (whom he considered to be distinct, yet related) had an estimated total population of 33,302 people. They were spread across the mountainous regions of northern Taiwan into rather compact settlements, known as alang, with an average of 165 people. Most households consisted of a married couple and their children, and some 90 per cent were patrilocal (Mabuchi 1974, 51–3). Each alang was divided into ritual groups that were centred on "influential men" and often bore their names. Entry or exit from such a ritual group was marked with a sacrifice of a pig. One influential man would be chosen as the village headman, but he had no power over the others as he was *primus inter pares* rather than permanent holder of a political position (Mabuchi 1974, 53). These were the groups that would organize headhunting expeditions. In pre-colonial days, they were launched against other or enemy groups, which, in a word derived from alang, were called *kaalang*. When Chinese and Japanese started entering Taiwan and making their way up into the mountains, especially in search of camphor, they also became victims (Roy 2022).

The Atayalic political dynamics can best be understood in contrast to other Formosan groups. The Paiwan of southern Formosa, with their hereditary ranks of nobility and commoners, could mobilize large groups of warriors. In the north, headhunting groups were miniscule in comparison, with records of Seediq headhunting by individuals or two or three men. Most headhunting expeditions were organized by the small ritual groups or up to the level of the hamlet, or alang (Yamada 2015, 242).

Various alang were sometimes capable of forming alliances with other groups, typically along a watershed. If some people moved to a different drainage system, perhaps because of resource depletion, they would in a generation or two cease contacts with their group of origin. This loss could eventually lead to conflicts over hunting territories and eventually to mutual headhunting (Mabuchi 1974, 186). Due to the terrain, there was a certain degree of territorial overlap, differential usage in different times of the year, and room for negotiation in ways that are not reflected in Cartesian mapping. Groups could grant permission for other groups (kaalang) to hunt on their territories as long as a community member was present (Roy 2022, 338). Nonetheless, Taiwan's rugged terrain shaped human and non-human interaction. Large swaths of mountain forests provided foraging opportunities for mammals but became contested hunting territories for people from adjacent areas, whereas rivers provided paths for communication and political alliances.[8] Headhunting usually took men across the mountains and often far beyond the areas they used for hunting (Mabuchi 1974, 180). Interestingly, until the colonial period, no mountain group recognized Formosa as an island surrounded by the sea, and only the coastal groups had a word for sea (184). The difficult terrain and the fact that most groups were hemmed in by hostile groups led to a situation in which peoples' worlds were limited to the mountains and forests in which they could safely hunt or gather plants. When one was the warrior, headhunting expeditions happened beyond the horizon of everyday life.

What this world view means is that all land on Formosa was recognizable as territory related to some human group. *Dxgal* meant "the earth we walk on" but had nothing to do with the planet Earth as we now know from constant media images and use of Google Earth. *Dgiyaq* meant actual "mountains," looming about the settlements, and the rugged terrain people crossed for hunting or headhunting. Each alang was a specific settlement, either the one where one lived, that of one's in-laws, or that of an enemy group, thus sites of emotional attachment. These were all places towards which one could point when meeting another person on the pathways and being asked *"Msa su inu?"* – the greeting that means "Where are you going?" Territory was thought of in relation to one's own group, to one's allies, or to one's enemies. The forests were all used by humans, either for slash-and-burn cultivation or for hunting and gathering – all activities that included modification of the forest and the exclusion of others. Headhunting was the main activity that took people far from their alang and through which the Seejiq and Truku probably first encountered peoples with states. Headhunting was thus an integral part of what Mabuchi called the "observation and hearsay sphere" of geographical knowledge (Mabuchi 1974, 180). It took people beyond their intimate life spheres, and they came back home to tell others what they had experienced.

A Phenomenological Reading of Headhunting

The following description of headhunting, in a translation by historian Paul Barclay, is that of Kondō Katsusaburō, a Japanese merchant in Puli. Eager to engage the aboriginal peoples and further Japanese colonial goals, he married into a local family and got himself adopted by Truku headman and power-broker Bassau Bōran. He published his experiences with the Atayalic/Seejiq/Truku people in twenty-nine installments in the *Taiwan nichinichi shinpō* 臺灣日日新報 (*Taiwan Daily News*) between 20 December 1930 and 15 February 1931 as "'Kondō the Barbarian' Tells His Life Story: A Key to Understanding the Truth about the Musha Uprising." This chronicle was an important publication for Japanese-language urban readers in Taiwan and Japan at the time, as people were still dealing with the emotional shock of the 27 October 1930 Musha Incident (to be discussed in chapter 6). It was thus as important at the time as would be today an undercover journalistic account of an Islamicist group in the Middle East. Although these publications have the effect and perhaps even the intention of justifying Japanese colonialism by portraying the aboriginal peoples as savages in need of a Japanese civilizing project (Ching 2001), these sources do provide the kind of detailed description needed to understand the experience of headhunting. Kondō's account, however, omits certain parts of the process, including the important steps of organizing an expedition, preparing for it, and the actual attack. He also does not discuss what happens if the expedition fails or if a member is killed or dies.

The Japanese anthropological and state accounts list "reasons" for headhunting (Simon 2012a). Many of those accounts simply make lists that confuse individual motivations for joining headhunting expeditions, reasons given by leaders of expeditions, and even functionalist anthropological explanations. Kojima, in his investigative report, provided a parsimonious list of only three reasons. The first is a description of a conflict resolution mechanism. In the event of a serious conflict within an alang, such as an accusation of theft or other crime that prevents people from hunting or farming together, the conflicting parties would consult a local leader. He would first try to negotiate directly with the parties involved, then consult bird oracles, but only suggest headhunting as a last resort. If it came to the latter, the two disputing sides would have to organize headhunting expeditions from among the men of the alang (Kojima [1915] 1996], 258ff). If both sides could convince enough people to join them, they would leave in different directions to hunt a head. The party that could success-fully bring back a head without having a member of their own party injured or killed was understood to have been judged innocent by the ancestors. If both parties came back with heads, the party that brought back a greater number of heads was considered to have won the case (Furuno 1945, 432). The guiding idea is that, as in hunting, only the morally righteous can succeed, since the ancestors punish wrongdoers with accidents when they are in the forests. This notion was also the key to understanding the story of Sita Duku, the female headhunter. The fact that she could kill a person and return alive was sufficient to prove her innocence.

Other factors were also involved. As his subsequent two reasons, Kojima lists retribution for the death of close kin and the need to prove male courage. Logically, since headhunting had to happen for ritual purposes anyway, retribution was less of a motivation than it was a jus-tification for selecting which group to attack. As for the need to prove male courage, Kojima found "almost no examples of this." It is more likely that this reason was individual motivation to join headhunting expeditions, as participation was necessary to gain social recognition as a man and obtain a facial tattoo. Suzuki (1932, 165) and others added to this reason that people went headhunting because it would help ward off infectious disease, and Furuno (1945, 431) notes the impor-tance of headhunting to agricultural rites. Kondō's account likewise indicates that headhunting happened in October, so at harvest time. This detail, therefore, is less an explanation of *why* people headhunted than it is a description of *when* they did so. Elders in Hualien similarly told me that headhunting was an important component of the har-vest rituals related to millet. The emotional connection between this plant and headhunting was so strong that, when I once asked an older farmer if he had considered growing millet, he replied with a look of horror on his face: "If we started growing millet again, we would also have to start headhunting again." All of these factors show that head-hunting was not random. It was embedded in relationships that people have with other people, as well as with other living beings, including hungry millet plants and divinatory birds. It was part of the mesh-work of mountain life. Unlike some practices of modern warfare, such struggles were never intended to annihilate the enemy or replace one people with another (Walis 2009, 51).

Preparations for Headhunting

Kondō focused on his personal preparations. As an outsider, he had
to burn the soles of his feet in order that they would become tough
and leathery like those of warriors. He failed to mention that the
entire ritual group had to prepare. Women prepared food. The men,
since women were not allowed to touch the weapons, sharpened the
knives. The group fell under ritual taboo, which meant that they had
to establish a new fire, abstain from weaving, and halt all relationships with other groups (Kojima [1915] 1996, 262). Since the ritual
groups were charged with headhunting and most of them lived in
close relations with others, the social costs were high for the entire
community.

   Headhunting began with ritual. A leader, either from one of the existing ritual groups or a newly appointed youth known for his hunting
skills, was appointed as "one who draws water" (Kojima [1915] 1996,
261). He began the expedition with ritual purification by using grass to
splash the warriors with water. He carried with him a talismanic bag
(like that carried by hunters), which included the queue of a previous
Chinese victim and was usually stored in the eaves of his house. The
warriors would make an oath to fight until getting a head – a ritual act
that would make it difficult to back out after this point, as it made the
desires of the group more important than the fears of any individual.
The warriors would then construct a hut near the settlement of the
chosen victims and establish a strategy for attack. At this point, any
man who had a nightmare was permitted to leave the expedition. The
warriors also observed the behaviour of birds and would abandon the
expedition if the sisil indicated impending disaster (Kojima [1915] 1996,
262). These preparations surely gave both individuals and entire groups
adequate options to back out and the chosen group an opportunity to
prepare for an attack. From this preparation, we can see that the leader
had to be charismatic enough to rally the men around him and to allay
the fears they certainly had about this dangerous action. The ritual itself
thus brought together individuals with their own motivations, goals,
and anxieties.

   Finally, the warriors would attack the settlement. In the past, they
would have used spears and knives, or in the distant past kill in close
combat with sharpened bamboo to cut off the head (Yamada 2015, 74),
but by the Japanese period they were armed with rifles and sharp steel
knives. Kojima reported that only in remote areas, where the number of
rifles and ammunition was still insufficient, would they use bows and
arrows (Kojima [1915] 1996, 272). They would kill any family members,

and even passers-by, and destroy property. After killing a victim, they would cut off the head and wash the brain from the back of the head. If the victim were Chinese, they would cut off his queue and place it in the ritual bag. They would place any of the victims' weapons in the trees for other members of their group to find them. If they were successful, they would return victoriously to the settlement in a festive ritual. One person told me that they played a four-holed flute (depicted in Yamada 2015, 254) to entice the soul of the deceased to accompany the physical head with them back to their settlement. The ritual upon return to the village is best understood by reading Kondō's description in its entirety. I thus leave the gory details to him.

"Kondō Is Adopted by Bassau Bōran"; "'Kondō the Barbarian' Goes Headhunting"
(translated from *Taiwan nichinichi shinpō* 臺灣日日新報, chapter 5, 13 January 1931, and chapter 6, 14 January 1931)

He waited for the annual headhunting expedition and its attendant festivities, which occur around October. In order to accomplish his aims, Kondō would have to go headhunting himself, and participate in their various martial exploits.

"With feet like those, you cannot come with us," they said to Kondō. What they meant was that Kondō had to temper his feet so that he could run upon rocks and mountainsides. It was part of his training to burn his feet daily with a bellows to toughen up – he did this for almost a half-month.

The reason why Aborigines can climb slate-like sheets of rock that stand vertically, or step down jagged stones, is that they burn the bottoms of their feet to prepare for it. In a word, they train by stepping on hot iron rods. Of course, they begin at a temperature that will not damage their feet and gradually raise the heat of the rods they walk upon. While he underwent this training, Kondō awaited the October headhunting season. Kondō, however, was a believer in the Shingon sect of Buddhism, and did not want to do any killing. But Kondō wanted to find out whether or not the Fukahori troupe's heads were around, so he would go along with the headhunters. They even called him their weak little "Japanese savage"; he served them as a lowly infantry grunt.

The time had come. October, 1897! The men set out in high spirits. After a few days of sleeping in fields and running around as if on a battlefield, they obtained their quarry, a head. They returned to the village's border singing their triumphs.

Here, like something straight out of an ancient Japanese military saga, they cleaned the head and set it up for display and viewing. They washed the neck, pulled the teeth out completely, shaved the hair, and then removed the filth from what remained of the face. Then they wrapped a white sash around the neck. They carefully wrapped the hair to bring home to use as medicine; the teeth were saved for jewelry. The afflicted will exchange a whole chicken and a melon for two or three of these hairs. The beautiful, unadorned heads were hoisted up. Now it was time to enter the village. The populace welcomed them, wearing festival finery. From here, the undertaking known as the "head festival" would commence.

Underneath a triangular white piece of paper, they tied a tassel made of fibrous paper fringes, which they hung from the top of the tallest tree in the village; this was a landmark for the descending ancestor's spirits. Under this they placed the skull shelf. They put the new head in the center, among all of the previously acquired skulls. An old woman known as the "guardian of heads" walked up to the fresh one and opened its eyes. Then she said a rather self-serving prayer to the departed soul:

"You are welcome here. I have been awaiting your arrival. This village is a good place, please stay here forever …"

Then she placed a slice of sweet potato into its mouth. From a pig killed for the festival, she skewered a little bit of meat, bone, and innards, putting them into the mouth, attaching it to the potato. This is not such a hard scene to picture; it looked something like a Taiwan festival pig with incense stuck in its mouth. After all of the preparations were completed, everybody gathered in front of the tree and called the ancestors' spirits towards the triangular paper in the tree. They offered saké to the head. The headhunting dance began. For a number of days, the people of Wushe danced and drank crazily. Kondō himself had been attracted to Aborigine country, drawn by a grotesque question, "why do the Aborigines hunt heads?" Now, according to Kondō, for the first time he was able to grasp the reality of headhunting. He says, "Aborigine men and women, it doesn't matter which, have a passion for heads, and a way of conceptualizing heads, which Japanese people would never understand." Kondō laughed and continued, "Maybe it would be better to have one's head taken by the Aborigines rather than just dying and being cremated in the normal way."

Source: Barclay (2008).

Such a ritual complex merits unpacking. First, it demonstrates how certain individuals used headhunting to augment their own prestige and social power. Men could become local leaders, demonstrating their position by keeping the skull racks in front of their homes. Women, known as *msapuh* (shamans), also played important roles in the rituals and subsequently took possession of hair and other parts of the head that could be used in healing rituals. The fact that people gained political and social power from headhunting requires one to nuance the idea that these are strictly egalitarian groups. The Seejiq represent themselves as strictly egalitarian, as I have illustrated in earlier publications (see Simon 2012a, 2012b). Another word for such egalitarian societies in anthropology is "acephalous" societies – derived from the Greek for "headless." Thinking through the phenomenological experience of headhunting, nothing could be further from the truth, except from the victims' perspective since they literally became headless. Indeed, the ritual groups collected heads, and individuals gained power for doing so. Women gained power as shamans and healers. Men gained prestige as leaders of ritual groups and could perhaps be chosen to represent the entire settlement or a confederation. If anything, the Atayalic groups should be said to form a many-headed or polycephalous society. Headhunting kept the Chinese out of the mountains, and competition between ritual leaders made it difficult for any outside interest to find a negotiator who could represent more than a few hundred people. If any groups wished to avoid external states, their claims to having no leaders could easily become part of the "art of not being governed" (Scott 2009). It would be best to say that headhunting was the basis of political power within communities, but the multiplicity of both severed heads and living political heads made higher level political organization extremely difficult.

Nowadays, many people evoke these days as a period in which everyone was equal, since all *rudan* (elders, as heads of ritual groups) participated in the consensual decision-making of the group, and in theory every man could eventually gain this status. People also emphasize that nobody was allowed to give orders or to accumulate wealth and power for themselves, as that was a violation of Gaya. It seems most likely that the leaders of ritual groups tried to augment their power, whereas the members restrained such power through various social-levelling mechanisms that could include reminding them of the Gaya of equality, social ostracism, or even leaving the settlement to move elsewhere. The fact that men could, at least theoretically, opt out of headhunting expeditions, even at the last minute by claiming to have had a nightmare, permits resistance to the emergence of monist power. I have elsewhere argued (Simon 2012a) that these societies were marked by oscillations, as some men tried to assert power and others tried to restrain them. Clastres and Scott have understood the mechanisms by which some societies rejected the emergence of hierarchies, but they also underestimated how some people did indeed emerge as local leaders, earning more power or prestige than others.[9] What is perhaps most important is that headhunting was a political ritual that allowed certain ritual leaders to draw people around themselves and thus give them power. As Barraud said about headhunting societies and political power, "it is above all at the level of ritual that the chief has a particular status" (Barraud 1972, 69, free translation by the author).[10]

The persistent idea that pre-colonial society was egalitarian and that leaders of headhunting expeditions were charismatic individuals who temporarily became "first among equals" is perhaps rooted in fact, but heavily tinted with nostalgia. Tgdaya elder Rosi Nabu, interviewed by Kumu Tapas, reflected upon the difference between the Japanese colonial period, when state authorities appointed a chief for them, and the pre-colonial period, when the authority of the chiefs was based on respect for their abilities. In her description of Mona Rudo, rebel leader in the 1930 Musha Uprising, she revealed that the leaders of headhunting expeditions were, at least by that time, relatively wealthy individuals. She explained that only men with livestock could lead the expeditions, because they had to provide the entire community with prodigious amounts of meat at the post-expedition feasts. Mona had greater flocks than anyone else (Kumu 2004a, 365–6). This explanation casts Mona's reputation as a lead headhunter in a new light, especially because at the time the Japanese authorities were gradually restricting hunting and replacing the lost protein with livestock (Kojima 2002, 99). Mona's military prowess is thus linked to his collaboration with the colonial authorities. At any rate, the men who joined the expeditions had to turn over the heads to the expedition leader, who placed them on a skull rack in front of his house and thus gained both power and prestige.

Becoming Men and Becoming Ancestors

The ritual of feeding the head (mkan hadur) was the most important part of the ritual, and afterwards, the forests were always full of abundant game, proving that the ancestors appreciated the sacrifice (Kaji 2011, 27–8). If the warriors successfully returned with a head, they would enter the village in triumph, where they were met by the ecstatic women of the community. In the film *Warriors of the Rainbow*, as well as in descriptions of headhunting in village conversations, people imagine it as a bacchanalian period of singing, dancing, and drinking. There are implications of male sexuality, as the returning young warriors were now eligible for marriage and were welcomed as heroes by the women. It was also a chance to socialize the children, as the boys too young to join an expedition would be encouraged to feed the heads (Kumu 2004a, 130). Some people told me that, as children, they were terrified to even walk past the skull racks.

The central point was that the head would be placed in front of the ritual leader's house. Leading men and women alike had roles in the ritual that followed, giving the head millet and alcohol as they enticed its soul to remain in the community. Singing, dancing, feasting, and drinking would last all night. According to elders, they would entice the soul to bring in other members of its group of origin, saying that they are welcome to remain and become the ancestors (*utux*) of the group that took the head.[11] Kojima documented the wording used by the Atayal: "Here, we let you drink alcohol. May you call your father, mother, and brothers to all come here. In the same way, they can be happy and live here with you" (Kojima [1915] 1996], 260).

This ritual made headhunting into what some elders still describe as an ethical act. Once, thinking more about the contrast between warfare and headhunting, I casually mentioned to one older woman that headhunting was probably not the savage, immoral action imagined by outsiders. She expounded on that idea, saying: "Right! We didn't just kill people. We fed the head. We welcomed it as our friend and ancestor." It was precisely this transformation of the enemy into a friend and ancestor that made this ritual beneficial to the community. From an emic perspective, noted McKinley, headhunters are "winning souls for humanity" (McKinley 1979, 125).

So far, this account overlooks what happened in the not unlikely eventuality that the expedition fails. The difficulties of the expeditions were enormous. First, they did it on relatively distant lands belonging to enemy groups, which meant that they were not entirely familiar with the terrain, potential hiding places, obstacles, or dangers. Second, they began by building a hut and conducting certain rituals, which probably made the targeted groups aware of what was happening and allowed them to mount resistance. There was thus always the possibility of failure, even injury or death on the way home after a successful raid.

Kojima documented that, if a member of the expedition died during an expedition, even if they had captured a head, they had to abandon both the body and the head. The warriors would return to an encampment outside their settlement, leave their weapons in the forest, and return to the village naked. The death of one of their own members required rituals of appeasement, and the ritual leader would have to sacrifice a pig to atone for the loss to the immediate family and to the ancestors. Since it was believed that sexual impropriety could lead to failure of an expedition, any person found to have committed adultery would also have to compensate for the failure of the expedition (Kojima [1915] 1996, 263–4). Even if the warriors just came home empty-handed, they had to re-enter the settlement in shame and disappointment, surely an important anti-climactic moment for the young men hoping to gain a facial tattoo. It is interesting to note that heads are always central to the ritual, in terms of both the victim's head and the warrior's head that became eligible for a tattoo.

The perspective of the victim is also often overlooked. In neither the Japanese ethnographic literature nor in my own records of village conversations have I found direct mention of what happens to the person who has been murdered or to his or her family and community, as the preferred subject position is always that of the headhunter.[12] People seem to have a vague notion that the flow of energy in heads is a zero-sum game, in which a gain in vitality in one community is matched by a loss elsewhere. Even the myth about the origin of headhunting in the sermon cited earlier evokes a sense that populations and, by extension, vitality should tend towards equilibrium. But very little is said about the phenomenological experience of the victim. A clue can be found from Palau, where Augustin Krämer documented similar headhunting rituals in his reports to the Hamburger Südsee-Expedition from 1908 to 1910. Krämer writes that the victim would be buried at the site of the murder, with a Pandanus or Musa fruit used to replace the head. The usual funeral ceremonies were not performed, and the family was considered impure and quarantined for a short period of time (Krämer 1926, 302). Headhunting is one of the "unlucky" deaths that people mentioned to me: deaths that happen when one is alone and away from home, when no family members are there to hold one's hand at one's last breath (Kim 1980, 225). People went to great lengths to avoid having their head cut off, even if it meant certain death. Suzuki wrote that, if attacked, people would rather commit suicide by jumping off a cliff (and dying intact in an inaccessible place) to avoid the capture of their heads (Suzuki 1932, 176). Clearly, nobody wanted to be ritually transformed into the friend and ancestor of an enemy group.

The Power of the Head

Headhunters and anthropologists alike have explained headhunting in terms of a spiritual life force or soul substance that was concentrated in the skull and could be appropriated ritually. There is broad consensus, in all headhunting societies studied by anthropologists, that skull racks were reservoirs of power (*mana*) that could guarantee good crops and protect communities (Needham 1976, 74). The question is how to understand "power." Early nineteenth-century anthropologists tended to use an analogy with radio transmission, which Rodney Needham thought was a misunderstanding by anthropologists thinking in terms of physics, energy, and the new technology of their times (82). Perhaps because they have read it in ethnographies, people told me that their ancestors believed that the heads held energy. If energy left the community, they would be threatened by infectious disease or crop loss. The idea is that this energy is in flux, that it can be lost or gained, and that it was enhanced by bringing in a skull from outside the community. It is probably less useful to think about power as cause and effect than to think of how the power of the ritual placed people within a larger experiential world of selves and other beings.

The treatment of the captured head gives clues to headhunting as a phenomenological experience. Warriors, already accustomed to watching the turning heads and watchful eyes of animal prey, were certainly even more aware of what their human victims were going through. Their final images of the victims were those of eyes bulging with fear and mouths crying for mercy. They carefully washed the skulls, emptying them of the brains, and triumphantly brought the heads back to the village. The heads were placed in a position of honour, from which shamans could open their eyes anew as seeing ancestors. They sang and danced in front of the heads so that the heads could see and hear. They fed the heads, expecting the heads to smell, taste, and finally hear their appeals to become friends and ancestors. McKinley thus argued that the most important reason for taking a head was because the face made it into a social person and thus capable of being transformed into a friend (McKinley 1979, 110). There is also a notion that the head, as recipient of the senses through the face, is a vector of power.

Headhunting is also characterized by the fact that it mobilizes members of one group against clearly defined other groups. Groups tended to form alliances along river watersheds and seek headhunting victims across mountains, especially in areas of conflict over hunting groups. The fact that initiated warriors had facial tattoos, and that the designs varied from one community to the next, made these into clear markers of belonging. When warriors encountered others, whether they be members of other tattooed groups, other aboriginal groups such as the Amis who had no facial tattoos, or the Chinese with long queues (during the Qing period), these ethnic markers made it possible for them to identify human groups just as easily as hunters could identify animals from morphological characteristics.

This point suggests, as did the anecdote that opened this chapter and the ethnographic evidence on how headhunters chose their victims, that the rituals were very much about reinforcing in-group cohesion and managing otherness, what McKinley called managing the "existential limits of the social world" (McKinley 1979, 95–6). He argued that the victim ethnic groups were perceived as not quite human. Living across the mountains, they were somehow associated with the realm of the spirits. Most likely, the rituals could be used by local leaders to stimulate adrenaline in the warrior groups and prime a species mental module that facilitated this intergroup raiding and homicide. The young men were motivated by a desire to prove their masculinity but also by a fear of ostracism if they did not sacrifice their own interests for their group. Nonetheless, it must have been emotionally very difficult for them to face a protesting victim, who could be a man or a woman, young or elderly, and bring back a head.[13] The ritual of feasting the head was a means of atonement, of re-humanizing the head and transforming it into a friend or ancestor. As killing and decapitation became easier with the introduction of steel knives and rifles, the psychological struggles likely only intensified. People would probably have eventually ended the practice themselves, even if the Japanese government had not prohibited it. The efficiency of the killing made it less of a sacred ordeal, less of a warrior tradition of hand-to-hand combat, and more of a cruel and simple homicide. Rifles emptied headhunting of its ritual efficacy.

Transformation of Headhunting

For contemporary Seejiq, one of the most salient features of headhunting is that it has ended. Yamada's (2015) survey of the archaeological and historical literature demonstrates that headhunting existed on Formosa for millennia, an argument that supports the hypothesis that headhunting was part of the Austronesian cultural complex that enabled prehistoric peoples leaving Formosa to conquer Oceania. Yet, headhunting is also linked to the wider political economic context. On Formosa, headhunting intensified with contact with Chinese and Japanese states. Especially in the earlier years of Japanese administration, better small arms were more easily available, which made homicide and the extraction of heads easier and less dangerous for the warriors. At the same time, expanded camphor extraction in the forests of northern Taiwan meant that there were more territorial conflicts between the Atayalic groups and the new colonial powers, as camphor workers and their superiors also became targets for headhunting (Yamada 2015, 212). Japanese police statistics show spikes in aboriginal homicides in 1914 and 1920, the first coinciding with Governor-General Sakuma Samata's "Five-Year Plan to Pacify the Savages" and the second with the 1918–20 influenza epidemic (Simon 2012a, 179). In 1920, aboriginal groups were thus still using headhunting as a means of addressing epidemics. In the following years, headhunting declined dramatically, leading Japanese administrators to claim success for their civilizing project.

The people probably made a conscious decision to abandon the practice. In New Georgia, as a heuristically useful comparison, headhunting was practised as rituals for canoe launching, an initiation rite for young men, and an arena for certain men to gain political power. In the 1880s, the introduction of the steel axe made homicide more efficient, leading to large-scale expeditions under the leadership of strongmen. The New Georgians, not least to limit the power of these strongmen, terminated the practice themselves. They justified the end of headhunting by the presence of British rule and reinforced the decision with conversion to Christianity (Zelenietz 1979, 104). If similar choices were made in Taiwan, it would be consistent with what I learned from conversations with older people in Seejiq communities. When people expressed disdain for the headhunting practices that they remember hearing about, it was less about the practice itself than about the fact that their own community members launched headhunting expeditions on behalf of the Japanese military to subdue other groups and received monetary compensation for each head (Kuo 2012, 204). They thus came to associate headhunting less with Gaya than with would-be leaders who collaborated with a colonial force. As demonstrated by the anecdote at the beginning of this chapter, they are proud of the fact that they gave up headhunting, a transformation facilitated by the adoption of Christianity as a new manifestation of Gaya.

This conversion *from* headhunting has become an important part of peoples' identities. In the summer of 2019, when I took a group of university students up the mountain to Skadang, our host Yaya told us about her ancestors. On her mother's side of the family, her great-grandfather was named Yakaw Abu, and her great-grandmother was named Alay Pajiq. Yakaw Abu was a great warrior. While everyone slept, it was his duty to sleep in a high tree so that he could remain on constant guard against enemy groups. Due to the success of his own exploits, he could maintain a rack full of skulls in front of his house. All these skulls had been brought back to the village by young men fighting under his command. When the warrior parties brought skulls back to the village, the women greeted them with ecstatic song and dance. They would give the head alcohol and welcome it to the community. Describing the practice as particularly cruel, Yaya said that they would even ask the head to bring them the head's whole family as future victims. Enchanted by the magic of the ritual, she described: "The heads would sometimes cry in sorrow. Or they would turn their head in anger away from our people." She explained that her great-grandmother was an eminent msapuh, one of the women healers who could draw immense power from these rituals. She lived to be 116 years old, never fell ill, and died simply of old age. She was capable of curing people of many diseases. But she was the first person in the community to convert to Christianity. Yaya said that her family has suffered greatly from poverty and from sickness, as God punished them for the terrible sins of headhunting committed by their ancestors. Yet, because they converted, the next generation will prosper. Yaya was not expressing pride that her great-grandmother belonged to a headhunting cult; she was proud of the early conversion to Christianity. When Yaya told this story, I could not help but remember my father's story about the Simons being Jewish. This telling is the intergenerational pride of the converted.

Despite social changes in Taiwan, people tried to keep what they found to be positive from headhunting, to find new ways of mgaya, or implementing Gaya. This attempt was certainly the case on Formosa by 1932, when tattooing had been eliminated and hunting for deer, muntjac, and boar had replaced headhunting as the most important coming-of-age ritual (Suzuki 1932, 88). People commonly told me that they replaced headhunting with the hunting of animals. There are indeed common features, beginning with the fact that they must identify the location of the target population and take lives. From the perspective of the young men, hunting has become the most important expression of masculinity and the central coming-of-age ritual. Headhunters and hunters observe many of the same taboos and rituals, including making offerings to the ancestors and observing bird oracles (Yamada 2015, 191–3), as well as transforming body parts into talismans, a boar tusk also being part of a head. In some Truku areas, I learned from some older people that they also substituted headhunting with hunting for animals as a divine ordeal to resolve intra-community conflicts. Older men earn prestige and solid reputations as morally upright individuals by demonstrating strong hunting skills. People now say that men must prove their skill at hunting in order to get a good wife and to enter

Figure 3.3. Animal skulls. As hunting for animals has replaced many social dimensions of headhunting hunters decorate their homes with animal skulls.

Source: Photograph by Scott E. Simon

Heaven after death. The skull racks are long gone, but people adorn the exterior or interior of their homes with animal skulls (figure 3.3), a new form of fetishism probably reflecting a belief that animal souls can also contain spiritual energy (Liu 2009). There are, of course, rather striking differences. People do not hunt merely to capture the skulls but rather to enjoy and share the meat, whereas they have never eaten human flesh as part of headhunting. Nor do people conduct elaborate rituals to transform the animals into ancestors.

The will to political power has certainly survived the end of headhunting, but would-be leaders easily found new arenas to advance their goals. In Formosa's southwest, the aboriginal Siraya people abandoned headhunting willingly under Dutch rule but soon embarked on "new routes to the achievement of traditional Sirayan values" (Shepherd 1995, 63). This change was certainly a precedent for what would happen in other communities under Japanese colonial rule. In the postmodern era of identity politics, it ironically includes the simulacra of headhunting in new contexts. The evocation of headhunting, and the use of fruit or dolls' heads as ritual substitutes, has drawn the attention of anthropologists in Indonesia (George 1996) as well as in Taiwan (Rudolph 2008). An event that I observed in 2006 likewise illustrates how the contemporary descendants of headhunters evoke this past in new circumstances.

Headhunting as Modern Ritual: The Taroko National Park

In early 2006, the Taroko National Park administration sent notices to all the local community development associations, inviting them to participate in a song and dance competition as part of the Buruwan Lily Festival at the national park headquarters. To my amusement at the time, the written notice explicitly said that participants were not permitted to carry real knives or firearms during their performances. I simply did not imagine that anyone would want to do so.

The event began, as usual, with speeches by local politicians. The township magistrate, a Truku woman, began by taking the microphone and, looking at the park superintendent, stated: "We have to remember that this land belongs to the Taroko people." Three people were introduced as the judges of the competition: a non-Indigenous university professor, the minister who had given the sermon about headhunting discussed earlier, and a local Truku politician – all three of them with a long history of social movement activism and protests against the park.

The performances then began. Nearly all of them included carefully prepared props, children in colourful weavings singing Truku songs, and dance. A tourist would surely have seen a performance of Truku culture. To everybody who organizes music and dance performances or seeks to revive traditional musical instruments and songs, this occasion was a treasured opportunity for cultural expression (Kaji 2011). A deeper meaning, however, was more evident to both park administrators and performers. Most of the performances evoked hunting traditions, even shooting at stuffed animals with bows and arrows or hunting rifles. In one group, the young boys re-enacted headhunting, with one boy brandishing a knife as he danced across the stage with an imaginary head in his hand. They sang a song celebrating the Truku division of labour, in which men hunt and protect their land by headhunting while women weave. Another group enacted a ritual sacrifice to the ancestors, explaining that it is the core of Truku culture. Members of a Catholic church actually killed a real chicken as part of their performance, leaving the area drenched with blood. Contrary to the instructions, they had indeed brought a real knife to the festivities. Most of them were declaring their right to hunt in the Taroko National Park, thus seizing agency from state authorities.

A third group, from the adjacent village of Tkijig, sent a handful of middle-aged men out to the performance arena wearing little more than banana leaves and painted tattoos but brandishing the large steel knives called *fandao* 番刀 (savage knives), which everyone associates with historical headhunting rituals (figure 3.4). One of the men took the

Figure 3.4. The knives are real. Anger and sarcasm about being asked to perform indigeneity, Taroko National Park, 8 April 2006.

Source: Photograph by Scott E. Simon.

microphone, looked at the park superintendent, and said: "You treat us like savages, so we will act like savages." He walked directly up to the judges' podium to say: "I want to speak to the park superintendent. We did not prepare a performance at all. The National Park says that we cannot kill animals. We shout out loudly, and the animals come out of their own free will. The little pig then pleads: 'Please don't kill me. I will sacrifice myself,' and we carry him down the mountain. We don't have to use our bows at all." They then shouted out loud and imitated the killing of a pig by attacking a bunch of leaves and sticks. The park superintendent took the microphone and said that they had not followed instructions, as they had failed to wear Taroko clothing, adding that it is improper of them to "dress like Indians."

At the conclusion of the competition, the organizers distributed prizes. The group from Tkijig was disqualified because of their overt insubordination to park authorities, and the local Presbyterian choir got the first prize. Each group took turns taking photos with the park superintendent. Taking the microphone into his hands, the owner of a private hotel in the park concluded: "This proves that we have ethnic harmony." When I talked to people about the performance afterwards, however, this harmony was far from evident. Some people criticized the men from Tkijig for their lack of decorum and pointed out that they had arrived at the performance already drunk. They accused the men from Tkijig of spoiling the event, which they saw as an opportunity for cultural resurgence, as long as they played by the rules. Others, however, praised them for openly challenging the park administration about hunting restrictions. Ichiro, the friend who had taken me to his mountain lodge, declared: "I never want to cooperate with the National Park again. They should realize that we are the only real masters of this land and that we are not their subcontractors." What was clear to everyone, however, was that bringing real weapons to the show was an intentional show of force. However playful they may have appeared, the use of weapons and the evocation of headhunting was an act of resistance with real undertones of violence. It was a declaration of sovereignty, even if it happened within the context of a tourist spectacle. It is interesting to note as well that each performing group basically replicated the groupings that would have formerly constituted small ritual groups and that it still took the emergence of local Big Men to make organization of the event even possible. In a postcolonial twist, the performers used the trope of the past to communicate their dissatisfaction with the much more powerful invaders of the present.

These public rituals emerge from a specific historical moment in Taiwan's Indigenous social movement. As documented by Michael Rudolph, the first "ancestor-spirits-ritual" had been organized in Tongmen Village, Hualien, in 1999 by the Taroko Cultural Construction Association with local government funding. This event was an attempt by local politicians, including one Presbyterian pastor, to forge and consolidate a Truku (Taroko) identity as distinct from the Atayal. They reconstructed "traditional" ritual by reading Japanese-era ethnographies and compacting a ritual that would have lasted several days into a one-hour performance preceded and followed by speeches from politicians and Presbyterian ministers (Rudolph 2008, 106–9). That Tongmen event provided the template for future public performances. Even the Tkijig joke about wild animals voluntarily sacrificing themselves in the Taroko Park, unbeknownst to me at the time, had been said at that event (Rudolph 2008, 123), making it rather stale humour to the experienced participants in such events. Nonetheless, the performance is efficacious in the sense of ritually reminding the Han Taiwanese that they are guests on Truku land and dependent on Truku ritual for the successful continuation of even such apparently hegemonic projects as the Taroko National Park. Such rituals thus subvert social reality in ways that are powerful to the participants (Rudolph 2008, 130).

Discussion

From a sociological perspective, it is significant that the Chinese word for "headhunting," chucao 出草, resurfaces regularly in contemporary Taiwan. When there is a protest demonstration for Indigenous rights, the Indigenous groups announce first in the media that they are going to chucao, sometimes even with a provocative photo of an Indigenous man defiantly raising a "savage knife" into the air. At one protest in Taitung against the proposed storage of nuclear waste on Paiwan territory, I was astonished by the large numbers of protesters who showed up with large knives and even hunting rifles. There is a large dimension of theatricality to such events, which begin with "traditional" ceremonies and to which many people wear their traditional regalia. The competition at the Taroko National Park was an interesting twist on this type of event. At one level, it was an example of local collaboration with a state-sponsored event, and it was surely understood as such by most observers and participants. Most performing groups embraced it to express their own culture in a public forum. Nonetheless, it was also an opportunity for some participants to resist the encroachment of the park on their territory in a publicly comic fashion. While the headhunting was simulated, the weapons were nonetheless real and wielded by several groups. We will come back to the moral dimensions of the contemporary Indigenous social movement in a subsequent chapter.

For the moment, it suffices to underline political dimensions of ritual that the former rituals of headhunting and the contemporary re-enactments of that ritual have in common. First, both are arenas in which local leaders manipulate differences between groups, or ethnic otherness, as they try to accumulate power in their own groups. To a large extent, the same families from the former ritual groups and small settlements of alang are still mobilized in these local political formations, albeit in new forms such as community development associations or church congregations. These families and clans now reside in agglomerated villages, as a result of both Japanese and ROC policies, but they evoke their former places and groups continually as they explain how each village came to be composed of different factions in the contemporary context. Headhunting, whether real ritual in the past or simulacra in the present, is still about relations between groups. Some, especially those who would like to gain power at wider levels of political organization, evoke this past as they deplore the difficulties they have in uniting different people. One of the community development association leaders who had organized a group at the Taroko National Park performance summed it up quite well: "Let me tell you about the problem of the Truku. We are too individualistic. Everybody wants to be a chief." In his view, Truku men still have the desire to gain power that formerly motivated men to organize headhunting expeditions.

Although the performers competing at the Taroko National Park took the event very seriously, other members of the community did not seem to take an interest in it at all. My observations over the years confirm those of Michael Rudolph, who noted that ordinary people find ridiculous the actions of would-be leaders, including those who apply for state funding to re-enact headhunting rituals (Rudolph 2004, 250). These ordinary people do not hesitate at all to accuse these emergent local leaders as collaborators who violate Gaya by accumulating wealth and power for themselves while most of their kin still suffer from poverty. By all appearances, they are still a society against the state, resisting the emergence of power from within their own ranks as well as from beyond their community. The evocation of Gaya continues to be used to both affirm local power and to resist it, which does not mean that the individuals who organize performances are insincere. If anything, they see these performances as important opportunities to assert their own cultural sovereignty in what may be the result of complex internal negotiations (Hatfield 2020).

With colonialism, headhunting was relegated to the past, sometimes as ethnic stigma, sometimes as ethnic pride, and sometimes in ritual simulacra that emergent leaders could still use to consolidate prestige in a very new sociological context. Whether ordinary people are nostalgic or reflect critically on the violence of their great-grandparents, they express the pain of their colonial situation and look for ways out of it. Yet, not even the most enthusiastic proponents of cultural renaissance would seriously consider a revitalization of headhunting, although some suggest so in jest. Old rituals have been replaced by new ones. The beat of the headhunting song is now re-created only in ethnographic recordings and in Formosan variants of world music. Nowadays, in ordinary life, that music has been replaced by the pious melody of Christian hymns. That change in Formosan lifeworlds is the subject of chapter 4.

Punic (hunting rifle) 獵槍

Figure 4.1. Hunting rifle (*venandi instrumenta*) takes a Truku name meaning "fire." In Tgdaya, rifles are called *halung* (pine), after the wood used to make them. From at least the 1860s, Formosans have enthusiastically acquired the most advanced rifles available. Nowadays, they are only allowed to use home-made, muzzle-loading rifles, but they remain important actors in Indigenous lifeworlds. In 1916, anthropologist Shinji Ishii observed: "Now nearly every savage fighting-man has a firearm, which he holds only second in value to his life, just as our Samurai looked on their swords in feudal times" (Ishii 1916, 23).

Source: Illustration by Biluan.

Chapter Four

Utux (Spirit)

The legacy of Christianity lays heavily on Canadian consciences. In the summer of 2021, as I was finishing my work on this chapter, Canadians embarked on a collective reckoning with the history of church-run residential schools. The remains of 215 children found on the grounds of a former residential school in Kamloops made a broad public aware of the trauma that had been caused to Indigenous peoples by state and church through forced removal of children from their families, abuse at the hands of strangers, neglect, and disease. Canada's National Inquiry concluded that residential schools were part of a larger project of colonial genocide because they were intended to eradicate Indigenous languages, cultures, and lifeworlds (Government of Canada 2019b). Knowing this history, it is difficult to imagine that Indigenous people anywhere could have a very different relationship with Christianity, one less tainted with violence and colonialism, even a positive one. Yet, since Christianity continues to be a defining part of Formosan Indigenous lifeworlds, I cannot ignore that social reality. This chapter will explore that complex relationship between Christianity and indigeneity. But just as the people in the villages do, I will embed it in Sədeq religious history. And in a way that enabled my field research, Christianity was their first point of contact with Canada.

While Canadian churches were interning Indigenous children in residential schools, the same churches were also sending missionaries abroad, including to Formosa. The best-known missionary was Scottish Presbyterian George Leslie Mackay (1844–1901) from Oxford County, Ontario, who founded schools, what became one of Taiwan's leading hospitals, and churches, showing a particular affinity with the island's Indigenous populations. His name is still a household name in Taiwan. The Roman Catholic Church also had French-Canadian priests. Although Christianity appealed to only a very small number of Han

Taiwanese, it spread rapidly in Taiwan's Indigenous communities, to the point where nearly all Indigenous people are Christian of one denomination or another.

Conversion began with the Sədeq, in particular those known today as the Truku. In 1929, Canadian Presbyterian missionary James Dickson visited Hualien and encouraged Ciwang Yiwal, a fifty-seven-year-old Truku woman who often attended church services, to study the Bible at the Presbyterian girls' school in Tamsui. She became a minister of the Woman's Missionary Society and returned to Hualien to preach (Covell 1998, 166). Referring to the 1930 violence on the other side of the mountains in Musha, missionary Ralph Covell summarized this mission history: "The tragic Sediq loss had prepared the context in which the gospel seed could be planted. Beginning with them – the chosen people – this seed was sown among all of the original inhabitants" (158).

As I mentioned in chapter 1, the Presbyterian Church would eventually become the cradle of Taiwan's Indigenous rights movement. In the integrationist period of Taiwan's history of indigeneity, as public schools were punishing Indigenous children for speaking their own languages, the Presbyterian churches provided some of the few contexts in which the languages were actively used and promoted. Canadian anthropologist Michael Stainton thus referred to "counterhegemonic Presbyterian aboriginality" (Stainton 1995). Even in the darkest days of Japanese colonialism and displacements or the subsequent Republic of China (ROC) martial law, Taiwan never had an equivalent to the residential schools or the "sixties scoop," which in Canada literally seized Indigenous infants from the arms of their mothers. How was Christianity in Taiwan different? How does it fit into Sədeq religious history? What differences exist within Christianity? How does it articulate with indigeneity and Indigenous resurgence? In this chapter, I begin with my own background, how Christianity first brought me to Indigenous Formosa. I then discuss pre-Christian forms of religion before exploring the diversity of Christian experience in Sədeq lifeworlds.

Where I Come From: My Own Experience and Family Background

Before I explore the winding trails that took other people from headhunting rituals to international gospel meetings, it is important for me to acknowledge the personal wayfaring that brought me to Taiwan. It was along well-laid paths that I met some people early in my fieldwork and others only later. The people who initially guided me to Indigenous Taiwan remain important parts of my lifeworld, and the experiences I shared with them colour my perceptions of the world around me to this day. As I recognize that knowledge emerges from interactions between the ethnographer and others, this episode is a non-negligible part of my heart journey.

In the summer of 2002, I had just completed my first year of teaching sociology at the University of Ottawa and had been getting acquainted with the Taiwanese-Canadian community. Steve Chen, whom I knew from the Formosan Association for Public Affairs, suggested that I enroll as a student in a one-week Urban-Rural Mission (URM) training for social activists at the Presbyterian Chang Jung Christian University in Tainan. The course would be taught by Ed File, a sociologist from York University in Toronto and minister with the United Church of Canada, and Albert Lin, a retired physicist and former legislator for Taiwan's Democratic Progressive Party (DPP), who also lived in Toronto. I was comfortable with this expression of Christian faith, because it promoted social justice in contexts ranging from Indigenous rights to same-sex marriage. I joined Taiwanese students for the entire week, and we studied, ate, and slept on campus, giving us a sense of comradery and fellowship. Although this experience gave me a new perspective on beliefs as a sensible truth (Jackson 2013, 98), it also coloured my initial perceptions of Indigenous Taiwan in a historically grounded way.

URM, a World Council of Churches (WCC) project since the 1960s, has become a worldwide ecumenical educational movement based on principles of social justice, community participation, resistance to oppression, and "resurrection" of the poor (David 1987). The goal of the training is to provide intellectual and organizational tools for grass-roots organizers among peasants, workers, and Indigenous communities.[1] URM graduates in Taiwan are known for having in 1988 toppled the statue of Wu Feng, a Confucian scholar official who had supposedly sacrificed himself to end the savage custom of headhunting. They subsequently succeeded in getting this racist story removed from school textbooks and in changing the name of Wu Feng Township to Alishan Township. Igung Shiban, the woman who first convinced me to do research with the Truku of Hualien, also launched her campaign against Asia Cement after participating in URM training.

I listened attentively as Ed File introduced URM with a lecture about how capitalism is expanding around the world, destroying the environment and causing poverty, thus needing organized resistance. Up to this point, I could only nod my head in agreement, since I was teaching sociology of development mostly from a perspective that looked at "development" as discursive hegemony and at social movements as resistance (Escobar 1995). I was even more interested when he demonstrated how

URM offered an answer to my students' frequent question: What is to be done?

This training set the tone for my own research agenda that, although unknown to me at the time, would stretch over the next two decades. Due to my emerging research interest in development in Indigenous communities, I joined a group of three university students, one primary school teacher, and one seasoned environmentalist activist to discuss what needed to be done on Indigenous issues. The training itself used a medical metaphor, asking participants to make a diagnosis of a social pain and then discover a cure. The subsequent process of discussion guided participants through stages of issue analysis, discussion of values by different stakeholders, strategic planning, and finally social action. Two young men, skilled hunters and theology students in training to be Presbyterian pastors, convinced us to work on the issue of the criminalization of Indigenous hunting. One of them even said: "Hunting means to Indigenous culture what the tea ceremony means to Japanese culture." They framed it as a cultural issue, with the need to organize resistance against the government's repression of Indigenous culture (Simon 2004). I was still more interested in development and the spread of capitalism, but I took note of the importance of hunting. Without URM at the beginning of my journey, I would probably not have eventually understood the perspectives of hunters or gained the knowledge that led me to the study of hunting lifeworlds, including relations with animals.

Although the activities of each day included prayer and hymns, the most important religious component was the concluding ritual at the end of the training. An imposing cross was placed in the centre of the room, and candles were distributed to everyone present. A pastor gave a dramatic sermon about how everyone in that room has a cross to carry, a mission to fulfil the work of God by empowering the poor and marginalized people in our societies. Heightening the emotional experience of the ceremony, the lights were dimmed, and each person lit a candle. We could see little but the face of each person illuminated by the small flame held in his or her hands. A pianist playing moving Protestant hymns heightened the emotional tenor of the event. One by one, as they felt moved, participants walked forward to the cross, said a prayer, and left their candle on the cross. Some people burst into tears as they promised to commit their lives to various projects of poverty reduction, environmental protection, gender equality, or Indigenous rights. Having spent a week immersed in lessons, prayers, and hymns, I also felt compelled to step forward. I still vividly remember that moment: the sight of flickering flames and wisps of smoke rising from the candles already laid on the cross, the scent of melting wax, the warmth of people I had come to love as their eyes gazed at me in full attention, but also memories of my Canadian grandmother who had taught me how to pray when I was a child. As I spoke to God, but equally aware of the living and deceased people around me, I said that I had completed my PhD and become a university professor, a job that gave me many opportunities and responsibilities. I prayed for a research grant that would permit me to do research with Indigenous people in Taiwan and also that I would be able to use the grant in a way that somehow could bring benefit to Indigenous communities. I then stepped back into the crowd, making way for the next person who would step up to the cross with a similar promise.

This inspiring moment set my intellectual priorities for more than a decade, motivating me to conduct long periods of field research and to share the message through publication. Memories of URM, regular attendance at Presbyterian churches affiliated with URM, and even solitary prayers in the dark of night as I was awakened by sounds at nearby Asia Cement sustained me through both homesickness in the field and the frustrations of academic publishing. During that same fieldwork, however, other people also encouraged me to reflect more critically on religion or on this particular expression of faith. This chapter is an attempt to do just that.[2]

Churches in Indigenous Communities

Christianity seems to have become an inescapable part of social reality in Indigenous Taiwan. Each Indigenous village is dominated by the presence of one or more churches. Some of them are modest one-story buildings adorned with red crosses; others are dominated by imposing steeples that draw one's attention upward towards the sky. In any case, the presence of churches rather than Buddhist and Taoist temples is usually the first visible sign that one has driven into an Indigenous village. Ethnographers inevitably make their ways to these churches, as pastors and priests are among the most knowledgeable and accessible informants. Accustomed to answering questions from inquisitive graduate students on day trips as well as from seasoned professionals who stay much longer, they have already elaborated articulate answers to most questions they may receive.

Churches are instant places for ethnographers to meet people, since people gather in churches for weekly services, holidays, baptisms, marriages, funerals, and prayer or Bible study groups throughout the week. They are important access points for foreign researchers because they allow researchers to enter Indigenous villages through social networks with long histories of collaboration between Westerners and Indigenous people. In many cases, including my own, there is already an established base of trust before the research begins. As early as 2000, when I was teaching anthropology at Dong Hwa University in Hualien, I had already visited the Ciwang Presbyterian Church in Bsngan several times and met people who encouraged me to do research in their village. In my first period of field research in 2005, I found a place to stay because the Presbyterian pastor introduced me to an elder from his church who had a house to rent. These connections are still an important part of my life. In my 2013 research in Nantou, I stayed in the Presbyterian Church, which had a set of guestrooms that are regularly rented to hikers. That is my base every year when I return to Buarung. Slowly, however, my wayfarings have also taken me to other denominations, which have very different approaches to indigeneity and spirituality. I also met people who are not interested in Christianity at all.

Anthropologists have ambivalent relations with churches. Those who seek to study traditional cultures find churches to be awkward presences, signs of colonial domination or unwelcome globalization. Some anthropologists struggle to work around this contemporary reality by seeking out the oldest informants possible and questioning them about rituals they experienced in childhood in ethnographic practices that glean valuable nuggets of information by bracketing off the experience of contemporary life. When anthropologists tried to filter out foreign influences to understand local cultures, Christianity was intentionally ignored for decades (Robbins 2007, 6). I remember being quite surprised once at a lecture at Academia Sinica because a senior anthropologist concentrated only on reconstructing from the memories of the elderly "traditional" rituals that have not been performed for over five decades, while completely ignoring the Christian churches that dominate the same village today. Maybe the crisis of representation in the 1990s made anthropologists more concerned about the consequences of such approaches. In the past fifteen years or so, there has been a proliferation of research on local conversions and adaptations to Christianity, especially in the anthropology of Oceania, spearheaded by the influential works of John Barker ([2004] 2016) and Joel Robbins (2004). This research shows that, around the world, people have adopted Christian beliefs and symbols on their own terms and in ways that validate their own lifeworlds.

Trying to move beyond debates about whether conversion to Christianity incurs a radical rupture from previous cultural ways or becomes integrated into local cultural frameworks, researchers have shown interest in vernacular, hybridized, or syncretic Christianities in the plural. To do so requires an examination of Christianity as not just a coherent system of beliefs but also as local institutional configurations (Barker 2014). Looking at religions as institutions brings us back to the materiality of belief and practices, since churches become as much a part of the landscape or local ecology as mountain ridges and river-beds. Just as the form of the mountains lead humans to create trails on relatively level terrain, religious institutions conduct humans to meet in particular spaces. They can thus become nodes for multiple pathways in the lives of human (and other) organisms, what Tim Ingold called knots in the meshwork of life (Ingold 2011, 70). They are places where various human paths intersect.

The church was an awkward part of my own positionality in the field, and not just because of my URM training. I was raised Anglican, which meant that I was familiar with weekly Mass similar to the Roman Catholic Church, yet also acquainted with the melodies of Protestant hymns used by the Presbyterian and True Jesus Churches. It was only after I had completed three years of research in Indigenous communities that I discovered my own family's historical connection with the Presbyterian Church of Taiwan. Inheriting my maternal grandmother's Bible collection, I discovered that ephemeral items such as church bulletins had been inserted among the pages. From them, I learned that my grandmother had been Presbyterian before her marriage and that her parents had participated in fundraising at Toronto's Bonar Presbyterian Church for George Lesley Mackay's missionary activities to Formosa. Whether I liked it or not, my own family history was entangled with that of the institution that so strongly shapes the contours of the indigeneity I had been studying. It was no coincidence that the Presbyterian Church was the place where I felt most at home and welcomed in my research. Although it was tempting to bracket out the religious dimensions when presenting my research in academic settings, my church-based activities in Taiwan also made it possible for me to justify my long absences from home to my parents, who were unfamiliar with anthropology. Those church networks also meant that I was closer to the Indigenous social movement than I might have otherwise been.

Theoretical Positioning towards Religion in Anthropology

Religion is one of the most central concerns of anthropology and one of the discipline's most challenging theoretical subfields. Some scholars have looked at religion as an individual question of faith, including those influenced by Freud, who saw faith as a form of neurosis, and those inspired by such thinkers as William James and Mircea Eliade, who thought that it emerged from direct experience with the divine. Focusing on the collective dimensions of religion, Marxist approaches have examined religion as a manifestation of underlying economic dynamics in society, ultimately as a mechanism by which the economically powerful groups in society exercise domination over others. Focusing on Christianity as if it were only a tool of Western colonialism and hegemony, as did the World Council of Churches Declaration of Barbados that launched international indigeneity, is a logical continuation of Marxism. Durkheimian sociology saw religion as the collective soul of society in a much more sanguine light but has said little about colonialism.

Some anthropologists have tried to combine attention to the individual and the collectivity, explaining religion in the context of human cognitive evolution (Atran 2002; Boyer 2001). Scott Atran looks at religions as by-products of human cognitive evolution, including pan-human emotional faculties and cognitive modules that lead humans to perceive supernatural beings in similar ways across cultures. Religions unfold in social contexts in which individuals have the opportunity to express commitment to their larger groups. Like Ingold, Atran uses the metaphor of the pathway, saying that religions do not exist apart from individual minds and their constraining environments, no more than a physical path can exist apart from the organisms that tread it and the ecological forms that restrict its location and course (Atran 2002, 267–8).

All these approaches, as useful as they are for understanding certain dimensions of the complex activities that we call religion, overlook the lived experiences of prayer and fellowship while seeking explanations in such things as neurotransmitters in the brain, colonialism, or social manipulation by political elites. Such notions can be better understood through the wider context provided by a phenomenological approach. Thomas Tweed does so by defining religions as "confluences of organic-cultural flows that intensify joy and confront suffering by drawing on human and suprahuman forces to make homes and cross boundaries" (Tweed 2006, 54). The aquatic metaphor is apt, as it leads us to anticipate a mixing of elements when religions merge, just as we would expect the waters, mineral content, and organisms to mingle at the confluence of rivers. Knowing the history of the Truku as disparate groups who migrated from Nantou to Hualien along different watersheds, I can stand at the confluence of the sparkling blue Skadang River and the grey waters of the Liwu River before they run into the Pacific Ocean. I have done that many times, imagining the encounters between the Toda and the Truku, the Truku with the Han Taiwanese or the Amis on the coast, a history of Japanese military conquest, and even earlier Dutch adventurers panning for gold. Human pathways have long followed rivers, and religions have long been a part of those encounters. Referring to gods, ghosts, and ancestors, as well as to human and non-human animals, religion allows humans to create homes and dwelling places but also to transcend boundaries between human groups and travel far into the legend sphere of imagination. This transcendence is precisely what people are sharing with me when they invite me up into the forests, guide me along rocky riverbeds, or even take me to church. I begin with an exploration of the pre-conversion religion.

Indigenous Religious Traditions

The Atayalic groups lived a religion in the sense of having a cosmology expressed through myths and rituals, of which headhunting was only a part. Their religion had no formalized theology and no creator deity (Kim 1980, 144) but did include stories about the first humans who emerged into life in the central mountains of Taiwan. I began this book with the story of Pusu Qhuni in order to root the book in an ontology shared by the people known today as Sediq and Truku. In another Truku story (Kim 1980, 148–50), the first woman emerged from pig dung and married a dog – beginning the eternal entanglement between humans, dogs, and pigs (Simon 2015c). Truku and Seediq cosmology thus includes a rich mythology about the first humans and their relationship with animals but has no need to look for internal logical consistency, which at any rate is mostly a Protestant preoccupation.[3] Like in most religions (Tweed 2006, 86), the people who wove these stories and transmitted them to others were concerned not about how the world came into existence but rather how particular people in specific instances took a place in that world. They were also concerned with maintaining a spiritual equilibrium with the other entities, human and non-human. We should also not forget the insight that telling these stories is a way of creating relations between the people who tell and those who listen to them.

   There was a spatial dimension to this cosmology, as the ancestral spirits were associated with the west, location of the setting sun and (for those in Hualien) the ancestral home in the mountain forests of Nantou. This place is Alang Utux, the home of the spirits. People became ancestral spirits through their own efforts, as only those who could prove their industriousness in life by weaving (women) or hunting (men) could cross the Rainbow Bridge (Hakaw Utux) into that realm after death. Humans and animals were associated with the east, the location of the rising sun and the ocean. This place is Alang Seejiq, the home of humans (Kim 1980, 170). This tradition is why some elderly people in Hualien told me stories about Nantou as if it were a mythical realm inhabited by all kinds of supernatural beings. Kim hypothesizes that this idea reflects the fact that these nomadic people were always moving through the mountains towards the east. As people moved further from their homeland in Nantou, their knowledge of physical geography transformed into notions of sacredness and metaphysical territory (160). One day in the fall of 2017, for example, as a Truku friend and I were preparing for a hiking trip in Nantou, one of the most elderly people in his community told us a story about *mssungut*, mythical little people as light as feathers who once terrorized and killed their people and thus had to be exterminated (Simon 2018, 162; see also the hermeneutical reading in Shen 1998, 194–8). These are fragments of earlier cosmologies. When we left the elder's house, my friend looked at me incredulously and said: "He seems to *really* believe that." He had never heard the story before.

The survey reports on the Formosan aborigines by the Taiwan Governor-General Office Provisional Taiwan Committee on the Investigation of Taiwan Old Customs include a volume on the Atayal (Kojima [1915] 1996) and separate reports in one volume on the Truku in Hualien and the Sediq in Nantou (Sayama [1917] 2011). These reports, published by the Division for the Aborigines (established in 1909) between 1913 and 1922, included sixteen volumes in two series. Although the authors consulted with anthropologists, they were administrators of the *riban* (savage control) project of the Japanese police (Shimizu 1999, 134). This form of "survey anthropology" was clearly part of the Japanese strategy to bring the Indigenous peoples under colonial rule (Barclay 2007), but the reports have such valuable information about customs before colonial sedentarization policies and conversion to Christianity that they have been translated into Chinese and are frequently consulted by Taiwanese anthropologists. The chapter on Truku religion includes belief in spirits (*utux*), a list of taboos, bird divination, dream interpretation, medicine women, and rain-making, in addition to an independent chapter about headhunting. Information is provided from Tgdaya, Toda, and Truku communities in Hualien. The chapter on Sediq religion follows the same headings, but with an additional category for malefic witches (*mhuni*). Information is provided from Truku, Tawsay (Toda), and Tkdaya (Tgdaya) communities in Nantou.

After the Indigenous peoples were pacified and settled on reserves, Formosa became a living laboratory as Japanese anthropology developed. Furuno Kiyota (1899–1979), sociologist and translator of

Durkheim into Japanese, conducted fieldwork in the 1930s on the ritual life of the Atayal (which included the Sediq and Truku). Influenced by Lévy-Bruhl's work on "primitive" religion, Furuno was interested in their animist beliefs. Rituals for sowing, reaping, seeking rain, and even headhunting were all oriented towards successful horticulture, especially the cultivation of two kinds of millet (Proso millet and Foxtail millet) on difficult mountainous terrain through swidden agriculture (Furuno 1945, 4). The Atayal believed that each person had only one soul (utux), which would enter some form of afterworld by crossing the "Rainbow Bridge" if he or she had lived properly by hunting or weaving. There were good utux, especially those who died at home while holding the hands of a loved one, but there were also bad utux, who had died alone or committed suicide and might linger in the mountains (7–11). At the harvest festival in July, the utux would all be invited to return to the village and eat (192). Humans, and even other animals, had to maintain a proper balance in this world by living a life according to the ancestral law of *Gaya*. People were in constant communion with the natural environment through these rituals, but also through individual practices in which they consulted ancestors through dreams at night and through sisil birds by day (Kaji 2011, 13). The main idea is that "although the human body dies, the spirit is not extinguished" (Takun 2012, 276).

There were political dimensions to these religious practices. The year was punctuated by regular rituals of horticulture, warfare, and healing, which meant that ritual leaders could enhance their local prestige and influence. In a strongly egalitarian society with no permanent positions of political power, men could gain power by organizing headhunting expeditions, in which case they became "Big Men" (*Qbsuran*), which literally means "big brother." Young men were motivated to join the expeditions by the promise of obtaining a tattoo and the possibility of marriage. Women could become medicine women (*msapuh*), specializing in rituals of healing and communication with the spirit world. Dakis Pawan discovered something that nobody ever told me during fieldwork: the horticultural rituals were sources of political power. Among the Tgdaya, the patriarchal hereditary position of horticultural ritual leader permitted Alang Paran to gain a leading position in a confederation of *alang* and allowed Walis Buni to become the grand chief of the Tgdaya (Kuo 2012, 140–1).[4]

Although I did not encounter any Seejiq or Truku traditionalists who repudiate Christianity and publicly affirm traditional religion like some Indigenous people in the Americas, syncretism was widespread. Many myths have been largely forgotten among the ordinary people, even as pastors, local scholars, and cultural nationalists peruse the Japanese-era ethnographies for stories that can become inspiration for sermons, new weaving patterns, and political speeches. Ironically, the translators of the Bible into local languages were frustrated by the reluctance of Christian converts to recite the old myths, which would have been useful for learning more about grammar, syntax, and vocabulary (Covell 1998, 265).

The most important rituals have disappeared. The horticultural rituals related to sowing, harvesting, and beseeching rain, which once gave ceremonial leaders great prestige, are no longer performed. During my research, I encountered only two msapuh, and one passed away the year after I interviewed her (figure 4.2).[5] Although the msapuh were consulted for many problems, they specialized in healing rituals. In the most basic ritual, she would hold a bamboo stick in her fist, ask a question of the spirits, and then open her hand with her palm vertical to the ground. If the stick fell under the force of gravity, the answer was no. If it stuck to her palm, the answer was yes. In this way, she could ask if the disease were caused by a spirit and, if so, whether the spirit desired a sacrifice of a chicken or a pig. Nowadays, because people have good health insurance and most Truku have converted to Christianity, most of their clients are non-Indigenous Taiwanese, as reported by the women themselves (Kaji 2011, 258).

Contrary to the optimistic expectations of missionaries, conversion did not eliminate all earlier beliefs and practices. Fear of spirits, blending seamlessly with Chinese concern about ghosts, is very common, especially regarding the tombs in the foothills near the villages and the mountain forests at night. Dakis Pawan attributes beliefs about maleficent ghosts to the influence of Christianity (Kuo 2012, 63). Some people acknowledge the presence of the ancestral spirits each time they drink alcohol by casting a few drops into the air and onto the ground. I will return to the question of ghosts later in this chapter. Some hunters still do small private rituals before entering the mountains. The most important way of communicating with the ancestors, however, is with the pig sacrifices that remain ubiquitous to this day. The Christian gospel may draw peoples' attention to a higher God, but it does not replace more mundane ancestral spirits unless local congregations make strong efforts to eliminate all old ritual traditions. Kaji Cihung sees three Christian approaches to the old religions. People either reject old practices as idolatry, see the ancestral spirits and deities of the churches as coexisting in parallel, or see them as stemming from two different hierarchical realities. This third approach, which accepts both "God above" (Utux baraw) and "ancestral spirits" (utux rudan), is that proffered by msapuh

Figure 4.2. *Msapuh* (medicine woman or shaman). Rabay Rubing, one of the last shamans, explains Gaya and her craft to a group of visiting law students, 8 November 2012.

Source: Photograph by Scott E. Simon.

Rabay Rubing, who says that God is the root (*pusu*; Kaji 2011, 31–2). In addition to being a traditional healer, Rabay is a devout Roman Catholic and has decorated her home in Catholic symbolism, with particular fondness for the Virgin. These different approaches can all be seen in attitudes towards the pig sacrifices, the most common public rituals in most communities.

Pig Sacrifices: The Core Religious Practice

The most important traditional rituals in contemporary Truku and Sejiq communities are rituals of pig sacrifice, a practice that exists in diverse variations throughout Southeast Asia and Oceania. People are always conscious of the presence of the ancestors, who are believed to have continuing powers to determine the well-being of the living through blessings or curses. If someone has violated Gaya, people in the community will suffer from hunting failure, accidents, illnesses, or even death. In order to maintain a good relationship with the ancestors, they must communicate with the ancestors through ritual sacrifices, the most common being the offering of a domestic pig. This ritual in Hualien is called *powda Gaya*, the literal meaning "moving through Gaya" suggesting transition or movement (figure 4.3). Taiwanese anthropologist Lin Ching-Hsiu classifies the powda Gaya rituals as either celebrations of blessings or atonement for infringements of Gaya (Lin 2011, 34). People tell me that they must notify the ancestors and ask their blessings or forgiveness for any major change in their lives. In the past, people would sacrifice a pig when individuals were adopted or left their alang and joined a new one, which is still the meaning of pig sacrifices at marriage. In this sense, the pig sacrifice is a paradigmatic *rite de passage* as a ceremony that takes people from one stage in life to another (Van Gennep 1969). These rites of passage happen within a larger context. Since hunting failure is the first sign of a violation of Gaya, the correct ritual equilibrium is necessary to ensure a continuing supply of wild game. Some Truku people thus describe the pig sacrifices as generalized reciprocity between generations. The living must provide domestic pigs (*babuy*) to the ancestors, who give wild boars (*bowyak*) in return. Darryl Sterk, studying in Nantou, interpreted both animal sacrifices and headhunting as blood sacrifices of *dmahur* (to) or *dmahun* (tg), rituals of reconciliation (Sterk 2020, 110–14). Following the explanations of my Truku informants, I have looked at these pig sacrifices (Simon 2015c) as a Maussian dynamic of exchange, in which the living people provide domestic pigs to the ancestors in exchange for wild boars provided to those who uphold the proper rituals.

Figure 4.3   The ritual of powda Gaya. A pig is being cut up for members of the community to celebrate a completion of a stream conservation project in the Taroko National Park.

Source: Photograph by Scott E. Simon.

The largest powda Gaya rituals are held at marriage, when up to a dozen pigs may be slaughtered. Depending on the ability of the groom, who provides the pigs as a form of bridewealth (Lin 2011, 39), these rituals reinforce the boundaries of the alang, or the smaller groups of "people who eat together" (Atayal: *nniqan gaga* [*Gaya*]; Kojima [1915] 1996], 232; Huang 2000, 7). Following Mabuchi, Lin calls this the "gxal group" (Lin 2011, 36). Members of the kin group expect to receive an equal share of the meat and can be called upon to contribute to the labour of the sacrifice. Since conflicts may occur if a household is forgotten, organizers make careful lists of meat recipients before the event.

There are many reasons to kill pigs. In addition to marriage rituals, people hold small rituals with close friends and relatives to mark a divorce, usually killing only one pig. They may also kill a pig to mark milestones in their personal lives, such as the purchase of a new car or a significant raise in salary. I once saw a household kill a pig and asked why. The mother, who seemed very happy, said: "Because my daughter had sex with a foreign worker." The sacrifice was thus simultaneously an atonement for the violation of Gaya against pre-marital sex and the public announcement of their engagement.

The divorce sacrifice reveals something about how ritual mediates various kinds of relationships. One dawn in April 2007 in Ciyakang, I was awakened by the screeching sound of a pig. When I went outside to investigate, the neighbours invited me to join them, contrary to most events, inside the house rather than in the courtyard. After the pig had been killed and cooked, we had a meal of barbecued pork, blood-rice porridge, and beer. Someone said that only the Truku cook rice in the blood. The newly divorced man explained to me that they must sacrifice a pig because divorce is a grave violation of Gaya and angers the ancestral spirits. Since the entire extended family is responsible for supporting each other, they carry the burden of guilt collectively. Without a sacrifice, the spirits would certainly cause illness or a serious accident to someone. But divorce is not a public event like a marriage, which is why they must eat inside. He said that the pigs cry especially loudly at a divorce, reflecting the strong feelings that the estranged couple still have for one another. "Only with the death of a pig does the blood turn black into red," he said, and the day becomes a happy occasion. The colour red here refers to the literal colour of blood but also to the colour as a symbol of happiness, which they all know from the use of red in Chinese-style weddings. He said that pigs do not cry at wedding sacrifices but instead die willingly for the happy occasion.

To give a more personal example, when I asked people in the first village how I could thank the villagers at the conclusion of my research project, my host Kuhon said: "Kill a pig." As Kim noted, any activity done for a special purpose is not complete if a pig has not been killed (Kim 1980, 191). I thus sacrificed a pig at the conclusion of my six-month research trips in three villages. At first, I found it psychological difficult to watch an animal be killed and die, especially knowing that I was responsible in real ways for its suffering and death. By the third time, however, I was able to help catch the pig and even hold it while it was being killed. In the past, individuals could join an alang through adoption by making the required sacrifice of a pig to seek the approval of the ancestors. People may have been thinking in those terms when, after public pig killings in the courtyards of my host family, they started calling me Walis Kuhon in Kele and Walis Takun in Gluban, both times in recognition of my relationship as someone learning from the older man in the family like father and son.

In Alang Ciyakang, where I did research in 2006, the social dynamics were different because I lived in a rented house. My landlord, moreover, who had just won a township election, was nervous about publicly killing a pig and sharing the meat, telling me it could be interpreted as illegal "vote buying" behaviour and get him into legal trouble.[6] He asked me to sponsor a barbecue in the courtyard of one of his supporters, best known as a representative of the DPP, and he himself stayed away. The people who had helped me with my research thanked me for sponsoring a neighbourhood party, but some people even took the meat home to eat it privately. It was as if, in each case, people had to decide whether a foreigner-sponsored pig kill is a ritual or a barbecue. Clearly, it depends upon the power of the host.

The pig sacrifice is, except when part of a divorce, always done in the front courtyard of a home or in a large public space such as the village basketball court. A large plastic tarp is laid out on the ground in preparation. Before dawn, the killing begins. Pigs scream in protest and horror as the men grab them by their legs to kill them. This audible sign attracts crowds of people and dogs who watch the ritual and socialize with one another. Usually, one man respected for his skills will kill the pig by plunging a large knife through the throat and down into the heart. The men carefully manipulate the pig so that the blood pulsating from its arteries will drain into a large bucket. After the pig has died and the blood has been drained, the men usually burn off the skin and any hair with a blowtorch. Some people also told me that they feel uncomfortable listening to the cries of the pigs. People judge the skill and moral rectitude of the man who kills the pig by evaluating the rapidity of the pig's death. If it dies quickly with little struggle, it is considered to be a clean death. If it struggles loudly and dies slowly, people cast doubt on the butcher. People say that a painful death produces bad taste in the meat because the flesh is filled with hormones produced by pain and stress. Empathizing with the pigs, they say that the pigs are "pitiful" because they must face death as a result of what happens between humans. Whether the humans are experiencing joy at marriage or sadness at divorce, the pigs must still die.

People describe the subsequent butchering of the meat in gendered terms, often citing the Chinese proverb that "men are in charge of the outside, women are in charge of the inside." The men collectively cut up the animal, beginning by chopping off the head and the legs. In a liminal moment, a man picks up the entire package of internal organs and carries them to an area outside the tarp where women are waiting with a water hose and buckets. It is a liminal moment because at some point, to separate the meat from the organs, either a woman must touch the meat or a man must touch the internal organs, both of which are described as taboo. So a man quickly does the job. The women then clean the internal organs while the men continue to cut the meat.

Figure 4.4 Traditional ancestor worship. An elder discretely leaves a piece of pork for the ancestors at a high spot.

Source: Photograph by Scott E. Simon.

It is very important to cut each piece of the animal into equal portions. If they plan to provide meat to thirty households of their kin-based alang, for example, they must divide the leg meat, the heart, and so on into thirty equal portions. Some of the meat is provided to everyone in attendance. They serve a blood soup, with the addition of intestines and stomach, which is eaten immediately. This soup is an important part of the ritual, as humans and spirits make contact only through the medium of blood (Kim 1980, 371). In some cases, they barbecue the ribs to share and enjoy afterwards. The undesirable body parts, such as the lungs and the ovaries, are given to the dogs. Although people express concern and even disgust about the slaughter, the ritual quickly transforms the pig into meat for distribution and feasting.

The religious dimensions of powda Gaya vary greatly according to community, household, and even individual preferences. Some families invite the Presbyterian pastor to pray before the pigs are slaughtered. Some people will wrap up a very small portion of meat and internal organs in a large leaf and discretely hang it from the eaves of a home or another high place as an offering to the ancestors (figure 4.4). Followers of the True Jesus Church reject entirely the rituals of ancestor worship, which they perceive to be the sin of idolatry, but pork is nonetheless purchased from a slaughterhouse and shared before weddings, suggesting that the effects of the sacrifice remain important even without the ritual appeal to ancestors. True Jesus believers are also much more careful to ensure that the pig they purchase is killed quickly and that the blood is drained rather than eaten, in accordance with their reading of the Old Testament, which somehow overlooks the prohibitions on eating pork. This mixture of old and new rituals, as well as the vigilant distinction between what is permitted and what is labelled as sinful superstition in pig sacrifices, demonstrates what happens at the confluence of different religious institutions and practitioners. This flow and ebb of religious practices and mutual influences has been part of Indigenous life since at least the colonial era.

Colonialism and Religious Change

The Japanese period, the first time in history that the Formosans were subject to state interference in their beliefs and practices, was a turning point. The Japanese stigmatized most traditional beliefs and practices as superstitious, tolerated organized religions (rather reluctantly in the case of Christianity, especially after the war began), and encouraged participation in civil ceremonies. All groups abandoned rituals of headhunting, apparently with no regret. Among the Atayalic peoples, the forced elimination of facial tattooing was more difficult. One elderly woman with traces of scars on her face told me that she was first obliged by her family to tattoo her face. The tattooing was painful, she said, but it was also a moment of joy and pride as she entered full womanhood. When the Japanese forced her to remove the tattoo, she felt only sadness and shame.

Japanese religion was also introduced. Colonial photographs document the construction of Shinto shrines in communities. In what is now the Taroko National Park, a Shinto shrine was erected in honour of Governor-General Count Sakuma Samata, who led the Battle of Taroko against the Truku people living there. People recall that their elders were forced by the Japanese police to pray at that shrine annually on 28 January. From a Japanese perspective, this annual prayer was a civil ceremony that incorporated the Truku into the modern Japanese Empire and demonstrated their loyalty. They encouraged the Sejiq to hunt in the forests, following their own customs and worshipping the ancestors, especially if they attended shrines as a patriotic duty (Covell 1998, 155). Their main goal was to Japanize Taiwan's Indigenous peoples, and Christianity was perceived as an impediment to that nationalist goal.

Older people told me that the Japanese associated Christianity with the United States and thus suspected any convert of being potentially an American spy.

In general, people avoided talking about Shintoism with me, and nobody seemed interested in the animist beliefs at its core. Most of them described it as an unwelcome colonial imposition. Only one person, an elderly Truku msapuh in Ciyakang, expressed traces of nostalgia. She described the Shinto manner of praying by clapping and ringing a bell, adding that Shinto gods were very efficacious. After the arrival of the ROC on Taiwan, she recounted, the new Chinese government demolished the shrine and tried to convert the site into agricultural land. No matter what crop they planted or how much fertilizer they used, however, the land remained barren. "The Japanese left," she concluded, "but their spirits remained." Perhaps these are among the ghosts that people fear in the forests. The following story, although I have published it elsewhere (Simon 2012b), is worth retelling in this context as it illustrates certain notions about the reality of the spirits of the dead.

A Personal Encounter with Utux

During my second period of fieldwork, I had attended a conference on indigeneity in Paris and, although suffering from jet lag, accepted an invitation to visit the hunting lodge of a friend up in the mountains. After having shared a large meal and a bottle of whisky, I was ready to go to bed and get a good sleep. My friend, whom I shall call by the pseudonym Ichiro, however, had another idea. He went into his room and emerged with a home-made hunting rifle, suggesting that we hunt some flying squirrels. With Ichiro in the lead, his son, his dog, and I followed him through the forest. By this time, my legs had learned to walk in the mountain forest, but I felt more and more tired as the effects of the whisky wore off. Eventually, I just wanted to lie down and sleep, but Ichiro pushed us forward.

The three humans in our party wore headlamps and shone them upward as we stealthily walked through the forest. Eventually, Ichiro pointed out the reflection of eyes up in the branches, aimed his rifle carefully, and shot into the branches. We could hear the squirrel fall through the leafy branches and land with a thump on the ground. Ichiro told me and his son to wait while he and his dog searched for the squirrel in the ravine. He soon emerged from the bush perplexed and empty-handed. We continued for about an hour, lights focused on the tree branches ahead. Ichiro pointed out another pair of eyes, shot the squirrel, which fell noisily to the ground and again was not to be found.

When the same thing happened a third time, he began to get nervous and said it is impossible that the squirrels would escape alive. He said that it must have happened because he neglected to make an offering to the spirits before entering the forest. He took a bottle of rice wine from his backpack, sprinkled it in front of him, and said a prayer to the spirits, including to his father, who had died on the same mountain by falling off a cliff. Ichiro insisted that he wanted to return with at least one squirrel.

Again, he found a squirrel, shot it, and it disappeared. As the sky began to grow light, Ichiro's son and I both asked to go back. Ichiro finally gave in but demanded that we run so that we could get back before dawn. I tripped over a vine and, trying to stop the fall, broke my wrist. The next day I had to go to the hospital for an operation on the broken bone. As I emerged from the anaesthesia, I dreamt about a man's voice, whom I understood to be Ichiro's father, telling me: "We Truku ancestors protected you in the forest to keep you alive. We need you to defend us too."

When I returned to Ciyakang with my arm in a cast, people greeted me with both concern and amusement. Many of the men teased me, saying that I must have had sex with a woman, since a violation of Gaya is often punished by a fall in the mountains. They were unwilling to accept my explanations that I was tired after a long trip back from France and after drinking whisky. Instead, one man just pointed to the cast and said: "You can't deny it. The proof is right there in your broken arm." Unlike Sita Duku, the woman headhunter discussed in chapter 3, I had obviously failed my moral ordeal. Other people, in much more serious tones, told us that we had failed to understand the meaning of the disappearing squirrels. Those were not flying squirrels at all, they said, but evil spirits who were following us in the forest. If you kill an animal and it disappears, it is in fact not an animal at all. After the first sciurine disappearance, we should have returned to the village immediately.

The msapuh offered a more detailed description of events. The evil spirits we encountered, she said, were the spirits of the Japanese soldiers who had died in the mountains. They knew about the war between the Japanese and the Americans but did not know that the war had ended. They thus tried to kill me. I would have fallen to my death if the Truku spirits had not intervened and saved my life, which is why I merely broke a bone. Of course, it makes little sense that the Japanese spirits would know about a war that began more than two decades after their deaths but not be informed about its conclusion. Nonetheless, it also gave new meaning to my dream, which I had recounted to no one, and the msapuh had no way of knowing. This experience, with the subsequent explanations given to me by Truku people about why it happened, gave me an emotionally salient insight into the continuing existence of traditional spiritual beliefs. Despite decades of Christian practice, everyone's explanation of why I broke my arm all included the presence of watchful ancestral spirits in the forest. Maybe I really had met Japanese ghosts and the spirit of Ichiro's father up on the mountain. At least, I had learned intimately about the context in which such beliefs are elucidated.

To summarize so far, the anecdotes described in this chapter reveal the strong presence of supernatural beings in human lives. Around the pig rituals, some people sense the existence of ancestral spirits who require regular porcine sacrifices in order to maintain spiritual equilibrium of some kind and to ensure continued success in the hunt for boars. People find pig sacrifices meaningful for moments of social transition that can include marriages, divorce, and even the conclusion of my research projects, saying that the ancestors must be kept informed and appeased when necessary because they enforce Gaya. My own run-in with the spirits led people to speculate about whether I was being punished for some unadmitted sexual impropriety and whether the Truku and the Japanese spirits are still fighting wars in Taiwan's central mountains. The shaman spoke out about Japanese supernatural beings. Just as she could detect the presence of Shinto Kamisama 神様 in the fields, she could also speak into existence military ghosts who fight to the death and beyond. Moreover, this experience tied me intimately to the people around me, especially Ichiro in a very particular way, as I also had come to perceive the same supernatural beings that other people had been telling me about. In fact, his wife told me afterwards that the fall would bind me and Ichiro together for the rest of our lives. I did not sense the presence of ghosts as I walked in the mountains, but I did hear Ichiro's father speak in a dream. Over three years, I offered pigs for sacrifice annually without even thinking about Truku or Tkedaya ancestors, but I did sense the presence of my deceased Canadian grandmother when I prayed in front of a wooden cross in Tainan. When I prayed with Christians of all denominations, we all acted as if we were speaking to someone capable of listening and answering our requests. A phenomenological approach is open to the possibility that we are indeed encountering *something*. As Tim Ingold wrote in his wonderfully titled essay "Dreaming of Dragons," we must abandon our imagined distinction between real life and the imagination if we wish to make space for religion, as well as for the beliefs and practices of indigenous peoples (Ingold 2013, 735).[7]

Conversion to Christianity: Local Accounts

The people themselves struggle to understand their mass conversion to Christianity. Some of them, especially Roman Catholics, say that their parents converted to Christianity at the conclusion of the Second World War because they had been reduced to poverty and sought food and clothing provided by the missionaries. Quite commonly, others point out commonalities between their old religion and Christianity, saying that they recognized in Christianity a better expression of their own Gaya. One member of the True Jesus Church said that people initially resisted Christianity but ultimately recognized it as the same Gaya, the difference being that the rules are written down in a book rather than in their own hearts. "Christianity helped us answer the one and only question unanswered by our old religion – what is the name of God?" he said. "The answer is Jesus." A Presbyterian Church elder was more explicit when he explained Gaya to me. He said that people accepted Christianity because it is based on the same three Gaya principles that formed the basis of their former ethical system: the importance of generosity, the need to take care of one's family and community, and fidelity in marriage. Ralph Covell even called it a "'functional substitute' for the old practice of head hunting" (Covell 1998, 164). He thought it gave them a new sense of identity, as they faced pressure to assimilate to a Chinese society. Dmahun, the blood ritual of reconciliation, became the word for Eucharist in both the Catholic and Presbyterian churches (Sterk 2020, 115).

Some people were less sanguine about their old religion. One elderly woman in her eighties, who may have witnessed headhunting rituals as a child, described the men running back to the village with a head and everyone dancing ecstatically around it. When I asked her about Gaya, she shook her head and said: "*Gaya truku naqih balay*" (Truku Gaya was really terrible). She said that some people still make sacrifices of rice wine or tobacco to the utux before farming or hunting, but that Christians should not do so. I was sometimes scolded by Christians when they saw me dipping my finger into my beer and splattering drops on the ground for the ancestors. Another woman criticized her neighbours for syncretism, saying: "There is only one God. You should not pray twice." Her son-in-law added: "You cannot worship both God and Mammon." Yaya, whose conversion story I recounted in chapter 3, said that her shaman grandmother converted to Christianity "because she immediately saw that Jesus had a magic that was even greater than hers."

There is strong power in the syncretic blend of Gaya and Christianity. In Hualien, Truku people talk about the misfortunes that may befall people who violate Gaya in important ways. This misfortune is called *rmuba*. In one case, a local politician took advantage of his position to rebuild the cable car that people needed to transport farming implements and goods up and down the mountain. People accused him of overcharging for this service. They also suspected him of enriching himself through various forms of corruption. When his son injured his head severely after falling down a cliff while hunting, people perceived it as proof that the father had seriously violated Gaya. The son eventually came out of his coma but had the intellectual capacity of only a five-year-old boy.

At church, people began to suspect that maybe his soul had left his body. As it turned out, the boy's great-uncle had committed suicide at the same spot decades earlier. Since the souls of people who die "bad" deaths may linger around the spot where they died and cause harm to the living, people deduced that the uncle must have captured the soul of the boy. They thus sought the help of a church elder, renowned for the strength of her prayers. She gathered the members of the congregation, and they went to the spot where the boy had fallen to pray. She gave them strict instructions to pray only to God and told them that they must not make even the smallest sacrifice to the ancestors. It is the only way, she said, that the prayers will be efficacious. Afterwards, the boy gained the mental capacity of a young teenager, albeit still younger than his age, and they declared the Christian prayer to have worked.

Even the most fundamentalist of believers do not reject the old religion entirely. Yaya described headhunting as a sin and shamanic rituals as a lesser magic, but did not deny the ontological validity of those practices. Her son-in-law, also a fervent Christian believer, did not deny the efficacy of headhunting either. He even said that the heads can still move and cry. The two realities coexist, which is why it is as important for some Christian believers to avoid any discussion of the old beliefs as it is to attend church. When they refuse to even utter certain words, like *sisil* or msapuh, it reveals a fear and a belief that these entities still have power and that old spirits may emerge if called upon. This coexistence is also why some people combine old and new practices, most notably hunters who may be devout Christians while in the village yet perform ancestral sacrifices in the forest. Yaya's daughter, one of the most fervent Christians I have met, told me how the old spirits still enter their worlds. When a relative passed away, she and his daughter were the only two people remaining at his wake at four o'clock in the morning. Suddenly, the *hghug*, the bird of death described as white with red feathers on its feet, flew around the front of the house and landed on the eaves in the back. She heard the dead man moving in his coffin.

She called his daughter, who heard it too, "but some force prevented us from walking into the room to see what was happening." The bird cried and flew away, after which they were able to enter the living room. This bird, she said, comes to guide the souls of the dead into Heaven.

Christianity and Indigenous Religion

Religious concepts take on new meanings in changing contexts. This situation is where words are most powerful. The Protestants have historically taken the lead in translation efforts, believing that people approach God more closely in their own mother languages, even in the face of government persecution when the Chinese Nationalist Party (KMT) was trying to convince all the people of Taiwan that they are Chinese (and thus trying to ban local languages; Covell 1998, 243). The Protestants incorporate some Indigenous concepts into their translations of Christian ideas. They refer to God as Utux baraw, which means the "Supreme Spirit." They also translate the Ten Commandments as the ten Gaya (*maxal Gaya*). For the Roman Catholic Church, translation has been less of a pressing issue, as the services are mostly in Mandarin Chinese. Whereas Protestants refer to God in Chinese as Shangdi 上帝 (highest emperor), the Catholics refer to Tianzhu (celestial lord). There have always been communications between these missionaries. Catholic missionary Ferdinando Pecoraro, in his Truku-French dictionary, thus illustrates the word utux with such similar attempts to translate God. These include Utux baraw, Utux tnpusu (original spirit), and Utux tminun (weaving spirit or creator spirit; Pecoraro 1977, 188; see also Kaji 2011, 242).[8] In the bilingual sermons of the True Jesus Church, and quite ironically considering the Chinese origins of that church, I heard God translated as the Japanese Kamisama 神様. Christians of all three denominations thus employ a syncretic vocabulary that emerged from local concepts, missionary work in the Chinese-speaking world, and even Japanese Shintoism.

The materiality of the churches is important for a phenomenological approach, especially in contrast to the old practices. Traditional religion looked westward, which meant upward into the mountains and towards the setting sun. There were also skull racks in front of the homes of local leaders. But what is most noticeable is that the old religions happened among the dense vegetation of the forests. This location is perhaps why some people, especially hunters, are comfortable with syncretic practices in which they worship the Christian God in the village church but still give offerings to the ancestors in the forest. At least, they can spatially segregate their seemingly contradictory practices.

Figure 4.5. Christianity at a time of ethnic politics, 2006. At the Ciwang Presbyterian Church, a sign to the right of the cross in Truku highlights the importance of ethnic "identity."

Source: Photograph by Scott E. Simon.

Churches are an innovation because they draw the attention of the worshippers directly upward towards the heavens. In Bsngan, this upward motion is most evident in the Ciwang Presbyterian Church that dominates the skyline. Because the church is built on a mountain slope, worshippers must first climb a steep set of stairs. There is a small chapel on the first floor, but services are more commonly held on the second floor, which has an imposing cathedral ceiling and long narrow windows. The decor is Protestant minimalism, with mostly white walls, but above and behind the altar in front is an imposing red cross. On both sides of the cross are slogans written in Chinese and Truku. During the time of my research, when the Truku had just been recognized as an independent people and were advocating for the creation of an autonomous region, one of the slogans said *rentong* 認同 (identity), promoting the politics of recognition (figure 4.5). The front area is elevated, with an altar, a pulpit for the pastor, and a piano. As people sit in the pews, therefore, their attention is drawn collectively towards the pastor and upward towards both the cross and the political slogan of the time. Ciwang Presbyterian Church also has a special outdoor feature: the cave where Ciwang, the first local convert, clandestinely held services during the Japanese period. People sometimes step outside and make a private visit to the cave between the Sunday service and the shared noon meal that usually happens on the plaza in front of that cave. Other churches all seem to follow this same general pattern. Fushih has two other Presbyterian churches in Minle, a neighbourhood settled in 1979 by the hamlets of Skadang and Xoxos when they were displaced in preparation for the creation of the Taroko National Park. In these smaller churches, as in the Presbyterian churches in the other villages I studied, there is still a large cross and a consistent attempt to draw everyone's attention to the front and upward.

The interior configuration of the churches is also important. The True Jesus Church is best known for practices of glossolalia (speaking in tongues). Their churches are also austere and plain and, like Presbyterian churches, draw the attention of the worshipper towards the front and upward. The men are seated on the left side of the church and the women on the right, but everyone looks forward to the altar for nearly the entire service. On the altar in each True Jesus church is a large bell. At the beginning of each service, the officiant rings the bell. Immediately, the entire congregation begins speaking in tongues. Closing their eyes, they clasp their hands in front of their chests, but with a constant up-and-down movement. Some people sway back and forth, whereas others flap their elbows. The sounds people make vary, but there tends to be a synchronization of pitch across the hall. The echoes reverberating through the hall make it difficult to identify where particular sounds are coming from or even if the voices are coming from the men's or the women's side. It feels as if a spiritual power, with the force of a strong yet gentle wind, has descended upon the crowd. It lasts for about ten minutes, concluding with a second ring of the bell. The rest of the service consists of Protestant hymns, a very long sermon sometimes given by guest speakers, and prayers. To conclude, there is a second period of speaking in tongues. As a non-member, I was told to simply recite the phrase "Hallelujah True Jesus" while everyone else spoke in tongues. Sometimes, however, I also felt as if my body were seized by an external force that made me move my arms and emit the same sounds as my neighbours. People called this sensation a blessing from the Holy Spirit, saying that it happens spontaneously to some people whereas others seek for years and never experience it. But the feelings are enhanced by the enclosure of sound within the churches.

The Roman Catholic churches in the villages are more modest in size, yet more colourfully decorated. In Fushih Village, which has imposing Protestant churches, the sole Catholic church is tucked away in an alley.

Figure 4.6. Roman Catholic Church, Nakahara, Nantou, 2007. On the right, the banner reads in Chinese characters: "Jesus is the Savior of all humanity."

Source: Photograph by Scott E. Simon.

While I was there, Mass was celebrated every two weeks by a French priest for a very small congregation. In Ciyakang, the equally small church was packed at the biweekly Mass. Near Gluban in Nantou, the church was a beautiful brick edifice in the neighbouring village of Nakahara (figure 4.6). It was built on a hillside with a commanding view of the Beigang River and the two Seediq villages of Gluban and Nakahara. These churches had statues of a bleeding Jesus on the cross and of the Virgin Mary, as well as the Stations of the Cross. They incorporated Truku or Seediq material culture, especially weavings, into the altar decorations and priestly vestments. The materiality of the Catholic churches, in contrast to the austere Protestant churches, is much more sensual. In addition to the visual appeal of the church art, vestments, and altar paraphernalia, there is the smell of incense and the taste of the bread and wine used in the sacraments. There is also the tactile experience of reciting the rosary by feeling the beads one by one. Frankly, I felt the existence of the Divine in the churches of all three denominations. As an anthropologist, I may feel compelled to explain those feelings as the result of the social environment around me, but the feelings are no less real.

The common social characteristic of churches is that they bring people together in collective activities that are, in principle, open to anyone who wishes to participate. In practice, however, people point out that there is a strong overlap between church membership and historical membership to a clan and alang. This overlap explains why in Minle, a recently established neighbourhood in Fushih, there are two Presbyterian churches within 200 metres from one another. One was established by people from Skadang and the other by people from Xoxos. They have only once attempted to merge the two churches, at a time when the pastor was from one village and his wife from another. Their joint activities lasted seventeen years but ended when that pastor retired. People identified to me the one Skadang man who continued to attend the Xoxos church years after the (re)establishment of an independent Skadang congregation as the exception who proves the rule. In all the churches, weekly services usually conclude with a collective meal, recalling colonial observations that, even within an alang, people tend to form small groups of "people who eat together" (Kojima [1915] 1996], 232; Huang 2000, 7). There is still room for individual choice. I met one farmer who had become a Seventh-day Adventist, attending church outside the village; one woman who had converted to the Japanese Soka Gakkai branch of Buddhism; and one woman who had adopted the folk religion of her Taiwanese husband.

Churches, just like alang from which emerge Big Men, need leaders. It is probably not a coincidence that the strongly egalitarian Atayalic peoples are mainly attracted to egalitarian Protestant institutions. The Presbyterian pastors are mostly trained at Taiwanese seminaries. Yu Shan Seminary in Hualien is known for its leadership in Indigenous and liberation theology. The Presbyterian Church attempts to place pastors in churches from their own linguistic group, if not their own community, so that they can deliver sermons and conduct services in Indigenous languages. They emphasize identity politics and language revitalization, making them somewhat "counterhegemonic" at times when the government focuses on Chinese identity politics (Stainton 1995). Yet, the church elders act very much like the councils of elders in the former alang because they can overpower the influence of Big Men. The True Jesus Church does not have pastors, but instead relies on local volunteers to deliver sermons and direct services.

The hierarchal nature of the Catholic Church resonates less with Atayalic egalitarianism. In addition, it is difficult for parishes to find qualified priests because of the celibacy requirement. As a result, they must rely on non-Indigenous and often even foreign priests. Since learning Chinese is already a challenge for foreigners, the priests rarely learn the local language. Since priests usually must take care of plural congregations, moreover, the Catholic churches have fewer activities and are nearly always empty. In Gluban, people recall quite fondly one American priest who learned to speak Seediq, even if they couldn't always understand him because of his accent. They were also impressed because he was just as skilled at hunting as any local man. While I was there, the priest was Vietnamese and hoping very much to get a position outside of Taiwan.

Orientation in Space and Time

A phenomenological perspective allows us to think of time and space from the perspective of the participants. In pre-colonial days, there was a strong overlap in the life sphere of the alang because horticultural rituals were performed on the land held by each group. These rituals thus defined membership in the alang. Headhunting and commerce took people beyond their homelands, and those experiences became new forms of knowledge, even though less present in everyday life and probably more selectively retained in memory (Mabuchi 1974, 182). The legend sphere has people thinking about their ancestral homes in the central mountains or about the ill-defined location of the Rainbow Bridge.

Christianity, which arrived in the communities after the sedentarization policies of the colonial period and the state-led stigmatization of old practices, provides new ways of making a home and orienting oneself in space. The local church activities define the space of the alang, since people attend church services on the weekends, as well as other activities throughout the week. Nearly every evening there is some kind of activity for Bible study, youth groups, or women's prayer groups. In all denominations, members of the congregations also take turns hosting prayer and study activities in their homes. Even in villages where people of different communities have been forced to share village spaces like community centres and basketball courts, these church activities demarcate space of specific groups. The True Jesus believers, because of their prohibition of alcohol, also tend to create social spaces where they can meet and socialize while drinking tea. These practices create a strong sense of in-groups and out-groups, which is spatially structured even within a single village. They are new ways of creating a sense of home, a dwelling place in the world.

Church members also decorate their sacred sites with great care. In the Roman Catholic churches of Nantou, weavings selected for the altar express their Sediq identity. People create their spiritual dwellings in sometimes idiosyncratic ways that reveal their own pathways through life. In the tiny Skadang Presbyterian Church, for example, the pastor and his family had made a pilgrimage to Israel and returned to decorate the altar with prayer shawls and a menorah, which made the church feel somewhat like a synagogue.

Island-wide church networks enlarge the observation and hearsay sphere for people of all three denominations. The Presbyterians are linked into networks across Taiwan through a system of local synods, theological seminaries, and a central church in Taipei. Sometimes they even organize trips to other parts of Taiwan as tourists, visiting other churches but also welcoming visiting delegations into their own midst. The True Jesus Church has a main church in Taipei, and the leaders circulate around the island, often showing up as guest speakers in other communities. The Roman Catholic Church, with a strong hierarchy and various orders of clergy, also has larger events. In formal events, the bishops enter the church with the flags of the Vatican and the ROC, celebrating Taiwan's only diplomatic alliance in Europe. All these events situate the Indigenous believers in space as also united with non-Indigenous people. These alliances can be used for many purposes, such as when Presbyterians in Hualien organized travel to Taipei to join a protest march against proposed same-sex marriage. At the same time, the Indigenous Yu Shan Theological Seminary in Hualien, known for the promotion of liberation and Indigenous theology, made a public statement in favour of same-sex marriage. The churches thus link people with island-wide networks that contribute to the circulation of political ideas in the communities.

Orientation in space links people to others in wider networks, but not without resistance. The Presbyterians, for example, have a long-standing history of support for Taiwan independence and networks of solidarity with Hoklo-speaking Christians and the DPP. On 29 December 1971, when US President Richard Nixon was planning talks with the Peoples' Republic of China and some members of the United Nations were calling for a transfer of Taiwan to China, the Presbyterian Church in Taiwan issued a "Public Statement on Our National Fate," advocating the right of self-determination for the people of Taiwan (Presbyterian Church in Taiwan 1971). Prominent Presbyterians, including President Lee Teng-hui and presidential candidate Peng Ming-min, have even more strongly supported Taiwan independence. Presbyterian seminaries even integrated the theme of Taiwan independence into their local variant of liberation theology. As a result, Presbyterian ministers often weave these themes of national self-determination into their sermons. In 2006, when DPP President Chen Shui-bian was accused of corruption and mass rallies of the "Red Shirt" movement were mobilized against him in Taipei, the Presbyterian ministers in two churches I attended defended him. Support for Taiwanese independence is not a popular stance in Indigenous communities, as we will see in chapter 5. In one community, congregation members disparagingly called their minister the "DPP minister" and argued that he inappropriately brings politics to the pulpit. In another Presbyterian church, I mentioned to a church elder that their minister has never discussed politics. "He would like to," said the elder, "but we won't let him. He used to preach for the DPP, but we told him that we will fire him if he continues."

Just as the Presbyterian Church links Indigenous believers with Hoklo networks and ideas of Taiwan independence, other churches orient them towards Mainlanders and relations with China in either of its two nationalist incarnations. The Catholic Church is the most obvious. Since the Vatican maintains diplomatic relations with the Republic of China (Taiwan), the Catholic Church is effectively Taiwan's last remaining diplomatic ally in Europe. As a result, the church hierarchy in Taiwan is heavily invested in maintaining a solid relationship between the Vatican and the ROC, and its leaders have long-standing personal relations with the Chinese Nationalist Party (Kuomintang, KMT). There are still people who hope that the Vatican will maintain relations with the ROC until China democratizes and the Catholic Church can operate freely across China. Seeing the Catholic Church on Taiwan as the custodian of Chinese Catholicism, they fear that Taiwanese independence would terminate forever their dreams of resurrecting the ROC. At the grassroots level, this fear can lead Catholics to oppose Taiwanese nationalism. During the 2006 Red Shirt movement, for example, the priest in the church I attended openly denounced President Chen. Based on conversations during field research, his congregation was staunchly pro-KMT. The Presbyterian Church thus orients believers towards an imagined Taiwan within global networks, whereas the Catholic Church encourages the faithful to identify with a cultural and historical China, while maintaining a distance from Chinese communism. The remaining congregation, the True Jesus Church, is more open to the Peoples's Republic of China.

The True Jesus Church, founded in 1917 as part of the Pentecostal movement in China, is simultaneously the most fundamentalist and the most Chinese church in Taiwan. One Saturday in 2013, I attended the True Jesus Sabbath service and was surprised to find that the guest speaker was from Xiamen, China. In a one-hour sermon, he argued that China has in the past, especially during the Cultural Revolution, oppressed religions. Nowadays, he claimed, China has fully implemented religious freedom, and the True Jesus Church congregations are full members of the Three-Self Patriotic Movement. In fact, the True Jesus Church is the only church that has always been completely autonomous of foreign missionaries. The speaker concluded by making the case that all True Jesus members should support the goal of unification of Taiwan with China so that everyone can again be a full member of the "Chinese family." He welcomed people to visit him personally in Xiamen so that they could see for themselves how vibrant the church has become in China.

After the service, at the Sabbath feast in the basement, I was a bit uncomfortable when the church women directed me to sit next to him at a round table. The guest was situated in an awkward place right next to one of the supporting pillars that holds up the church building and is intended to protect the structure during earthquakes. As we conversed throughout the entire meal, he enthusiastically repeated his message to me individually. I politely told him about the two years that I had spent in Zhejiang Province. We enjoyed tea and cookies after the meal, and then the church leaders escorted him to his car so that he could move on to the next village and their afternoon church service. I remarked to one of the women that he had spoken only to me for most of the meal. "Didn't you notice?" she replied. "We asked him to sit between you and the pillar because none of us wanted to talk with him." In spite of such moments, the True Jesus Church still orients people towards China just as much as the Presbyterian Church tries to direct their attention away from China. In another village, a young and very enthusiastic member of the church insisted to me that the True Jesus Church is the only legal church in China and has millions of believers. Although I had lived in China and attended church services for two years, he would not believe me when I said that the Three-Self Patriotic Church is the only legal church in China and that Pentecostal congregations are often forced underground as illegal house churches. He did not see it as problematic at all that the True Jesus Church has to accommodate itself to the surveillance of the Chinese Communist Party if it is to carve out any social space at all in China.

In terms of orientation in imagined space, Christianization has most dramatically changed the legend sphere. Even as some Presbyterian ministers weave traditional legends and new interpretations into their sermons, those myths have largely been replaced with biblical stories. People tend to think of Israel rather than of the central mountains in Nantou as the Holy Land. Due to the work of George Lesley Mackay, who founded churches, schools, and a hospital in Taiwan, Presbyterians have made Canada into a legendary place in their geography of the world. More recently, they imagine Canada and New Zealand to be models of Indigenous rights. The expanded accessibility of aeroplane travel takes believers to these places, and they return to share stories at church. Their imagined geography of the world is that much vaster than it has ever been in history. They now situate themselves in space not only vis-à-vis their enemies in a nearby watershed but also in terms of potential alliances with people they have never seen in distant lands. Christianity makes it possible for beliefs to both create homes and cross boundaries into distant lands. This is the context in which people start saying that Gaya belongs to everyone.

These churches also help orient individuals in time. The most obvious means is the way in which rituals guide individuals through their own life cycles of birth, reproduction, and death by means of baptisms, marriages, and funerals. The sermons also orient individuals and congregations in biblical time. Due to the annual cycles of biblical readings, people can imagine themselves as part of a human history progressing from the creation of the earth, through the fall of Adam and Eve, the tribulations of Jewish prophets, redemption through Christ, and finally to a promised messianic future for all. Many Presbyterian pastors combine these teachings with traditional myths; for example, one pastor says that a certain mountain in Nantou, where the first man and the first woman emerged from a giant boulder called Pusu Qhuni, is the actual site of the Garden of Eden. Others embed their own history within the timeline of Christianity, contrasting the headhunting past to their post-conversion lives.

The rituals of the church, as mundane as they may seem at times, intensify joy and confront suffering. Some of the Presbyterian services, influenced by charismatic movements, use drums and other percussion instruments in ways that transform hymns into shared ecstasies of joy. In the same services, prayer is marked by waving hands in the air, jumping and dancing, and fervently grasping the Bible at one's chest while pleading to God for healing or other blessings. I noticed that the charismatic services drew visibly more people to church than the pastors who tried to spread political messages about Taiwan independence (a subject for chapter 5). As I got to know the family histories of individuals, I was also amused to notice that the most charismatic pastors and believers, the ones whom people go to for prayers and healing, were also the ones who said their family members were shamans in the past. The early missionaries noted the existence of the same phenomenon. As Covell said, these "Christian shamans" are "different only in degree, not in kind, from their ancestral cousins" (Covell 1998, 265). I have come to believe people both when they say that conversion is a rupture with the past and when they look for continuity between ancient Gaya and the gospel. Conversion is attractive to so many people, and possible, because Christianity is simultaneously both a rupture with some parts of the past and a continuity that gives people a comfortable sense of stability.

Discussion

A phenomenological approach to the spread of Christianity, rather than a study concentrated on doctrines, beliefs, or political economy, focuses on religions and religious change as the unfolding of pathways from the perspective of the individuals walking on them. Changes to those pathways over time have happened due to historical circumstances, including colonialism and the spread of a capitalist world system that brought Christianity to distant parts of the world, but they happen according to the forms of local ecological constraints and the agency of individuals wayfaring through their own lives. I must admit that, in the early years of my research at least, I felt most comfortable in church. In addition to providing instant connections with the village, it made me feel a sense of continuity with my own past and even the presence of my own ancestors around me. It took years before hunters made me feel just as comfortable (even more comfortable, in fact) while walking through the forest, and introduced me to animist ways of living with forest beings.

Colonial history changed the location and form of the pathways in dramatic ways. When the people were still living in the mountain forests, they were animists of a special kind with a fetish for human heads. In those circumstances, sacred space was diffused throughout the forest. There were places where hunting was forbidden, stones that marked the burial sites of ancestors, temporary sites for horticultural rituals, and skull racks in front of the homes of charismatic Big Men. People encountered their religion, which was above all a cultivated relationship with ancestral spirits (utux) and animals (*samat*), through a rich complex of rituals and myths. Furuno, after a lifetime of studying "primitive" religion and animism in Taiwan and elsewhere in Southeast Asia, concluded that these religions are not expressions of primitive thought or different cultures but rather a part of our common humanity. He even concluded his theoretical synthesis of his lifetime work by describing their religions as "invisible churches" (Furuno 1971, 370). Much of that has been lost forever, even as belief in ghosts persists and the pig sacrifices seem to be increasingly elaborate.

Colonial policies of sedentarization that forced the people to move down the mountains brought great change. Suddenly, they were living in permanent villages and along paved roads that led to other villages. This move facilitated the arrival of missionaries, both foreign and local, who established new churches. These same roads also brought in construction materials for the churches that are now an important part of village ecologies. Churches have become spaces where people congregate, making them nodes in the intercrossing pathways of villagers and visitors alike. They have also become places where certain ideas are channelled and take on reality through emotionally salient music and rituals. It is important to avoid overstating the change that happened in this mass conversion by depicting it as a violent rupture with the past. People have constantly told me that their elders accepted Christianity relatively easily, albeit after initial resistance, because they perceived it to be consistent with their own Gaya but without the headhunting.

Awareness of the social dimensions of religion suggests other continuities. One continuity that people explicitly pointed out to me is that the church congregations, by and large, overlap with the membership of the alang. They are thus formed by people who would, even in the absence of the church, find other circumstances for mutual support and eating together. There are notable exceptions of people who leave one congregation to join another, most common when a man or a woman decides to join their spouse's church. People describe this transfer as a matter of personal choice. Even people who do not attend church regularly find themselves brought into these community rhythms by participation in major holidays or the life events of marriages and funeral wakes.

Attention to the social dimensions, within the colonial context, reveals important differences in the relationship between Christianity and Indigenous peoples in Canada and Taiwan. In Canada, the residential schools were an external imposition, part of a larger genocidal attempt to destroy Indigenous cultures, languages, and religions.[9] In Taiwan, on the other hand, Christianity was brought into most Indigenous communities by Indigenous leaders like Ciwang. From the days when Ciwang held prayer services in a cave to today's services in the Ciwang Presbyterian Church, Indigenous people themselves have been in charge of the churches. In Canada, Christianity was the religion of the settler majority and part of the pressure on Indigenous people to assimilate. In Taiwan, where the settler majority believe in a mixture of Taoism and Buddhism, Christianity has offered a form of resistance against pressures to assimilate. It is no coincidence that the churches nourished Indigenous political demands. They were created by strong Indigenous people who were already trying to create autonomous space for themselves in a situation that often oppresses and marginalizes them. The

URM retreat that set me on this path is an example of Christianity creating affordances for Indigenous resurgence. At the same time, other individuals prefer to hold back silently, worshipping the ancestors in hunting rituals and pig sacrifices but seeing little reason for weekly church attendance.

In both Taiwan and Canada, Christianity came with the upheaval of colonialism and territorial dispossession. In Taiwan, the mass conversion to Christianity is in some ways like the crosses that Sediq believers placed at Pusu Qhuni. Gaya, like that boulder, is still present; it permeates the lifeworlds of Sediq and Truku people to different extents and in different ways in different churches. The institutions of Christianity were built to spread a foreign faith, but today they also provide affordances for Indigenous resurgence, as if the vegetative roots of Pusu Qhuni have spread vines around the crosses and created something new. This thought reminds me of the First Nations leader in Canada who, while deploring the residential schools, also said that the education he gained there is precisely what made it possible for him to fight the system that oppresses his people. Christianity and colonialism are intertwined in history, even if they are not necessarily experienced as such in the lifeworlds of either believers or sceptics. Taiwan is unique only because that historical process is refracted through a very different history of Japanese and Chinese colonialisms.

Traditionalists, sharing their old rituals when they took me into the mountains, taught me that there is a place for spirituality beyond the confines of the church walls. This idea is also what they teach their own young when they enter the forests and tell stories about Pusu Qhuni. It is surely no coincidence that the mass conversions happened between 1950 and 1990, when the forests were being felled, hunting was being criminalized, and people were being extracted from the forests through welfare colonialism, developmentalism that stigmatized rural life as backward, and job-led urbanization. It is a sign of Indigenous resurgence when people still maintain the ancient practices and even share them with curious foreigners.

Finally, is Christianity a form of oppression? I think that it can be a part of cultural imperialism. Over the years, I have had people refuse to answer my questions about msapuh, the divinatory sisil bird, or even Gaya in general, saying that these are superstitions and it is a sin to even discuss them. This thinking is cultural imperialism. There is also the risk that people identify the dominant religion as more prestigious, but here is where Taiwan's experience of non-Western colonialism differs. Christianity is not the dominant religion in Taiwan. In some ways, conversion is a clever strategy by the least powerful in the society to seek alliances with even more powerful outsiders. Conversion can thus also be a way of seizing agency, of maintaining the host position in the mountains rather than conceding territory to Han-controlled Buddhist monasteries or Taoist temples that are often built on mountains in China or in non-Indigenous parts of Taiwan. It is very important that the Christian churches were the only autonomous Indigenous-led organizations in Taiwan until 1984, which makes churches potentially anti-oppression forces. But even as churches are sometimes tools of cultural imperialism and sometimes sources of liberation, they are simultaneously arenas of political competition, which is evident, as shown in this chapter, when KMT, DPP, or even Chinese Communist forces try to manipulate believers. This aspect was visible to me during the peak of the Indigenous name rectification movements, as I will discuss in chapter 5. There is no unequivocable answer to the question of whether churches are oppressive or liberating, and we must live with that. To insist that Christianity liberates is blind faith, but anti-Christian ideology can also become another form of fundamentalism. What is important is that Indigenous people use their own Gaya to find their way to church, within the church, and sometimes past the church. Even when some ministers and believers say there is a conflict between the old and the new religions, the old traditions remain alive. People take what they choose from Christianity and graft those elements on to old ways of inhabiting the world. Anthropologists have the professional duty to understand and respect the diversity of those individual and community choices, even when they don't match our own ideological predilections.

Most Indigenous people in Taiwan identify in one way or another with Christianity, but I have encountered individuals who think otherwise. Once as I stepped out of my house on a Sunday morning, crossing the street with a hymnal and a Bible under my arm, someone cried out to me and said: "Don't waste your time with that church stuff. You should come and join us for a drink instead." When I walked around the villages with a social survey and asked what church people belonged to, the vast majority automatically ticked off the box for the Catholic, Presbyterian, or True Jesus Church. A few people, however, pointed at the written question on the form and said: "What if I don't care?" One Rukai friend even once deplored to me the presence of churches up and down the east coast, describing Christianity as a foreign religion that prevents them from affirming their own traditions and thus from asserting their own political sovereignty. Despite these individual interrogations about the meaning of the churches, however, these same individuals inevitably must enter these buildings as they attend funerals and other community events. When they do so, Christianity clearly demarcates the Indigenous peoples from the overwhelming majority of Taiwanese who practice Buddhism, Taoism, and Chinese folk rituals. No matter what individuals may think about Christianity, it is still a way in which all Formosan Indigenous peoples collectively and most individually make home in an uncertain world. The churches are likely to be an enduring part of their social reality for yet a very long time.

Bowyaq (wild boar) 山豬

Figure 5.1. Wild boar (*Sus scrofa taivanus*), the most prized game animal of
all, can be found in mountains up to 3,000 metres. Boar approach human
habitation, to the annoyance of farmers. Hunting boars is a real test of
manhood because they are ferocious and can attack the hunter. They are
hunted by rifle, with dogs, or by trapping. They can weigh well over
100 kilograms, which makes it an ordeal to carry the body back down the
mountain. Boars reproduce quickly, with litters up to twelve piglets. The tusks
are made into talismans.

Source: Illustration by Biluan.

Chapter Five

Lnglungan (Heart)

Atayal society is certainly egalitarian, autonomous and republican. If one could call it a political system, one could say that it is an unparalleled democratic system.

– Kojima [1915] 1996, 235

Just as colonial anthropologists like Kojima found much to admire in Indigenous political systems, people today recall with nostalgia their egalitarian past. Kaji Cihung argued that Truku groups (*alang*) had four special characteristics. First, they were organized around kinship, with all people contributing to decisions about important issues. Second, those with special skills would exercise leadership by carrying out important collective duties. Third, alang constituted hunting groups and, in case of conflicts, warrior groups, both led by men who had proven their abilities. Fourth, similar groups organized rituals (Kaji 2011, 65). Stressing the egalitarian ethos of these institutions, people in Hualien refer to people who emerge as leaders as *pngalan kari* (according to his words), since proven skills gave their words more weight than that of others. Older people who had proven their worth were respected as elders (*rudan*). In Nantou, people said they referred to influential people as older brother or sister (*qbsuran*). Pecoraro translated *mdudul* as "the chief, one who leads, conducts, exhorts" (Pecoraro 1977, 54), but also glossed *tama* (father) as "chief" (293). There is no consensus in the communities about whether chiefs and grand chiefs (of confederations of alang) were ancient traditions or colonial inventions, but men who demonstrated selflessness, courage, and skills became leaders, and sometimes these characteristics were passed on to their sons (Kuo 2012, 40–1). Even in those cases, their leadership was justified by skill rather than by inheritance. Anthropologists may think of such societies as egalitarian, acephalous (literally "no head"), or societies against the state, but the most important dimension was that no community affair was decided by one single person. If there was a chief, he was a community's representative to the outside world and helped to resolve community conflicts but had no ability to give orders. Unlike modern capitalism, there were no classes of people who accumulated far more wealth or power than others, and there were no formal institutions of command. In the age of Indigenous resurgence, people are concerned that this egalitarian ethos has been gradually replaced by a society of money, a violent (power-based) society, and elections that wreak havoc within each alang (Shen 1998, 76).

Sometimes, an alang would come to be identified by one core leader. Likewise, a confederation of alang had one influential alang as a nucleus. It is thus no coincidence that the people feel such an affinity with the sisil, a bird with a very similar kind of sociopolitical organization. People told me that they are like the sisil because they are small, but egalitarian, and like to cooperate and share. In an oft-told story, the sisil became the partner of the people in ancient times when, after the crow, the black bulbul, and all the other birds failed to move a giant boulder, the sisil were able to do so. The people were amazed that only the smallest bird of the forest could achieve this feat, but it was because the sisil knew how to cooperate (Kuo 2012, 291). This tale is reminiscent of the way in which, on Turtle Island, the Nishnaabeg and the salmon converge in the way they govern and organize themselves, based on an intimate relationship in a local ecology (Simpson 2011, 87–8). In this chapter, I hope to show how these egalitarian ontologies shape the way the people make ethical decisions, including how they participate in electoral campaigns, make voting decisions, or join social movements. People refer to leaders they respect as qbsuran and, as discussed in chapter 1, to would-be leaders who depend on external politicians (in Chinese) as zhengke 政客.

As I discussed in the introduction, breakfast diners and grocery shops were important locations for my field research and are especially important political arenas at election times (Simon 2010a). Since I arrived in the field with strong Marxist inclinations, I embraced these sites for their access to working class or "ordinary people" who love to simply hang out and chat. These people often get overlooked by anthropologists, especially those who prefer to interview elderly people known for the depth of their traditional knowledge or the local cultural entrepreneurs who may run weaving workshops or other projects with state support. The ordinary people are difficult to interview. If asked, they are likely to refuse by saying: "There is no reason to interview me.

My life is not interesting, and I have nothing to say." Doing research with ordinary people became a kind of slow research in which I could develop friendships with people and gain insights from snippets of daily conversation rather than from formal interviews. Although the days began in breakfast shops, I was often able to accompany people throughout the day, even joining them in the rice fields at harvest time in one village because they were short of workers. Breakfast shops thus proved important as an entry point into the lives of ordinary people and insights into their ethical reflections.

Conversations in these shops revealed lifeworlds I would never have encountered through formal interviews with people accustomed to the sensitivities of academics. In the first village where I did research, one older woman loved to reminisce to me about the good old days of Presidents Chiang Kai-shek and Chiang Ching-kuo (both Chinese Nationalist Party, KMT), whom she portrayed as generally caring about the welfare of Indigenous people. She contrasted them to the supposedly corrupt President Lee Teng-hui (KMT) and Chen Shui-bian (Democratic Progressive Party, DPP), whom she depicted as benefiting financially while fomenting Hoklo Taiwanese ethnic nationalism. I had to suppress the urge to argue, because the two Chiangs are usually described among academics, Indigenous activists, and Presbyterian ministers as brutal dictators. Although I initially dismissed such judgments as the result of successful brainwashing by the KMT, I eventually realized that KMT adherents are more numerous than supporters of the Indigenous social movement. It was my duty to respect and understand those perspectives.

In the modern era, most political and economic innovations involve a new relationship with money, known as *pila* in Sədeq languages. Pecoraro thought this word, which also means "silver," was a loan word from the neighbouring Amis peoples, saying that the Truku previously had no knowledge of it (Pecoraro 1977, 199).[1] In the breakfast shop, customers exchange hard-earned money for food, whereas the entrepreneurs get up before dawn to cook breakfast and earn their money. Workers come to the breakfast shop in the hope of being picked up by labour contractors for a day of work in exchange for money. In their conversations, people may accuse others, especially political leaders but also entrepreneurs, pastors, and the like, of violating ethical norms and selling out their community in exchange for pila. People always sigh when they say: "In the end, it's all about money."

Sədeq people claim that money is a relatively new and foreign introduction. Older people even told me they remember a childhood in which they did not have money. They tend to discuss money as a corruptive, impure substance that has replaced the traditional modes of sociality such as labour exchange for farming. They contrast the ethical dilemmas of their current colonial situation with nostalgic memories of an era when people followed *Gaya* by sharing and gave no thought to money. Like Christian faith, these were moral ideas that I shared with the people before I arrived. This time, instead of having learned the moral code at home or in church, I had acquired it in graduate school. The ideas of Karl Polanyi (1886–1964) have had a profound influence on economic anthropology and our ideas about the consequences of economic development. He argued notably that the expansion of capitalist markets destroyed traditional ways of life based on reciprocity and redistribution (Polanyi 1967). Falling in line with this kind of thought, I had gone to Taiwan looking for evidence of the destructive nature of capitalism, and these grocery shop conversations gave me plenty of it. For example, shop owners evoke Gaya as a form of social pressure when they extend credit indefinitely to alang members for unpaid goods, knowing that they will never be repaid. And, since Gaya encourages sharing, they were often reluctant to take money even from me, a visiting anthropologist, for food or drinks. They thus imagine pila as a social evil, which can be contrasted to an innocent pre-colonial Gaya. Money is an important part of how people imagine ethics.

The Ethics of Indigeneity: A Theoretical Dilemma

Attention to the ways in which people learn and live ethics, as I hope to demonstrate in this chapter, may contribute to a better understanding of a dilemma that has perplexed Taiwanese and foreign scholars studying indigeneity in Taiwan. Since the 1980s, there has been a vocal Indigenous rights movement in Taiwan. Beginning in the late 1990s, state promotion of local identities and multiculturalism has led to a proliferation of workshops and studios for such things as Indigenous art, weaving, and other forms of material culture. Since 2000, and especially with the 2005 passage of the Basic Law on Indigenous Peoples, the state has paid increased attention to Indigenous rights. Most visibly, the state uses images of Indigenous people in soft diplomacy abroad and inevitably begins ceremonies, such as the inauguration of the president of the Republic of China (ROC) every four years, with Indigenous singing and dancing. In 2016, Democratic Progressive Party (DPP) President Tsai Ing-wen made an official apology to Taiwan's Indigenous peoples and set up a Presidential Office Indigenous Historical Justice and Transitional Justice Committee. The paradox is that Indigenous people overwhelmingly reject the politicians who have brought them a discourse of multicultural indigeneity. When they enter the ballot box at election time, most of them vote for the conservative KMT, which downplays ethnic difference at the same time as it promotes its version of Chinese citizenship. The paradox appears when the same people can talk about being oppressed in a colonial situation, the injustice of having lost their land, or the ongoing importance of Gaya in their lives, but then judge very harshly the people in their own communities who emerge as activists with solutions to their problems. Most people refuse to vote for the parties that promise the greatest improvements in Indigenous rights. What is happening?

If we focus on individuals and how they learn ethics, a distinction between morality and ethics is important. Charles Stafford distinguishes between morality as structure, for example, churches and their teachings, versus ethics as agency, for example, how persons negotiate moral rules and frameworks (Stafford 2013, 4). Ethics draws attention to the role of reflection, judgment, and agency. Ethics can be studied in settings such as breakfast shops because they are the sites of explicit and conscious deliberation that emerges within conversations. I found that ordinary people tended to be very unambiguous in explaining how their lived experiences lead them to certain ethical conclusions. When they make judgments about good and bad people, ethics and morality are not intellectual problems as much as they are parts of interpersonal and emotional relations (106). Michael Lambek similarly argued that ethics is less a set of rules (which might be very culturally specific) and more a sense of judgment about one's life and the lives of others. Ethics has more to do with keeping to certain paths, commitments, and relationships, albeit with freedom to change if one can reconcile the new direction with what is being left behind (Lambek 2010, 55).

Thinking about indigeneity as an individual ethical issue on the physical pathways of life casts everything in a new light. Ordinary people, like the ones waiting for work in the breakfast shops every morning, do not read the United Nations Declaration on the Rights of Indigenous People (UNDRIP) or even Taiwan's Basic Law on Indigenous Peoples and then reflect upon what action needs to be taken to implement them. They may be curious about Indigenous peoples elsewhere in the world, and inquisitively engage visiting anthropologists in conversation about supposedly more progressive countries like Canada and New Zealand, but they do not look to foreign legal precedents as guides to action in their own lives.

I find it useful to think about indigeneity through the metaphor of traction, because it allows for the possibility of grabbing or not the hearts of individuals. Anna Tsing focuses on the metaphor of friction, which may slow us down and impede progress but is also the source of traction "where the rubber meets the road" (Tsing 2005, 6). If indigeneity is like a vehicle that some people can take to arrive at their chosen destinations, it still must follow the form of the terrain to get them there. Since it follows roads, it can only go to some destinations and not to others. Since these are difficult mountain roads, however, even the best jeep may gain enough traction to get them uphill only in some places, whereas in others it may lose traction and slide back down the slope. Moreover, there are other people on the path, and some of those people may represent obstacles, and there are also paths leading in different directions. People decide what indigeneity means to them, and how far it can take them, amid the criss-crossing of paths taken by many people along the pathways of their lives. It is a teleological fallacy to assume that indigeneity will gain traction everywhere that the symbols of indigeneity are introduced by states or other external actors. None of the international forces that grasp the cosmopolitan imagination, not even global markets or liberal election practices, can enter local communities without coming up against friction caused by the local terrain and the people who carve the paths through it. Indigeneity, like discourses of development, can furthermore be used by individuals to promote their own agendas. Indigeneity then becomes subject to the same ethical examination as development, democracy, churches, or any other innovation. To understand indigeneity's bumpy trajectory in Taiwan, I begin with some of their own concepts of ethics that are deeply rooted in human hearts.

Ethical Concepts

Sədeq peoples have rather clearly defined ideas of morality, which, as we have seen in previous chapters, is discussed in terms of Gaya. There are many ways of thinking through daily ethical situations. The Truku language has a rich vocabulary of body words as metaphors for emotions (Lee 2015). The heart (*Inglungan*) is the site of ethical reflection, based on the root verb of this word which means "to think, to reflect." A person with a good heart (*malu Inglungan*) is someone of good character, whereas a person with a bad heart (*naqih Inglungan*) is someone of ill intentions. Someone without a heart (*ungat Inglungan*) is ungrateful and insensitive to others. Table 5.1 shows examples from Pecoraro's dictionary for use of the word Inglungan.

Two other ethical concepts are relevant here. People value generosity very highly. The word for generous being *mhuway*, the way to say "thank you" is to acknowledge that "you are very generous," as in

Table 5.1. Truku words for the heart

Truku	Literal meaning	Emotional state or ethical stance
Malu Inglungan	good heart	a good person
Naqih Inglungan	bad heart	an ill-intentioned person
Mslagu Inglungan	straight (direct) heart	a loyal person
Mkere Inglungan	solid heart	a persevering person
Msbalay Inglungan	true heart	a peaceful person of good humour
Muwit Inglungan	tired heart	a discouraged person
Meydang Inglungan	scattered heart	a distraught person
Muutux Inglungan	ghosted (possessed) heart	a crazy person
Dha Inglungan	other (two) heart	a disloyal person
Ungat Inglungan	no heart	an insensitive, ungrateful person

Note: Spellings are adapted to modern standardized Truku.
Source: Pecoraro (1977, 148).

mhuway su balay (thank you very much). The corollary is that stinginess is a serious moral fault. Even at the micro-event of an afternoon snack, a person who eats alone rather than sharing is said to be like a rat (*qowlit*). At a larger social level, and true to their political ontology, those who gain reputations for generosity also increase social prestige and can achieve a certain degree of political power. Those who are perceived as accumulating wealth or power for themselves, however, are criticized for their avarice and can lose influence. People also think it is important to empathize with the situations of others and to feel pity with those in need. This sentiment of tenderness and affection for others called *sgealu* or *galu* has a long list of possible inflections, including *pgalu* for "provoking pity." Since Truku speakers lengthen the first vowel for emphasis, someone who is very deserving of pity is *pgaaalu bi* (Pecoraro 1977, 67).

Although these ethical concepts may be derived from Gaya, it is possible to make a distinction between Gaya and everyday ethics. Gaya is usually described as a list of taboos and in terms of the relationship between the group or the individual with the ancestors or with God. Ethical concepts are more about the emotional states of individuals and the ways in which individuals are supposed to interact with each other. In contemporary Taiwan, Indigenous people must deal with those different ethics – and different ethnics – on a nearly daily basis. They live in a political context in which different nationalist imaginations are associated with different ethnic groups. The alang thus becomes emotionally meaningful as the starting point of ethical thought, not least when the definition and recognition of Indigenous nations is at stake.

Ethnic Groups and Boundaries

The people who leave the breakfast shops in the morning make an abrupt transition in social worlds. Since the Indigenous people I worked with live on reserve land in mountain townships, where non-Indigenous people cannot legally purchase land, their villages are ethnic refuges of a sort. In the villages where I did research, over 90 per cent of the population are classified as Sediq or Truku. The settlements are compact and densely populated, which means that people wake up every morning to the cadence of their family members and neighbours speaking a Sədeq language or Sədeq-inflected Mandarin. They may commute up to an hour to get, for example, to a school in Hualien or to a construction site in downtown Taichung. When they arrive in those cities or towns, they are surrounded by incense-filled Taoist and Buddhist temples rather than austere churches and by the clamour of Taiwanese or Taiwanese Mandarin. Hardly a day goes by when they are not reminded of their place in a multicultural society and, to be very precise, on the lower rungs of that society.

Sociologists classify Taiwan's population into four main ethnic groups. Of these four ethnic groups, the state keeps detailed population statistics only on the Indigenous groups. The Indigenous people constitute only about 2 per cent of the population. The numerical majority, constituting about 72 per cent of Taiwan's population, are the Hoklo people, descendants of migrants who arrived from Southern Fujian Province of China and began settling the western plains of the island in the seventeenth century. Some 13 per cent are Hakka, a term which means "guest people," because even in China they are said to be wanderers who arrived from the north. These people came to Taiwan from Guangdong shortly after the Hoklo had settled in Taiwan's most fertile plains and thus had to settle for lands in the foothills where they were more likely to have conflicts with the Indigenous people. Together, the Hoklo and Hakka people are called in Chinese *benshengren* 本省人, which literally means "people from this province." Quite confusingly, the anthropological norm is to translate this term into English as "Native Taiwanese," which some readers may mistakenly identify as meaning Indigenous. I prefer to call them "Han Taiwanese," using the term "Han" in recognition of their historical roots in China. Finally, there are the "Mainlanders" who came from China to Taiwan with Chiang Kai-shek and his government after the Second World War.

In Mandarin, they are called *waishengren* 外省人, "people from other provinces." They represent about 13 per cent of the population.[2] This taxonomy does not include the *pingpuzu* 平埔族, or plains aborigines, who tend to get lumped in with the Hoklo (see chapter 1).

These ethnic groups are by no means bounded categories or entities but rather bundles of human relations defined by centuries or (in the case of Mainlanders) decades of interaction. There is intermarriage between the groups, which means compromises about which language to speak at home with children, and people mix in the workplace. As Fredrik Barth taught us long ago (Barth 1969), ethnic groups are not the natural product of different cultures; rather, they are created by negotiations between groups as individuals cross boundaries, shift identities as needed, and strengthen in-group identity by emphasizing certain cultural traits as ethnic markers.

There are differences between ethnic groups in terms of phenomenological experience. The Han Taiwanese and Indigenous groups were in Taiwan before 1945, which means that individuals from these groups remember their grandparents speaking Japanese or recounting memories about the Japanese on Taiwan. The Mainlanders came from China, and many of them had served in the military, which means that their grandchildren grew up hearing about their struggle against the Japanese. The Han Taiwanese are more likely to have agricultural land and to spend their work and social lives in long-standing merchant and temple networks. The Mainlanders are more likely to come from families with careers in the public service, education, or state-run enterprises. The Han Taiwanese tend generations of graves, whereas the Mainlanders can at best remember their ancestors in China. There is also a history of residential segregation, so many Mainlanders live in or have memories of visiting grandparents in the "Military Dependents' Villages" established by the government around the island, just as Indigenous people have their rural home communities to visit. Urban Indigenous youth visit their home villages on weekends and during summer vacations. Waishengren 外省人 used to be a legal category, as province of origin was written on peoples' ID cards, but nowadays only Indigenous people have household registration documents that label them by ethnicity, Indigenous status giving access to affirmative action measures and other benefits.

The Indigenous groups have their own ethno-sociology, which is inflected with ethical judgment. In Hualien, the Truku refer to the Hoklo people as Teywan, a derivation of "Taiwan" usually said in a pejorative tone of voice. In Nantou, the Seediq follow the example of the neighbouring Atayal by referring to the Hoklo as *kmukan* (often pronounced *mukan*), a pejorative term derived in folk etymology from the Mandarin Chinese words for "mother" and "fuck" (Stainton 2006, 398). This word does not mean "motherfucker," as Stainton suggested, although it certainly has the same emotional value. When I asked Seediq people why they use that term, they explained that the Hoklo people have a habit of swearing "*Gan ni nia*" – which means "Fuck your mother!" The Seediq find this language offensive. Since it is a major violation of Gaya to speak about the sexuality of female relatives, they use it as a marker of the moral inferiority of the Hoklo people.[3] The Truku in Hualien refer to the Hakka, for whom they reserve an even stronger dislike, simply as *ngay-ngay*, poking fun at the incomprehensible sounds of their language. Finally, the Hualien Truku refer to the Mainlanders somewhat fondly as *ibaw*, which is probably derived from *yibao* 義胞 (righteous compatriots), an honorific term for the last wave of refugees who arrived from China and the offshore islands of Fujian and Zhejiang Provinces in 1955. Some people I encountered jokingly said that the Mainlanders are ibaw (#1 compatriots), whereas the Indigenous people are *sanbao* (#3 compatriots), a pun referring to the homonym in Taiwanese pronounced Mandarin of *chanbao* 山胞 (mountain compatriots, the old legal term for Indigenous people).[4] In Nantou, Mainlanders are called *Telu*, derived from the Chinese word for "mainland," whereas the Hakka are called *Khilan* (Chien 2002, 28). The Japanese might be called *tanah tunux* (red heads) in Nantou because of the rising sun symbolism on their headbands or *rungay* (monkey) in Hualien because the same symbol reminded people of the red colour on the rear of a monkey disappearing up a tree. The different names I collected for ethnic groups in Hualien and in Nantou reflect the particular social entanglements of each alang.

What about the word for Indigenous peoples? A Presbyterian pastor suggested I use the term *tnpusu*, which means "rooted." They are thus the people who are rooted in the soil of this land, whereas all other people have drifted in from somewhere else. Pecoraro chose to inflect the word alang as *tn'alang* to mean "one who is from this *terroir*, indigenous" (Pecoraro 1977, 3). I found that ordinary people, when asked how to translate "Indigenous" into their language, preferred the word *seejiq* (human being), but qualified as *seejiq balay* (real people). In Hualien, one young man (in the year 2019) even insisted that he is not *Seejiq balay* but rather *Truku balae*, suggesting that local identities are stronger than abstract national ones. One Presbyterian minister in Bsngan explained that *Truku* has come to mean "an outstanding, upright person," but in Hualien alone. No matter what, everyone seems to employ a wider logic of identifying the living inhabitants of the mountains as somehow more authentic and more morally upright than those of the plains. By the same logic, which people reported to me with apparent pleasure, the native Formosan dogs from the mountains are called *huling balay* (real dogs) as opposed to the pet breeds of the plains. The small fish of the mountain streams are called *qsurux balay* (real fish), as opposed to ocean creatures or purchased fish. Both of those mountain animals are considered superior to others of the same kinds. Coming back to human ethnic groups, few people in daily life try to find a word in their language for "Indigenous." They all revert to the Mandarin Chinese *yuanzhumin* 原住民, a linguistic habit that reveals the foreign nature of the concept. Unlike the iconic ngay-ngay, it is still more of a legal category than an expression of immediate experience.

I learned the meaning of this linguistic differentiation one evening when, around a table covered with meat and beer, I practised my language by putting together such phrases as *Seediq Amerika* and *Seediq Nippon* (American people and Japanese people). When I arrived at *Seediq Kmukan*, everyone roared in laughter. "That is impossible," someone said. "*Kmukan aji seediq*" (literally "They are not human"). What he meant is that they do not have the ethical foundation of full humanity. Kmukan and Teywan, pejorative ethnonyms with strong emotional salience, reveal learned expectations about the way the world works, how to interpret events, and how to plan for the future. In social interaction, they fill in missing or unambiguous information, which is what makes communication possible when people share certain worlding practices. When people say the word Kmukan, they usually continue by telling a story about being cheated of their wages, losing a piece of land, or some other negative experiences of discrimination. Their distrust of the Teywan makes them rather wary of anyone who talks about Taiwan independence, which they associate with Hoklo ethnic nationalism.

Across Taiwan, each Indigenous community has different dynamics of ethnic relations depending upon the demographic weighting of each group and local histories of settlement and interaction. In Hualien, I met elderly Mainlander men who had married local Truku women. As young military conscripts, they had been brought to Taiwan with the promise that they would one day retake the Chinese Mainland and return home. Once in Taiwan, they were assigned the work of reconstructing and modernizing the Central Cross-Island Highway through the mountains from Taichung to Hualien. Some of them chose to settle in their new location, married local Truku women, learned the Truku language, and raised their children as Truku. As a result, many Truku identify with Mainlanders as members of their extended families, as uncles and great-uncles if not direct grandparents. Many of the local politicians come from these families, successful because they have the social capital needed to communicate effectively with both local voters and with Mainlanders, who have historically dominated the KMT.[5]

Relations with the Hoklo are far more tenuous. My field notes are full of stories that people told me about unscrupulous Hoklo investors who cheated them of reserve land through various means. One common strategy was to make a business partnership in which the Hoklo entrepreneur would supply the capital for construction of a small hotel or other enterprise and the Indigenous person would provide the land, agreeing to equally share the profits. The Hoklo entrepreneur could subsequently find some way to get the Indigenous partner to forego profits or even cede the property. In one case, the Hoklo investor constructed the frame of the building and then asked the Truku partner to pay for the windows and doors, claiming that the contract did not cover these costs. When the Truku partner was unable to come up with the cash, he signed over his rights to most of the building. Although the Indigenous partners continue to hold legal title to reserve land, they are often unable to enforce those rights, saying that the courts would require them to compensate the Hoklo partner for all construction costs if they tried to take back the property. In some cases, the Indigenous partner ends up responsible for any property taxes, whereas the Hoklo partner takes the profit from the business.

More ubiquitous are conflicts with Taiwanese labour contractors. One evening in Nantou, as I stopped by the small grocery store, the men gathered at the table in front invited me to join them for a beer. The mood was serious, and one of the men said that I should document what they had experienced for my research. They had all just completed a construction project in Taichung. Once the work was finished and it was time to get paid, however, they were told that the subcontractor had filed bankruptcy, was unable to pay their wages, and had "run away." I asked how it is possible for a construction company to "run away," especially since the names of the firms are always clearly documented on public posters on the construction sites. That is only the main contracting firm, the men explained, but in fact the work is done by very dense networks of subcontractors, which means that they cannot locate the individuals on their own and they lack the means to hire lawyers. In cases like this one, all these men can do is return to their village, drink some beer, and swear "Kmukan!"

People also told me stories about bosses who failed to pay required contributions for their health insurance. In agriculture, people also claimed that the Kmukan cheat them by paying lower than market prices for their crops. If I had done my fieldwork just a few years earlier, I would have heard stories about predatory Kmukan purchasing Indigenous girls from impoverished parents for urban sex markets (Rudolph 1993). Everyone has the experience of overhearing Taiwanese people call them in Hoklo *hoan-á* 番仔 (savage), a far more insulting term than the arguably patronising "mountain compatriot." Discrimination based on perceptions of ethnic difference is an important part of their lives.

These emotionally charged life experiences give people different impressions of other ethnic groups. In terms of ethics, people accuse the Hoklo of being dishonest and motivated only by money and the Hakka of being stingy, but they only explain these details explicitly to foreign anthropologists. Within the group, it suffices to say "Kmukan," "Teywan," or "Ngay-ngay" to evoke these negative connotations. One elder informant summed up the Indigenous perspective on ethnic relations by saying: "The Kmukan want our land and our labour. The Mainlanders only want our votes." These personal experiences with other ethnic groups colour the ways in which ordinary people deal with the wider Taiwanese society, including through interactions in religious and political networks. Ethnic relations became even more complex when the new freedoms brought by democracy provided the possibility for political entrepreneurs to create new Indigenous ethnic groups. Although I will discuss ethnogenesis more closely in chapter 6, I introduce the issues here, focusing on the close relationship between ethnogenesis and electoral politics.

Ethnogenesis and Indigenous Social Movements

Taiwan's Indigenous rights movement began in Taipei as part of wider demands for democratization that eventually led to the 1987 lifting of martial law. In 1983, a group of Indigenous students founded the magazine *Gaoshan Qing* 高山青 (Green of the High Mountains). In December 1984, the Alliance of Taiwan Aborigines (ATA) was founded to unite Indigenous peoples of all ethnicities and took a leading role in organizing street demonstrations. Among their most prominent goals was "rectification of names" (*zhengming* 正名), which led to adoption of the term *yuanzhu minzu* 原住民族 (Indigenous peoples). There was also the "return our land" (*huan wo tudi* 還我土地) movement, asking for reform of the reserve land system and return of traditional territories under state control, as well as "enter the Constitution" (*ruxian* 入憲), which led to the inclusion of Indigenous rights in the constitutional amendments of 1994 and 1997. The ATA also began sending independent delegations to the UN Working Group on Indigenous

Populations in Geneva (Allio 1998b). In the 1990s, name rectification campaigns led the government to adopt the term "Indigenous
peoples" and to permit individuals to use their Indigenous personal
names on official documents. In the 2000s, name rectification concerned defining the boundaries of ethnic groups. In 2000, there were
nine officially recognized Indigenous groups. That number by 2017
had increased to sixteen.

As groups sought recognition, the Presbyterians were important
leaders for both the Truku and the Sediq. In fact, those identities overlap with the areas covered by two different Presbyterian synods (Hara
2003, 2004). The Presbyterians brought to the table the theological argument that all peoples are liberated through sovereignty. This notion is
the basis of Presbyterian support for both Taiwanese independence and
for Indigenous sovereignty, as well as its attempts to unite Indigenous
and Han Taiwanese. For local people, the movement for name rectification and Indigenous sovereignty appeared as intrinsically related to
electoral politics. The debates were animated by the same local leaders, and involved ethical choices for individuals about how to position
themselves in relationship to other people in their communities and
with other ethnic groups outside the village. Ethnogenesis, the recognition of new ethnic groups, is debated among living people, but just like
the introduction of Christianity, it is rooted in the colonial experience.
The local leaders who introduce these innovations to their community
always find it difficult to gain traction at first, but if they do, they can
substantially transform the community and how individuals imagine
their place in the world.

Name Rectification, State Legibility, and Presbyterian Indigeneity

The designation of official ethnic names for Indigenous groups is useful primarily to states, which need a strong degree of legibility for
governance. When the Japanese colonial state arrived on Formosa,
most Indigenous groups identified themselves simply with the word
for "human" in their language but did not think of that word as representing a political unit of any kind. Rather than trying to imagine
the world as composed of large nations or cultures whose members
do not even know one another, they thought in terms of the names
of local groups (such as the alang) or temporary confederations.
Members of different alang were often mutual enemies after generations of conflict over hunting territory and headhunting (Lin 1996,
780). The Japanese colonial ethnographers found it difficult to classify the island's ethnic groups. Kojima, for example, recognized that

members of local groups with such names as Musha, Troku, Tawca',
Tawsai, and Taroko all used easily recognizable variants of "Sədeq"
to call themselves human beings and distinguished themselves from
the neighbouring groups who call human beings "Atayal" or "Tayal."
Nonetheless, there were cultural and linguistic similarities. The Japanese, moreover, already had the habit of grouping the Atayal, Sədeq,
and Saisiyat together as "northern savages" (*hokuban* 北番), and these
groups all had similar customs of facial tattoos. For Kojima, this grouping was sufficient reason to write about them collectively as the Atayal
(Kojima [1915] 1996, 5).

The Japanese government finally classified all of the groups listed in
the preceding paragraph as Atayal, but Japanese officials left sufficient
contradictory documentation behind that could be used for future generations in different ways. For example, Kojima preferred Atayal, but
only two years after his report was published, Sayama ([1917] 2011)
wrote separate volumes on the Sediq and the Truku. As people got
accustomed to state classifications, they began to refer to themselves as
Atayal, even if they also knew they belonged to the subgroups of "Eastern Sədeq" in Hualien and "Western Sədeq" in Nantou. Because of the
history of the Taroko Incident and settlement in new villages in Hualien, the Truku there also started to form a new identify for themselves
(Hara 2006; Lin 1996, 780). Within those groups, there was consensus
that, due to the history of migration along different watersheds, they
could refer to themselves according to the geographical names of their
places of origin in Nantou. These subgroups were the Truku, Tgdaya,
and Toda (Hara 2003, 212). Missionary Ralph Covell, presumedly following local use, called them all Sediq, whether they were in Hualien or
Nantou, whereas Father Ferdinando Pecoraro, also presumedly following local use in Wanrong, used the name Taroko, as if it were an element
of great Indigenous pride.

After the transition to the Republic of China (ROC), the Presbyterian Church became an important player in the politics of recognition.
In 1960, the Taroko Synod was formed with thirty congregations in
Nantou and Hualien. In the early 1980s, they made the first request
to the Ministry of the Interior to change their ethnic name to Taroko,
although there was no consensus about the Chinese characters to use
for the name or about the geographical boundaries of the group (Lin
1996, 779). Throughout the 1990s, as the government promoted local
identities, there was a proliferation of non-governmental organizations
(NGOs) promoting both the ethnonyms Truku and Sediq (and variants thereof) through cultural activities and symposiums. In 1998, the
Presbyterian Church founded the Sediq Synod in Nantou. These two

synods because a new source of ethnic identity and arenas for political competition.

Debates about name rectification intensified after 2000, when DPP Chen Shui-bian was elected president. The DPP, and Chen in particular, emphasized the right of Taiwan to self-determination and sovereignty. They were thus much more open to, and even promoted, Indigenous demands for sovereignty. In Hualien, township magistrate Huang Hui-bao, with the support of the Taroko Synod, mobilized township resources to promote a Taroko identity and gathered signatures on a petition to submit to the government. On 14 January 2004, Premier Yu Shyi-kun of the Executive Yuan announced that the Taroko were to be recognized as the twelfth Indigenous people in Taiwan, supposedly with the hope of gaining votes in Hualien for the DPP in the elections of that year (Simon 2012b, 191–2). The precipitous recognition of the Taroko frustrated Sediq nationalists in Nantou as well as in Hualien. As a result of their intensified lobbying, Chen Shui-bian's lame duck government made the Sediq Taiwan's fourteenth legally recognized Indigenous group on 23 April 2008. In her analysis of these debates, Japanese anthropologist Hara Eiko argued that the Truku could force their will more easily in Hualien where they constituted 92.5 per cent of the local population, whereas in Nantou a nearly equal demographic balance between the Truku, Tgdaya, and Toda forced them to lobby for a more inclusive name (Hara 2003, 2004). But in both Nantou and Hualien, ordinary people associated name rectification with electoral politics.

Shen Ming-ren (Pawan Tanah) opposed Truku name rectification for four reasons. First, he stressed the "blood relations" between the people in Nantou and Hualien, saying that it is unfair and a violation of Gaya for those in Hualien to seek an independent political status without their Nantou relatives. Second, he deplored the fact that the leaders of the movement seemed to prioritize political factions in the government over their own Gaya. Third, it would create more small Indigenous groups, whereas unity would give them more political power. Finally, the people on both sides of the mountain speak the same language, albeit in three distinct dialects. He thought it would be better to be called Seejiq, their shared word for human, rather than use a place name meaningful to only some people among them. He deplored the fact that the name rectification was led by the Taroko Synod of the Presbyterian Church, as if the establishment of that synod meant more to them than centuries of shared history (Shen 1998, 56–63).

In both Hualien and Nantou, I found that ordinary people were cynical about name rectification and autonomy projects, which they described as strategies by their political elites to create new positions for themselves. One person in Nantou told me:

> They have placed flags all over the village to promote Sediq name rectification. This does nothing to help ordinary people. Everyone will continue to work during the day and to drink in the evenings. There are already two social classes in the village: the cadres and the workers. The cadres monopolize all of the advantages for themselves, and the result is growing disparity between the rich and the poor. This is not good. We had a good life in the past. We lived from hunting, and we were able to ensure that everyone was equally well fed.

To provide another example, I was once sitting outside drinking beer with a group of men in Gluban when Watan Diro, a local Presbyterian pastor involved in the Sediq name rectification campaign, stopped his car, rolled down the window, and asked if I wanted to leave with him. I told him I was busy and would contact him later. After he drove away, one of the men said: "Why would you even think of leaving with *him*? Don't you know that all people who wear neckties are evil?" Watan, an Urban-Rural Mission (URM) graduate, was fully confident that Sediq name rectification is no less than the will of Jesus. Recalling his reputation for close ties with the DPP, villagers accused him in conversation of getting involved with oppositional politics in order to make personal gain. The accusations were spurious, but most importantly for this analysis, these local people were making daily ethical decisions about which political groups they should support. People tended to associate rhetoric of Indigenous rights with the Democratic Progressive Party (DPP), which they identified as the ethno-nationalism of the Hoklo. This connection made it difficult for Indigenous rights, even the right to determine the name and limits of one's own Indigenous group, to gain traction. People continued to make ethical decisions about which group to support based on their own set of personal relations.

Ethnic Relations and Politics: The National Level

Ethnic relations become accentuated during electoral campaigns, during which individuals also make ethical deliberations about which candidates to endorse and for whom to vote. The election cycle is also the most important social context for understanding many other dynamics in these small Indigenous communities. Many events and activities, including village-level projects for employment training to township-level "traditional" festivals, are organized with future elections in mind.

Even wedding feasts, as they bring together large numbers of people, are political events because elected officials take the podium and congratulate the young couple.

National-level politics are part of the story, probably the least important for most local people, but need to be understood to put Indigenous politics in a broader context. Since the 1990s, when Taiwanese people began voting in direct elections for national legislators and a president, the two main parties have been the Chinese Nationalist Party (Kuomintang, KMT) and the Democratic Progressive Party (DPP). The KMT and allied parties are collectively known as the "pan-blues," whereas the DPP and allied parties are the "pan-greens." Since the KMT came to Taiwan with the Republic of China in 1945 and ruled as a one-party state for four decades, the pan-blues are Chinese nationalists. In their imagined nationalism, all inhabitants of Taiwan are Chinese nationals. The strongest supporters of the KMT and related parties are the Mainlanders. The "dark blues" have an almost jihadist faith in the need to reunify the Chinese motherland, even if it means temporary compromise with their former enemies in the Chinese Communist Party while waiting for China to democratize, but the ultimate goal is to resurrect the Republic of China. The darkest blues think that national unification is more important than democracy. The "light blues" are more Taiwan-centric and simply think that the KMT is the most appropriate ruling party for Taiwan. In their view, the KMT is better at managing the economy and less likely to unnecessarily provoke China, and is thus "non-ideological." Many Indigenous people appreciate the pan-blue slogan of "ethnic harmony," even if they disagree with the associated idea of "we are all Chinese." Some people even told me that Chineseness can embrace all forms of ethnic difference. From this perspective, indigeneity can appear as a way of fostering ethnic rivalry and conflict, usually done for personal gain. Indigenous people who favour the blues are even likely to reject claims of the Hoklo to be Taiwanese. Quite commonly, they said: "The Hoklo and the Mainlanders are all from China. We Indigenous people are the only real Taiwanese."

The DPP, founded in 1986, arose from the social movements of the 1980s that promoted democratization, ethnic pride, and Taiwanese nationalism. In their imagined nationalism, the Han Taiwanese (Hoklo and Hakka) as well as the Indigenous peoples have been oppressed by the KMT since 1945 and need to affirm together a strong Taiwanese identity that is different from China. The fundamentalist "dark greens" argue that it is important to overthrow the Republic of China and declare an independent Taiwan, whereas the "light greens" accept the Republic of China as the manifestation of Taiwan's legal independence from the

People's Republic of China. Since the green camp seeks to demarcate a Taiwanese national identity that is distinct from China, they have not hesitated to mobilize Indigenous symbolism to this purpose for both domestic and international audiences. Unfortunately, such practices lead many people to the cynical conclusion that the state employs the rhetoric and symbolism of indigeneity *only* to demarcate a non-Chinese identity for Taiwan (Ku 2005; Rudolph 2006: 46fn12). In August 2016, when newly elected Tsai Ing-wen made a highly publicized apology to the island's Indigenous peoples for 400 years of colonization, Indigenous activists as well as foreign observers questioned whether she was sincere or whether this apology was just a way of gaining the attention of the international liberal media.[6] The questions here are how these larger nationalist yearnings gain traction or fail to do so in Indigenous communities and how these dynamics relate to local political behaviour. For individuals, political belonging is an ethical dilemma, as they either show loyalty to or risk the appearance of betraying important people in their lives.

Politics are very much about interpersonal relations, and not just in Taiwan's Indigenous communities, in ways that shape how voters relate to the different nationalist imaginations offered to them. After the 2000 presidential election, in which DPP candidate Chen Shui-bian unexpectedly won the election, Taiwanese sociologist Wang Fu-chang analysed statistical correlations between ethnic relations and election results in Taiwan's 359 townships, as well as data from a 1999 national survey on ethnicity. He found that Mainlanders have the highest degree of ethnic political consciousness. Hoklo living in areas of Hoklo demographic preponderance are more likely to believe the narrative that they are oppressed by Mainlanders. Hoklo who have daily interaction in areas of greater ethnic diversity are more likely to seek harmonious ethnic relations and are thus less attracted to DPP ideology. In terms of voting behaviour, this trend leads to very high support for the KMT in the few areas dominated by Mainlanders (and Indigenous areas), high support for the DPP in the southern and northeastern townships dominated by the Hoklo, and less support for the DPP in mixed areas (Wang 2002). This dynamic continued in the 2004 elections (Wang 2004–5) and, as far as I can see, to this day. Wang's model provides the big picture for Taiwan, but ethnographic research provides the fine-grained details needed to understand how social interactions lead to specific political behaviours in small communities.

Indigenous voters, like Mainlanders, are hardcore pan-blue supporters. The small Indigenous sample size in the 1999 survey meant that Wang could not fully discuss Indigenous ethnic identity and voting behaviour in his study. His maps, however, show clearly that the thirty Indigenous townships voted strongly in favour of the pan-blues in the 2000 and 2004 elections. The same pattern held in 2008 (Simon 2012b, 141) and in subsequent elections. Even in 2016 and 2020, when the DPP won both the legislature and the presidency, the Indigenous townships voted overwhelmingly in favour of the pan-blue candidates. Tsai made great efforts to reach out to Indigenous voters, even by claiming that her grandmother was Paiwan. As a result, Tsai won in a few mixed townships where Indigenous people live in closer proximity with the Hoklo. None of those places, however, have the legal status of Indigenous townships. Despite claiming Paiwan ancestry, Tsai did not win in the Paiwan townships, but in 2020, a Paiwan woman was elected to the Legislative Yuan on the DPP ticket. In 2019, after Daniel Han Kuo-yu took over the KMT leadership and became the presidential candidate, Indigenous people became some of his most enthusiastic supporters. People explained to me that he is the most likely person to establish a close economic relationship with China. One Truku woman told me directly: "We have to vote for him because he is a Mainlander. China won't trust anyone but a Mainlander."

Sediq and Truku voters remained faithful to established patterns. I consulted the 2016 and 2020 township-level election results for president in the three townships where I did fieldwork. These are the Truku-majority townships of Hsiulin and Wanrong in Hualien and the Seediq-majority Ren'ai Township of Nantou. In the combined results of these three townships in 2016 (table 5.2), DPP candidate Tsai Ing-wen gained only 24 per cent of the vote, compared to 52 per cent for the KMT candidate Eric Chu and 24 per cent for the pan-blue maverick candidate James Soong. This breakdown contrasts to national-level support for Tsai at 56 per cent, Chu at 31 per cent, and Soong at 13 per cent. In 2020 (table 5.3), the charismatic KMT candidate Daniel Han managed to gain the loyalty of Indigenous voters who had previously supported Soong, but Han lost in Taiwan overall. Support for Tsai remained low.

These results are consistent with the decades-long pattern in which the Indigenous voters distrust the Hoklo-dominated DPP and show preference for pan-blue parties. Since the KMT is the mainstream party preferred by Mainlanders, a strong KMT outcome reveals the strength of the local Mainlander-Indigenous political alliance. James Soong, a maverick Mainlander politician, deserves special mention. For his PhD thesis in political science at Georgetown University, he did research on the strategies of the Chinese Communist Party to cultivate patronage networks and political support among Chinese minority nationalities. As governor of Taiwan Province from 1993 to 1998, he was able to put

Table 5.2. 2016 presidential election results

Township	Green	Blue		Eligible ballots, n
	Tsai Ing-wen (DPP), %	Eric Chu (KMT), %	James Soong, %	
Hsiulin (Truku)	27	49	24	6,518
Wanrong (Truku)	21	61	18	2,575
Ren'ai (Seediq)	23	51	26	6,679
Combined Truku/Seediq	24	52	24	15,772
Taiwan general results	56	31	13	12,284,970

Source: Central Election Commission, ROC (https://db.cec.gov.tw).

Table 5.3. 2020 presidential election results

Township	Green	Blue		Eligible ballots, n
	Tsai Ing-wen (DPP), %	Daniel Han (KMT), %	James Soong, %	
Hsiulin (Truku)	26	71	3	8,350
Wanrong (Truku)	22	75	3	3,209
Ren'ai (Seediq)	21	76	3	8,212
Combined Truku/Seediq	23	74	3	19,771
Taiwan general results	57	39	4	14,300,940

Source: Central Election Commission, ROC (https://db.cec.gov.tw).

this strategy into practice himself by tactical distribution of infrastructure contracts to his local supporters in Indigenous villages. In 2000, he failed his independent bid for the ROC presidency and formed the People First Party (PFP). As we will see in the discussion later in this chapter, Indigenous elections tended to be a race between the KMT and the PFP supporters. It was only in 2020 when the Indigenous voters turned their back on Soong. A close look at local elections further reveals how individual's political decisions are rooted, not in abstract notions of nationalism or indigeneity but in ethical decisions about how to relate to the people in their daily lives.

The Politics of Indigenous Townships

It can be said everywhere that politics is local, but that is even more the case in Indigenous Taiwan. Taiwan has separate political institutions for Indigenous and non-Indigenous communities. This division is important at two levels. First, the state makes a legal distinction between "mountain Indigenous peoples" and "plains Indigenous peoples." Confusingly, neither of these categories includes the plains aborigines (ping-puzu 平埔族). This distinction is based on Japanese-era classifications in which some groups perceived as more primitive lived on reserve land, whereas other supposedly advanced groups had access to private property. After the ROC came to Taiwan, they kept these legal classifications, renaming them somewhat confusingly as "mountain-mountain compatriots" (*shandi shandi tongbao* 山地山地同胞) and "plains-mountain compatriots" (*pingdi shandi tongbao* 平地山地同胞). These categories are now called "mountain Indigenous" and "plains Indigenous." In what was probably a compromise with local Indigenous leaders who had emerged during the colonial period, the new government consolidated the areas of mountain-mountain compatriots into thirty mountain townships. One of the main tasks of mountain townships is to manage reserve land, which to this day remains state property even though Indigenous people have the right to buy and sell housing and usufruct rights between Indigenous individuals. Each mountain township has a township office with an elected magistrate, who by law must be Indigenous, and a township council, which may include non-Indigenous members. Each township is further divided into villages, with elections for village mayor and the heads of local neighbourhoods. Since 1950, this system has been called "local autonomy."

Second, the Indigenous people and non-Indigenous people have a separate form of representation in the Legislative Yuan. Since the constitutional reform of 2005, legislators have been selected in a predominantly single member district electoral system. This type of system means that non-Indigenous people vote for both a member of the Legislative Yuan from their geographical district as well as for a party list for "at-large" members. Indigenous voters, on the other hand, must vote on a separate ballot according to their legal status as mountain or plains Indigenous. Since 2005, there is a quota of three mountain Indigenous and three plains Indigenous members for the Legislative Yuan. Although direct elections for the Legislative Yuan were first held only in 1992, this system of quotas for Indigenous legislators was based on precedents in the now-defunct Taiwan Provincial Assembly. Most Indigenous people, even if they have migrated to urban areas, keep their rural household registration and return to the villages to vote in elections. The system raises the costs for Indigenous candidates and voters alike. Indigenous candidates for the Legislative Yuan campaign across Taiwan, rather than just in a local district, which means that they incur the same transportation expenses as presidential candidates.

Indigenous voters who live outside the communities of their household registration pay for train or car transportation to return home and vote, making Election Day into a festival day in which all the villages are crowded with people who would ordinarily be elsewhere.

Since the beginning of local elections in the 1950s, the KMT has deftly cultivated local patronage networks based on kinship and friendship to mobilize support for its candidates. In order to avoid conflict within patronage networks, candidates tend to avoid ideological platforms that could alienate even a minority of faction members (Bosco 1994, 31–2). In other words, they tend to emphasize their personal competence, history of service to the community, and supposedly non-ideological subjects such as "development." The KMT manages its relationship with local factions between elections through the work of "People's Service Stations." Their representatives throughout the year make regular rounds of local villages, eating and drinking with groups of people and sharing their interpretations of current events in casual conversations. They promise to help people resolve problems with the government and maintain a good reputation of carrying out these promises efficiently. Since the KMT is considered (especially in Indigenous communities) to be the party of Mainlanders, they sometimes assert a role for Mainlanders in these contexts as the allies and protectors of Indigenous people. When James Soong left the KMT in 2000 to form his People First Party, the politics of Indigenous communities became divided between factions loyal to the KMT and those faithful to Soong.

At the village level, influential individuals emerge as what are called in Taiwanese *thiâu-á-kha* 柱仔腳, which literally translates as "stake" (as for a tent) and means that they root the party in local soil (Bosco 1994, 35). This word, even in Indigenous communities, is always used in Taiwanese rather than in Mandarin or Indigenous equivalents in casual conversation. In the Indigenous communities, these individuals are frequently the village mayors, the chairs of farmers' associations, or the presidents of local community development organizations.

Between elections, the thiâu-á-kha try to consolidate their own power and influence by taking control of local NGOs, gaining state resources and distributing them locally. In the villages where I did fieldwork, the county government required local villages to establish community development associations (CDAs). There was always one village-wide CDA, but also a diversity of other CDAs with Indigenous themes specializing in such things as cultural development, arts and crafts, ecotourism, or song and dance. The CDAs are all eligible to apply for state funding for various projects. When I did my research in Hualien, I observed CDAs apply to the Council of Labour Affairs to fund employment training.

Without exception, they applied to train people in Indigenous handicrafts, such as the manufacture of glass beads or handmade traditional musical instruments. Although they claimed in their grant proposals that graduates of these short-term programs would subsequently be able to produce crafts for the tourist markets, there were no attempts to create such markets. Everyone involved was very clear (and very honest with me) about the fact that the students were there for the temporary wages they were offered to participate, and the organizers were there to cultivate patron-client ties for subsequent elections. Here is where ethics came into play. Those thiâu-á-kha who could cultivate a reputation for generosity with ordinary people gained larger followings, but all of them were subject to accusations from their opponents of using these opportunities to accumulate personal wealth and political power. In my field research, I heard many people be reproached as naqih lnglungan (bad-hearted) or as *duhi* (thieves), but I rarely heard a word of praise for any of these people.

To sum up so far, Taiwanese society is composed of diverse groups of people who, through decades of interaction, have learned to perceive themselves as belonging to what they describe as four main ethnic groups. The relative newcomers, Mainlanders from China, brought their political system with them when they replaced the Japanese after the Second World War. In order to govern, they put in place a political system in which they could gain legitimacy by cultivating local elites loyal to them. In the mountainous areas, they were entirely unfamiliar with the languages and customs of the Indigenous groups, but they had to create new relations with these people accustomed to dealing with the Japanese through a system of reserves, tribal councils, and elected chiefs. They modernized the reserve system by permitting Indigenous people to buy and sell housing and usufruct rights among themselves, and they cultivated a new local elite by incorporating them into thirty mountain townships with modern local elections. During this time, subaltern Mainlanders settled into those communities and married local women. In some communities, the result was the formation of a KMT-dependent political elite in societies where people took pride in their egalitarian ethos of Gaya. As development accelerated interaction between ethnic groups, even those who had been in hostile relations for generations, ordinary people found themselves in daily ethical dilemmas about how to relate to others. Their conscious ethical reflections are especially important at election time, but also as they think forward about what it means to be Indigenous, or even Taiwanese, in a rapidly changing world.

Election Time

Electoral campaign periods, especially for village and township elections, are the most boisterous periods of the year in Indigenous communities.[7] Every day in local elections, groups of people enthusiastically parade through the streets, going from village to village (figure 5.2). Trucks equipped with loudspeakers broadcast campaign slogans and blaring music. The candidate may arrive standing on the back of a pickup truck or jeep, adorned with a red sash announcing his or her name and political affiliation, but may also jump off the vehicle to mix with people on the street and shake hands with those who come out of their homes to watch the spectacle. Crowds of supporters follow the vehicles on scooter and on foot. In places where groups of people habitually socialize, such as in breakfast shops and small grocery stores, the campaign teams stop to chat and distribute campaign pamphlets. The day ends at the campaign headquarters of the candidate, which may be behind the gates of an enclosed villa or out in the open in front of a local general store. Usually large red tables are rented from local wedding caterers, and a large feast is prepared with food and drink for those who have decided to publicly support a candidate. Due to the high frequency of elections and local by-elections, I was able to participate in election campaigns in every village I studied. As a foreign anthropologist, I also had a privileged vantage point compared to local people. Only I could move from group to group and take a place at each table without anyone questioning my loyalty. They knew, after all, that I was ineligible to vote.

Local people describe their behaviour in electoral campaigns as being culturally particular compared to elections in Han Taiwanese communities and also to elections in other countries. People were very inquisitive with me during elections, asking how elections are run in Canada and if I had ever been involved as either a supporter or a candidate. They imagine, and my own experience so far seems to confirm their intuitions, that their elections are among the most festive and raucous elections of all. They conjure up images of the West, supposedly home to more mature democracies, as a place where people calmly and rationally make private decisions about how to vote. They argue that even urban Taiwan, which they often know from personal work experience, is closer to that democratic ideal. They contrast those presumptions with descriptions of their own elections as stressful periods of social pressure, corruption, and even conflict that can break out into violence.

Electoral campaigns are consciously organized according to previously existing forms of social organization. As we have seen in previous

Figure 5.2. Local election parade. Supporters distribute campaign literature in a village electoral parade, 2006. This candidate intentionally downplayed his Indigenous identity and promoted development as a "non-ideological" KMT platform.

Source: Photograph by Scott E. Simon.

chapters, several kinds of groups with overlapping memberships are important in the lives of each village. All villages are political administrative units created by the state. The people who live there were forcibly moved to those locations in both Hualien and Nantou during the Japanese period from their original hamlets up in the mountains. They still remember those hamlets and identify strongly with this clan-like alang. Church congregations also bring people together in social constellations that roughly overlap with alang membership. Within that larger context, there are also smaller groups of people, the "people who eat together," whom one can see in predictable groups eating in front of their homes in the evenings or gathered in the breakfast shops and general stores throughout the day. These groups usually collectively support one candidate. At the township level, each alang hopes to elect one of their own to the township council in the belief that it is the only way to get adequate service from the government after the election.

Work groups are also important. In contexts where agriculture is important, people used to have a tradition of daily labour exchange (*madas jiyax*) in which families would take turns helping each other at planting and harvest time. This practice is also called *smbarux*, or "labour in return" (Kaji 2011, 63). These same groups of people who would help each other in farming also tend to prefer working together when subcontractors come to the villages looking for workers for plantations or construction sites. In the past, people would work together all day, finishing the day with a pig as payment. In the early days of democratic elections, the KMT used this existing labour system to mobilize votes. I was told that they provided a pig in the early days, but later they paid with chickens or even cash. As a result of this historical practice, which is now perceived as "corruption" by contemporary standards, it is now forbidden for the candidates or campaign organizers (thiâu-á-kha 柱仔腳) to kill pigs before an election or shortly thereafter. From the perspective of the participants, they already spend their lives eating and socializing with the same group of people in the village. When elections happen, they feel obliged to support the candidates of their group, which happens in very public events of street processions and feasts. They benefit from this support through the generous offering of food and drink, and sometimes even with cash wages for the time they spend working on the campaign.

These elections are very expensive, which leads to accusations of corruption. The candidates provide the thiâu-á-kha with a budget to mobilize a predetermined number of votes. If they receive a budget of NT$300,000 for 100 votes, for example, they will say that the candidate purchased the votes for NT$3,000 per vote. In places where the stakes are high, as in Hsiulin Township where officials interact with Asia Cement and the Taroko National Park, the cost is especially elevated. In a village election I studied in 2006, people estimated that the winning candidate had spent more than NT$3,000,000 (CAD$130,434) for her campaign. People were not at all surprised, when I told them about candidate spending limits in Canadian parliamentary elections, to discover that it costs more to become elected as mayor of an Indigenous village of 2,000 people in Hualien than to run for member of Parliament in a riding in Toronto. Calling out what they described as a deficiency in their own democratic system, they pointed out that the candidates do not have their own funds to finance the campaigns, and the costs far exceed the salary that a person can expect to earn during one mandate. Candidates must therefore borrow money from influential people, usually those connected with mining and construction companies, and are thus indebted to them. In Hsiulin Township, for example, a local construction boss has won several successive elections as a member of the township council. Although he is the only non-Indigenous member of the council, he finances the campaigns of the other members and can count on their loyalty when they choose the township chair. Perceptions of corruption carry risks for the politicians and their allies. In fact, in the three years of my initial research, I saw one elected township politician, one thiâu-á-kha, and one non-Indigenous supporter with mining connections accused of vote buying, convicted, and imprisoned. When ordinary people see politicians chasing after money for themselves, rather than taking care of their constituents, they conclude that the politicians are naqih lnglungan (bad-hearted) or even ungat lnglungan (heartless).

The thiâu-á-kha use various psychological ploys to ensure support for their candidates. The banquets, efficacious use of music to stir up emotions, and parades all have the effect of enhancing solidarity among the core members, but those loyalties are public and chosen long before the election according to ties of affection called *ganqing* 感情 in Mandarin. The ethical dilemma is that everyone has personal ties with more than one person. In an election, a family may have to choose between, for example, voting for the husband's cousin, the wife's uncle, or the man who provided them both with a spot in a vocational training course. Some thiâu-á-kha themselves told me that they can convince some individuals with a bottle of rice wine or a red envelope with some cash discretely slipped in their pockets. There is little faith in the secrecy of the votes. Some voters are convinced, because they have been told so by the thiâu-á-kha, that the ballots are marked in ways that candidates know who voted for them. But probably the most effective strategy is to manipulate already existing ties of kinship and friendship.

Personal ties are often discussed and mobilized in terms of the Chinese concept of ganqing. This Chinese concept has been very productively used in the anthropology of China and Taiwan ever since the early work of Morton Fried based on his 1947–8 fieldwork in Anhui Province. For him, ganqing (which he spelled *kan-ch'ing*) was an expression for "the primary institutionalized technique by which class differences are reduced between non-related persons" (Fried 1953, 103). Contrasting this concept with friendship, a relationship between equals, he argued that rural tenants and agricultural workers were far more concerned about cultivating good ganqing than were the landlords and labour bosses. Mayfair Yang embeds her discussion of ganqing 感情 within a wider study of *guanxi* 關係 (relations), noting that it is a quality of "emotional feeling" in any long-standing emotional commitment, even between friends or close relatives. Her example, which she contrasts to the supposedly impersonal human relations in the West, is that of eating together in China, where one person pays for everyone in order to create a sentiment of indebtedness to the host (Yang 1994, 121). The thiâu-á-kha are skilled at creating these emotional bonds and a sense of indebtedness among the common people, just as the higher echelons of the KMT create such emotional ties with them.

The discourse of ganqing and culturally specific ways of cultivating it were certainly brought to Taiwan's Indigenous communities by Mainlanders working through the Peoples' Service Centres of the KMT, but those forms of interaction were not without precedent. During the Japanese period, the Japanese military and police officers similarly cultivated friendships through drinking and feasting with local leaders and influential people (Barclay 2003). Moreover, none of this cultivation is incompatible with traditional ethics. The relationships between "the people who eat together" were already important, even between non-kin. Moreover, people place a high value on the "loyal heart" (*mslago lnglungan*) and a need to take action based on affection. Quite often, there are ethical debates about the relationships between different ethnic groups, as I saw in 2007 during a by-election in Ren'ai Township of Nantou.

A Puppet Election

In Taiwan, the decade of the 2000s was marked by questions of ethnic identity, including in Indigenous politics. In 2004, the Truku in Hualien, who had since colonial times been classified as Atayal, gained state recognition as an independent group. As we will see later, electoral logics also played an important role in that somewhat pyrrhic victory. After the 2004 recognition of the Truku, influential people in Nantou in collaboration with allies in Hualien launched their own campaign for recognition of the Sediq as independent from both the Atayal and the Truku. One of the main proponents was Chen Shih-kuang, who was elected as township magistrate of Ren'ai Township in 2005. After the election, he and two thiâu-á-kha were accused and found guilty of corruption for having paid NT$5,000 to a villager for his vote. The Taichung Superior Court declared the election invalid and called for a by-election (Tseng 2006).[8]

The subsequent election was largely about ethnic identity or defining the appropriate place for the Sediq peoples of Nantou within a larger Chinese-dominated context. The KMT nominated Ke Shih-mei, a thirty-eight-year-old nurse and Chen's wife, as their candidate (figure 5.3). The opposition candidate was Zhang Zixiao, who already

Figure 5.3. Township magistrate election. KMT candidate Ke Shīn-mei emphasized her Indigenous identity.

Source: Photograph by Scott E. Simon.

had a reputation for being a political maverick locally and nationally.[9] As a PFP candidate closely allied with James Soong, he had already lost two township magistrate elections in 2002 and 2005. In 2006, he mobilized busloads of demonstrators from Ren'ai to descend on the streets of Taipei in massive "red tide" protests (Shih 2007) against the suspected corruption of DPP President Chen Shui-bian. Zhang rejoined the KMT after the protests but was expelled in 2007 amid accusations that he was an "opportunist" and threatened party unity in Nantou. Supporters of both candidates described this conflict as a struggle between the "blue army" (KMT) and the "red army" (PFP). Because the election occurred only one year before the 2008 presidential and legislative elections, national political leaders took it very seriously. KMT leader Ma Ying-jeou and KMT Indigenous legislator Kung Wen-chi came from Taipei to support Ke in public rallies, whereas James Soong and Indigenous legislator Lin Chunde took the stage with Zhang.

Ethnicity was at the centre of the campaign. Supporters of Sediq name rectification rallied around Ke. To emphasize her gender and ethnic identities, they decorated their campaign headquarters and rally platforms with boldly red Sediq weavings, which paradoxically meant that members of the "blue" camp appeared in red clothing. Ke's teams began and ended their campaign activities with Sediq song and dance. Even her campaign trucks blared Sediq music as they wove their way through the various villages of the township. Zhang, on the other hand, minimized his Indigenous identity, stressing instead the theme of "ethnic harmony" and portraying himself, as the son of an Atayal mother and Mainlander father, to be the most capable person to ensure a good relationship with the more powerful Chinese. In contrast to the colourful clothing of Ke, he wore a simple golf shirt in his campaign. His supporters hung banners all over the township saying "Abandon the marionettes. Elect talent!" The term "marionette" evoked the colourful ethnic clothing of Ke's campaign but was meant to both accuse her of being manipulated by a corrupt faction and to poke fun at her use of gaudy clothing to promote a distinct (and supposedly narrow) ethnic identity. Zhang's campaign trucks broadcasted Protestant hymns and speeches against corruption. Supporters of Sediq name rectification acted as if their beloved political project were on trial. They depicted it in terms of Gaya as a struggle between good and evil, especially because Ke affirmed her Sediq identity whereas Zhang represented assimilation and collaboration with the dominant Chinese.

After a rather subdued election, with strong police presence intended to prevent candidates from offering feasts and drinks on the day of the vote, Zhang was announced the winner. With a voter participation rate of 67 per cent, he won with 3,951 votes against 3,500 for Ke. In the evening, the thiâu-á-kha calculated their own losses and gains. Estimating that Ke had spent about NT$1,000 per vote and Zhang NT$2,000, both sides even admitted to me that they had delivered some red envelopes in the middle of the night. One of them laughed at the candidates for having engaged in such lavish campaigns, saying that "the candidates pay out a lot of cash, and often the people take from both sides. In fact, both candidates lost. The ordinary people won." After Zhang's inauguration ceremony, which some Sediq leaders told me fulfils the functions of their traditional peace ceremonies, Sediq nationalists sought Zhang's support for their goal of gaining legal recognition of the Sediq. Not only did they obtain Zhang's help, but they also got support from the Council of Indigenous Peoples (CIP). They did not trust the incoming KMT, nor ironically their own friend Ma Ying-jeou who would soon become president, to invest the necessary political capital needed for name rectification. In 2008, shortly before the national-level elections, the CIP announced that the Sediq were recognized as an independent group. The newly recognized groups, nearly a decade later, would provide the basis for creating new political arenas when the government decided to create band councils similar in some ways to those that exist in Canada.

Creating Band Councils

The legal need for precisely delimited groups such as Sediq or Truku goes far beyond the emotions of identity politics. Both UNDRIP and Taiwan's Basic Law are based on the foundation of Indigenous inherent sovereignty, a *sui generis* right emerging from the fact that the Indigenous peoples were present on a given territory before the external imposition of a state that marginalizes them and thwarts their ability to define and implement their own life projects. This concept calls for an imagined indigeneity, not as a variant of multiculturalism but as an institutionalized nation-to-nation relationship. In order to negotiate with the state and other interested parties, each Indigenous nation must have a governance structure that is recognized as a legal person capable of negotiating contracts and enforcing them. The emerging legal framework of indigeneity in international customary law is based on the assumption that it can be done only through the establishment of Indigenous governance structures that are at arm's length from the state. In Taiwan, the creation of Indigenous self-government would mean that Indigenous communities or nations could decide on development projects such as Asia Cement on the principle of free prior informed consent. It also means that they could establish and manage their own hunting and trapping regimes in a way that is both faithful to their own cultural traditions and sustainable for wildlife. In Taiwan, Indigenous leaders and scholars debate whether governance is best done at the local level, either within the boundaries of administrative villages or more traditional units like the alang, or at the level of larger national confederations like the Sediq or Truku Nation. But the government seems to be promoting lower level autonomy rather than larger confederations that resemble nations.

In May 2017, I attended a meeting in Bsngan about a state-led initiative to create local level band councils (*buluo huiyi* 部落會議) with the boundaries and populations to be decided by local consensus. People, quite expectedly, argued vociferously about whether this council should be organized according to the existing village boundaries, within which they already manage a community development association, or according to membership in the socially more relevant five alang that co-constitute the village. The proponents of both positions were all village elites whom people recognized from township-level politics, electoral campaigns, community development associations, and churches. These included fervent proponents of Truku identity but also prominent dissidents who still affirmed Sediq identity. One pastor argued that the legal autonomy promised by the new band councils was the only way to create a government based on Gaya, whereas an older person said this proposal reminded him of the tribal councils created in the Japanese period. Others asked what would be the role of people who have migrated to other parts of Taiwan. Again, when invited to join meetings or support this innovation, ordinary people had to make difficult ethical decisions. Some of them were not interested at all when the same elites they recognized from electoral competition suddenly proposed a new form of politics.

There is a reason for us to take this meandering route from breakfast shops to ethnic relations to elections and then to an emergent band council. After all, the campaign parades take a similar path, zigzagging through the countryside from village to village, from breakfast shop to general store, and back to the campaign headquarters for collective feasts at the end of each day. Throughout the day, people make ethical decisions about whether or not to join a parade, which parade to join, whether they should hide inside their homes, or avoid voting altogether by pretending that they absolutely have to spend that week in Taipei. They all know that they are making a collective decision for leaders who will have an influence on the relationship that their village and township has with a state they all perceive as an external imposition. They also know that the results will influence their relations with other ethnic groups in what is becoming a multicultural Taiwan. Experience teaches them that whenever local elites promise them something, whether it be a development project or an ethnically themed festival, those elites are trying to cultivate support for the next election. From this "inside" perspective, it makes sense for ordinary people to ally with the Mainlanders who brought them their familiar political system of "local autonomy" and who have nurtured emotionally laden relations of ganqing with them for decades, even if they are simultaneously cynical about their own local leaders and accuse them of violating Gaya by accumulating private wealth and power. The alternative seems to be an alliance with the ethnic Taiwanese, and so far their experience with them has been worse. In this wider political context, anyone who arrives with promises of name rectification, sovereignty, or even social justice appears as one political entrepreneur among many. Even with the best ideas derived from international discussions of indigeneity, it can be difficult for political entrepreneurs to gain traction and local support.

Discussion

This chapter, as part of an understanding of Sejiq and Truku as emergent social relations within a context of electoral politics, delved into the difficult problematics of electoral politics and Indigenous politics as a continual process of ethical reflection. Along with churches and schools, democratic institutions such as elections and political offices are historically a colonial imposition on Indigenous peoples. But, as they did with Christianity, the Sədeq peoples have adeptly transformed democracy to fit their own needs. The primacy of the alang and groups of people who eat together at campaign time shows how the people incorporate political innovations into existing forms of social relations. The number of political offices, many reserved for Indigenous people, provides sufficient opportunity for individuals drawn to leadership positions and, in the egalitarian ethos of Gaya, the ordinary folk also have means of keeping individual ambition in check, not least through gossip. People interpret institutions of indigeneity, including legal recognition of peoples and the establishment of new political organizations, as part of this wider political field. These are all ways in which local communities negotiate their place with other peoples or ethnic groups within a colonial situation.

Elites and ordinary people alike accept or reject political parties and other institutions within an ethical process of the heart that is based most of all on relations with other people, and that depends very much on individual circumstances. So far, this process has led to the seemingly paradoxical situation in which Indigenous communities vote for the KMT rather than for more progressive parties that more fervently advocate Indigenous rights. The KMT has been very successful at building up relations with Indigenous communities through intermarriage, development projects and workshops, the continual work of KMT cadres who help people resolve conflicts with the state, and seemingly trivial conversations daily in breakfast shops and grocery stores. The election fixers understand the importance of heartfelt communication, which is why they invest so much time building relations with ordinary people between and during electoral campaigns. Social activists trained in urban Taiwan or academics well versed in international Indigenous rights law fail to gain understanding at the grassroots, especially because they are not present in the villages and taking part in daily conversations.

This chapter shows that ordinary people have come to dwell in a physical and social landscape that is shaped by their own labour but also by the imposition of outsiders. Over the past century, they have been physically displaced by the Japanese, adopted subaltern Mainlanders who gave up hope of returning to China, and been swindled by Kmukan entrepreneurs trying to exploit their land and labour. Their villages, as well as the surrounding forests, mountains, and fields, are all shaped through these interactions between different groups of people. Most ordinary people have already achieved a sense of comfort in this place where they have reserve land as a retreat, but have then joined alliances with Mainlanders in the Kuomintang in township and national politics.

People make their ethical decisions within this larger context. They are asked to join election campaigns, vote for candidates, sign petitions, participate in demonstrations, send their children to native language instruction, and join in cultural festivities. They are most likely to cooperate with the people they know best and with whom they share established relations. If would-be leaders become elected politicians and then monopolize the benefits of power without sharing in ways perceived as stipulated by Gaya, ordinary people accuse them of being ill-hearted (naqih lnglungan). If those same leaders get involved in oppositional politics or campaigns for name rectification or autonomy, people also perceive that they are just trying to create new positions of power for themselves. This situation creates ethical dilemmas for ordinary people at every election.

The ramifications of people's political choices are of great consequence. When people are being asked to vote for a particular candidate, change their household registration data to a new Indigenous group, or show support for the creation of an Indigenous autonomous zone, they are being asked to choose between competing political ontologies. People have a clear awareness of their colonial situation, but simultaneously embrace the benefits of democratic citizenship. People know that state-centric indigeneity, including proposed autonomous zones and the more recent Presidential Office Indigenous Historical Justice and Transitional Justice Committee, are all forms of relationships with the state. They judge their leaders who engage with all of these state institutions based on values of Gaya and alang. An ontology based on Gaya was about relations between people in face-to-face relations where heart mattered more than money. Gaya had nothing to say about the borders of ethnic groups or about Indigenous nations imagined as coloured shapes on maps. People are cynical because they know that the state, like money, is foreign to Gaya.

When considered from within the existing meshwork of social relations, it makes sense that ordinary people react to political innovations with suspicion and even cynicism about the motivations of their proponents. They were initially slow to accept being called "Indigenous" rather than "mountain compatriots," and "Truku" or "Sediq" rather than "Atayal," but those identities eventually took root. When I first started my research, few young people seemed interested in name rectification, but fifteen years later, they strongly identified as either Sediq or Truku. Those new identities have gained traction, and they influence the ways in which people view their place in the world.

Most people still find it difficult to understand why "Indigenous self-government" promoted by Han Taiwanese in the DPP is an improvement over the "local self-government" promoted by Mainlanders in the KMT. For them, these different projects are more closely intertwined with personal ethics and inter-ethnic loyalties than with abstract national politics. This way of thinking means that politics, local and national, is more about maintaining good relations with kin and neighbours than about taking a stand on apparently remote issues such as Indigenous rights or cross-strait relations. It is precisely this distrust of authority, even of those would-be leaders who promise new state-based institutions of indigeneity, that makes the people who follow Gaya so egalitarian, autonomous, and republican to this day.

Huling (dog) 土狗

Figure 6.1. Formosan mountain dogs (*Canis familiaris formosanus*) are members of the community and usually permitted to roam freely. They are medium-sized, with a height around 50 centimetres and a weight around 16 kilograms. Hunters prize them for agility, balance, attention to game, and ability to obey commands. People used to hunt with five to six dogs that would encircle a boar or other animal until the hunter could stab or shoot it. Now, due to restrictions on hunting, it is more common for a hunter to take only one dog for companionship or to retrieve flying squirrels from steep ravines. Real people – *seejiq balay* – consider it barbarian to eat dog meat.

Source: Illustration by Biluan.

Chapter Six

Tminun (Weaving)

It was late at night, and it had already been a very long day for the township and village politicians in Wanrong Township. In the late morning, most of the villagers had attended the inauguration ceremony for the newly elected village mayors (figure 6.2). Six village mayors had been elected, in addition to the township magistrate and members of the township council. Only one woman, in a neighbouring village, had been elected. A political ritual unfolded in a hall duly decorated with the tricolour Republic of China flag, reminding everyone present that they are citizens of Republican China. The crowd dutifully sang the national anthem, swearing allegiance to the Three Principles of the People, the modern Chinese political philosophy of liberty, equality, and fraternity that everyone had learned in primary school. Although most people probably do not reflect on the meaning of the lyrics, the song is addressed to "our party," admonishing the leaders of the country to serve the people with diligence and courage "with one heart and one virtue."[1] At the conclusion of the national anthem, the crowd followed instructions from the master of ceremonies to bow three times to a portrait of Dr. Sun Yat-sen, who is credited with founding the Republic of China (ROC) in 1911.

The brief ceremony was planned to stress an ethic of public service. The township magistrate, who had himself just been inaugurated in a separate ceremony, took the podium and gave a speech. He reminded the new mayors that they had all promised during their campaigns to serve the people, and now the actual work must begin. He said they should all follow the example of an exemplary village mayor, who had served five terms. Whenever there was a typhoon, he said, the mayor never waited for help to come from outside the village. Instead, he immediately went to work before the storm with his own bulldozer to clear the stream of stones and debris and thus lower the risk of floods.

Figure 6.2. Mayoral inauguration, Hualien, 2006. Republic of China symbolism is designed to instill loyalty to the state.

Source: Photograph by Scott E. Simon.

As soon as the storm had passed, he was the first person to emerge from his house to begin clearing the roads of fallen trees. "This is only one example of the service expected from a village mayor," the magistrate said. "You must remember that, from now on, all of the problems of the villagers are your own problems." He reminded them, as well, who holds the reins of power. Village mayors can propose new projects, but only the township can make decisions about the budget. The tasks of the village mayors are to carry out the administrative orders of the township government. The mayors were then called to the stage and lined up in front of Dr. Sun Yat-sen's portrait. Raising their right hands into the air, they swore allegiance to the Republic of China and to the welfare of their villages. The township magistrate distributed plaques of recognition and welcomed them as new servants of the people. At the conclusion, the township office sponsored a celebratory banquet, allowing each elected mayor to invite about a dozen supporters, friends, and family members. Not a word was said about the prospect of creating a Truku Autonomous Zone – even though this issue was one of the main local political topics in the summer of 2006.

Many stories were told that day. In the morning ceremony, the township leaders wove politicians and citizens alike into a narrative of the nation, the Chinese Republic, and the Chinese Nationalist Party (KMT) that represented it at the local level. But at night, as we relaxed in the privacy of his home, the re-elected mayor spun for me a much more local story. I had spent the afternoon learning about the machinations of the township council, as the incumbent council chair unexpectedly lost his position when one of his supporters suddenly ran for the position himself and won. At the end of his own day of celebrating, the mayor took out the bottle of wine that I had given him after my trip to France and poured us both a glass. "You came to Ciyakang at the wrong time to study development," he said. "People worked hard when the economy was brisk. Nowadays, there is not enough work so people have become lazy. Most people just work for two days and rest for five. They only go back to work after the booze has been drunk." There are more important issues at stake, he said.

People love to tell stories about the past in an oral genre that they call "weaving the words of elders of times past" (*tminun kari rudan sbiyaw*). The mayor told me the story of his grandfather Walis Yakao. This name was familiar name to me, since my own Truku name given to me in a different village was Walis. In Ciyakang, when I introduced myself as Walis, people often recalled: "Ah! Like our Walis Yakao!" Offering to fill in the details for me, the mayor explained that Walis Yakao was his grandfather, who had been an important leader a century earlier. "There was no law back then," he told me, "so headhunters were considered to be heroes who protected their ancestral territory." Walis Yakao, he continued, was well known for his prowess as a warrior, having killed many people and even taken the lives of many Japanese. In gory detail, the mayor described how his grandfather "could cut off a head as easily as if he were cutting the head of a chicken, and the person would not even feel it." He would then throw the head into a sling and carry a set of heads on his back to return triumphantly to the village.

Walis Yakao's headhunting drew him across the central mountains to Nantou. Once he had arranged a meeting with Mona Rudo, the fearsome leader of the Tgdaya Mhebu clan (discussed later in the chapter). After crossing Hehuan Mountain, he entered an Atayal community and announced to them that they should not sleep at night since he was planning on cutting heads. When they went to sleep as usual, Walis cut off three heads while they were sleeping and fled the village. Walis apparently escaped all immediate repercussions, but two generations later, these homicides have not been forgotten. "If anyone from our village goes there," the mayor said, "the people ask if we have heard of Walis Yakao. They want to know which clan we belong to. No matter what we say, they are likely to beat us up. Even if ten of us go together, we are in danger."

Bringing the story back to his own experience, the mayor explained the supernatural ramifications of history. Headhunting was such a terrible evil, he said, that it brings bad luck not only to the perpetrator but to his offspring for three generations. The ancestors, after all, must enforce the laws of *Gaya*, and that means punishing those who have murdered. This retribution explains the poverty that Walis Yakao and his entire family experienced. "I am the third generation," he said, pointing out that he is now forced to atone by serving the people humbly. Only in the fourth generation, that of his son, will his family know prosperity and a good life. By then, we had finished the bottle of wine. He set the empty bottle on the floor, picked up the wine glasses, and escorted me to the door.

This narrative, which is obviously incomplete and probably full of historical inaccuracy, could easily be dismissed as drunken ramblings. Although I cannot know for sure what it meant, there was probably a personal reason why the mayor, at the conclusion of one of the busiest days of his career, would go out of his way to summon me to his house and tell me this story. He had probably spent the entire day thinking about the changing nature of political power and where he, as grandson of an infamous headhunter, fits into the wider scheme of things. The fact that this conversation happened on the day of his inauguration is not fortuitous; political crises and elections can provoke surges of memory as people imagine new futures for themselves and their communities (Cole 2006). It is salient that the mayor placed himself, not as a humble public servant amid the unfolding story of the Chinese nation, a narrative carefully retold by state and party, but rather as an individual and grandson with a precarious position in relations between communities on two sides of Taiwan's Central Mountain Range. This election occurred only two years after the Truku gained legal recognition as an ethnic group, when Truku leaders were advocating for the creation of an autonomous region including counties in both Hualien and Nantou and when opposition to that project was gaining traction in the Nantou highlands. This story is thus an appropriate starting point for an exploration of memory and its importance in shaping the political landscape of indigeneity in contemporary Taiwan.

Quite strikingly, in every village where I have done research, young and old people alike have told me stories on their own initiative about what happened to their families and to their villages during the Japanese period. They make it clear that the Japanese period was the first time in history that they knew the power of the state and the force of state law. They also make it clear that the state was imposed on them through violence. This violence may seem suspended at times, but always remains a possibility. People in Hualien and Nantou have very different stories to tell. In Hualien, people talk about the 1914 Battle of Taroko, in which the Truku people resisted the modern Japanese military for nearly three months before finally submitting to state power. In Nantou, they talk instead about the 1930 Musha Uprising, about how Mhebu leader Mona Rudo organized a violent uprising against the Japanese, provoking military reprisals that still traumatize the survivors and their families. This chapter is structured around the memories of these two historical events. How have the Sediq and the Truku woven together stories and new political identities? It is the story of how the people of Pusu Qhuni established identities as two distinct Indigenous peoples.

Weaving

I called this chapter "weaving" (*tminun*) for several reasons. As mentioned earlier, oral storytelling is called tminun kari rudan sbiyaw (weaving the words of the elders of past times). In the communities I studied, human sociality was based upon eating and drinking together, frequently around a firepit or a makeshift grill in front of peoples' homes. In the winter, people value this time of huddling around the fire together, but in the heat of summer they venture into the mountains to relax while soaking in a cool stream. Wealthier people may create welcoming places in their homes or courtyards to entertain guests with tea or alcohol. In these contexts, people love to share stories of the past. I was amazed at their ability to do so, aware that I am unable to tell stories about what my great-uncles did at the beginning of the twentieth century. But I do not have the burden of trying to hold a small community together in the context of cultural imperialism. The choice of the verb "to weave" is fitting, since it highlights the creativity of the genre. Storytellers may take familiar themes and base their stories on actual historical incidents, but they make the stories relevant to their current situations as if the past and the present constitute the warp and woof of a new creation. This way of storytelling is what Mario Blaser called "storied performativity," since there is a direct connection between stories and practices in these worlding or ontological practices (Blaser 2013, 552).

Tminun is also important because it values the work of women. In traditional cosmology, the people said that men can cross the Rainbow Bridge into the land of the ancestors only if they have demonstrated competence as hunters and warriors, whereas women must demonstrate their abilities in weaving. Weaving is a prominent theme in public dance performances and in native language instruction. It is so important to Indigenous identity, in fact, that the only woman candidate in the mayoral electoral race in Ciyakang had prominently displayed Truku weavings in her campaign activities. State funding is made available to weaving workshops, and thus nearly every village has one or more weaving workshops. The women who run the workshops carefully research the weaving patterns of their ancestors, often perusing old ethnographies and photo collections for inspiration and authenticity. They say that their weavings all contain stories. Straight lines may represent the Rainbow Bridge, for example, and diamonds may represent the eyes of the ancestors (*dowriq utux rudan*) who are always watching the living for any violations of Gaya. Weaving is thus a way of telling stories to future generations and keeping a rich cultural heritage alive. The clothing made from such weaving is rarely worn in daily life. It is instead brought out for special occasions and cultural performances. People are more likely to use some weavings to decorate their homes. Smaller, less expensive items such as covers for mobile phones are more commonly seen. The high cost of weavings, as opposed to factory-made clothing imported from China, makes it impractical to wear such items in the workplace or while farming. In any case, weaving puts memory into physical form. In the era of Indigenous resurgence, the presence of weaving, because of the stories in the patterns, reminds people that they are Sejiq or Truku.

Sejiq Truku Approaches to Memory

Curious to know if the Truku have a culturally specific understanding of memory, I asked Kuhon Sibal in Hualien how to say "I remember." Much to my initial surprise, he gave a very cognitivist reply, saying *skuun ruqi* (to deposit in the brain). As an example, he said: "*Kana skuun ska ruqi mu,*" which literally means "It's all deposited in my brain." The metaphor evokes images of saving things on computers, and that certainly works for him. His computer is full of digitalized historical photos of the Japanese conquest, grant proposals for various forms of state funding to Indigenous groups, email threads, and years of Facebook feeds. The word *skuun* is used for bank deposits, but also for burials.

The fact that the idiom refers to the brain is important. "You can also say I stored it in my head (*tunux*)," he explained, "but it is better to say the brain (*naojiang* 腦漿 in Chinese)," using as his Chinese gloss the term that means the cerebellum and other parts of the brain that get exposed when the skull is crushed. It is the same character that is used for paper pulp and soy milk. I verified this Truku wording with two other elders in Hualien and two in Nantou, getting the same answer. Moreover, I noticed that, unlike native speakers of Chinese, who would simply say "I remember," elderly Truku speakers have a tendency to say "I remember it in my brain." This linguistic habit is thus a translation from a Truku original. They explicitly draw attention to the process by which short-term memories are transformed into long-term memories. They may imagine ethics as belonging to the heart, but they attribute memory to the brain.

As an anthropologist, I am more interested in social memory. Kuhon may have drawn my attention to psychological processes, but in social life the most important memories are those that are shared in conversation and those that take concrete form in social memory. In conversation, which forms the basis of ethnographies such as this one, people enter into what Tim Ingold called a common stream of consciousness (Ingold [1986] 2016, 226). In conversation, people recall events, symbols, and ideas that establish and maintain relationships between the individuals engaged in talk. Based on shared memories, powerful people in a community can find ways to select memories and give them concrete form. Social space is thus never neutral; it is always a product of struggle between conflicting groups of people (Halbwachs [1950] 1980; Lefebvre [1974] 1991; Simon 2003a).

The description of the township hall at the beginning of this chapter is a good example of this social space. It is intended to focus attention on the ROC and its symbols, subordinating the people in that space to one avatar of the Chinese nation, eliminating other possibilities. It is based on the ontology of the modern nation-state in a way that obscures and marginalizes Indigenous ontologies. But Indigenous people keep other memories, such as those the mayor shared with me, and struggle *within* Indigenous nations also takes form in social space. These are ontological struggles about what exists. People reflect on such questions as the following: Are we in the Republic of China, interacting as citizens in a modern democracy? Or are we on unceded Sejiq or Truku territory, trying to seize agency as Indigenous peoples? Is it possible to be both at the same time? These are not easy questions to answer, which is why many ordinary people brush them off, saying it is all political strategies of local elites and has nothing to do with them.

During my field research, competing local factions evoked their memories in conversations as ways of drawing me into their lives. When I first arrived in Hualien, Kuhon Sibal was eager to demonstrate to me his Christian heritage. He told me the story about his father, who had converted to Christianity and took the initiative of founding the local True Jesus congregation. "The Japanese tried to suppress Christianity," he said, "because they suspected that all Christians were potentially spies for the Americans." He said that the Japanese thus arrested his father and planned to execute him. They imprisoned him in a small bamboo hut. A typhoon struck in the night, and the violent winds destroyed his makeshift prison. He was able to escape into the woods and avoid punishment. This story thus contrasts the negative colonial past with the present, in which Taiwan and North America are closely linked and share religious freedom. He was using memory to weave together our friendship.

The following year, another person told the same story in a different context and with the addition of another detail. This person, a fervent proponent of Truku nationalism, held a long-standing grudge against Kuhon and a retired Presbyterian minister because both of them had opposed the creation of an independent Truku Nation and supported forming a Sediq Nation. He was especially furious that the minister was suddenly accepting a daily fee to help the township office draft a Truku dictionary. He told me that the minister had a lifelong tendency to choose sides for personal gain, thus violating Gaya concerning both loyalty and avoidance of personal gain. "During the Japanese period," the person recalled, "he even collaborated with the Japanese police. He was the leader of the Takasago Youth Corps and spied on us for them. He is the one who told the Japanese where to find Sibal and imprison him." After the Japanese left, the person telling the story argued, this man faked conversion and became a minister so that he could take control of donations in food and clothing coming in from American churches. I questioned the person, saying: "Maybe his conversion was a genuine change of heart, like St. Paul on the road to Damascus." The person insisted, however, that all those who support Sediq nationalism are disloyal and only out for personal profit. During this time, which was also the time of the election evoked earlier, Truku and Sediq proponents were making mutual accusations against each other, not only to visiting anthropologists but also in church sermons and on nationally broadcast television shows. This context of wider political conflict is important to keep in mind in the following discussion of the Truku Battle and the Musha Uprising.

The 1914 Battle of Taroko

Because Truku leaders were re-evaluating their own history while I was doing research, they were eager to share their thoughts with me. When I evoked the Musha Uprising, they told me that almost nobody in Hualien identifies with Mona Rudo. Instead, they think about their history in terms of three important local "incidents." The first was the 1896 Hsincheng Incident, which happened one year after Japan acquired Taiwan. In the Hsincheng Incident, Truku men killed thirteen Japanese soldiers in revenge for the rape of a young Truku woman. The Japanese sent troops, including a battalion of warriors from the Amis, but gave up trying to conquer the Truku after four failed attempts. In the 1906 Weili Incident, the Truku were angry at the Japanese for cutting camphor trees on their territory without their consent. Truku warriors killed twenty-five Japanese officers and took sixteen hostages. The Japanese reacted by sending in one hundred Japanese and five hundred Amis troops, but the Truku maintained their territorial autonomy in the mountains. Details of these incidents figure in the written history of the Atayal (Walis and Yu 2002). In the oral accounts that people told me, people seemed quite interested in the role played by Han Taiwanese merchant Lee Ah-long, who had organized the Truku violence. The Japanese killed Lee Ah-long first in their reprisals for the Weili Incident.

For the Truku in the Hualien highlands, the historical turning point happened in 1914 (figure 6.3). Governor-General Sakuma Samata, a general whose military career included suppression of the 1874 Saga and the 1877 Satsuma Rebellions in Japan as well as an 1874 punitive expedition against the Paiwan of Formosa, obtained funding from Japan's twenty-fifth Diet for his "Second Five-Year Plan to Manage the Aborigines" to last from 1910 to 1914. In what historian Paul Barclay calls a "scorched earth" campaign, the goal was to eradicate the mountains of the peoples who were seen as obstacles to rational land surveys, modern forestry, and capitalist accumulation. The overall strategy was to encircle communities with military force. The guard lines, known as *aiyūsen* 隘勇線 in Japanese, consisted of electrified fences, landmines, and armed guard posts. As the military moved the guard lines further into the interior, the Indigenous groups would be unable to leave the restricted areas to trade for such important goods as salt and would eventually become desperate enough to surrender (Barclay 2018, 104–6; Linck-Kesting 1978; Walis and Yu 2002, 154–5).

Japanese troops began attacking the Truku highlands with troops arriving from both Musha in the west and Hualien in the east, sending in over 6,000 troops equipped with the most advanced military

Figure 6.3. Battle of Taroko. Japanese soldiers planning their attacks on the Truku.

Source: Special Collections & College Archives, Skillman Library, Lafayette College.

equipment at the time. The 2,000 to 3,000 Truku warriors were equipped only with bows and arrows, as well as a limited number of hunting rifles (Walis and Yu 2002, 155). The Truku resisted for nearly three months before surrendering in August (Hara 2006, 62). The Japanese military erected triumphal arches throughout Taiwan and celebrated with military parades. By Japanese accounts, Sakuma returned to Japan, where he had an audience with Emperor Taishō on 19 September 1914 (Barclay 2018, 110). He died on 5 August 1915 and became a deity in state Shinto. Most of the Truku communities were involuntarily relocated into new villages in the Hualien foot-hills and plains, where they were organized into "savage reserves" (*banjin shoyōchi* 蕃人所要地) and encouraged to take up agriculture in policies based on the American frontier model (Yan and Yang 2004, 232–3). Twenty-eight hamlets refused to move (Masaw 1978, 109), which is probably part of the reason why subsequent Japanese documents reported that the Indigenous people were not reduced to submission and that "some of them *may still remain incorrigible at heart*" (Barclay 2018, 110, emphasis in the original). One of those hamlets was Skadang, which people have not abandoned to this day, despite the construction of the Taroko National Park on their lands.

Individual Memory and the Battle of Taroko: Life Histories and Storytelling

By the time I began my fieldwork in 2004, there were no people alive with personal memories of the battle. Nonetheless, people made constant reference to this historical set of events as well as to other dimensions of the Japanese period, retelling what they had learned from elder members of their own families. They drew parallels between resistance against the Japanese and their own experience dealing with the Taroko National Park. Young men described with pride, using the first-person pronoun "we," how their ancestors, without modern weapons, lured fully armed Japanese troops into a narrow canyon and then decimated them by unleashing boulders on them from above. The lesson was that human ingenuity and knowledge of the terrain can overcome technological superiority. Sometimes they contrasted policies, saying, for example, that the Japanese allowed them to hunt and even provided them with rifles and ammunition, whereas the contemporary overlords arrest them for catching animals with rusty traps leftover from the Japanese period.

Even as my own research interests focused more on contemporary issues of development and resistance, local people were doing their own research on the Battle of Taroko and shared their interpretation of events with me on their own initiative. One such person was Kuhon, who in 2001 and 2002 had conducted life history interviews with 102 elderly people between the ages of 80 and 100 years of age. In 2003 and 2005, he even went to Japan to visit Sakuma's grave, do archival research, and interview members of Sakuma's family. He published excerpts from selected life history interviews in two volumes, one about women's (Kuhon 2010) and one about men's (Kuhon 2014) experiences. He invited me to write a preface to one volume. Kuhon's two books are coloured with his own political proclivities. He refers in the titles to "Truku people" (plural of person) rather than to a "Truku people" (in the sense of a nationality), preferring to depict his interviewees as speakers of Truku, Toda, and Tgdaya who are all "Seejiq balay." True to his lifetime of service to the Chinese Nationalist Party, the preface to his second book embeds the interviews within a Chinese nationalist narrative in which he traces the origin of Taiwan's Indigenous peoples to China and portrays the 1945 turnover of Taiwan by the Republic of China as a liberation from repressive colonial rule. Kuhon's goal was to promote pan-Sediq identity, but he did it from within a Chinese nationalist framework.

Kuhon's books provide valuable glimpses into how a generation of Truku experienced the upheavals of the twentieth century, a period that saw their integration into states for the first time in history. Kuhon is not the only local grassroots scholar to write about the Battle of Taroko and to give me his books. Taroko nationalist leader Tera Yudaw justified his agenda for Taroko political autonomy within a history of resistance against the Japanese in Hualien (Tera 2003). That book was followed by more detailed historical works by younger scholars in Hualien (e.g., Shen 2008; Siyat 2004), and there is a constant stream of publications to this day. I focus on Kuhon's works, however, because he was one of the main influences on my field research. In addition, the presentation of the life histories in the words of the elderly people is more personal and conversational than what one would read in a professional history. The oldest informant was a woman born in 1904, who describes hiding in a cave and watching as the Japanese military destroyed their homes and crops (Kuhon 2010, 195). The youngest was a man born in 1949. Although Kuhon interviewed people across Hualien, some of his interviewees were also people with whom I interacted during my own field research. Unfortunately, Kuhon did not publish the questions he had asked them, nor did he reveal how he selected which stories to publish. He was, after all, a retired policeman trying to document his people's history and not a professional historian.

The transcripts of the life narratives reveal several themes. Many informants simply apologized for having forgotten the stories that their parents had told them about the Battle of Taroko. Some said that their parents had never talked about it. Many of the narratives begin with pre-colonial practices such as headhunting, describing the Toda as perpetual enemies, and tattooing, revealing the personal pain experienced both while getting tattoos and while removing them when required by Japanese authorities. Since most of the memories are from the latter years of Japanese administration, many of them talked about the Japanese instruction offered in elementary schools, expressing nostalgia about personal relations with their teachers. They discussed the Kōminka campaign, in which Japanese authorities tried to impose Japanese lifestyles, and the war, when the Japanese recruited young men for action in Southeast Asia and Oceania. They described the Japanese authorities as strict supervisors of poorly paid or forced labour but also spoke about the positive aspects of such strict social order, such as a lack of crime. They tended to be proud of their Japanese military service.

One of the major overarching themes was movement along physical trajectories in the mountains. People recalled the difficult forced labour of carrying heavy burdens of lumber, supplies, or official documents across treacherous terrains in service of the Japanese administration.

Women recalled their life trajectories of moving from their natal families to their husband's families in patrilocal marriages. Most of all, people recalled the trauma of their families and entire communities being forced to move from their mountain homes to the plains.

The difficult terrain figures importantly in their descriptions of Japanese invasion routes, with recognition that long-term resistance was possible only because of their own knowledge of the terrain. Emax Yudaw, for example, described the community of Kbayan, which resisted the Japanese most ferociously. Emax was only one of many to evoke the strategy that the people of Kbayan used to defeat the well-armed Japanese troops. They lured the troops into a steep valley with steep cliffs on both sides. This valley was a dangerous trap, as the villagers were waiting on top to launch an avalanche of boulders and trees onto the unsuspecting troops (Kuhon 2014, 103). This shared social memory, in fact, is one that Truku people in Hualien have repeatedly related to me over the years. The name Kbayan, high up in the mountains and uninhabited, means "the village we protect" (Kaji 2011, 146). Emax described the slow process by which the Japanese troops brought one community after another to surrender.

The narratives emphasized Truku agency. In another story that I heard rather frequently in fieldwork, many people described how, as Sakuma led his troops through the mountain forests, Truku warriors shot and killed him. There seems to be a broad understanding that Sakuma was killed and buried around a place called Slagu Qhuni (Kaji 2011, 147; Kuhon 2014, 105). Since *qhuni* means "tree," this story tells that Sakuma's soul was reclaimed by the forest he hoped to conquer. The stories contradict one another about who killed Sakuma. Some assert that nobody knows who fired the fatal shot, whereas others claim in full confidence that their own father or grandfather killed Sakuma. Yudaw Pisaw, a Presbyterian minister who was also one of my Truku language instructors, explained the situation:

> Some people out on a hunting expedition must have surrounded Sakuma's encampment. Since they started to shoot at him simultaneously from different positions, each person thought that he was the one who fired the fatal shot. Therefore, there are so many interpretations. (Kuhon 2014, 94)

This story is commonly told in the community. One senior hunter, whom I call Karaw here, once told me that he can show me the precise location where Sakuma was buried and the stones that mark his grave. Unfortunately, Karaw passed away from liver disease shortly before we could make that expedition.

Sakuma's death is an important part of local cosmology. When Karaw recounted to me the story of Sakuma being killed, I revealed my own scepticism. I said that Japanese accounts have him returning to Taipei, marching in parades, going back to Japan, meeting the emperor, and then dying at home a year later.[2] Karaw replied, in a serious tone of voice that revealed full conviction, that the Japanese had replaced Sakuma with an imposter in order to fool the local people into believing that Sakuma had lived and had conquered them. I said that I found it unlikely that an imposter could fool Sakuma's own family, even to the extent of having the intimate experience of dying and the body prepared for the funeral. Karaw poured me another beer and turned the conversation to other issues. Perhaps I simply didn't understand at the time that it is not important whether Sakuma really was killed by Truku warriors. These stories make it possible for people to assert their own collective agency as part of a larger story. The story of a Truku warrior killing Sakuma is a potent ontological claim. The Truku know the territory they inherited from their ancestors and, as people of Gaya, they will protect it against even the most powerful outsiders by all means necessary.

Back to social memories of the Battle of Taroko, some people interviewed by Kuhon asserted Truku agency even at the final surrender. Their defeat may have been partly caused by the superior weaponry of the Japanese military, but the Truku were able to outwit them on the dangerous terrain and even kill their leader. The final decision to surrender, however, came not from direct pressure from the Japanese but from within. Several people referred to a devout Christian woman named Pai Ciwan, who had studied in Japan and understood the Japanese. Travelling by foot to all of the Truku communities, she urged people: "Do not continue to fight against the Japanese. You will only sacrifice more of our people. The Japanese have many troops, and their weapons are superior. We Truku should stop sacrificing ourselves this way" (Kuhon 2010, 60). Kado Kimi explains this person was Ciwang, founder of a Presbyterian congregation, who was trained by the Japanese and sent by Japanese authorities to dissuade the people from violent resistance. "There is no point in resisting," she said, "because the Japanese soldiers are as numerous as ants" (Ai 2015, 12). These stories thus explain the end of Truku battles as resulting from the pathways of one Truku woman urging her people to choose peace rather than destruction.

Most of the stories shared in the books are about events that happened after the 1914 battle. After the Battle of Taroko, the Japanese erected a Shinto shrine to Sakuma at Tpdu – which, now named T'ien-hsiang after a Song Dynasty Chinese politician, is one of the central tourist hubs in the Taroko National Park. The Japanese also erected a Sakuma shrine in Dowmung far to the south. Every year on 28 January, everyone was required to go to these shrines and pray. In a manner reminiscent of contemporary practices in the Taroko National Park (see chapter 3), young people from different villages were invited to participate in song and dance competitions at these events.

Kuhon's books end with no conclusion. From 102 interviews, Kuhon chose to publish the stories of 40 women and 24 men, translating them himself from Truku to Mandarin Chinese. Although he selected the stories to share and abridged them considerably, they all speak with their own voices. The result is a cacophony of unique voices, describing the divergent pathways taken by different individuals over the past century. Sometimes their stories converge. The Japanese period was the definitive moment when the Truku lost their former way of life and their ability to live autonomously in the mountain forests. The Battle of Taroko and the subsequent forced displacement to the plains was a traumatic experience for all. But there were also differences. Some communities resisted the Japanese intrusion to the bitter end. Others surrendered quickly in the face of an overwhelming military opponent, and some even fought for the Japanese. They described pre-colonial conflicts between the Truku and Toda groups, and Japanese military actions seem to have only deepened those conflicts. Reading these life histories, especially in the context of hearing the same and similar stories told in village conversations, makes it difficult to imagine how people with such divergent paths can possibly come together to forge their way forward as a "Truku Nation" or a "Seediq Nation." That takes a more conscious effort of social memory. With so many divergent individual memories, it is inevitable that any effort to shape social memory is met with discontent.

Constructing a Truku Nation

From 1996 to 2004, the Truku of Hualien held a series of research workshops, conferences, and cultural events to construct a Truku identity separate from the Atayal and Seediq. This project meant emphasizing stories other than the larger saga of migration over the mountains from Nantou to Hualien. Since the Seediq had their history of Mona Rudo and the Musha Uprising, the Truku had to draw attention to their own bravery. The story of Truku hunters killing Governor-General Sakuma Samata during the Battle of Taroko was thus useful in constructing a Truku history and identity (Hara 2006).

By 2005, when I began long-term field research in Bsngan near the Taroko National Park, Truku leaders from the township office and Presbyterian Church networks were already making plans to establish a Taroko Autonomous Region.

The Taroko National Park had to deal diplomatically with the Truku. On 12 June 2005, on our way to Skadang, a group of students and I stopped at the visitors' centre. Chin Hsang-Te, a Truku MA student studying tribal mapping with his supervisor Chi Chun-Chieh, gave us a tour of the special exhibit he had curated there. He had purchased photos, postcards, and period items at antique stores and other places in Japan so that he could show his narrative of how the Japanese had come to Taiwan and violently taken over Truku territory. He deconstructed the Chinese nationalist narrative, told elsewhere in the visitors' centre, that Mainlander soldiers working under the leadership of Chiang Kai-shek had built the road across the central mountains. In fact, Chin said, the roads were already there. They were hunting paths, carved over centuries of walking on them, but were improved upon by the Japanese military in order to conquer the Truku and were only broadened and paved by the Chinese. The exhibit ended with a photo of a Truku man in traditional clothing gazing longingly at the mountain forests. The caption stated that the Japanese "and other colonizers" (an only slightly veiled reference to the Taroko National Park administration) have taken over Truku territory and that "we" (the Truku people) are still not able to return.

This final photo and caption sparked local controversy. The park manager accused Chin of encouraging dangerous "ethnic consciousness" and demanded that he remove the photo. Chin held his ground, saying that if he could not exhibit that photo, he would simply tear down the entire exhibit. Not wishing to exacerbate the already existing tensions with Truku communities, the manager backed down and let the exhibit open, but then subsequently refrained from publicizing the existence of the exhibit. When I asked local people what they thought of the exhibit, nearly everyone said they had not even heard of it.

While I was doing research in Hualien from 2004 to 2006, Truku activists began lobbying the government to establish Taiwan's first Indigenous autonomous zone. From the literature they were producing, I could see that their plans were to incorporate three townships in Hualien and one township in Nantou. A map even identified the mountainous region in Nantou as "Teluwan District," and population statistics said that 6,574 people inhabited five villages (Siyat 2004, 171–2). Tera Yudaw writes that Teluwan is a Chinese equivalent of *Truwan*, which means "homeland" in Truku. The Truku had originated there, and there are still Truku people living in that district (Tera 2003, 17). Just like in Hualien, Tera explained to me, there are Truku, Toda, and Tgdaya people, which is why it is better to call the new Indigenous political identity by the new, more inclusive name of Taroko. I asked him what the people in Nantou think of these plans. "Everyone supports it," he assured me. From Kuhon, however, I knew that some people preferred to be called Sediq, and not everyone, even in Hualien, supported the movement to establish a Taroko Autonomous Zone. I decided to make a trip to Teluwan District on my own.

Early in the morning, I set off by bus with a Canadian graduate student and his visiting girlfriend. The Hualien bus, which has a daily run in the morning to take workers up to the fruit orchards of Lishan (Slamaw), left us midway at a restaurant at Dayuling. After a wait of several hours, we continued our journey on a Taichung-bound bus from Lishan. We got off at the village of Chunyang. Wanting to ask for directions, I approached the first person I saw on the street and asked for directions to the township office. As we chatted, I showed him the map of Teluwan District. He grabbed the book, his eyes protruding from his head with excitement, as he turned the pages and looked at tables and maps showing his village as part of Truku territory. He invited us into his car and immediately drove us to the Ren'ai Township Office, where he introduced us to Takun Walis at the Civil Administration Office. They took us out to lunch in a nearby restaurant and explained to us that the Truku from Hualien had never consulted them. As far as they were concerned, explained Takun, they are Seediq, not Truku, and these claims to incorporate them as part of a Taroko Autonomous Region exhibit the same raw will to power as Japanese or Republic of China colonialism.

In subsequent years, even as the Seediq of Nantou took a different political path, Truku identity crystallized in Hualien. The Truku continued their promotion of commemorating the Battle of Taroko, even hosting a centennial international conference in 2014 and unveiling a memorial in the heart of the village (figure 6.4). The memorial is crowned with a rather abstract limestone statue. At the top is a motif recognizable from weaving patterns to represent the eye of the ancestors. The body of the statue appears like a conglomeration of balls. It could be that each one represents an individual community and that this statue represents the unity of the different Taroko communities who fought against the Japanese in the mountains. There are two commemorative plaques. The plaque on the back has a long, detailed history of battles between the Japanese and individual communities, even with precise details about the contributions of individuals. A smaller plaque on the front, decorated with a symbol for the eyes of the ancestors, is reproduced on page 251 (figure 6.4).

The writing on this monument is very different from the historiography promoted by Kuhon. Kuhon documents the diversity in the community, even specifying if the interlocutors speak Truku, Tgdaya, or Toda, whereas this plaque portrays a unified Taroko people. Kuhon prefers to refer to his informants as Truku people (the plural of "person"), whereas this monument uses a vocabulary of Indigenous peoplehood. Kuhon makes a great effort to place his story within a narrative of

---

Commemorative Script of the Battle of Taroko

The Truku had established a relationship with nature of "the land is our blood, the forest is our home." On this basis, our ancestors came from TRUWAN and, following the teachings from our ancestors, planted together, hunted together, and worshipped the ancestral spirits together, from generation to generation protecting their homeland of mountain forests. After the Japanese acquired Taiwan, they entered eastern Taiwan in 1896, gradually encroaching upon the traditional territory of our people, causing the serious conflicts of the "Hsincheng," "Weili," "Sanzan," and "Jiawan" Battles. On 31 May 1914, the historically largest scale Battle of Taroko began. The Japanese side employed sophisticated weaponry and over 10,000 troops of soldiers and police to attack all of the villages on the upper Liwu River. At the time, the entire population of our people was around 9,000 people. Although there were only about 3,000 able-bodied youth, they used their courage to resist, colouring the mountain forests with blood, fighting until 23 August, when they finally announced the end. This year marks the 118th anniversary of the Truku battles against the Japanese. In order to cherish the historical traces of the courage of our ancestors' protecting homes and defending land, and in order to pray for the tranquility of the spirits of our ancestors who sacrificed themselves in the mountain forests, and simultaneously encouraging our descendants to awaken the collective historical memory of our people, and to forever protect the homeland passed down by the ancestors, we establish this marker.

Hsiulin Township Office, 15 October, (ROC) Year 103 (2014)

Figure 6.4. Memorial to the Battle of Taroko. Commemoration of this founding historical event is important in the construction of the Truku Nation.

Source: Photograph by Scott E. Simon.

the Republic of China and Chinese resistance against Japan. The main text on the monument does not even mention the Republic of China and is written entirely from a perspective of indigeneity. It is telling that the commemorative plaque mentions only the end of the battle, saying nothing about a surrender. Instead, it explicitly calls upon the youth to awaken their historical memory and to continue to protect their home garden. The implication is that colonialism has not ended and that the people must continue their acts of resistance. This thinking is an affirmation of sovereignty as much as it is a declaration of identity. Although the monument was created in 2014, at the 100th anniversary of the Battle of Taroko, it refers to the 118th anniversary of Taroko battles against the Japanese. It thus refers to a longer history, beginning with the Hsincheng Battle of 1896. Ironically, the plaque is dated in the calendar of the Republic of China rather than the internationally recognized Gregorian calendar, thus marking it as created in the year 103 of the

Republic of China. This limestone statue may very well remain in the village for decades, giving concrete form to the ideals of Taroko nationalism. But what about the Nantou side of the mountains?

The 1930 Musha Uprising

Let's begin with an insider's perspective, that of a teenage girl, as recounted to Kumu Tapas. Toda elder Labay retold her story of being taken by her teacher to Musha on 26 October 1930 at the age of seventeen for a sports event at the school the following day. After a day's walk, they slept in a grass hut in the Tgdaya community of Paran (Musha). Although they heard rumours of a planned uprising, they were told that it had nothing to do with them. Labay reported:

> The whole night we could hear the calls of the crows: Qa, Qa, Qa. The calls of the crows made it impossible for me to fall asleep the whole night. There was a whole flock of crows that came together and made a very loud noise. It is said that the cries of the crow carry an omen of misfortune. Our elders always told us: "If you hear the crows cry out, someone will surely die." (Kumu 2004a, 86)

The following morning, Labay indeed witnessed one of the most violent episodes in the Japanese colonial period. On 27 October 1930, Japanese and Indigenous people gathered at the school in Musha for a sports event. It was no ordinary sports event. It was part of a Shinto commemoration for Prince Kitashirakawa Yoshihisa, member of the royal family and military leader, who died on 27 October 1895 in Tainan during the Japanese invasion of Formosa. He was elevated to a Shinto deity (*kami* 神) and enshrined in most Shinto shrines in Taiwan, most likely the Shinto shrine constructed in Musha in 1932, as well as in the Yasukuni shrine in Tokyo. Toda, Tgdaya, and Truku schoolchildren from all over Nantou were forced by their teachers to attend this event, even if it meant walking great distances and camping near the school grounds in Paran the night before. As the Japanese national flag was being raised, some 300 men allegedly led by forty-eight-year-old Chief Mona Rudo attacked and beheaded 134 Japanese men, women, and children, as well as, by accident, two Taiwanese who were dressed in Japanese clothing.[3]

The 1930 Musha Uprising, usually known as the Wushe Incident (in Chinese), and its enigmatic leader Mona Rudo is familiar to everyone in Taiwan. Long before I began doing research in Indigenous communities, I knew about this incident simply from reading debates about historiography and nationalism in Taiwanese newspapers. It has also been intensely researched by Taiwanese and foreign scholars (Barclay 2018; Ching 2001), and been the subject in Taiwan of novels, comic books, and films. The tragedy has been popularized in a comic book by Ch'iu Jo-lung (2004), made into a novel by Wu He with both French (Wu 2011) and English (Wu 2017) translations, and made into several films, including the 2011 blockbuster *Warriors of the Rainbow* by Taiwanese director Wei Te-sheng. Taiwanese people all learn about Mona Rudo in civics education as a hero of the Republic of China who struggled against colonial Japan. Since I came to Taiwan from Montreal, which had not so long ago lived through the 1990 Oka Crisis pitting Mohawk resisters against Quebec security forces, I imagined Mona Rudo and the Atayal to be great Indigenous heroes like the Mohawk Warriors.[4] I was thus more eager to learn about the Atayal (as both Sediq and Truku were then called) than about any other group in Taiwan.

On my own initiative while I was working in Taipei and before embarking on Indigenous research, I took the train down from Taipei to Taichung and the bus via Puli up into the mist-filled mountains of Nantou. The first stop on my pilgrimage was in Wushe, where I stopped to photograph the tomb of Mona Rudo, read the commemorative plaque, and reflected on his anticolonial movement. I went further up the mountain to the village of Chunyang, which local people said they still call Sakura ("cherry blossom" in Japanese) Village. I purchased some weavings from an elderly woman who cheerfully conversed with me in Japanese. I spent the night in a hotel at the Lushan Hot Springs, where I chatted with one of the women hotel employees. She told me that the Han Taiwanese have taken over the hot springs, which in the pre–name rectification days she identified as being on Atayal traditional territory, leaving the local Indigenous people to do only manual labour. I returned to Taipei with ideas for an anthropological study of development and resistance among the Atayal. My Taiwanese friends cautioned me against romanticizing Mona Rudo as an anticolonial leader. "He was no Republic of China hero," they would say. "He had never even heard of the Republic of China." The memories were contested in Taiwan and well beyond Mona Rudo's home territory. Back then, I imagined that Wushe was Mona's community, and I had absolutely no knowledge of the social complexity of what I had walked through in Wushe, Lushan, and Chunyang. I was happy to have practised my Japanese with an elderly weaver who had been alive at the time of the Musha Uprising, but I had no idea about the complexity of calling that village Chunyang (in Chinese), Sakura (in Japanese), or still another name that nobody had yet evoked to me.

In 2007, everything finally came together for me to begin field research in Mona Rudo's community or, more accurately, in the community of survivors of the incident he caused. Even the most fervent Truku nationalists encouraged me to go to Nantou to gain a new perspective on their Truwan. I had met Seediq legal scholar Awi Mona in Ottawa, and he advised me to do field research in his father's village of Qingliu, Gluban in Tgdaya language, where the survivors of Musha have been living since 1931. Awi himself is from the same clan as Mona Rudo. Kuhon Sibal drove me up from Hualien to the home of Takun Walis, where I would stay for the next six months. I was immediately struck by the fact that Takun had erected a North American style tipi in his yard, just at the entry to the village, as a symbol of his Indigenous identity and solidarity with international Indigenous peoples. Takun explicitly requested that I not ask elderly people about the Musha events, since it evokes painful memories and people are tired of being bombarded with the same questions by a constant stream of professors, graduate students, and journalists. He instead provided me with publications, including his own conference paper and transcripts of interviews with Musha survivors. I was happy to focus on my own topic of development and resistance. As the months passed by, however, the people of Gluban brought up Musha on their own initiative, recalling it quite casually in conversations and raising critical perspectives in formal, taped interviews. I took careful note of the way in which Musha is a part of their contemporary lives, especially among younger generations.

Because it happened during the Japanese period, I usually refer to the "Musha Uprising," using the Japanese name for the town that had been built in the community of Paran. It is usually called the "Musha Incident" or the "Wushe Incident," but I think that the word "incident" downplays the fact that this affair refers to a long chain of events, from the initial uprising against the Japanese to the subsequent reprisals. Looking for Seediq names reveals local ambivalence. On the ninetieth anniversary of the events in 2020, a Seediq language page on Facebook related three different interpretations from Gluban. The first is rather negative. Mkuni Paran literally means "the Paran insanity or loss of reason," implying that the Seediq warriors had killed so many Japanese in an act of collective madness. This term also appears as the Seediq translation on the Chinese Wikipedia page of the events. The second is Kmciyuk Tanah Tunux, or "rebellion against the red heads [Japanese]." The third is a transliteration of the Japanese into Musya Jikeng.

Facts of the Musha Events

In comparison with the Battle of Taroko, there are detailed statistics and a vast historical literature on the Musha events. Before exploring how the events are recalled, evoked, and represented, it is useful to provide a brief chronology of events as well as statistics about the casualties. Reference to a single "Musha Incident" on 27 October 1930 allows the event to be represented as heroic nationalism, while covering up local conflicts, pathos, and intergenerational suffering. Even here, I must make difficult decisions about which events to include and which to exclude. By October 1930, Musha was already considered by the Japanese to be a model Indigenous village, with such modern facilities as a post office, school, medical clinic, and shopping street. The Japanese considered Musha to be living proof that they managed Indigenous populations more successfully than the British or the Americans. They were taken by surprise by the apparent sudden nature of the uprising, but it clearly was the product of decades of pent-up frustrations about the nature of colonial violence. That is all a matter for historians. I focus here on the historical events as evoked in village conversation, and I use the statistics that are displayed in Gluban at the Survivors' Memorial Hall to illustrate the tragic trek that brought their village to this spot.

The popularization of Musha narratives has kept the names of persons and places alive in memory. The main figure was Mona Rudo, but his sons Tado Mona and Baso Mona did more of the fighting. Mona's daughter Mahung Mona survived the war and, although she did not bear children afterwards, adopted a child and was subsequently remembered as an important ancestor in Gluban. Pihu Sapu and Pihu Walis from Gungu were blamed in Japanese investigative reports for having planned the uprising (Nakakawa and Wakamori 1997, 202) and figure prominently in the film *Warriors of the Rainbow*, but are less frequently mentioned in Gluban Village conversations. For villagers, the most emotionally salient figures seem to be Hanaoka Ichirō (Dakis Nobing) and Hanaoka Jirō (Dakis Nawi), two Seediq men who were trained to be Japanese policemen. Most names, especially those of the Japanese, seem to fade from people's active memory. Walis Buni is evoked as a local leader who was more respected than Mona Rudo. The instigators of the uprising tried to gain the support of the chiefs of all twelve Tgdaya groups. Only six chiefs gave their assent, but they could not prevent individual men from joining out of their own choice. The six groups that participated in the uprising were Mona

Rudo's Alang Mhebu, as well as Gungu, Drodux, Suku, Buarung, and Tgdaya Truwan. Buarung was formerly Toda (Taosai), but ritually joined the Gaya of the emerging Tgdaya Confederation at the end of the Qing period (Deng 1998, 16). Walis Buni, a ritual leader and chief of Paran, tried to convince the rebel leaders to make peace with Japan and did not allow Paran to join the uprising. Instead, his groups sheltered Japanese and Indigenous people alike as they fled the violence. After his death, he was honoured by the Japanese for his benevolence (Kuo 2011, 105–6).

Table 6.1 is a chronology of events preceding, during, and after the Musha Uprising of 27 October 1930. Events that people brought up in fieldwork conversations are discussed further on. The other events come from historical studies but seem to be evoked more selectively in public discourse and even in private conversations.

Conquest by the Japanese, 1895–1911

People tended to refer to this period in rather general terms, characterizing the Japanese as very effective military invaders. They said that the Japanese were very careful to map out the local territory, investigate demographics, and, most importantly, to understand which groups were in conflict over hunting territories or historical grievances. This preparation allowed them to make allies with some groups and instigate them to launch headhunting expeditions against recalcitrant groups targeted by the Japanese in a policy known as "using savages to suppress the savages." As mentioned earlier, Renzhiguan, "the pass where people stop," is the historical barrier between settlers and Indigenous groups. After successfully repelling the Japanese there, the Musha groups started calling the Japanese *Banah tunux* (red heads) because of the rising sun symbol on their headbands. People talk about how the Japanese extended a fortification of electric fences, slowly tightening control around Indigenous groups so that they could not hunt or trade with other communities, thus leading to starvation and forced surrender. As each group surrendered, the Japanese forced them to participate in ceremonies swearing allegiance to the emperor. The surrendered groups were then required to provide labour for the further construction of the electrified blockades and help pacify other groups. They were sometimes willing to wage armed battles against other groups, especially if the appointed leaders were eager to settle old scores and if young men wanted to prove their bravery through headhunting.

Table 6.1. Chronology of events leading up to and during the Musha Uprising

Date	Name of event
17 April 1895	Signing of the Treaty of Shimonoseki
1901	Japanese forces, based in Puli, begin encirclement of Musha "savages" with electric fences
29 April 1902	Battle of Renzhiguan – Japanese repelled by Musha warriors led by Walis Buni
5–6 October 1903	Sisters' Incident – Japanese instigate Bunun to kill Musha people
November 1905	Seven Musha groups surrender to the Japanese
30 May 1906	Musha Surrender Ceremony
January 1907	Mhebu and Boarung Surrender Ceremony
July 1907	Nantou Toda and Truku groups surrender
January 1909	Mona Rudo's sister Ciwas Rudo married to Japanese police officer Kondō Gisaburō
1909–10	Battles against Toda and Truku for control of Hehuan Mountain
1911	Prominent chiefs, including Mona Rudo, taken on a tour of Japan
September 1913	Japanese ban on headhunting and facial tattoos begins with ceremonies of public oaths at village police stations
31 May–23 August 1914	Battle of Taroko – Japanese forces sent in via Nantou
1916	Kondō Gisaburō commissioned to Hualien and disappears
September 1920	Slamaw Incident – Tgdaya troops (perhaps with Mona Rudo's involvement) used to punish rebels at Lishan
7 October 1930	Fight between Mona's son Tado Mona and Japanese policeman Yoshimura Katsumi
27 October 1930	Musha Uprising: Tgdaya warriors attack sports event in Musha, killing 134 Japanese
28 October–20 December 1930	"First Musha Incident": Japanese punitive expedition against the six rebellious groups, eventually with help of Toda and Truku groups; collective suicide of Musha women by hanging in the forest near Mhebu
25 April 1931	"Second Musha Incident": Toda warriors kill unarmed Musha survivors held in detention camps
6 May 1931	Survivors of the Musha Incident moved to Kawanakashima (Gluban)
15 October 1931	The final reckoning: at a surrender ceremony in Puli, thirty-eight suspected rebels are arrested and sent to detention, where they die one by one from "illness"

Sources: Barclay (2018); Ch'eng (2006, 233–9); Deng (1998); Fujii Shizue (1997, 191–3); Chien, Iwan, and Kuo (2002); Nakakawa and Wakamori (1997, 111–18); Simon (2012b, 75).

Sisters' Incident, 5 October 1903

In Gluban, people told me about this massacre called the "Sisters' Incident" as the event that brought the Tgdaya people to surrender. It also caused some of the anti-Japanese resentment leading up to the Musha events. In the oral stories, the Japanese military encircled the Tgdaya with barriers of electric fences to enforce a blockade that made it impossible for the people on the inside to obtain salt, gunpowder, or other needed items. As the communities began to suffer, especially without salt for cooking needs, two sisters who had married into a Bunun community invited the Tgdaya to come to their village for trade. This invitation, however, turned out to be a trap set up by the Japanese military. The Bunun prepared a feast and offered their guests copious amounts of alcohol. As the Tgdaya slept off their drunkenness, the Bunun attacked. Some 130 people were killed, leaving only around a dozen to return to their village. As a result of this massacre, the Tgdaya groups gradually surrendered to Japan over the subsequent few years. Although Gluban people told me this incident was eventually one of the causes of the Musha Uprising, it may also be a reason why she Tgdaya groups did not participate (Chien 2002, 31). Those villages had not yet recovered from their casualties and were not willing to fight. People also told me that they resent the Bunun for this massacre to this day.

Of course, the events of 1930 to 1931 have defined the village of Gluban. The history is illustrated with photos and written documentation at the Survivors' Memorial Hall on the site of the former Shinto shrine. In 2007, although the building had already been completed, the government had still not approved the construction or connected it to the electricity grid. It was thus accessible only through prior arrangements. There is also an outdoor memorial. The data in table 6.2 is based on that exhibit. It shows how the six rebel communities lost 76 per cent of their population as a result of Japanese reprisals. Those who survived were mostly women and children. After relocation to Kawanakashima, some people committed suicide or died of new diseases because they were not accustomed to the warmer climate. Thirty-eight others were detained and died in prison, which left a population of only 275 people in 1931 to found the new village (Chien 2002, 39).

How Ordinary People Evoke Musha

Local people do not speak about the "Musha Incident" as a single event on 27 October 1930. Instead, they speak about the "First Musha Incident" as the entire process of warfare between the Tgdaya people and

Table 6.2. Musha population (six rebel groups), reflecting fatalities, 1930–1

Alang	Original population		Survivors of First Musha Incident	After Second Musha Incident	Total fatalities
	Total	Warriors			
Mhebu	231	53	75	63	168
Truwan	28	8	21	21	7
Buarung	192	56	137	54	138
Gungu	269	53	64	39	230
Suku	231	68	120	25	206
Drodux	285	57	144	96	189
Total	1236	295	561	298	938

Source: Information panels in the Gluban Survivors' Memorial Hall, visited in 2007.

the Japanese military (who elicited the help of the Toda and Truku) between October and December of 1930. They also refer to a "Second Musha Incident" of 25 April 1931, in which Toda warriors at the instigation of the Japanese attacked and killed unarmed Tgdaya detainees at two detention centres. Although the survivors rarely talked about the actual violence of these battles with their children, there are still moments when those memories are passed on from generation to generation. Once when people took me to a restaurant, for example, they told me that the restaurant is located at Drodux, the location of one of the detention centres where innocents had been killed. The simple enunciation of that memory certainly placed a damper on the whole afternoon. Conversations tended to focus around (1) speculations on the reasons for the Musha Uprising; (2) using the history to reflect upon contemporary existential dilemmas; and (3) questioning the leadership or moral standing of Mona Rudo.

Recalling the Musha Uprising

There were obviously multiple factors that led to the violent uprising against the Japanese. At the Memorial Hall, historical panels explain six "distant causes" and five "near causes." The distant causes were (1) the Japanese established colonial political power; (2) the Japanese exploited mountain resources; (3) changes in the traditional life and mode of production of the Seediq Nation; (4) divisions between ethnic groups and the Japanese policies of "using savages to control savages"; (5) failure of the policy of "Japanese-to-savage" marriages; and (6) conflicts between the existing culture of the Seediq Nation and the Greater Japan culture of the colonizers. The near causes were (1) resentment against forced labour; (2) the radical instigation of Pihu Sapu and Pihu Walis; (3) drinking quarrels at Gungu and Mhebu; (4) failure of the Japanese policy of "savage administration"; and (5) Japanese police intimidation and corruption. The Japanese governor-general of Taiwan, immediately after the uprising, attributed it to dissatisfaction about the pain and delayed wages of the forestry workers, the instigation of Pihu Sapu and Pihu Walis, and the rebelliousness of Mona Rudo (Nakakawa and Wakamori 1997, 202). Leo Ching notes that the Japanese finally came up with eleven reasons for the rebellion, all of which characterized the motives as circumstantial and personal, thus deflecting all criticism of colonial authority itself (Ching 2001, 143). Gluban people, however, do criticize the colonial authority. They even go further by suggesting that they still live in a colonial situation.

Ordinary people reflected on these causes of rebellion as they reflected on their own lives. Workers who had not received their own wages from Taiwanese bosses as promised, for example, did not hesitate to recall that poor labour conditions and withdrawal of wages in the Japanese period led to anticolonial violence. While waiting for the bus from Gluban to Puli one day, I noticed that someone had posted a handmade no-trespassing sign by the forest explicitly stating that non-Indigenous people (*pingdiren* 平地人, literally "flatlanders") should not illegally cut down trees or plant vegetables. The sign read, in a way meant to be threatening: "The people here are a fierce people, the descendants of the Musha Incident." The implication is that they might react with another violent rebellion if they are mistreated by more recent settlers, even in the twenty-first century.

Women were more likely to attribute the anticolonial violence to the Japanese violation of Seediq Gaya. When I asked one woman to explain her comment that the Japanese mistreated women, she said that once a Japanese man had married a local woman. He then was transferred to Hualien and disappeared. She said that he must have simply found another wife in the new village. When I suggested that maybe he had died in the course of his work, she dismissed that idea entirely. She was recalling, I would learn much later, the fateful marriage of Mona Rudo's sister Ciwas Rudo to Japanese police officer Kondō Gisaburō, who did indeed disappear. Apparently, Ciwas was even with him when he fell down a cliff and died. Her brother Mona Rudo was furious when she returned to Musha and did not receive the same financial compensation as the daughter of the chief of another community. Japanese policeman, moreover, were known for sexually approaching local women and even reputed to see some into prostitution. This behaviour all violated Seediq notions of sexual morality (Deng 1998, 59).

People recalled two drinking events that supposedly enflamed anti-Japanese resentment. After our Japanese conversation class in Puli, somebody light-heartedly reflected on the common Taiwanese difficulty distinguishing the Japanese sounds *k-* and *g-*. Takun said that the word *baka* (enough) in Seediq sounds like the Japanese word *baka* 馬鹿 (idiot). He told the story of the Gungu chief Buhuk Nokan, who had trapped a wild boar and a muntjac. On his way home, he stopped at the police station and, treating the police officers as adopted kin, offered them some of the meat. The officer cooked the meat along with some vegetables and served Japanese saké. Everybody was already drunk when Buhuk wanted to go home and turned down the drink by saying "*baka da.*" Buhuk was larger and stronger than the police officer. But thinking the officer would simply realize his linguistic mistake, he did not fight back. Three Japanese policemen beat him. When he returned home, he told people that his open injuries had been caused by carrying the wild boar. It was only after he died a week later from internal bleeding that the police visited his home and his family learned what had happened. His younger brother Tado became chief (Kuo 2011, 134–6). The people of Gungu, instigated by Pihu Sapu and Pihu Walis, were still resentful of this murder and wholeheartedly joined in the Musha Uprising. Only 39 people out of a community of 269 souls survived the subsequent reprisals.

The other drinking event, dramatized in the film *Warriors of the Rainbow*, is also used by historian Paul Barclay to introduce the existential dilemma of Japanese colonial rule (Barclay 2018, 43). On 7 October 1930, Japanese police officer Yoshimura Katsumi passed through Mhebu and ran across a wedding celebration. Mona Rudo's son Tado invited Yoshimura to share a drink of alcohol. Probably, if Tado offered the drink in the way people often served me alcohol, he expected Yoshimura to drink from the same cup with their lips touching. Tado's hands were bloody from having butchered an animal, which may have been a pig sacrifice and is portrayed as such in the film. Not only did Yoshimura brusquely refuse the drink, a public snub of Tado's offer of friendship, but he beat Tado with a cane when he realized that Tado had stained his white uniform with blood. Tado and his brother beat Yoshimura. The following day, Mona Rudo took bottles of millet wine to the police station to apologize. The branch chief, Sugiura Kōichi, refused the apology and even promised severe punishment. This response angered Mona's family so much that Tado Mona's group killed Yoshimura in the first wave of attacks on 27 October. People usually brought this incident up to me in dark humour. Delighted when I pressed my cheeks to theirs to drink beer or accepted game meat from their hands, my hosts would say: "It's a good thing you are not like that Japanese police officer." The past lives on in the present.

The most iconic figures, as people thought through their own existential dilemmas, were two Gungu men Hanaoka Ichirō (Dakis Nobing) and Hanaoka Jirō (Dakis Nawi), who trained as police officers. They are recalled as having conflicting loyalties to both their own clan and community, and to the state that provided them with education and the chance to advance in a new kind of career. They are known, along with their wives, for having worn Japanese clothing, speaking Japanese, and succeeding in the Japanese school system. Hanaoka Ichirō, who attended teachers' training at the Taichung Normal College, had even studied English (Uno 2002, 144). People recall, using the Chinese pronunciation of the Japanese characters for their names, that these two men knew about the plans for the uprising but were ambivalent about whether they should inform the Japanese authorities or join the rebellion. Unable to decide, they instead committed suicide. More than once, over a round of drinks, a man has suddenly said to me that he identifies with these brothers and understands their psychological dilemma, unsure if he would side with the Republic of China or with the Seediq if there were another violent conflict. People in certain social roles, such as teaching, politics, and policing, used these historical personages to discuss their own personal conflicts about the meritocratic career ladder and more local community loyalties.

People also refer to the Musha events when discussing why the Sediq gave up headhunting. Although Japan banned the practice and related facial tattooing in 1913, the number of headhunting events recorded in Japanese police records continued to rise until 1920. Because it was believed that taking heads was necessary to ward off infectious disease, the 1918–20 Spanish influenza epidemic seems to have provided adequate incentive to launch violent expeditions (Simon 2012a, 179). Deng Shian-yang interpreted the epidemic as one of the reasons why the Tgdaya were willing to help the Japanese suppress the Slamaw at Lishan (Deng 1998, 39). People told me that the Japanese police were hypocritical and opportunistic. While they forbade headhunting in most circumstances, they took advantage of the pent-up desire of Indigenous groups to hunt heads to recruit them as warriors to suppress other groups. They said that the turning point was the military repression at Musha, when the Japanese paid the Toda to bring back Tgdaya heads, paying different rates for capturing a child, woman, man, or, most of all, a chief.

Hostilities remain. Even after the ROC came, said one woman, a rumour spread around Gluban that the Slamaw people from Lishan were coming to kill them. The men armed themselves with bows and arrows, as well as knives, and went up to the mountain pass to wait for the Slamaw. They left instructions to the women that, if they did not come back within three days, the women should kill a chicken and eat it before committing collective suicide. Fortunately, the rumour turned out to be false, but the people of Slamaw still resent Mona Rudo and are hostile towards his clan. The descendants of the Slamaw group faithfully boycott attending the township's annual memorial ceremony for Mona Rudo. They were also furious about how Mona Rudo was heroized in *Warriors of the Rainbow*.

Questions about Mona Rudo as a Hero and the Aftermath

Even in Gluban, where Mona Rudo (figure 6.5) is most prominently evoked publicly as an anti-Japanese rebel and an Indigenous hero, some people gave me harsh criticism of the man. One woman said that she found it especially ridiculous when people portrayed him as a Chinese hero. "If China considered him one of their own," she said, "China would have made an international protest about the Japanese oppression of Indigenous people [on Taiwan in 1930], *but they never did*." On the second day of the uprising, she recalled, Mona Rudo passed by her father's home. He declared his intention to commit suicide and said: "Whoever finds my body will surely earn a lot of money because the Japanese will pay for it." Indeed, on 30 October, Mona summoned his female relatives, including his wife, sisters, and daughters-in-law, and his children to a workshed, where he killed them all and burned the building to remove the evidence. He fled into the mountains and committed suicide by gunshot in a cave (Nakakawa and Wakamori 1997, 97). "A real hero would have fought to the end," said that woman, "like my father and my uncle. But Mona was a coward." Mona's corpse was indeed sold to the Japanese, who displayed it in the Taikoku (Taipei) Imperial University Department of Anthropology. Even after the arrival of the ROC, it remained at what became Taiwan National University until it was finally buried at Wushe in 1974 (Nakakawa and Wakamori 1997, 98). Some people said that Mona was, in fact, a bloodthirsty collaborator of the Japanese. They mentioned his trip to Japan and argued that he had become completely assimilated. "This," said the woman, "is why he said 'the Japanese are as numerous as the leaves on the trees in the forest.'" The comments of common people often came with a resigned sigh as

Figure 6.5. The enigmatic Seediq chief and rebel Mona Rudo. Mona Rudo (middle) as a young leader before the Musha Uprising.

Source: Unknown photographer, Wikimedia Commons. Originally from 海老原耕平『霧社討伐寫眞帖』共進商會，昭和六年 [Kohei Ebina's "Written Posts of the Wusha Crusade" and Gongjin Chamber of Commerce, Shōwa 6 (1931)].

they said that, if they had refused to listen to Mona, they could have averted disaster.[5]

The people of Gluban apparently learned a lesson from this rebellion, as one man explained while telling me about the anti-government protests across Taiwan in March 1947 (now known as the 2:28 Incident). Four young men from Gluban were studying at Taichung Normal University. When communist organizer Hsieh Hsüeh-hong was recruiting rebels, they went to learn about the uprising and took guns. Although other Indigenous men participated, most notably when Tsou warriors occupied the Chia-yi airport, the Gluban men used the rifles to go hunting for a week. "Having survived Musha," the man said, "they knew that there they can't win an armed struggle against a government. Moreover, the ROC had just won a war against the Japanese, so they must be very strong." After the rebellion, these young Gluban men turned themselves and the rifles over to the police. They were arrested and imprisoned. "But those Mainlanders liked the people from Musha," he said, "because we had fought against the Japanese. Mainlanders hate the Japanese. So they were lenient and gave them light sentences."

Putting the Musha Events into a Wider Perspective

In 2004, Presbyterian minister Kumu Tapas, who is of both Toda and Truku heritage, published her MA thesis in theology as two volumes of life histories. These volumes, of more than 400 pages each, are a valuable historical source because they contain detailed transcripts of personal accounts from all three dialect groups and beyond. Framing her analysis within both feminist theology and postcolonial thought, Kumu is interested in uncovering forgotten histories, which she says is a form of "historical amnesia" (Kumu 2004a, 5). As a Presbyterian minister in the Sediq Synod and a native Truku speaker, Kumu is very conscious of the emotional and social cleavages being created as related groups on two sides of the mountains pursue separate legal identities in the name rectification movement (16). Dakis Pawan criticized these books, although based on detailed interview research, as having a biased perspective and oversimplifying history (Kuo 2012, 257–8).

The most creative dimensions of Kumu's work are that she brings in perspectives beyond Gluban and provides details on the gender-specific existential dilemmas faced by women. The first of these is important because, as part of Seediq recognition, Tgdaya perspectives have been prioritized, but there is a need for further reconciliation with Toda and Truku people. The second is important because, in a society that tended towards patrilocality, women were more likely than men to move from one community to another. They thus have dual loyalties, both to their parents and siblings in their communities of origin and to their new families in their communities of marriage. The Sisters' Incident (discussed earlier in the chapter) is an example of those conflicts.

Kumu's book enlarges our perspective on Musha because, unlike the majority of works that focus on Gluban and thus the six communities that revolted, she looks at the six Tgdaya communities that did not support the uprising, as well as at the Truku and Toda communities that allied with the Japanese. As communities took positions, they did so after careful deliberation by their tribal councils and opinion leaders.[6] Those who opposed joining the rebellion tended to be those who had been on the organized tours to Japan and saw the futility of resisting such a powerful country, as well as the Toda and Truku groups who had historical grievances against Mona Rudo and his allies (Kumu 2004a, 56).

Women had very different perspectives throughout the events. As Dakis Pawan told Kumu in 2000, the women of the rebellious groups initially opposed the attack on the school, but once it happened, they had no choice but to support their men. Once they were attacked by the Japanese, their main goals were to protect their children and those of others (Kumu 2004a, 74).

Kumu introduces an important local concept into the discussion: *pngqeydin*, women who married into a community from another group. There are pejorative connotations to this word, as it implies that the women come from other groups, or *kaalang*, which may be enemy groups. Their experience highlights the dynamic that each community (*alang*) is composed of various families that may have divergent interests. In the past, Siyac Nabu (Tgdaya) told Kumu:

> Even if two families had kin relations [through marriage], each alang is a society composed of many families ... So, two families establishing kin relations would not influence the headhunting behaviour of other families ... Once they brought back a head and killed pigs, everyone in the village was invited to celebrate together. (Kumu 2004a, 258)

In the headhunting days, this custom implied that a woman might have to dance around the head of a deceased sibling, silently enduring the emotional turbulence that experience would cause. Women, however, could also leak information to their brothers about an impending headhunting expedition, a behaviour that earned *pngqeydin* a reputation for being potential spies. After the Musha Uprising, such women were also accused of spying for the Japanese (Kumu 2004a, 264). Intermarriage also created psychological conflicts for the men. One man told me about a Toda man in his family. As they ambushed the Tgdaya rebels in a stream, they engaged in hand-to-hand combat. In the heat of the moment, he did not recognize the man with whom he was fighting. Just as he stabbed his opponent, the rebel cried out the word for agnatic relatives – "*Anay!*" It was too late to stop the momentum of his arm, and he killed his brother-in-law. He felt guilty about that for the rest of his life.

During the uprising, women did their best to save women and children, regardless of nationality. Walis Cumeyq told Kumu:

My younger sister was called Away Cumeyq. She once carried away a Japanese child, that was the child of [Japanese police officer] Kojima-san … At the time, she had not yet married … While running away, she passed through Mriqi and dressed Kojima's child in Seediq clothing to prevent him from being killed and beheaded by Tgdaya people. The Tgdaya people just told her: "There is no reason for you to run. We are not going after you." (Kumu 2004a, 158)

Whereas most narratives describe heroic battles, Kumu's informants describe the difficulties faced by refugees, not least getting food. Many of the Truku people could not flee up the mountains to their homes and ended up taking refuge downstream in Songlin. One Truku man told his story of escaping from the school grounds, seeking refuge with other Truku in Songlin Village, and then helping some Japanese escape to Puli. Framing his story in familiar cultural terms, he told what happened after the people of Songlin had taken care of and fed him:

The Japanese appeared at Songlin. My teacher had wrapped up his hand, as if he could not move it. They all cried out: "Save us! Save us!" They told us: "While we were escaping, there was a group of Japanese who saw a bird screeching and flying horizontally in front of them." This is our Seediq inauspicious omen … If a sisil cries and flies in front of our eyes, it means that a great disaster is coming … Because they could not understand the message being conveyed by the sisil, they had the fate of being brutally murdered at Mhebu. (Kumu 2004a, 156)

The narratives collected by Kumu provide a new twist on the story. When the women from the rebellious groups committed collective suicide, only one woman survived. She was Obin Tadaw, the wife of Hanaoka Jirō, who was pregnant.[7] Dakis Pawan explained that Obin's husband, in his last words, had told her to flee and to give birth in order to continue the next generation (Kumu 2004a, 301). His colleague, police officer Kojima Genji, whose child had been saved by Away Cumeyq, in turn saved a sixteen-year-old Tgdaya youth Pihu Walis from death at the hands of the Toda because he recognized him as a friend and classmate of his son (296). At the age of eighty-six, Obin related that the Japanese police asked her to marry this younger boy, and she initially refused because he was younger than she (303). This young couple subsequently did well in the remaining years of the Japanese period, as he became a physician and she became a midwife with education provided by the Japanese. In the years after 1931, the Japanese forced the people around Musha to gather every year for a peace ceremony (305). They also constructed a collective grave for the Japanese victims of the Musha Uprising.

The end of Japanese colonialism brought the Republic of China (ROC) to Taiwan, with both challenges and opportunities for these people. After Japan handed Taiwan to the ROC, Pihu and Obin, who had been using Japanese names, adopted the Chinese names Gao Yong-qing and Gao Cai-yun. Gao Yong-qing became magistrate of Ren'ai Township, demolished the collective grave, and established the commemorative monument to Mona Rudo (Kumu 2004b, 194). The people interviewed by Kumu did not hesitate to point out the hypocrisy of local leaders who benefited from collaborating with the Japanese but then immediately after 1945 portrayed themselves as anti-Japanese rebels and promoted the glorification of Mona Rudo in order to profit from the anti-Japanese sentiment of the incoming Chinese. This turnabout, however, underscores the main point of this chapter that social memories are evoked and promoted in struggles for political power.

Aftermath of the Musha Events

Japanese policy after Musha effectively reshuffled the cards in ways that created the communities that I got to know during field research. Gluban was created as Japan resettled the survivors in the plains north of Puli, where the survivors of the rebels would be easier to control. The Japanese forced them to take up rice farming, which they resented at first but is now very important to their social identity. Among those survivors were fifty-four people from Buarung, thirty-nine from Gungu, and sixty-three from Mhebu. In order to prevent the Tgdaya from returning to their home villages, the Japanese moved a group of Truku to Buarung and installed the Toda in Gungu. Buarung has since 2013 become one of my regular field sites, and the Truku inhabitants do not seem to mind using the old Tgdaya place name. Gungu is now called Chunyang, but some local people still recall that they called it Sakura (Cherry Blossom) Village during the Japanese period.[8] The old Tgdaya name of Gungu is intentionally omitted, as its evocation would only serve to recall the most violent conflicts between the Tgdaya and the Toda, people who must still live and work together. Mhebu is now a hot springs resort, the one I visited years previously, and dominated by Han Taiwanese entrepreneurs. Although I initially perceived that situation as a displacement of Indigenous peoples by "development," I have come to see it from a new perspective. People in neighbouring Buarung, many of whom work in the hot springs, tell me that they prefer not to inhabit that valley. It was the site of violent battles, and the nearby forests were the place of collective suicide. Because they recollect the stories that they have heard about events that happened there, people just say in general: "It is a bad place."

There are many bad places up in those hills. In the summer of 2013, while doing fieldwork up in Toda territory, I was enjoying tea with some men in a workshed on the hill behind the school. The man who works there told me that, while he was sleeping there, "something black" passed by. He said he ignored it because he believes in Jesus. Later, "something black" pushed him down the hill while he was sleeping, causing a bloody head injury. He snuck around the school, to avoid frightening the children, and sought medical help. People explained to me that the site is haunted because it is the spot where the Japanese buried 103 heads after the Musha battles. This site is probably Hrhalung, the place on a hill by a school where the Japanese buried the heads of the Tgdaya people who had been killed by the Toda; it was even photographed by the Japanese in commemoration (Kumu 2004a, 211). Another school employee recalled seeing "something white" at the same place. The white colour, he explained, means that the phantom is not malevolent. It is dangerous to fall asleep there, however, because the ghosts can still cause bodily harm.

Constructing a Seediq/Sediq/Sejiq Nation

Considering the many ways in which the ghosts of the Musha battles still haunt the mountains of Ren'ai Township, it takes great will to unite the people of these formerly enemy communities under one political project. As the Truku in Hualien advanced on their project of legal recognition, the Seediq/Sediq/Sejiq (3S) were not far behind. In 1998, the Presbyterian churches in Nantou formed the Sediq Synod in Nantou and began demanding legal recognition as an independent people (Rudolph 2008, 115fn8). Language education became an important political tool. Unlike in Hualien, where the leaders produced pedagogical materials in Truku only, those in Nantou had to prepare separate classroom materials in Truku, Tgdaya, and Toda (Hara 2004, 97). They established several non-governmental organizations (NGOs) under the name of Saideke (the Chinese pronunciation, usually written in Chinese characters 賽德克) to promote the new ethnonym. The earthquake of 21 September 1999 was a turning point. For the first time, financial aid was distributed to them as Sediq rather than Atayal. During the reconstruction of their communities, they changed the names of churches from Chinese names to local ones (Hara 2004, 99). All of this change took diplomatic finesse. The leaders of the movement had to consider discordant perspectives on the Musha events, which remain very much alive in family memories and are even reinforced by discussions of ethnic identity. In order to carry out this project, they kept all three spellings of the ethnonym when writing in their own languages, but reached a consensus on one Chinese term. Emphasizing the theme of reconciliation, they incorporated into their events the symbolism of *psbalay* or *dmahur*, a ritual in which conflicting groups expressed their differences, announced peace through a ritual burying of stones or sacrifice of a pig, and then feasted together.[9] When the 3S gained legal recognition in 2008, they killed a pig at the grave of Walis Buni (Walis 2009, 132). In the 2000s and 2010s, the Toda initiated no fewer than four *mddahun* (the reciprocal form of dmahur, thus meaning reconciliation) with the Tgdaya to create and strengthen the 3S Confederation. Darryl Sterk found that the Tgdaya do not want to be continually reconciled, especially as they have nothing to be sorry for. He suggested that the Toda know that the Tgdaya have not quite forgiven them (Sterk 2020, 116).

It proved far more difficult to manage relations with potential co-ethnics on the other side of the mountains. One of the main Truku proponents from Hualien told me that his team had once driven up the mountains to Nantou with a pig in their truck. They wanted to invite people to psbalay but were brusquely turned away. They ended up taking the pig down into a valley and eating it among themselves. The Truku leaders were especially frustrated with political elites back home in Hualien who, rather than supporting their goals, sought alliances with political actors in Nantou. Both sides accused the other of obstructing their projects, feeding deep-seated animosity.

Conflicts intensified after 14 January 2004, when the Executive Yuan officially recognized the Truku. Since the Democratic Progressive Party (DPP) government had apparently done so with the goal of gaining Truku votes in the upcoming elections, 3S nationalists accused them of employing the old Japanese strategy of "using savages to control savages." During the next three years, in televised debates, publications, websites, and public hearings, both sides used a rhetoric of history, ethnography, and social memory to argue for the legitimacy of their chosen ethnonym. On 7 April 2006, the 3S advocates presented their formal request to the Council of Indigenous Peoples. At that meeting, National Cheng-chih University ethnologist Lim Siu-theh argued that, by all objective criteria, the two sides constitute one single ethnic group, and if they can't reach consensus, they should agree upon a third ethnonym to be called Taroko or Sediq (Wu 2006). 3S nationalists were furious with the anthropologist for not supporting their cause.

On 12 January 2007, the leaders of the emerging 3S Nation met at the William Sia Memorial Camp for a loyalty oath ceremony sponsored by the Ren'ai Township Office. They distributed a handbook, which is a strong cultural declaration of their new confederation as a sovereign Indigenous nation. It describes their bond with hunting dogs and the divinatory bird sisil that links them to nature, and summarizes a large number of founding myths. The document refers to Mona Rudo but is critical about how politicians have misused this cultural heritage in a combination of political ideology and Taiwanese official ceremonialism. It is an important ethnographic and political document. The organizers found it so important that they published it in all three regional languages, as well as translations in Chinese, Japanese, English, and French.

The English version, read by KMT legislator Kung Wen-chi (Truku Yosi Takun) and probably translated by him, is as follows:

The Rally to Pledge "Renaming of Sediq/Seejiq/Seediq"

1. I swear I will remain the blood of Sediq Toda/Seejiq Truku/ Seediq Tgdaya, and keep my tribe from any contempt by exploits of academic uses.
2. I persist the admonition passed down by my forefathers, Sediq Balay/Seejiq Balay/Seediq Bale, that is, my "tribal" name as the symbol of self-defined ethnicity.
3. I will not abandon the origin of my tribe, even if there are changes from outside circumstance.
4. By the rights given by U.N. Declaration on the Rights of Indigenous Peoples, and A New Partnership between the Indigenous Peoples and the Government of Taiwan signed by the President Chen Shui-bian and Indigenous peoples in Taiwan, we request the government of Republic of China respect and support our tribe's will of renaming us as "Sediq/Seejiq/Seediq."

Swearer: Seejiq Truku Yosi Takun (Kung Wen-chi)

One cynical township employee described to me the people at the swearing ceremony with their right arms held out in front of them, saying they "looked like Nazis." This comment shows how difficult it can be to convince local people about innovations in the institutions of state-centric indigeneity.

Negotiations with the government continued, and my Seediq friends asked me to join them. At their request, I wrote an essay giving my opinion about Seediq name rectification, arguing simply that choosing one's own ethnonym is a fundamental part of self-determination consistent with both international and national law (Simon 2008). This essay became expert testimony in their 2008 meetings with the Council of Indigenous Peoples. In early 2008, they again had a series of difficult negotiations, requiring a delicate balance after a potentially rules-changing election, with both the lame duck DPP Executive Yuan and the newly elected KMT President Ma Ying-jeou. Fearful that the change in government could delay or even derail their aspirations, the Seediq celebrated when they gained legal recognition on 23 April 2008, just one month before the inauguration of the new president. They followed legal recognition in Nantou with the reconciliation ceremony of dmahur.

In the subsequent years, people simply got used to the new legal identities, just as they had got used to being called *yuanzhumin* 原住民 (Indigenous) in the 1990s. There is no longer confusion about the ethnonyms. The Council of Indigenous Peoples has settled on the Chinese *Tailuge* 太魯閣 and the romanized "Truku" for one group, as well as the Chinese Saideke 賽德克 and romanized "Sediq" for the other. As I revise these pages in March 2022, Taiwan now has 33,246 people registered as Truku and 10,812 as Sediq. As can be expected, people have largely accepted the identities promoted by the township office and household registration bureaus in their place of residence. Hualien County thus has 23,242 registered Truku, but only 948 Sediq. Nantou County has 6,881 registered Sediq, but only 138 Truku. About one-third of the population of each group is spread across Taiwan's urban areas. In Hualien, the entire Toda-speaking village of Alang Tausa (see map 3) in Tsuo-hsi Township chose collectively to join the Sediq, even though they are very far away from the other Sediq communities in Nantou and separated from it, if we follow roads, by a vast tract of what is now claimed as Truku territory. Truku nationalists in Hualien were surely disappointed by this move, which betrays their goal of creating one unified Truku Autonomous Zone all the way down the Hualien coast. But this decision reinforces the idea that 3S and Truku confederations are more about relationality than about modern notions of territoriality. Through face-to-face encounters and the mutual weaving of stories, they created two new Indigenous nations that are no longer subordinate to the state category of Atayal. The freedoms they gained during Taiwan's democratization allowed them to assert their own political identities after decades of cultural imperialism.

Discussion

Colonialism took violence to new extremes due to the introduction of more advanced weaponry, but also because Japan in the Meiji era was competing with European colonial powers who otherwise might have reduced Japan to a colony. Japan had the will to conquer Formosa, subjugating land and human labour alike to an extractive mode of production never seen before in the mountain highlands. The memories recalled and evoked in this chapter reveal that colonialism was not a genteel matter of signing treaties and spreading civilization. Rather, it was a violent expropriation of land, forests, and human settlements that met with great resistance by people who wished to retain their autonomy and ways of life. It was a process of warfare that lasted for decades. In fact, it would not be an exaggeration to say that all of Formosa was transformed into the society we know today as Taiwan through tribulations of warfare and bloodshed. If the island itself could speak, it would attest to the human violence brought in by the Dutch, Spanish, French, Americans, Chinese, Manchurians, Japanese, and the Republic of China. It is no wonder that even in Han Taiwanese communities, temple inscriptions commemorate ancient violence, and people feel compelled to make ritual food and drink sacrifices every July to hordes of hungry ghosts. This ritual is not superstition. It is atonement for spilt blood. But all of this history is not the main point of this chapter. As ramie stalks are to weavings, these memories are the raw materials from which other stories are woven.

The main point of this chapter is to explore the nature of memory, how individual memory is woven together to become social memory and how that contributes to the political aspirations of nationhood. Here is where Claude Lévi-Strauss's observations in *Savage Mind* remain very relevant:

> Each episode in a revolution or a war resolves itself into a multitude of individual psychic movements. Each of these movements is the translation of unconscious development, and these resolve themselves into cerebral, hormonal or nervous phenomena, which themselves have refer-

ence to the physical or chemical order. Consequently, historical facts are no more given than any other. It is the historian or the agent of history, who constitutes them by abstraction … *History is therefore never history, but history-for.* (Lévi-Strauss 1966, 257, emphasis added)

Memories are the stuff from which nations are built. Ernest Renan famously wrote: "The essence of a nation is that all individuals have many things in common, and also that they have forgotten many things" (Renan [1882] 1990, 11). Through memory, and through forgetting, political actors in Hualien and Nantou have constructed two new Indigenous nations. There are important differences between the two places, and I think that a phenomenological attention to embodiment and movement highlights an important one. The Truku live their memories of the Battle of Taroko in different ways than the Seediq live theirs of the Musha War. The Truku of Hualien have all been moved to the plains. They were evicted from the places where their defining moment happened in what is now the Taroko National Park. The Seediq, for their part, are still living amid the haunted ruins of memory. Memories of the Musha Uprising, unlike the Battle of Taroko, were woven together in new ways to make a monument (figure 6.6), a site of pilgrimage, and an annual ceremony in the cycle of township politics. This monument, too, gives the Seediq physical signposts and decades of personal memories from which to construct their national belonging.

In our era of Indigenous politics, in Hualien a Truku Nation was born. From people speaking the same three dialects, a Seediq/Sediq/Seejiq Nation (or 3S Confederation) was also born on the other side of the mountains. For the leaders and strong supporters, this achievement is a liberating moment in history, the awakening of national consciousness that may one day lead to political autonomy and self-government. For many ordinary people, however, all of this name recognition appeared during the process of ethnogenesis as a political struggle about household registration classifications and the socioeconomic advantages that come with them. To the more cynical among them, it all looked like elite competition for state resources. But that is only part of the story. The practice of making confederations based on personal relations between alang is a political ontology that predates the modern ideas of territoriality that undergird modern projects of name rectification, autonomy, and self-government. The foundation of Gaya is the autarky of the alang, and these confederations respect that principle. The challenge is to make these fluid dynamics legible to a modern state based on a very

Figure 6.6. Musha Survivors' Memorial, Gluban, 2007. Commemorating the tragedy of the Musha Uprising and suppression.

Source: Photograph by Scott E. Simon.

different ontology. But people are very skilled at making new syncretic alternatives and bringing them to life. Watan Diro told me in 2019: "We used to say that Gluban means the place where we wash the skulls. Now, we say it is a place where people gather together." As people get used to new identities and build communities based on shared values and face-to-face relations, reconciliation is possible, even among previous enemies.

Gaya as a Pathway to the Future

The main point of this book was to explore the contemporary and universal meaning of *Gaya*, a concept that can be translated as "sacred law" or "customary law" but also as a way of life, culture, or ontology. The Atayal cognate is Gaga, and the Toda is Waya, but they are the same. Although Gaya emerges from the historical and social circumstances of the people on Formosa who came to be called Atayal, Truku, or Sediq, it is relevant more broadly as an Indigenous legal tradition that still provides alternative ways of thinking beyond the extractive institutions of the Westphalian nation-state and developmentalism. Because Gaya is about human relations, but also about human relations with animals and the entire living world, it resembles the Algonquin law of *Ginaway-daganuk* that "acknowledges the web of life or the interconnectedness of all things" (McDermott and Wilson 2010, 205). Gaya is the key to a "good life" (*malu kndsan*; Shen 1998, 27), like the Nishnaabeg *mino bimaadiziwin* (Simpson 2011, 13). I did not need to go to Taiwan to hear Indigenous teachings about industrial society, but because I started out in Chinese studies and then met the people who guided me towards the mountains of Formosa, that is what happened. As I was learning by wayfaring, Seejiq Truku made my heart receptive to teachings from closer to home. I listened carefully when elders told me: "You, too, are seejiq," pointing out that I am just as subject to Gaya as everyone else. They also taught me that the price to pay for violating Gaya is disaster in the form of such things as typhoons, epidemics, and injury. Their experience says much to indigeneity and Indigenous resurgence for the twenty-first century. I think that no matter where we may be on the planet, as the powerful living beings that humans are, we can no longer afford to ignore the traditional teachings of Indigenous peoples and other forms of land-based wisdom.

Each of the ethnographic chapters of this book is constructed around a Seejiq Truku concept. *Samat*, the animals of the forest, remind us of the interconnectedness of human and animal lives. Gaya is most evident in the actions of the tiny sisil birds who guide hunters to prey, communicate the will of the ancestors to the living, and serve as a model for political organization. In contemporary Taiwan, these ways of relating to other lives are weakened by state laws that criminalize many hunting practices. *Mgaya*, the implementation of Gaya, is about the warrior ritual traditions that were stigmatized as primitive headhunting under the forces of cultural imperialism. Mgaya was never about random violence and, as human sacrifice has been replaced with animal sacrifice, it is still about protecting the sovereignty of one's community, sharing, and working hard. This loyalty to the face-to-face group, the *alang*, now animates Indigenous resurgence. Social movements even reappropriate *chucao* 出草, the Chinese term for headhunting, as a call to protest and resistance. *Utux*, the spirits of the forest and of the church, converge in unexpected ways as realities that influence peoples' lives. *Lnglungan*, the heart, provides ethical deliberation about how to live with others by placing an emphasis on equality, autonomy, and sharing, even in a colonial situation with elections and new political institutions of indigeneity. *Tminun*, weaving, is about how people creatively weave together new relationships, new identities, and forms of Indigenous resurgence. All of this knowledge should demonstrate that, despite the predictions of generations of anthropologists, state administrators, and even some Indigenous authors, Gaya lives. Gaya is not a cultural curiosity. It is a pathway to the future.

In 1992, Pawan Tanah and a team of researchers went high up in the mountains to Truku Truwan to interview Apay Kumu, a woman who was at the time 105 years old and thus could remember most of the colonial history depicted in this book. Passing on the words of her father, she said:

> From ancient times to the present, Truku lives were self-sufficient because of hunting and growing millet. Without depending on the outside world, we lived like that for thousands of years. Just by obeying Gaya, we could live from our surroundings, taking wild plants and fruits, and ate to our full ... Nowadays, modern people seem to have material conditions, life quality and a space for activities all one hundred times greater than our generation. But, I get the general impression that they are missing something by losing the respect for the ancestral spirits and taking a foreign religion as the basis of life ... Gaya is the alang and the mutual interdependence and order that arises within it. (Shen 1998, 66–7)

These were the teachings that local intellectuals and ordinary people imparted to me over the past twenty years. In retrospect, I think that the questions people asked me were just as important, if not more so, than the questions I asked them. Do you farm? Do you hunt? How can you possibly leave your parents behind? Don't you find it sad that you don't have children? They were guiding me to reflect on the relationships I have with the plants and animals around me, with the people who preceded me and made me who I am, and with the generations of the future. These are also teachings about Gaya. Few people seemed to envy the way that I could fly in jets to come to Taiwan for field research, leave fieldwork to attend a conference in Europe, and still teach in Canada. If anything, they expressed abhorrence at the idea that I would leave my family to come to Taiwan, incomprehension when I said I had to do it for a "career," and pity because I was in the unfortunate circumstance of being alone far away from home. Their kindness shepherded me in the intellectual direction that become this book and shaped my own personal values. They taught me the importance of the heart journey.

Everyday sociality is enough to demonstrate the continuity of Gaya. In 1869, while working as a commissioner in the Chinese Customs Service, American official Edward C. Taintor visited one of these groups in Hualien.[1] I cringed when I read his portrayal of them as people who "stand at the very lowest point in the scale of civilization" (Taintor 1874, 4). He portrayed their hunting practices, their tattoos, and the ways in which men gain prestige through headhunting, all topics that the Atayalic peoples now affirm as their shared heritage. Yet, I also read in delight as he described men pledging friendship by drinking together from the same cup and how, most of all, people valued the gift of a sacrificial pig (25–6). I found pleasure in this description because, 150 years later, it is still the world that I experience and have come to love. The Indigenous peoples of Formosa, after 400 years of colonialism, refuse to accept characterizations of their lifeways as primitive or backward. Instead, they affirm a very different ontology of what it means to be human, and they are willing to share it with others. By drinking from the same cup, they affirm that we are not merely atomized individuals but rather kindred spirits brought into communion with one another through sharing. I see this idea as akin to the "shared breath" of sociality and ritual in Indigenous North America and beyond (Siragusa, Westman, and Moritz 2020). It is the wonder of everyday Indigenous resurgence.

Even the abandoned practice of headhunting needs to be put into a broader context. Anthropologist Janet Montgomery, who visited the island from 1916 to 1918, relativized the practice in the context of the

First World War. She wrote: "What is war between 'civilized' races, except head-hunting on a grand scale; only with accompanying mangling and gassing and other horrors of which the island *seban* ('raw savage') knows nothing?" (Montgomery [1922] 1997, 201). Unlike warfare, headhunting never had the goal of eliminating an enemy group or occupying territory. Violence may indeed be "an aspect of our humanity" (Jackson 2013, 171). But, in terms of cruelty and loss of human life, headhunting pales in comparison to the twentieth century of two atomic bombs, Nazi concentration camps, or the suffering of First Nations children in Canadian residential schools. The increasingly visible climate change, loss of biodiversity, and war are making it clear that modern industrial society is rendering the planet inhospitable to life itself. People who feared to venture into the next mountain valley due to caution about succumbing to headhunting surely had much smaller ecological footprints than the people of today who assume they can go anywhere they wish on the planet at low cost and with little risk.

Indigenous People in the Republic of China on Taiwan Today

Of course, Indigenous peoples live amid other members of society. Part of the problem, as highlighted in theories of oppression such as those of Iris Young ([1990] 2011), is that Indigenous people and other minorities are oppressed and marginalized in political structures created by more powerful groups. When Seediq and Truku people say that they returned to the village because they encountered discrimination in the cities, I believe them. They talked to me frankly about being refused housing, jobs, or rental space in public markets because they are Indigenous. People tell them directly that they do not want Indigenous people around "because they drink too much." Overt racism is also an issue for young people seeking marriage partners, since Han Taiwanese families can and do reject potential Indigenous spouses for their children. As recently as the summer of 2020, I encountered a Han Taiwanese man who called his Indigenous neighbour Igung Shiban the pejorative *hoan-á* 番仔 (savage) to my face (Simon 2021c, 20). Sediq and Truku people are fortunate because they have the option of staying in, or returning to, the alang. The kin-based community of the alang is their way of making home in an often-hostile world.

The affirmation of the local community does not mean that Indigenous people fail to assimilate to the wider society. Because I did my research in rural communities, I surely have missed out on the existence of thousands of other people who have successfully made lives for themselves among Han Taiwanese in the cities. I have sometimes heard stories about Indigenous people who have made successful careers beyond Taiwan, including investors in China and even one opera singer in Europe. In the rural villages, I also met people who expressed pride in having been assimilated. These latter ones are memorable because they are rare. In one case, a tea plantation owner in his mid-thirties boasted to me that he has few Indigenous friends. He uses only his Chinese name, practises Chinese martial arts, and having internalized negative stereotypes about Indigenous people, says he drinks tea rather than beer. A second person was a subcontractor in the tunnel construction industry who, in one of the elections I studied, presented himself as the candidate of "development." He also used only a Chinese name and had nothing but ridicule to express about Indigenous cultural or political initiatives in his own community. It is perhaps not mere coincidence that both these men have chosen careers that destroy the mountains and forests. They may have turned their hearts away from Gaya.

In trying to comprehend these dilemmas, the problem arises that neither constructivist theories of nationalism nor social movement theories work for understanding the situation of Indigenous peoples. The idea of the nation as an imagined community rests on the European experience. It is based on ontological notions that states possess exclusive sovereignty over territories, people relate to the state as individuals, and cultures are the colours of polygons that fill in space on maps. Gaya is a different ontology, not just one culture among many in multiculturalism, because it points to the *existence* of other things. Gaya rejects state-centric political thought, instead focusing on the reality of the alang and the possibility of creating broader, flexible confederations that come to life through ritual. That is how both the Truku and the Sediq have come into being as peoples, even as state discourse (and some of their proponents) represents them as discrete cultures with exclusive territories. Social movement theory is related to this latter representation because it assumes that what exists are citizens seeking to further their interests by lobbying the state. Scholars using this framework in Taiwan describe only the options of elite competition or assimilation into the broader society. In these theoretical approaches, culture is just part of the toolkit of political strategy. Such approaches fail to see the existence of something much deeper: namely centuries of resistance to the state based on ethical relations between peoples and with the spirit world.

The crux of the matter is that the Indigenous peoples on Formosa live in an enduring colonial situation. Gaya (or the equivalent in other groups) has been challenged by the imposition of state law ever since Japan militarily subdued the mountain peoples in the first two decades of the last century. Republic of China (ROC) law, which was brought to Taiwan and implemented as soon as possible after the Japanese war defeat in 1945, is from Indigenous perspectives no less colonial. This colonial aspect has been most evident in land laws, which justify the occupation of Indigenous territory by both the Japanese and ROC states to this day. It has also been painfully obvious in laws about hunting, trapping, and protection of wild animals, as those state laws have been used to detain, fine, and imprison Indigenous men who are simply carrying out subsistence and ritual activities on the land of their fathers and grandparents. As I have shown in preceding chapters, the people are very capable in daily life of determining land use, hunting, and solving conflict within their communities by referring to Gaya.

Indigeneity often fails Indigenous peoples. As I discussed in the introduction, Taiwan's Basic Law encapsulates Indigenous peoples by labelling them as tribes that exist with approval of the state. The problem is that the state sets the priorities. Article 13 of the Basic Law, for example, decrees: "The government shall protect indigenous peoples' traditional biological diversity knowledge and intellectual creations, and promote the development thereof. The related issues shall be provided for by the laws" (ROC Ministry of Justice [2005] 2019). It is revealing that the Legislative Yuan, with its six Indigenous lawmakers, passed the Protection Act for the Traditional Intellectual Creations of Indigenous Peoples in 2015 to promote "cultural development" through an intellectual property rights regime that puts traditional religious ceremonies, music, dance, songs, clothing, and so on, under the purview of the state (ROC Ministry of Justice 2015). This act prioritizes a world of individual entrepreneurs, artists, and consumers. Lawmakers and other state officials have done nothing to protect hunters or recognize them as holders of biological diversity knowledge. To the contrary, the state treatment of Bunun hunter Talum Suqluman and hundreds of other Indigenous hunters who have been arrested continues to marginalize and stigmatize their way of life.

As indigeneity has taken root in Taiwan, the Sediq, Truku, and other state-recognized Indigenous groups are in the process of establishing local band councils under state supervision, creating national councils on their own initiative, and promoting other ways in which their legal traditions can be at least partially recognized in state-centric legal pluralism. Not least of all, they would like to create institutions in which Indigenous groups can manage hunting on their traditional territories according to their own legal norms. Some would even like to create autonomous Indigenous governments. These political actors meet with stiff resistance from non-Indigenous (and even some Indigenous) people, who deny the legitimacy of unwritten Indigenous law and, only capable of seeing positivist state law, affirm that "all people are equal before the law." Not recognizing the authority of Gaya, they think that state laws about hunting (or other things) should be applied without discrimination on Indigenous and non-Indigenous alike.

This conflict between Gaya and ROC law is why the word "indigeneity" is part of the subtitle of this book. A focus on indigeneity, the state-centric institutions for governing Indigenous peoples and territories, shows that Indigenous peoples are in an ongoing colonial situation. They are still ruled by outsiders. Yet indigeneity, as opposed to a declaration of independent statehood, allows certain groups who existed on a territory before the arrival of others to affirm certain rights within existing state law. Indigeneity is a form of encapsulation as much as it is a source of hope.

Indigeneity created the conditions for the legal recognition of the Truku and Sediq nations. Their national histories are only just beginning, since we can date them to the legal recognition of the Truku on 14 January 2004 and the Seediq/Sediq/Sejiq (3S) on 23 April 2008. I was privileged to witness the births of these proud nations. Both of their national days are celebrated as moments of liberation by the people who created them. It is important that both Indigenous nations were created through confederations of small communities that unite by ritual means. They were both created by a social process infused with Gaya, which, like any other legal innovation, was contested. They are based more on relations, which form the basis of negotiations over use of territory, than on abstract notions of territoriality to which individuals would relate as citizens.

Indigeneity and Indigenous Resurgence

We can learn much about relations between Indigenous peoples and the encapsulating societies by reflecting on the difference between indigeneity and Indigenous resurgence. Anthropologists are probably most familiar with indigeneity, the legal and political structures that frame Indigenous-state relations. Examples of indigeneity are legal instruments such as the United Nations Declaration on the Rights of Indigenous Peoples (UNDRIP) and Taiwan's Basic Law on Indigenous Peoples, but also political arrangements such as quotas for Indigenous lawmakers in Taiwan's Legislative Yuan or co-management regimes in national parks. Anthropologists have been cautious about these innovations, even warning against the "cunning of recognition" (Povinelli 2002), which justifies ongoing state rule and can further marginalize Indigenous peoples. The dangers of cooptation, even deepening of assimilationist and oppressive structures, is why Indigenous thinkers like Taiaiake Alfred, Glen Coulthard, Audra Simpson, Leanne Simpson, Namoh Nofu Pacidal, and Pawan Tanah emphasize instead outright refusal or an alternative Indigenous resurgence. Indigenous resurgence is what happens when Indigenous peoples affirm and exercise self-determination outside of state structures and paradigms. I hope that this book shows that Indigenous resurgence emerges in the daily life of ordinary people.

There are many ways in which we could contrast indigeneity and Indigenous resurgence. Indigeneity focuses attention on oppression; Indigenous resurgence focuses on affirming pride. Indigeneity is about classifying people; Indigenous resurgence is about how we are related. Indigeneity is state centric and seeks to integrate Indigenous peoples into existing structures; Indigenous resurgence dares to imagine a new system. Indigeneity is focused on *human* rights; Indigenous resurgence boldly includes all lives. In Taiwan, indigeneity becomes visible in public when village elites compete for positions dealing with the state. Indigenous resurgence can be seen in such subtle moments as when Indigenous people refuse to eat with chopsticks from individual bowls, eating instead with their hands from a shared pot. Indigeneity and Indigenous resurgence are based on very different political ontologies. Indigeneity is couched in the language of written laws, constitutions, and state-protected rights, whereas Indigenous resurgence is rooted in Indigenous languages and stories. This difference was expressed forcefully by Leanne Betasamosake Simpson when she said we have debated long enough with Audra Lorde on whether "the master's tools can dismantle the master's house." Instead, she proposed that it is time to build a new house (Simpson 2011, 32). Building the new is a process that is happening in Taiwan as well as in Canada.

There are important attempts to combine the projects of reconciliation and Indigenous resurgence. In Canada, it has become a point of convergence for Indigenous peoples, anthropologists, and other scholars (Asch, Borrows, and Tully 2018). Indigenous people hope that the new institutions of indigeneity are better than previous state paradigms of assimilation, which is why they embrace such events as the UN Permanent Forum on Indigenous Issues. Indigenous activists from Taiwan take pride when they can access UN facilities that are denied to their unrecognized encapsulating state. In Taiwan, Indigenous peoples have historically found the Presbyterian Church to be a place to nourish Indigenous languages and ontologies. With democratization, they could create a broader movement for Indigenous rights, and the result has been new institutions of indigeneity. Within the affordances of those institutions, a new form of Indigenous resurgence has become possible. Anthropologists must come to an understanding of Indigenous resurgence, as we can act as allies of Indigenous peoples to decolonize the discipline. Indigenous anthropologists often lead the way. One first step is to think beyond culture.

Ontology, Indigenous Resurgence, and Human Rights

With the much-heralded ontological turn in anthropology, there has been debate about whether ontology is just another word for culture (Carrithers et al. 2010). Culture, as used in anthropology, emerged from the ontological assumption that there is one reality but different cultural representations of it (Blaser 2012, 52). An example would be to study beliefs about the sisil, assuming that ornithologists study the reality of the bird's life as *Alcippe morrisonia* and anthropologists explore how the Sediq or Truku represent it culturally as an emissary of the ancestors. A social anthropologist might look at the sisil as a cultural symbol used in identity politics. This one-reality approach preserves the notion that biologists understand how this species is related to other birds of its species or genus in an evolutionary and genetic way, and ethologists best understand the foraging behaviour of mixed-species flocks. It would consider the Sediq-Truku way of lumping together different kinds of birds (sisil and friends) as at best an ethnographic curiosity, and perhaps even as a lack of taxonomic skills. The ontological turn in anthropology entertains the possibility that the sisil really do communicate messages from the ancestors and that "sisil" is not limited to one "species." Political ontology is the study of what happens when ontological worlds collide, an example being when the state criminalizes the daytime hunting practices that once entangled seejiq and sisil pathways in the forests. Political ontology is also open to the idea that the sisil is more than a nationalist symbol; it can even be a model for imagining alternative ways of living politically.

The Sediq and Truku are very aware of the limits of culture. There are surely limits to culture as imagined through coloured maps of Taiwan's sixteen Indigenous peoples. Hunters have been very frustrated by understandings of hunting as a cultural right, especially when officials use culture as a way of limiting the hunters' activities. They found it unreasonable that they were asked to register the date, place, and species of animals to be caught before hunting. Some local officials have refused to grant permission to individual hunters, arguing that hunting is only cultural if it is embedded in collective ritual performance. Talum Suqluman, whose legal case was discussed in chapter 2, was even sentenced to prison on the grounds that his hunting rifle was different from those of other men in his village and thus not in accordance with local culture. Culture can thus be a form of entrapment. It is an act of Indigenous resurgence when people instead insist on using the term Gaya.

Indigenous peoples do not reject human rights; they insist on the right to redefine them. In this spirit, Takun Walis (2012) characterized the Musha Uprising as a human rights action. Gaya puts humans at the centre of a different ontological basis for rights. The most obvious difference is that Gaya does not imagine a right to own land. That is modern state ontology. Instead, Gaya emphasizes the responsibility of the true person to protect the land, because the land and the person who takes care of it belong to each other. This view does not exclude farming. In fact, people say that it is a violation of Gaya to sell land that their parents have cleared and cultivated, which suggests that people belong to the land, rather than the land belonging to them, but not in some abstract way. People belong to the land that they have transformed through the labour of farming or cultivating hunting territories and traplines. This notion is an ontological difference. Likewise, the forests are not resources to be exploited by mines, national parks, or trekking companies; rather, they are the realm of the ancestors, which needs to be entered with awe and respect. Sharing with others is more important than accumulating wealth for oneself. In fact, one could even say that the obligation to share largely precludes the possibility of selling "resources," or the gifts of the ancestors, for personal accumulation (Walis 2009, 40). Gaya provides for each alang to nourish its own collective hunting territory but also furnishes mechanisms for conflict resolution. The people of Gaya are skilled at setting boundaries between groups but also at burying stones in ceremonies of reconciliation and at creating confederations. The core is relationality, not territoriality, managed by local autarky rather than an overarching state. By affirming Gaya as the basis of human rights, these people are offering us a new ontology, which they proclaim as universal. The traditional autarkic nature of Sediq politics is a reminder that all rights emerge from very local forms of self-determination. In the long run, these principles of Gaya may be far more important to everyone than a mere redistribution of rights in the existing state-centric modern framework.

Indigenous Resurgence and the Decolonization of Anthropology

If the ontological turn permits an anthropological engagement with Indigenous resurgence, it can be part of our process of decolonization and indigenization of the discipline. It is a Western or even colonial ontology to even posit the idea that I, the researcher, am an anthropologist who studies the "culture" of such-and-such people, with "nature" in the background as a source for food or myth-making. It is in fact awkward to assume that the identity of the anthropologist is always the objective outsider. People reminded me of that when they said: "You, too, are human."

Indigenous resurgence can even challenge the assumptions of Marxist political economy. Once, after participating with a visiting Truku delegation in a sweat lodge ritual in Unama'ki (Cape Breton, Nova Scotia), the Mi'kmaq elder who led the ceremony and I sat at the table and conversed. When I brought up the subject of colonial extraction on Indigenous lands, he made it very personal. "The problem won't be solved," he said, "until you, too, realize that you are also Indigenous" (Simon 2012b, 209). After that, it became my responsibility to figure out the meaning of his teaching. Obviously, it does not concern legal status or identity politics. Something more profound is happening.

Indigenous people in both Taiwan and Canada sometimes challenge the idea of classifying people into distinct cultures and ethnicities. Seediq thinker Dakis Pawan reminds us that notions of distinct and exclusive peoples, ethnic classification, and ethnonyms were introduced by the Japanese (Kuo 2012, 96). This point resonates with the teaching of *Comis* Dominique Rankin, who said: "For us, where a human being comes from geographically is not very important. Long ago, when we came across representatives from a different Nation, we often said that we had discovered 'new faces' from the East, the South, the West, or the North" (Rankin and Tardif 2020, 26). He also notes that the term "Algonquin" is foreign to his people's vocabulary and that their own name for themselves, Anicinape, simply means "human being" (26). Pawan Tanah says that the transcendent question, above all the discussions of ethnic names that usually mean human, is to ask: "What kind of human are we?" (Shen 1998, 44–5). When such leaders teach us that we are all human and all subject to the same sacred law, we should take these ideas seriously. Relegating those notions to someone else's culture only justifies business as usual.

When I first met Algonquin elder Comis (Grandfather) William Commanda in his community of Kitigan Zini, he invited me and Seediq legal scholar Awi Mona into his home. He showed us the Welcoming and Sharing Three Figure Sacred Wampum Belt, which dates to the early eighteenth century. The belt depicts three figures, an Algonquin in the centre holding the hands of the French and the English, with a cross as witness. The meaning of the belt is that we all have responsibilities to care for the life-givers, to respect and love each other, and to share the land according to its law (also discussed in McDermott and Wilson 2010, 206). Comis William Commanda asked me to embrace that teaching as reality and as the law that we must follow, not to write about it as Algonquin culture.

These personal encounters are part of a much larger awakening, as Indigenous elders across Turtle Island (North America) and around the world see the immediate risks posed by environmental destruction and speak out. In the traditional teachings of Turtle Island, the prophets speak of a time in which the "light-skinned race" will have to make a choice between the road of unceasing technological development or the road of spirituality. If they choose the wrong road, there will be destruction. If they choose the right road, the Eighth Fire will usher in a new era of peace, love, brotherhood, and sisterhood (Rankin and Tardif 2020, 139). This teaching explains why it is important for everyone to learn from Indigenous knowledge and embodied wisdom. As the entire world is dealing with the ravages of the COVID-19 pandemic, as well as violent weather related to climate change, Indigenous leaders in the United States have even offered up a "red deal" based on Indigenous teachings to save our earth (Red Nation 2021). These teachings resonate with those of Sediq and Truku elders who said that people lived by Gaya for thousands of years and that it served them very well.

As we reflect upon a world supervised by utux, the concept of *rmuba* (misfortunes that occur due to violating Gaya) should serve as a warning to us. Over the years, Sediq and Truku people have speculated to me about whether their situation of poverty and ill health is not retribution for their ancestors who misused their traditions of headhunting. They ask to reflect upon how our moral failings contribute to such disasters as epidemics, typhoons, and landslides. This perspective should encourage us to think about what our lifestyles are doing to the planet. From a moral perspective, industrial-sized deforestation and fossil fuel emissions are surely much greater violations of Gaya than anything that could ever be imagined by people whose lives are focused on the well-being of the alang.

Despite the differences between them, anthropologists of various theoretical leanings are also walking on this path. Tim Ingold, for example, sees the root of the ecological crisis in the Western metaphysics of alienation of humanity from nature. Rather than relativizing indigenous views, which he opposes, he suggests that indigenous hunters and herdsmen have the best ideas on how to proceed in the future (Ingold 2000, 76). Maybe he is right to reclaim the non-capitalized word "indigenous," if we imagine a future era when everyone takes care of the land, but we are not there yet. Even Philippe Descola, who seemingly classifies all human societies into four discrete ontologies, notes that they coexist potentially in all human beings (Descola [2005] 2013, 233). Ontologies are thus ways of seeing the world, not discrete categories into which anthropologists can place the cultures they study. Descola's psychological insight explains why, in the highlands of Formosa, even I could be taught to see the reality of sisil and utux.

Coda

Coming back to Formosa, Gaya means many things to many people. It means being generous with others, protecting the interests of one's family, remaining loyal to one's spouse, and defending the territory of one's alang. It means living in accordance with the rhythms of nature, never taking more than one needs from the forest. Anyone who succeeds in upholding Gaya will be rewarded by the ancestors with hunting success or other signs of blessing. Such a person is *seediq balae* – truly human!

This way of life was perpetuated for centuries, if not for millennia, by the peoples who roamed the forests of northern Formosa, eventually taking them from Pusu Qhuni, the rock from which the first people emerged in ancient times, to the glistening waters of the Pacific Ocean. As stateless people, what anthropologists would call acephalous societies, they knew nothing of states, population statistics, or ethnic groups. If they said they were *sejiq truku*, they simply meant that they were people from a place called Truku, the terraced lands of the central mountains. They continued to live autonomously from any state until after the Japanese took Formosa in 1895.

The encounter between the Indigenous peoples and the state was a shock for all parties involved. The Japanese did not know how to deal with these people who, unlike the Han Taiwanese who had been on the island for more than two centuries, seemed to have no permanent settlements, writing system, or government and appeared to thrive from a state of permanent warfare. Since these people lacked recognizable state organization, the Japanese thought them to be outside the rules of civilized warfare or diplomacy, even the legal equivalent of animals. It was only with the imposition of the state, census, and household registration classifications and eventually multicultural indigeneity that they were classified as Atayal, before claiming themselves the identities of Truku and Seediq. It was only with official multiculturalism that they became an ethnic group opposed to others, no longer merely the peoples native to Formosa, or indigenous with a lower-case "s," but Indigenous as contrasted with being Mainlanders, Hakka, or Hokkien.

The words are important. *Seediq* as an Indigenous nation or *seediq* as human, Indigenous with a capital "I" or a lower-case "i" are all ways of expressing different forms of sociality, different political statuses, and ultimately different ontological categories. The sociological lesson is that peoples have all been incorporated into the colonial state and the capitalist world market, where they engage in political struggles to affirm the best possible place for themselves. It is only in this colonial situation that they become Indigenous. Decolonization, indigenization, and reconciliation hold out the promise of erasing those differences, inviting everyone to become truly human.

Anthropology asks us to probe deep questions, asking what it means to be human at the confluence of biology, society, and history. Showing how humans and others meet on pathways while wayfaring, their spirits and bodies mingling with one another, we can think about the ontological reality of the world as meshwork. In Taiwan, hunters and trappers have taught me to perceive this meshwork in the sound of wind rustling through bamboo, the cry of the sisil bird, the call of the muntjac, and the rising crescendo of cicadas in the summer. If I hear a dog bark, I know that humans are not far behind. Along with my Indigenous friends, I feel a sense of alarm when I hear chainsaws in the forest or dynamiting at the mine. I have learned well the lessons that the hunters and trappers hoped to share with me. Somehow, the pathways they shared with me have also made me a bit more seediq, a bit more human.

The pristine world that the first humans entered when they stepped out of the giant boulder called Pusu Qhuni no longer exists. Formosa is the immediate context of Pusu Qhuni. There are still mountains and forests, and they cover about 60 per cent of the island. But they are criss-crossed by electric lines and roads. In some places, forests have given way to cabbage farms, tea plantations, hydroelectric dams, tourist resorts, and military facilities. Indigenous people have also contributed willingly to some of those projects, as I saw vividly in the form of highland Indigenous-owned tea and cabbage farms. The inaccessibility of much of the island, as well as the diversity of microclimates from the tropical coasts to high mountain peaks, means that it is still a haven to species of plants, birds, amphibians, reptiles, and mammals found nowhere else on the planet. Nonetheless, the island is fragile.

The meshworked world in the mountains of Formosa is now threatened not just by development and highway construction but also by the global warming and species extinction that threatens the entire planet. The island is likely to experience more frequent and stronger typhoons, which means there will be more violent landslides in the mountains just as the coastal areas will become flooded from rising sea levels. Gregory

Bateson thought that the ecological crisis was not only caused by technological progress and population increase but also by a Western intellectual "hubris" or arrogant attitude towards the world that seems to dominate all living things with science (Bateson 1972, 496). Taiwan, the centre of the world's semiconductor industry, has embraced that technology as well as the attitude of conquest. Indigenous people are not immune from that hubris, but at least Gaya is a reminder that another relationship with the world is possible.

Anthropology has tended to neutralize other views on nature by characterizing them, not as lessons for the future but as other cultural constructions of reality. This outlook is partly why I avoided writing a book about the Seediq or the Truku and their construction of nature. Instead, I wrote about them as the people who emerged from Pusu Qhuni, whose society was transformed by the arrival of the state. They resisted the workers looking for camphor and the military that sought to occupy their land, but eventually took a place in Taiwanese society as Indigenous peoples. Not everyone with a household registration labelling them as Indigenous has a close relationship or deep knowledge of the island's forests. Some trappers and hunters, however, have taught me a lot about animals, plants, and Gaya. They assert that they know best how to preserve the environment, the proof being that animals and plants still thrive on the territories they nurture.

The world needs more seediq balae, people able to hear the voice of the sisil in the forest, lest the rhythms and melodies of life's symphony arrive at an irrevocable finale. If we are to get there, we all must answer some basic questions. On Turtle Island, some people are asking: "Are we willing to light the Eighth Fire?" On Formosa, one can ask: "Is it time to return to Pusu Qhuni?"

Indigenous Peoples and Relations with China

In a book about Taiwan, the proverbial elephant in the room and the potential political sensitivity is the relationship between Taiwan and China. The People's Republic of China (PRC), although it has never ruled Taiwan for even as much as a single day, insists that Taiwan is an integral part of its sovereign territory. Experts in international relations even see Taiwan as one of the world's potential flashpoints, where a major war could break out if China were to invade a recalcitrant Taiwan under its Anti-Secession Law of 2005 and the United States were to defend Taiwan under its Taiwan Relations Act of 1979. What does *Gaya* say to this issue?

On 2 January 2019, Xi Jinping, secretary-general of the Chinese Communist Party (CCP) and national chairperson of the PRC, gave a speech on the fortieth anniversary of the "Message to Compatriots in Taiwan." He began his speech with a summary of Chinese history from the CCP perspective: the nineteenth century was a century of humiliation for China, during which China lost Taiwan to Japan, and Taiwan was kept outside of the PRC only due to foreign interference. The return of Taiwan to China is thus a necessary step in national rejuvenation. He extended an olive branch of peace, saying that "we people on both sides of the Taiwan Straits are of one family." Yet the threat of violence was still present: "We do not renounce the use of force and reserve the option of taking all necessary measures."[1]

Taiwanese political leaders did not fail to reply. On the afternoon of that speech, President Tsai Ing-wen (Democratic Progressive Party, DPP) rejected Xi's call for "one country, two systems," even as she expressed willingness to engage in negotiations on a government-to-government basis authorized and monitored by the people of Taiwan. She said quite bluntly that "China must face the reality of the existence of the Republic of China (Taiwan)" and must not use intimidation to pressure the Taiwanese to submit.[2] This message clearly resonated with Taiwanese voters. In the January 2020 presidential election, Tsai was re-elected with 57.13 per cent of the vote, far more than the 38.61 per cent garnered by her main opponent Daniel Han Kuo-yu of the Chinese Nationalist Party (KMT), who favoured economic and political rapprochement between the two sides.

A week after Xi's speech, the Indigenous leaders serving as members of the Presidential Office Indigenous Historical Justice and Transitional Justice Committee (established by Tsai in 2016) replied. They said that Taiwan has been the motherland of the Indigenous people for more than 6,000 years and has experienced waves of colonizing powers, the Republic of China (ROC) being only the most recent. Their statement was independent of the president's views. In fact, they boldly stated: "We are not content with the current state of Taiwan, the sovereign state that has been built upon our motherland." They affirmed that each of Taiwan's Indigenous peoples has the equal right to self-determination, based on being humble to the land, respecting other lives, and coexisting with other groups of people. They said: "The national future of Taiwan will be decided by self-determination of the Taiwanese Indigenous peoples and all the people who live on our motherland."[3]

These positions represent three different ontological claims. Xi assumes that the PRC is the only China that exists, having replaced the ROC everywhere except in the recalcitrant Province of Taiwan. Tsai affirms that the ROC still exists as an effective state and that only mutually respectful negotiations can resolve political differences. The Indigenous leaders point out that both the ROC and the PRC are foreign to Taiwan. Their statement situates sovereignty in the people, who freely establish relationships with one another, rather than in states. Xi and Tsai are thinking in terms of coloured polygons, whereas the Indigenous leaders prioritize entangled lines of engagement.

Having spent so much time in Indigenous communities, I know that the work of the Presidential Office Indigenous Historical Justice and Transitional Justice Committee is contested, as is every political institution of indigeneity. In 2016 and 2020, when Tsai's party won by a large margin, Indigenous people voted for the KMT, and in each community, people are very outspoken about their scepticism towards the DPP. Over the past five years, people have shared with me their concerns that this committee will not achieve its stated aims and that their lives will not be improved. They say that this committee is just one more way in which the government instrumentalizes a discourse of Indigenous rights in order to increase international support. Just as anthropologists are coming to see state sovereignty itself as an ontological project that justified dispossession and the creation of legal regimes of difference (Bonilla 2017), these Indigenous people are making a radically different ontological claim. Under the non-interference principles of Gaya, neither the president, nor a committee in Taipei, nor even the people I happened to encounter in the villages have the right to decide for the hundreds of small autarkic groups that are spread across Formosa.

Over the years, I have been struck by the nonchalance with which Sediq and Truku people think about cross-strait relations and the future of Taiwan. They often echo Xi's metaphor of the family, but with a twist, saying that cross-straits relations are a conflict between Chinese people and, since they are not Chinese, have nothing to do with them. The settlers, who began arriving from China in the seventeenth century, may be of one family with people across the Taiwan Strait, but for the Indigenous peoples, they are not even distant kin. Indigenous people usually say that they have already lived under successive waves of colonial rule, but they are still there. If anything, they are the only real Taiwanese and have maintained their ways of life to the present. No matter who rules Taiwan, some people say with optimism, we can still live as we wish. They are confident that Gaya has existed for thousands of years; that it has been resilient in the face of other colonial powers; and that it can therefore also survive PRC rule. Knowing how the PRC weighs heavily on the lives of minority peoples, most recently through the "terror capitalism" (Byler 2022) that subjects Uyghur and other Muslim minorities to constant surveillance, mass detention, and genocide, I disagree. I think that the institutions of Taiwan's liberal democracy provide much greater affordances for genuine Indigenous resurgence and that incorporation into the PRC would destroy any hope of effective Indigenous autonomy.

When I ask Indigenous people about their opinions on Taiwanese independence, they nearly always oppose it. This stand does not mean they would like to become part of the PRC. They simply equate talk of Taiwanese independence with the DPP, a party they associate with an ethnic group in a numerical majority that is historically responsible for the dispossession of their land and their current marginalization. Most people seem content with maintaining the status quo, which in Indigenous communities means an affective alliance between Indigenous people and the Mainlanders of the KMT as part of the Republic of China. In each election, they end up choosing what they see as the lesser of two evils.

There is another possibility, especially if we imagine beyond the ontology of the Westphalian state with exclusive sovereignty over well-defined territories. In fact, the root of the conflict between China and

Taiwan is that they both claim this kind of sovereignty, the concept of which comes historically from Europe, over the same islands. Proponents of "Indigenous independence" (e.g., Liu 2021; Namoh and Lee 2016) are now trying to envision ways in which Taiwan's Indigenous peoples could first declare independence, paving the way for Taiwan as a whole to maintain its autonomy from China.

In the immediate context, I am worried about the possibility of a Chinese invasion of Taiwan. I hope that the international community includes the rights of Indigenous peoples in their deliberations as they decide how to deal with this possibility. The United Nations Declaration on the Rights of Indigenous Peoples (UNDRIP) explicitly acknowledges in the preamble that Indigenous rights are based in the right of self-determination of all peoples, by which they can freely determine their political status. I take this statement to mean that the Indigenous peoples of Formosa and Orchid Island have the right to decide for themselves if there is any change in their political status, irrespective of whether the change is annexation into the PRC or even encapsulation in a newly independent Republic of Taiwan. UNDRIP hopes that the days of states making unilateral decisions on behalf of Indigenous peoples has ended. Article 30, moreover, stipulates military activities shall not take place on Indigenous lands or territories without their consent, except (typical for UNDRIP) if states find it justified by larger public interest. In this spirit, Seediq former legislator and chair of the Council of Indigenous Peoples Walis Beilin suggests, in the event of conflict, putting Formosa's Central Mountain Range under UN supervision as a non-militarized zone (Walis 2009, 21). This proposal makes perfect sense from his Indigenous perspective. The PRC-ROC conflict is a relic of the unfinished Chinese Civil War, which had nothing to do with the Indigenous peoples, who were still getting used to living with Japan at that time. As a matter of fact, most inhabitants of Formosa had nothing to do with the Chinese Civil War until they suddenly had to accept the presence of millions of refugees and the imposition of a new state. That past history suggests that the system of state sovereignty itself is the problem for Indigenous peoples, not the question of which state represents China to the world.

In a world of Gaya, the state would recede from the scene, leaving behind face-to-face communities (*alang*) that could create confederations flexibly and as needed through repeated rituals that the Truku call *psbalay*, the Sediq call *dmahur*, and the Atayal call *sbalay* (a word President Tsai uses to refer to reconciliation). It may be impossible to ever bring a state-free world into existence. But, by attending to such alternatives, anthropologists draw attention to how the PRC, the ROC on Taiwan, Canada, and in fact most states are based on the same modern ontological base, even as they coexist with different mixes of ontologies everywhere. In spite of the differences between them, modern states all posit the state as the arbitrator of human rights of its citizens and are dedicated to resource developmentalism and non-stop economic growth. The job of anthropology is to relativize that model and to understand it in its various contexts. Indigenous resurgence offers different ontologies, both in human pasts and in our shared future. Perhaps Indigenous peoples can help states and their fellow citizens find a more workable equilibrium for a good life together as truly humans and beyond.

Glossary

Note on Ethnonyms

Before the name rectification movements discussed in this book, anthropologists and linguists classified the Atayal people into three dialects of Sediq, Squliq, and Ci'uli. Although the Sediq were often further categorized geographically into West Sediq (in Nantou) and East Sediq (in Hualien), there was also consensus that the main linguistic differences had evolved over three to four centuries of migration through three different river watersheds, creating the Truku, Tgdaya, and Toda dialects. Japanese police also referred to the Truku people of Hualien as the Taroko. Because most of my research was done in Truku linguistic communities in Hualien and Nantou, I have privileged Truku in the book and written the glossary in Truku. Nonetheless, if my interlocutor was using Tgdaya or Toda, I have written the words in that language throughout the book. When necessary, I specify the dialect in parenthesis, for example, *seejiq* (tr), *seediq* (tg), *sediq* (to). The legal English names of the ethnic groups now are Truku and Sediq, and both ethnic groups include speakers of these three dialects.

These languages are currently in the process of being standardized. For this glossary, I have relied most heavily on the Truku, and sometimes Sediq, entries in the online dictionary of the Aboriginal Language Research and Development Foundation (https://e-dictionary.ilrdf.org.tw). When people gave me alternative spellings in the field, I retained those when I thought it was important for my work to reflect local usage. Elders gave me their perspective on this entire process when I asked them to help me with my spelling. They told me that their language is traditionally a spoken language, with great variation between communities and speakers, and, moreover, that important parts of what is conveyed in spoken language such as intonation and emotion are lost when trying to capture it in the written word. This valorization of the living spoken word over what is ultimately a state-sponsored project of standardization is itself a form of Indigenous resurgence.

Truku and Sediq Vocabulary

Alang, a highly flexible, partly kin-based, territorial organization with clearly defined membership[1]

Anay, agnatic relatives, spouses of siblings or cousins

Babaw dxgal, "on the (whole) earth," nature (see dxgal)

Babuy, pig, sleeping in

Baka, enough

Balay, true, very

Banah (tr, Hualien), red; so *banah tunux* (red heads) means Japanese

Bhring, spirit energy (especially hunting), luck, a sharpshooter

Bowyak, wild boar, struggling, breaking free, busy

Bqan sari, "taro sprouts"

Bubu, mother, trunk of a tree

Dukung (tr), leader

Bungu qhuni, tree nodules or lumps

Cina sari, "old taro," the starchy corm or bulbotuber of the taro plant

Dha, two, other; so *dha lnglungan* means other hearted, disloyal, duplicitous

Dgiyaq, mountain, or hunting territory

Dheran (tg), soil, earth, world (see tndheren)

Dmahur (to), dmahun (tg), to ladle, blood rituals of reconciliation, Christian Eucharist

Dowriq utux rudan, "eyes of the ancestors," a weaving pattern

Duhi, thief

Dxgal, earth, territory, that from which living creatures grow

Gaya (tr and tg, Waya in Toda), ancestral or sacred law, culture, cultural ontology

Klaway (tr), swallows

Gxal, relatives, the people who eat together and expect shares of pig sacrifices

Hakaw Utux, Rainbow Bridge, the entry to the spirit world

Hghug, a bird that serves as an omen of death

Huling, dog

Huma, to plant (vegetables, herbs, flowers, etc.), so mhuma is farming

Ibaw, Mainlanders, Chinese officials and refugees who came to Taiwan with Chiang Kai-shek beginning in 1945, but especially after 1949

Ini klgug, "things that don't move," plants

Kaalang, people from other communities, foreigners
Karat, sky
Kari, language, to dig
Kbuyu, tall grassy underbrush; thus *knbuyu* "emerging from the grass," headhunting, as translation of *chucao* 出草 (Chinese)
Khilan (tg, Nantou), Hakka people
Kmciyuk, rebellion; so *Kmciyuk Banah Tunux* as "rebellion against the red heads" (Japanese), the Musha Incident
Kmukan (or mugan), a pejorative term for Hoklo Taiwanese
Kndsan, life (*malu kndsan*, good life)
Kumay, bear (animal)
Kuwi, insects
Kuyuh (Hualien Truku only), girl or woman (compare qrijil)
Lmglug, to shake, to move, movement, thought, (by extension) animals
Lnglungan, heart
Lubuy, a bag (hunters may carry small bags with talismanic animal parts)
Madas jiyax, daily labour exchange, literally "to carry the day"
Malu, good
Maduk, hunting
Maxal, ten; *maxal Gaya* being the Ten Commandments
Meydang, separated from or scattered; so *meydang lnglungan*, a distraught heart
Mdudul, to lead; originally as in "to lead along a path," but later meaning chief
Mgaya, "to implement Gaya," the process of headhunting
Mhuni, witches
Mhuway su balay, thank you, literally "you are very generous"
Mirit, Formosan serow (a mountain goat), to disobey
Mkan hadur, ritual of feeding the head after headhunting
Mkere, solid
Mkuni Paran, "the Paran insanity," Musha Incident
Mqribaq, "behind the mountains," Nantou, people in Nantou
Mneudus, living things
Mneudus mkarang dxgal, "living things that crawl on the ground," *karang* meaning crab as a noun and thus "to crawl" as verb
Mneudus ska qsiya, "living things that swim in the water"
Mneudus skaya karat, "living things that fly in the sky"
Msapuh, doctor, witch, shaman
Mslagu, straight; thus *mslagu lnglungan* for "loyal heart"
Mssungut, a mythical race of tiny, bean-sized people

Mtraqil (or mtlaqel), warfare

Muetsipo (from Masaw 1998, Mssbu), "shooting to kill"; Mccebu (tg), shooting on a large scale, warfare

Muwit, tired; thus *muwit lnglungan* for "discouraged heart"

Muutux (from utux), insane

Naqih, bad, evil

Nanak, only

Ngay-ngay, Hakka people

Nklaan hidao, "belonging to the place where the sun rises," Hualien

Nniqan gaga (Atayal), clan, "people who eat together"

Pada, Formosan Reeves muntjac (a small deer)

Patas, book, reading

Pgalu, to provoke pity

Pila, money

Pngalan kari, "according to his word," used for leaders

Powda, to rely on, to pass through, to share, rites of transition, wedding announcement

Pngqeydin (tr, Nantou; pnqeyjin, tr, Hualien), women who married into a community from a different group

Psakur, "working the earth," farming

Psaniq, tabu, forbidden things, female genitalia

Psbalay, to reconcile, to flatten out, to escape from a trap (animals)

Psidul (tg), psidar (tr), black drongo (a bird)

Psima, shrike (Hualien), Japanese white-eye (Nantou)

Ptasan, tattooing, school

Pusu, root

Pusu Qhuni, "root of the tree," the giant boulder in the central mountains from which the first humans emerged in the beginning of time

Qbhni (tr, Hualien), birds

Qbsuran, elder siblings

Qduda (tr, Nantou), birds, some identify it as only the Steere's liocichla (*Liocichla steerii*)

Qhuni, tree

Qowlit, rat, mouse

Qrijil (tr, Nantou), girl or woman (compare kuyuh)

Qsiya, water

Qsurux, fish

Quyu, snake

Rapit, flying squirrel

Rmuba, curse, misfortunes that befall people who violate Gaya in important ways

Rudan, elders, kinship, parents, old and tough food

Rungay, monkey

Ruqi, brain, brain pulp; *kana skuun ska ruqi mu*, I remember (store) everything in my brain

Samat, game animals

Sapah, family, home

Sari, taro

Sbiyaw, a long time ago, in the past

Seediq (tg), **sediq (to)**, **seejiq (tr)**, human, person, other people, personality, human nature

Seejiq tnpusu, Indigenous people, literally "rooted people"

Sgealu, to love, to pity, to depend upon

Sipil, black bulbul (bird)

Sisil, grey-cheeked fulvetta, a small, wild bird used in divination

Skaya, to fly

Skuun, to deposit, store, save; to bury

Smbarux, mutual labour exchange between families

Snaw, boy or man

Snegul, to follow

Spi, dreams

Spian skeeman, dreaming at night

Spriq, grass or weed

Swayi, younger siblings, same generation

Swiraw, Taiwan whistling thrush (a bird)

Tama, father, has also come to be used for "chief" and "God"

Tanah tunux (tg, Nantou), red; so *tanah tunux* (red heads) means Japanese

Telu, Mainlanders; see also Ibaw

Teywan, Taiwanese

Tminun, weaving

Tminun kari rudan sbiyaw, storytelling, literally "weaving the words of the elders of the past"

Tnalang, one from a place, Indigenous

Tndheren (tg), property owner, "sovereignty"

Tnbgan, "domestic" animals, literally "place where feeding happens"

Tnpusu, from the origin (see also utux tnspusu, seejiq tnpusu)

Tuku, Formosan striped squirrel

Tunux, head

Udus, life, living

Ungat, to not have

Utux, spirits, ancestors, ghosts, shade, mental illness

Utux baraw, "God above," one of the names for the Christian God

Utux rudan, ancestral spirits

Utux tminun, "Weaving God," another name for the Christian God

Utux tnpusu, "Original God," another name for the Christian God

Place Names
(long-term field residences marked with an asterisk*)

This list is not a comprehensive list of Truku or Sediq communities. It is a list of place names mentioned in the book, places where I did field research. Again, spellings are being standardized. I relied on the *Encyclopedia of Indigenous Communities* (Lim 2018) and Taiwan's Indigenous Peoples Portal of the Council of Indigenous Peoples (http://www.tipp .org.tw/tribe.asp), but I also consulted local people.

*Alang Bsngan, Hualien, corresponding roughly to Fushih Village, composite of alang moved down the mountains during the Japanese period, at the confluence of the Liwu River and the Pacific Ocean

*Alang Buarung, Nantou (Alang Fuji from 1931–45), Tgdaya until the Musha Incident, composite of five Truku alang since 1931

*Alang Ciyakang, Hualien, composite of Truku alang moved down the mountains during the Japanese period, in the plains on the Ciyakang River

*Alang Gluban, Nantou, composite of six Tgdaya alang formed by the survivors of the 1930 Musha Incident (called Kawanakashima in the Japanese period), in the plains on the Beigang River

Alang Mhebu, Nantou, historical, now site of Lushan Hot Springs

Alang Paran, Nantou, formerly the largest Tgdaya settlement, now 70 per cent non-Indigenous, administrative centre known as Musha (Japanese) or Wushe (Chinese), 1,148 metres above sea level

*Alang Qlgi, Hualien, also called Kele in Chinese, composite of Truku alang moved down the mountains during the Japanese period and some Toda families, next to Bsngan and part of Fushih Village

Alang Sadu, Nantou, Truku alang, 1,800 metres above sea level

*Alang Skadang, Hualien, legally part of Fushih Village, Truku alang with a traditional settlement in the Taroko National Park and a settlement with the people of Alang Xoxo in the Minle District of Fushih Village

Alang Snuwil, Nantou, formerly Alang Gungu (tg) until Musha Incident, when the Japanese resettled it with Toda, after which it became Alang Sakura ("cherry village" in Japanese), 1,200 metres above sea level

Alang Toda, Nantou, Toda, 7 kilometres north of Alang Bwarung, 1,200 metres above sea level

Alang Tausa, Hualien, Toda, the only Sediq village in Hualien

Alang Tkijig, Hualien, Truku, on the Pacific coast adjacent to Bsngan

Alang Tpdu, T'ien-hsiang, Hualien, 485 metres above sea level, now a tourist centre in the Taroko National Park

Dgiyaq Silung, Nenggao Mountain 能高山 (Nenkaw in Truku)

Spitay (in Chinese, *Renzhiguan* 人止關), the "barrier where people stop" that marks the transition from Han to Sediq territory on the road up from Puli[2]

Chinese

Baoliudi 保留地, reserve land

Benshengren 本省人, "Native Taiwanese" or Han Taiwanese, speakers of Hokkien and Hakka who have settled Formosa since the seventeenth century

Buluo 部落, "tribe," band or village community (not exactly the same as alang)

Buluo huiyi 部落會議, band council, a recent innovation since 2016

Chucao 出草, "emerging from the grass," headhunting

Chuantong lingyu 傳統領域, traditional territory

Daziran 大自然, nature

Ganqing 感情, feelings, affection

Guanxi 關係, relations

Guo 國, country, state

Huan wo tudi 還我土地, "Return Our Land," a slogan of the Indigenous rights movement

Laobaixing 老百姓, "the old one-hundred surnames," ordinary people

Naojiang 腦漿, the cerebellum and other parts of the brain

Pachong lei 爬蟲類, reptiles

Pingdi tongbao 平地同胞, plains compatriots (a legal category within Indigenous peoples)

Pingdiren 平地人, plains people, non-Indigenous

Pingpuzu 平埔族, "plains aborigines," not recognized by the state as Indigenous

Ren 人, person

Rentong 認同, to identify, identity, recognition

Ruxian 入憲, to enter the Constitution

Saideke 賽德克, Sediq/Seediq/Sejiq

Shandi tongbao 山地同胞, mountain compatriots (a legal category within Indigenous peoples)

Shengfan 生蕃, raw savages, outside of Qing rule

Shoufan 熟蕃, cooked savages, under Qing rule

Tailuge 太魯閣, Truku

Tuzhu 土著, savage (used at the United Nations to translate
   "Indigenous people")
Waishengren 外省人, Mainlanders, who came to Taiwan after the
   Second World War
Wenhua 文化, culture
Yibao 義胞, Mainlanders, from a word originally for refugees from the
   Dachen Islands
Yuanfen 緣分, destiny
Yuanzhumin 原住民, Indigenous person (sing.) or people (pl.)
Yuanzhu minzu 原住民族, Indigenous people (sing.) or peoples (pl.)
Zhengke 政客, pejorative word for opportunists in politics
Zhengming 正名, name rectification, used for state recognition of
   Indigenous peoples
Zu 族, "tribe" as a legal category, imagined as a large territorial unit,
   similar to a "nationality" in Stalinist usage

Taiwanese

Huan á 番仔, savage
thiâu-á-kha 柱仔腳, foot of a stake or pillar, a supporter for an
   electoral candidate or party

Japanese

Baka 馬鹿, idiot
Daishizen 大自然, "big nature," Nature
Hokuban 北番, northern savages
Kijun 帰順, submission
Jiken 事件, incident
Kami 神, god
Kamisama 神様, gods
Kōminka 皇民化, "imperialization," assimilation campaign of the
   1930s
Shizen 自然, nature
Takasago minzoku 高砂民族, Formosan Indigenous peoples
Yamabushi 山伏, Japanese mountain ascetic

Algonquin

Anicinape, human
Comis, grandfather

Debwewin, personal truth in one's heart
Ginawaydaganuk, "the interconnectedness of all things," Algonquin
  law
Kokum, grandmother
Te-nagàdino-zìbi, Gatineau River

Notes

Introduction

1 I dare not credit this story to a single author; this version is a composite version of what I have learned through many conversations over the years. I have read it as an "Atayal" story (Rimuy 2002, 16–21), and it appears across the Japanese and Chinese language ethnographic literature. I have heard it told, sometimes in a version with one man and one woman, in church sermons. People discuss it in both Nantou and Hualien, although different communities and different interlocutors have their own variations and interpretations. Shen Ming-ren (Pawan Tanah) attributes the story of two men and one woman to the Atayal and the story of one male and one female, who were in fact deities, to the Sədeq. Showing the close relations between humans and animals, he also provides origin stories based on a primordial woman deity giving birth to the first humans (or the first Truku and Toda) after mating with a pig or dog (Shen 1998, 43–4).

2 Pusi Qhuni is a descriptive name of the boulder. The larger place, with its forests and water, has a name, but in respect for its sacred nature, people do not usually say its name (Kaji 2011, 52).

3 I borrow the strange spelling "Sədeq" from Utsurikawa (Utsurikawa, Mabuchi, and Miyamoto 1935, 36) and use it very sparingly throughout this book, only when I wish to refer collectively to all the peoples but without using one of their languages (to the exclusion of others) or the official state term. The "ə" marks it as foreign. In my earlier book (Simon 2012b), I used "Sadyaq" in the same way and even as the book title.

4 Attentive readers will also note that I spell the name of Igung's father as Shiban and that of her brothers' father as Sibal. They had the same father but spelled his name in different ways on their respective publications. This spelling variation reflects the fact that the language is still in the process of standardization and that standardization of written language is not a priority for many people.

5 The ROC Council of Indigenous Peoples website publishes monthly population statistics.

6 The Qing Dynasty (1644–1912), initially founded by Manchurian invaders, developed into a multi-ethnic confederation as they expanded the borders of China through military conquest. They began settler colonization of Taiwan in 1683 in a process of Indigenous dispossession that was coeval with European settler expansion in the Americas. Since the 1911 Chinese Revolution, the Manchurians have themselves been displaced in China. When they ruled all of China, they stressed their unique culture and protected Manchuria as the national heartland. They are now considered to be only one of fifty-five national minorities in the People's Republic of China and, after a complex history with both China and Japan, are assimilated into Chinese language and national culture, their territory simply labelled as China's "Northeast" (Narangoa 2002).

7 The "i" in "indigenous" is uncapitalized in the English text of the law.

8 In 2006, the Taroko (Truku) Autonomous Region Promotion Team similarly voted to use the term "Taroko Nation" in all English documentation (Simon 2010b, 64). For full disclosure, they did so after I had explained to them the Canadian usage of a vocabulary of First Nations. In 2012, a group of pan-Indigenous activists founded the Taiwan First Nations Party and, because of the Canadian inspiration for their name, invited me to serve as their consultant.

9 Darryl Sterk, professional translator of Sediq languages and Mandarin into English, found that alang has connotations of "band" or "clan," but finally settled on the term "village community" for his book (Sterk 2020, 142).

10 Kaji and Tera, local scholars with no linguistic training, both gave this explanation and probably learned it from interviewing elders, but translator Darryl Sterk and anthropologist Skaya Siku (private communications) have told me that the etymology is based only on the root -ruku, meaning plateau.

11 As is the norm in anthropology, I use a pseudonym for Pisaw and other non-public figures.

12 Quotes from conversations and interviews are my own translations.

13 The root is tabu, "to feed," so tnbgan literally means "places of feeding" (Darryl Sterk, personal communication). This contrast with samat is thus based on the location of the animal – in the forest or in the village. This way of thinking is very different from Western notions of domestication (Simon 2015c).

1. Introducing Taiwan and Its Indigenous Peoples

1 Thanks to Paul Barclay for pointing this fact out to me. For some discussion about why these maps came to be and what they mean, see Maier (2016) and Branch (2014).

2 I learned this linguistic nuance from discussions on Facebook with Darryl Sterk, who was doing research on the dictionaries, and confirmed through private messaging with Sediq intellectual (and Presbyterian pastor) Watan Diro.

3 Publicly available statistics in Taiwan are far more comprehensive, up to date, and transparent than in Canada. Transnational statistics are not easily comparable, as there are fine differences in methods and definitions, but nonetheless are useful in drawing general comparisons. I chose 2017 because that is the last year for which I found roughly comparable Canadian statistics.

4 I had the honour of doing the simultaneous interpretation of Namoh's presentation at the North American Taiwan Studies Association meetings in Toronto in 2016. He is Amis and represents a new generation of Formosan Indigenous intellectuals and activists engaged in radical political resurgence.

5 The triad of Heaven, Earth, and Human is a common Chinese trope, which Pawan used as a cultural translator between Truku and Chinese. Thanks to Darryl Sterk for pointing this out.

6 These place names are summarized in the glossary at the end of the book.

2. *Samat* (Forest Animals)

1 Some hunters encouraged me to do research on their ecological knowledge, with the logic that simply the presence of a foreign scholar studying the topic would strengthen the position of hunters against the state. That became my research priority for more than a decade.

2 The gender of the protagonists, however, is not always specified in the telling of the story.

3 Interestingly, Pecoraro defines the same word, which he spells *mudus*, as including all living things, including plants, but also things that move, such as the hands of a watch (Pecoraro 1977, 114).

4 Because hunting is still not completely legal, it is necessary to use a pseudonym and to conceal the identity of the location of this experience. Since this event happened well more than a decade ago, the statute of limitations has long passed.

5 This bird is referred to in Hualien dialect as *sisin* and in Nantou dialect as *sisil*.

6 Thanks to Darryl Sterk for pointing out the broader connotations of the word. Even in English, to say that someone "has gall" is to say that they have chutzpah, which is a form of courage.

7 People quickly took a liking to hunting at night because mammals are easier to find. Hunters now illuminate their path with headlamps or shine flashlights into the trees to find the reflections from animals' eyes.

8 Japanese anthropologist Mori Ushinosuke documented this belief as a white bird with red feet that invoked misfortune on the enemy, saying that its name *hawun* is related to the word *mahawun*. Kim, referring to Japanese studies, said he found nobody who had heard of this belief and concluded that it is unlikely to exist since he has never seen it in the Truku area (Kim 1980, 198). I never saw such a bird, but two informants said they had and that the person in the house where it roosted died shortly thereafter. They were unable to identify the bird in field guides for me, saying that the bird exists but does not appear in the books. The problem, it turns out, was that we were looking at photos of birds we think of as night birds: owls and nightjars. After discussing this issue with Takoshima Sunao, who documented similar beliefs among the Puyuma about the black-crowned night heron (*Nycticorax nycticorax*; personal communication), I went back and asked the same people about this bird. Seeing pictures of the night heron, they said with certainty that it is the bird that forebodes human death.

9 *Qbhni* has a slightly different semantic range in the two communities. In Hualien, the category of birds is simply called qbhni. In Nantou, Truku speakers refer to birds collectively as *qduda*, even as some elders report that *qduda* should refer only to small birds (particularly the Steere's liocichla) and that there is a forgotten higher level category that includes small birds plus raptors and larger game birds, the proper collective word being qbhni. The different lists produced in the two communities reflect the kinds of birds they encounter and thus reveal much about Truku migration from Nantou to Hualien (Simon 2015a).

10 Some of their neighbours pointed out to me the irony that some of the same people who now hunt and promote hunters' rights formerly earned a living from forestry, even in what is now the Taroko National Park.

11 The precondition of ownership is the relationship of belonging together, which is very different from, say, the idea that an absentee landlord can own an apartment complex in a distant city (Sterk, personal communication) or that a corporation owned by unrelated shareholders can legitimately claim a mountain and mine it.

3. *Mgaya* (Headhunting)

1 Headhunting is important beyond Taiwan, and similar social dynamics of ritual re-enactment with surrogate heads occur both there and elsewhere (Cauquelin 2004; Schröder and Quack 1979; George 1993, 1995, 1996; Hoskins 2002; Rudolph 2008). The presence of this institution is documented throughout Southeast Asia and Oceania, and was once one of the central topics of anthropological discourse about the region. It was a central part of

the "Austronesian complex" of warrior and age-class societies (Désveaux 1996, 145) that attained dominance over other peoples as they migrated from Taiwan throughout the Pacific Ocean (Blench 2014, 16).

2 *Mgaya* is a very difficult word. Anthropologist Masaw Mowna, himself Truku, glossed the term in Atayal as "Me-gaga" (*Mgaga*) and in Sədeq as "Pe-gaya" (*Pgaya*) (Masaw 1998, 216). Suzuki has マガガヤ (*magagaya*) and ブガーヤ (*bgaya*; Suzuki 1932, 162). Both authors say it means implementation of the law. Although Pecoraro uses mgaya for "to observe the law," he just uses *Gaya* for headhunting, with one definition being "la LITURGIE de la chasse et du coupage de têtes" (the LITURGY of the hunt and cutting of heads; Pecoraro 1977, 70; all caps in the original). Pawan Tahah calls it *Mo-Gaya* (Shen 1998, 136), whereas Kaji calls it *pgaya* (Kaji 2011, 317), even as he seems much more interested in *mkan hadur*, the ritual of feasting the head (27). Puzzled by the contradictory spellings in the literature, I consulted both professional linguists (who told me that *pgaya* is correct) and village elders in Hualien (who insisted on mgaya). I sided with the elders to better reflect my fieldwork experience.

3 Le marque sur le corps, égale sur tous les corps, énonce : tu n'auras pas le désir du pouvoir, tu n'auras pas le désir de soumission.

4 Masaw was writing before the current standardization of the Truku language. Since then, Truku language specialists have decided not to write the short ə vowels. He seems to have formed this word from the stem *sipo* (now written *sbu*). The Truku online dictionary now glosses warfare as *mtgjiyal* and *tmgjial*, based on the root *jiyal* (to take, to trap). Likewise, for Pecoraro's gloss, the closest I could find was *pluqih* (to wound). According to Truku linguist Apay Tang (personal communication), the correct terms should be *mssbu* for "shooting to kill" and *mtraqil* or *tmjiyan* for "warfare."

5 Kim's confusion about birds demonstrates the usefulness of watching animals as part of our ethnographical practice.

6 The version the woman elder shared with me is no longer available on the internet as part of Truku language education, but ROC Ministry of Education (2010) presents what seems to be a revised version.

7 I asked this woman elder's husband, a senior pastor and skilled hunter, if Duku is meant in the sense of *tuku* (striped squirrel) here. He said yes but had no explanation why she carried the name Duku, except to say it is probably her father's name. He said that Duku was the name of a historical person and was not meant as a metaphor of any kind. It is an example of someone named after an animal as a child.

8 Robert McKinley argued that, across Southeast Asia, riverine settlement patterns were conducive to headhunting ideologies until the formation of the state (McKinley 1979, 111).

9 The anarchist utopia imagined by some anthropologists (e.g., Barclay 1982) has probably never existed in a human society. In these cases from Taiwan, similar to what David Graeber observed in another Austronesian community in Madagascar (Graeber 2004, 55), it is probably best to think of the imagined egalitarian past as part of identities that emerge from political processes of "ethnogenesis." In this case, a desire to live free of Japanese (and then Chinese) domination was transformed into a desire to live free of all hierarchies. In Taiwan, it is easy to conflate these community-based discussions with anthropological discourse that labels Atayalic groups as "egalitarian" because they are not societies "ranked" into nobility and ordinary people like the Paiwan.

10 C'est surtout au niveau du rituel que le chef a un statut particulier.

11 Some reports indicate that the head was treated differently if it were from another aboriginal group or if it were Chinese (Yamada 2015, 253). A less elaborate ritual for Chinese heads would suggest that they were considered somehow less than human and could not be incorporated as ritual ancestors.

12 Kado Kimi (Ai 2010) made an important contribution in a 2010 conference paper by providing detailed stories from the perspective of the victims He also wrote about the tragedy of those who failed to gain a head and were even counter-attacked. Thanks to Jen-Hao Randolph Cheng, his son-in-law, for sharing this conference paper with me.

13 This point was precisely the one made by Kado Kimi in his story about his grandfather and two uncles who took the heads of a young woman and her children while they were digging sweet potatoes. Before she was murdered, the woman pleaded with them to spare them and cursed the headhunters by saying that their lives would be short if they killed her. Indeed, all three died before the age of fifty, whereas a brother too young to join them lived into his seventies. Kado's point is that headhunting was anything but courageous, as the men targeted even women, children, and infants (Ai 2010).

4. *Utux* (Spirit)

1 One of the first international documents of indigeneity, the 1971 Declaration of Barbados, was the product of a meeting between the World Council of Churches and anthropologists, specifically from the Ethnology Department of the University of Berne (Stefano 1997). These origins of global indigeneity, although they influenced Taiwan, are important to note but remain beyond the scope of this book.

2 I presented this chapter as an invited lecture in the Contemporary Taiwan Indigenous Studies Series, Centre of Taiwan Studies, School of Oriental

and African Studies, University of London on 21 June 2018 as "Making God's Country: A Phenomenological Approach to Religious Conversion among the Seediq and Truku of Taiwan." There is thus some repetition of paragraphs in this chapter and the book chapter (Simon 2021b) that also emerged from that lecture, even if this book has a larger scope and has evolved in a different direction.

3 The Truku are not alone in having two different origin stories; indeed, there are two different origin stories in Genesis, one in which God created both men and women in God's image and another in which He made woman out of Adam's rib.

4 There seems to be a contradiction between the idea that this society was an acephalous one with no permanent leadership positions and the presence of a hereditary position that was a source of political power. In my article about headhunting (Simon 2012a), I tried to resolve this paradox as "oscillation" between two competing drives in society: some men tried to gain political power and the group tried to limit their ambitions. People consistently told me that their society was egalitarian, and this notion was also reported in both Japanese and post-1945 Taiwanese ethnographies. The distinction between egalitarian (Big Man) and hierarchical (chief) societies (Huang 1986) is useful as ideal types, but may also reveal political drives that are latent in all societies, even as one drive may become dominant in a particular historical situation. The contrast between an egalitarian past and the still colonial present is a strong political commentary that imagines pre-colonial life as free of the kind of coercive power held by Japanese colonial police officers, or even by the legislators, courts, police, and conservation officers that restrict the lives of Indigenous people today. Walis Buni is a good example of non-coercive power because, although he did not support the 1930 uprising, he also had no power over the leaders of six other communities to prevent it (see the discussion of the Musha Uprising in chapter 6).

5 Just as I am putting the finishing touches on this manuscript, I have gotten to know Rabay's grandson, who has taken over her practice. Perhaps a new historical trajectory of shamanism, with male as well as female shamans, is beginning, including a resurgence of non-binary genders and non-heteronormative sexualities.

6 Kim documented competing candidates during elections in the 1970s killing pigs for doubtful reasons, with the hope that people who took the meat would feel obliged to vote for them. Some people refused to participate and told Kim that sharing meat from a sacrificial animal creates obligations more binding than ordinary bribes because of the ritual (Kim 1980, 376).

7 The lower-case in "indigenous" reflects usage in the original text.

8 Hoping to make the Truku language (which he calls Taroko) accessible to French speakers, Pecoraro spelled *Utux baraw* as *Otoç balao*. He also writes *Otoç mtinun*.

9 Even in Canada, the residential schools are only part of the history of Christianity in Indigenous communities. For example, when I accompanied a delegation of Truku and other international Indigenous activists to the Mi'kmaq community of Eskasoni (Nova Scotia), they showed us their Catholic church and pilgrimage site as a valued part of their community. Long-term field research in any First Nations community would probably reveal important local diversity such as that described in this chapter.

5. *Lnglungan* (Heart)

1 Everyone told me that money was introduced in the Japanese period. Darryl Sterk, however, documents that *pila* is a Mon-Khmer loanword that originally meant "silver" and was used in Seediq before the Japanese arrived. This finding suggests that the Seediq were linked in pre-colonial times to trading networks that extended well beyond Formosa (Sterk 2021, 62). The fact that the word is non-Chinese suggests to me that it even predates the arrival of Han settlers on the island in the seventeenth century.

2 In the absence of updated population figures, these percentages come from Corcuff (2002, 163).

3 Kumu Tapas explains that this word is derived from *tmikan*, which means "to thresh rice." The action of threshing rice is forceful, like the hostility people have towards the Han Taiwanese. *Tmukan* thus means the enemy that must be attacked (Kumu 2004b, 53).

4 In "standard" Mandarin, people roll their tongues to pronounce the *sh*- sound. Taiwanese people find this sound difficult, and thus most people, including Indigenous people, usually make only the *s*- sound. In Taiwan, the words for "three" and "mountain" are thus homonyms, which would not be the case in most of China.

5 This arrangement resembles the Japanese colonial practice that Takun Walis calls "pacifying the savages through intermarriage" (Takun 2012, 280) in which Japanese police officers took local wives.

6 These publicly stated doubts have serious consequences at United Nations Indigenous events when state-sponsored indigeneity is perceived as a manipulative strategy to gain international space and thus easier for Chinese diplomats to suppress (Miller 2003, 193). Yet, the exclusion of Taiwan from official sessions of the UN Permanent Forum on Indigenous Issues means that grassroots NGOs cannot air legitimate grievances or seek the aid of the UN to pressure their government.

7 For anthropological interpretations of Indigenous elections in Taiwan, see Allio 1998a; Ku 2008; Simon 2010c; Yang 2005.

8 I have discussed this election in a previously published article (Simon 2010c). I place my interpretation of it here in a wider theoretical context.

9 In this case, I made the literary choice of using modified Wade-Giles for the name of Ke Shih-mei and pinyin for Zhang Zixiao, with the intention of showing the more localized identity of Ke and the identity of Zhang with Greater China.

6. *Tminun* (Weaving)

1 This vocabulary annoys some supporters of other parties, who say that the language of "our party" refers to the Chinese Nationalist Party and is thus inappropriate for a multiparty democratic country.

2 According to Japanese records, Sakuma slipped 36 metres down a cliff on the morning of 26 June 1914. He received military medical aid for four or five days before stabilizing. He returned to Taipei, finished his term as governor-general, and went back to Japan. He died while slipping in his bath at the age of seventy-two (Hara 2006, 62–3).

3 I learned about this event from reading an explanatory panel in the photo exhibit at the Gluban Survivors' Memorial Hall.

4 Unbeknownst to me until writing this book, I was not the first person from Canada to entertain this notion. On 4 October 1930, the *Globe* reported Rev. George William Mackay's observation that "the Tayal Tribe is considered the 'Iroquois' of Formosa" as the fiercest of the island's groups (Globe 1930, 13).

5 Dakis Pawan, who is from Gluban, argues that everyone in Gluban views Mona Rudo unequivocally as a hero (Kuo 2012, 259–60). After the movie *Warriors of the Rainbow*, the men loved to talk about Mona as a hero. It is perhaps important that most of the negative sentiments I heard were from women, most of whom would have married into the community from outside. But most of the people I met seemed to have nuanced views and felt a need to ponder carefully on the ethics of the rebellion.

6 In her discussion of tribal councils and throughout the book, Kumu tends to refer to chiefs as one type of "opinion leader" among others (Kumu 2004a, 56). The term "tribal council" is appropriate because it refers to an institution created by the state as a tool of colonial rule. In actual practice, the councils were infused with the traditional norms of *Gaya*, which meant that political prestige was based on one's ability. In this case, it was the ability to persuade others through oratory skills.

7 Her name is spelled Obing Tadao in standardized Truku, but I follow Kumu's pre-standardization usage here.

8 The new local name is Alang Snuwil, which means "cherry blossom" in Toda. The village is also divided into smaller alang, each of which maintains a distinctive identity.

9 Although these words refer to the same ritual, there are linguistic differences. In Nantou, Sediq Toda and Seediq Tgdaya refer to *dmahur/dmahun*. Seejiq Truku refer to *msahur*, and the Hualien Truku call it *psbalay* (Watan Diro, personal communication).

Conclusion

1 I thank Aaron Valdis Gauss, professor at the National Taitung University, for bringing Taintor to my attention.

Epilogue

1 For an English translation of Xi Jinping's speech, see Taiwan Affairs Office of the State Council (2019).

2 For an English translation of Tsai Ing-wen's speech, see Office of the President, Republic of China (Taiwan) (2019).

3 For an English translation of this statement, see Presidential Office Indigenous Historical Justice and Transitional Justice Committee (2019).

Glossary

1 Although the Truku dictionary glosses it as "community, region, country," this last meaning is obviously a recent semantic extension. I have never heard anyone use the term that way. People use the Japanese *koka* to mean country or state.

2 Darren Sterk argues that *spitay* is a loanword from the Japanese *subitai* (garrison; Sterk 2020, 155), which would make this place name a recent innovation.

References

Notes: Atayalic names do not have surnames, but rather the name of the individual followed by the name of the father (patronym). Names of Atayal, Sediq, or Truku authors are thus listed by personal name without a comma between their personal name and patronym. When authors have both a Chinese and an Indigenous name, I use the Indigenous name here, unless it does not appear on the original publication. Spellings of Chinese names (including capitalization) follow the preferences of the authors when their publications have appeared in English or when they have expressed their preferences to me. When those preferences are unknown for authors writing in Chinese, Wade–Giles pinyin is used in accordance with traditional usage in Taiwan.

Ai, Chung-chih (艾忠智, Kado Kimi). 2010. "出草是英勇的行為嗎：太魯閣族獵首習俗的再詮釋及反省" [Was headhunting courageous behaviour? Reinterpretation and reflections on Truku headhunting customs]. 全國原住民族研究論文發表會 [National Indigenous research thesis presentation forum], Chiayi, 21 October.
– 2015. "被遺忘的歷史：太魯閣戰役在地觀點" [History that has been forgotten: Local perspectives on the Truku battle]. 8th Taiwan-Japan Forum on Aboriginal Studies, Conference on History of the Truku War, Hualien, 30–31 October.
Alfred, Gerald R. (Taiaiake). 1995. *Heeding the Voices of Our Ancestors: Kahnawake Mohawk Politics and the Rise of Native Nationalism*. Toronto: Oxford University Press.
Alfred, Taiaiake. 2005. *Wasáse: Indigenous Pathways of Action and Freedom*. Toronto: Broadview Press.
Allio, Fiorella. 1998a. "Les austronésiens dans la course électorale." *Perspectives chinoises* 50 (November–December): 46–8. https://doi.org /10.3406/perch.1998.2361.

– 1998b. "La construction d'un espace politique austronésien." *Perspectives chinoises* 47 (May–June): 54–62. https://doi.org/10.3406/perch.1998.2300.

Anderson, Benedict. 1983. *Imagined Communities: Reflections on the Origin and Spread of Nationalism*. London: Verso.

Andrade, Tonio. 2008. *How Taiwan Became Chinese: Dutch, Spanish and Han Colonization in the Seventeenth Century*. New York: Columbia University Press.

Arriagada, Paula, Tara Hahmann, and Vivian O'Donnell. 2020. "Indigenous People in Urban Areas: Vulnerabilities to the Socioeconomic Impacts of COVID-19." *StatCan COVID-19: Data to Insights for a Better Canada*, Statistics Canada, catalogue no. 45-28-0001. https://www150.statcan.gc.ca/n1/pub/45-28-0001/2020001/article/00023-eng.htm.

Asch, Michael, John Borrows, and James Tully, eds. 2018. *Resurgence and Reconciliation: Indigenous-Settler Relations and Earth Teachings*. Toronto: University of Toronto Press.

Assembly of First Nations. 2018. "First Nations Post-Secondary Education Fact Sheet." https://www.afn.ca/wp-content/uploads/2018/07/PSE_Fact_Sheet_ENG.pdf.

Atran, Scott. 1990. *Cognitive Foundations of Natural History: Towards an Anthropology of Science*. Cambridge: Cambridge University Press.

– 2002. *In Gods We Trust: The Evolutionary Landscape of Religion*. Oxford: Oxford University Press.

Barclay, Harold B. 1982. *People without Government*. London: Kahn & Averill.

Barclay, Paul. 2003. "'Gaining Confidence and Friendship' in Aborigine Country: Diplomacy, Drinking, and Debauchery on Japan's Southern Frontier." *Social Science Japan Journal* 6, no. 1 (April): 77–96. https://doi.org/10.1093/ssjj/6.1.77.

– 2007. "Contending Centres of Calculation in Colonial Taiwan." *Humanities Research* 14, no. 1: 67–84. https://doi.org/10.22459/HR.XIV.01.2007.05.

–, trans. 2008. "Serial III: Kondo Katsusasboro among Taiwan's Atayal/Sedeq Peoples, 1896 to 1930." *The View from Taiwan* (blog), 23 November. https://michaelturton.blogspot.com/2008/11/serial-iii-kondo-katsusaburo-among.html.

– 2015. "Playing the Race Card in Japanese-Governed Taiwan: Or, Anthropometric Photographs as 'Shape-Shifting Jokers.'" In *The Affect of Difference: Representations of Race in East Asian Empire*, edited by Christopher Hanscom and Dennis Washburn, 38–80. Honolulu: University of Hawai'i Press.

– 2018. *Outcasts of Empire: Japan's Rule on Taiwan's "Savage Border," 1874–1945*. Berkeley: University of California Press.

Barker, John. 2014. "The One and the Many: Church-Centered Innovations in a Papua New Guinean Community." *Current Anthropology* 55, no. S10 (December): S172–81. https://doi.org/10.1086/678291.

– (2004) 2016. *Ancestral Lines: The Maisin of Papua New Guinea and the Fate of the Rainforest*. Toronto: University of Toronto Press.

Barraud, Cécile. 1972. "De la Chasse aux têtes à la pêche à la bonite. Essai sur la chefferie à Eddystone." *L'Homme* 12, no. 1 (January–March): 67–104. https://doi.org/10.3406/hom.1972.367239.

Barth, Fredrik. 1969. *Ethnic Groups and Boundaries: The Social Organization of Culture Difference*. London: Allen & Unwin.

Bateson, Gregory. 1972. *Steps to an Ecology of Mind: Collected Essays in Anthropology, Psychiatry, Evolution, and Epistemology*. Northvale, NJ: Jason Aronson.

Bellwood, Peter, James J. Fox, and Darrell Tryon, eds. 1995. *The Austronesians: Historical and Comparative Perspectives*. Canberra: Australian National University Press.

Bessire, Lucas. 2014. "The Rise of Indigenous Hypermarginality: Native Culture as a Neopolitics of Life." *Current Anthropology* 55, no. 3 (June): 276–95. https://doi.org/10.1086/676527.

Blaser, Mario. 2009a. "Political Ontology: Cultural Studies without 'Cultures'?" *Cultural Studies* 23, nos. 5–6 (September): 873–96. https://doi.org/10.1080/09502380903208023.

– 2009b. "The Threat of the Yrmo: The Political Ontology of a Sustainable Hunting Program." *American Anthropologist* 111, no. 1 (March): 10–20. https://doi.org/10.1111/j.1548-1433.2009.01073.x.

– 2012. "Ontology and Indigeneity: On the Political Ontology of Heterogeneous Assemblages." *Cultural Geographies* 21, no. 1 (January): 49–58. https://doi.org/10.1177/1474474012462534.

– 2013. "Ontological Conflicts and the Stories of People in Spite of Europe: Toward a Political Ontology." *Current Anthropology* 54, no. 5 (October): 547–68. https://doi.org/10.1086/672270.

Blaser, Mario, and Marisol de la Cadena. 2018. "Introduction. Pluriverse: Proposals for a World of Many Worlds." In *A World of Many Worlds*, edited by Marisol de la Cadena and Mario Blaser, 1–22. Durham, NC: Duke University Press.

Blaser, Mario, Harvey A. Feit, and Glenn McRae, eds. 2004. *In the Way of Development: Indigenous Peoples, Life Projects, and Globalization*. London: Zed Books.

Blench, Roger. 2014. "The Austronesians: An Agricultural Revolution That Failed." Paper presented at the 2014 International Conference on Formosan Indigenous Peoples, Contemporary Perspectives, Academia Sinica, Taipei, 15–17 September. http://www.rogerblench.info/Archaeology/Oceania/Blench%20Austronesian%20Taipei%202014%20agric%20failed.pdf.

Bonilla, Yarimar. 2017. "Unsettling Sovereignty." *Cultural Anthropology* 32, no. 3 (August): 330–9. https://doi.org/10.14506/ca32.3.02.

Boretz, Avron. 2011. *Gods, Ghosts, and Gangsters: Ritual Violence, Martial Arts, and Masculinity on the Margins of Chinese Society*. Honolulu: University of Hawai'i Press.

Borrows, John. 2010. *Drawing Out Law: A Spirit's Guide*. Toronto: University of Toronto Press.

Bosco, Joseph. 1994. "Faction versus Ideology: Mobilization Strategies in Taiwan's Elections." *China Quarterly* 137 (March): 28–62. https://doi.org/10.1017/S0305741000034032.

Boyer, Pascal. 2001. *Religion Explained: The Human Instincts That Fashion Gods, Spirits and Ancestors*. New York: Basic Books.

Branch, Jordan. 2014. *The Cartographic State: Maps, Territories and the Origins of Sovereignty*. Cambridge: Cambridge University Press.

Brass, Paul R. 1991. *Ethnicity and Nationalism: Theory and Comparison*. Newbury Park, CA: Sage Publications.

Brown, Melissa. 2004. *Is Taiwan Chinese? The Impact of Culture, Power, and Migration on Changing Identities*. Stanford, CA: Stanford University Press.

Byler, Darren T. 2021. "Anti-Colonial Friendship." *American Ethnologist* 48, no. 2 (May): 153–66. https://doi.org/10.1111/amet.13020.

‒ 2022. *Terror Capitalism: Uyghur Dispossession and Masculinity in a Chinese City*. Durham, NC: Duke University Press.

Carrithers, Michael, Matei Candea, Karen Sykes, Martin Holbraad, and Soumhya Venkatesan. 2010. "Ontology Is Just Another Word for Culture: Motion Tabled at the 2008 Meeting of the Group for Debates in Anthropological Theory, University of Manchester." *Critique of Anthropology* 30, no. 2 (June): 152–200. https://doi.org/10.1177/0308275X09364070.

Cauquelin, Josiane. 2004. *The Aborigines of Taiwan, Puyuma: From Headhunting to the Modern World*. London: Routledge.

Chandler, Michael J., and Christopher Lalonde. 1998. "Cultural Continuity as a Hedge against Suicide in Canada's First Nations." *Transcultural Psychiatry* 35, no. 2 (June): 191–219. https://doi.org/10.1177/136346159803500202.

Chang, Lung-chih. 2008. "From Quarantine to Colonization: Qing Debates on Territorialization of Aboriginal Taiwan in the Nineteenth Century." *Taiwan Historical Research* 15, no. 4 (December): 1–30. https://www.ith.sinica.edu.tw/quarterly_history_look.php?l=e&id=69.

Chen, Chao-chieh, and Fushing Hsieh. 2002. "Composition and Foraging Behaviour of Mixed-Species Flocks Led by the Grey-Cheeked Fulvetta in Fushan Experimental Forest, Taiwan." *Ibis: International Journal of Avian Science* 144, no. 2 (April): 317–30. https://doi.org/10.1046/j.1474-919X.2002.00020.x.

Ch'eng Shih-i 程士毅. 2006. 原住民族與台灣史 [Indigenous peoples and Taiwanese history]. Puli: Taiwan Taritsi Cultural Association; 埔里：台灣打里摺文化協會.

Chi, Chun-Chieh, and Hsang-Te Chin. 2012. "Knowledge, Power and Tribal Mapping: A Critical Analysis of the 'Return of the Truku People'" *GeoJournal* 77, no. 6 (December): 733–40. https://doi.org/10.1007/s10708-010-9374-6.

Chien, Amy Chang, and Amy Qin. 2021. "Taiwan Court Upholds Laws Restricting Hunting." *New York Times*, 8 May 2021, A10. https://www.nytimes.com/2021/05/07/world/asia/taiwan-hunting.html.

Chien Hung-mo 簡鴻模. 2002. "Alang Gluban (清流部落) 生命史調查研究" [Investigative research on the life histories of the Gluban community]. In Chien, Iwan, and Kuo 2002, 15–53.

Chien Hung-mo 簡鴻模, Iwan Beilin 依婉 貝林, and Kuo Ming-cheng 郭明正, eds. 2002. *Ltlutuc Knkingan Sapah Alang Gluban* 清流部落生命史 [Life histories of the Gluban community]. Puli: ROC Taiwan Indigenous Peoples Association; 埔里：中華民國台灣原住民同舟協會.

Chinese Human Rights Association 中國人權協會, ed. 1987. 臺灣土著的傳統社會文化與人權現況 [Taiwan aboriginal traditional society and culture and human rights situation]. Taipei: Dajia chubanshe; 台北：大佳出版社.

Ching, Leo T.S. 2001. *Becoming "Japanese": Colonial Taiwan and the Politics of Identity Formation*. Berkeley: University of California Press.

Chiu, Fred Yen Liang. 2000. "Suborientalism and the Subimperialist Predicament: Aboriginal Discourse and the Poverty of State-Nation Imagery." *Positions: East Asia Cultures Critique* 8, no. 1 (Spring): 101–49. https://doi.org/10.1215/10679847-8-1-101.

Ch'iu Jo-lung 邱若龍. 2004. 霧社事件：台灣第一部原住民調查報告漫畫 [The Wushe Incident: Taiwan's first graphic Indigenous investigative report]. Taipei: Yushanshe; 台北：玉山社.

Ciwang Teyra, and Hsieh (Wendy) Wan-Jung. 2023. "Carrying Historical Trauma: Alcohol Use and Healing among Indigenous Communities in Taiwan." In *Indigenous Reconciliation in Contemporary Taiwan: From Stigma to Hope*, edited by Scott E. Simon, Jolan Hsieh, and Peter Kang, 121–44. London: Routledge. https://doi.org/10.4324/9781003183136.

Clastres, Pierre. 1974. *La Société contre l'État*. Paris: Les Éditions de minuit.

Clifford, James. 1988. *The Predicament of Culture: Twentieth-Century Ethnography, Literature, and Art*. Cambridge, MA: Harvard University Press.

Clifford, James, and George E. Marcus, eds. 1986. *Writing Culture: The Poetics and Politics of Ethnography*. Berkeley: University of California Press.

Cole, Jennifer. 2006. "Malagasy and Western Conceptions of Memory: Implications for Postcolonial Politics and the Study of Memory." *Ethnos* 34, no. 2 (June): 211–43. https://doi.org/10.1525/eth.2006.34.2.211.

Corcuff, Stéphane, ed. 2002. *Memories of the Future: National Identity Issues and the Search for a New Taiwan*. Armonk, NY: M.E. Sharpe.

Coulthard, Glen Sean. 2014. *Red Skin, White Masks: Rejecting the Colonial Politics of Recognition*. Minneapolis: University of Minnesota Press.

Covell, Ralph. 1998. *Pentecost on the Hills of Taiwan: The Christian Faith among the Original Inhabitants*. Pasadena, CA: Hope Publishing House.

David, Kenith A. 1987. "An Introduction to Urban Rural Mission." *International Review of Mission* 76, no. 303 (July): 319–23. https://doi.org/10.1111/j.1758-6631.1987.tb01534.x.

Davidson, James W. 1903. *The Island of Formosa, Past and Present*. New York: MacMillan.

Dawley, Evan N. 2015. "Closing a Colony: The Meanings of Japanese Deportation from Taiwan after WWII." In *Japanese Taiwan: Colonial Rule and Its Contested Legacy*, edited by Andrew D. Morris, 115–32. London: Bloomsbury.

Deng Shian-yang 鄧相揚. 1998. 霧社事件 [Wushe Incident]. Taipei: Yushanshe; 台北：玉山社.

Descola, Philippe. 2011. *L'écologie des autres : L'anthropologie et la question de la nature*. Versailles: Éditions Quæ.

– (2005) 2013. *Beyond Nature and Culture*. Translated from the French by Janet Lloyd. Chicago: University of Chicago Press.

Désveaux, Emmanuel. 1996. "Contrôle de naissances et classes d'âge : une cas limite." *L'Homme* 36, no. 138 (April–June): 143–9. https://doi.org/10.3406/hom.1996.370081.

Dirlik, Arif. 2018. "Taiwan: The Land Colonialisms Made." *boundary 2: An International Journal of Literature and Culture* 45, no. 3 (August): 1–25. https://doi.org/10.1215/01903659-6915545.

Engels, Friedrich. (1902) 2021. *The Origin of the Family, Private Property and the State*. Chicago: C.H. Kerr. Online version by Alexander Street Press.

Escobar, Arturo. 1995. *Encountering Development: The Making and Unmaking of the Third World*. Princeton, NJ: Princeton University Press.

Feld, Steven. 1982. *Sound and Sentiment: Birds, Weeping, Poetics and Song in Kaluli Expression*. Philadelphia: University of Pennsylvania Press.

Flanagan, Thomas. 2000. *First Nations? Second Thoughts*. Montreal: McGill-Queen's University Press.

Forth, Gregory. 2004. *Nage Birds: Classification and Symbolism among an Eastern Indonesian People*. London: Routledge.

Frank, Andre Gunder. 1998. *ReOrient: Global Economy in the Asian Age*. Berkeley: University of California Press.

Fried, Morton H. 1953. *Fabric of Chinese Society: A Study of the Social Life of a Chinese County Seat*. New York: Praeger.

Friedman, Kerim. 2018. "The Hegemony of the Local: Taiwanese Multiculturalism and Indigenous Identity Politics." *boundary 2: An International Journal of Literature and Culture* 45, no. 3 (August): 79–105. https://doi.org/10.1215/01903659-6915593.

Fujii Shizue 藤井志津枝. 1997. 理蕃：日本治理台灣的計策 沒有砲火的戰爭(一) [Savage control: Japan's strategy for governing Taiwan in a war without artillery fire]. Taipei: Wenyingtang; 臺北市： 文英堂出版社.

Furuno, Kiyoto 古野清人. 1945. 高砂族の祭儀生活 [The ritual life of Takasagozoku]. Tōkyō: Sanseidō; 東京：三省堂.

– 1971. 原始宗教の構造と機能 [The construction and function of primitive religion]. Yokohama: Yūrindō Shuppan; 横浜：有隣堂出版.

Gehl, Lynn. 2014. *The Truth that Wampum Tells: My Debwewin on the Algonquin Lands Process*. Halifax: Fernwood.

– 2017. *Claiming Anishinaabe: Decolonizing the Human Spirit*. Regina: University of Regina Press.

George, Kenneth M. 1993. "Lyric, History and Allegory, or the End of Headhunting Ritual in Upland Sulawesi." *American Ethnologist* 20, no. 4 (November): 696–716. https://doi.org/10.1525/ae.1993.20.4.02a00020.

– 1995. "Violence, Solace and Ritual: A Case Study of Island Southeast Asia." *Culture, Medicine and Psychiatry* 19, no. 2 (June): 225–60. https://doi .org/10.1007/BF01379413.

– 1996. *Showing Signs of Violence: The Cultural Politics of a Twentieth-Century Headhunting Ritual*. Berkeley: University of California Press.

Globe, The. 1930. "Formosa Tribes Busy Chopping Off Heads If Their Crops Fail." *The Globe* [1844–1936], 4 October, 13. https://www.proquest.com /historical-newspapers/formosa-tribes-busy-chopping-off-heads-if-their /docview/1354223565/se-2?accountid=14701.

Government of Canada. 2019a. "Canada Reaches Lowest Poverty Rate in History." https://www.canada.ca/en/employment-social-development /news/2019/03/canada-reaches-lowest-poverty-rate-in-history.html.

– 2019b. *A Legal Analysis of Genocide: Supplementary Report of the National Inquiry into Missing and Murdered Indigenous Women and Girls*. https://www .mmiwg-ffada.ca/wp-content/uploads/2019/06/Supplementary-Report _Genocide.pdf.

Graeber, David. 2004. *Fragments of an Anarchist Anthropology*. Chicago: Prickly Paradigm Press.

Halbwachs, Maurice (1950) 1980. *The Collective Memory*. Translated by Francis Ditter and Vida Yazdi Ditter. New York: Harper & Row.

Hara, Eiko 原英子. 2003. "タイヤル・セデック・タロコをめぐる帰属と名称 に関する運動の展開 (1) : タロコにおける動向を中心に" [The development of the identity movement of the Atayal, Seediq and Truku: Centred around Truku tendencies (1)]. 台湾原住民研究 [*Taiwan Indigenous Research*], no. 7, 209–27.

– 2004. "タイヤル・セデック・タロコをめぐる帰属と名称に関する運動の展 開 (2): 南投県セデックの動向を中心に" [The development of the identity movement of the Atayal, Seediq and Truku: Centred around tendencies of the Nantou Seediq (2)]. 台湾原住民研究 [*Taiwan Indigenous Research*], no. 8, 94–104.

– 2006. "佐久間左馬太台湾総督に関するタロコ族の記憶と「歴史」の構築" [Truku memory and construction of "history" relating to Taiwan Governor-General Sakuma Samata]. 台湾原住民研究 [*Taiwan Indigenous Research*], no. 10, 60–71.

Harrison, Henrietta. 2001. "Changing Nationalities, Changing Ethnicities: Taiwan Indigenous Villages in the Years After 1946." In *In Search of the Hunters and Their Tribes: Studies in the History and Culture of the Taiwan Indigenous People*, edited by David Faure, 50–78. Taipei: Shung Ye Museum of Formosan Aborigines.

Hatfield, D.J.W. 2020. "Good Dances Make Good Guests: Dance, Animation and Sovereign Assertion in 'Amis Country, Taiwan." *Anthropologica* 62, no. 2: 337–52. https://doi.org/10.3138/anth-2019-0030.

Hauptman, Laurence M., and Ronald G. Knapp. 1977. "Dutch-Aboriginal Interaction in New Netherland and Formosa: An Historical Geography of Empire." *Proceedings of the American Philosophical Society* 121, no. 2 (April): 166–82. https://www.jstor.org/stable/986525.

Henderson, James (Sa'ke'j) Youngblood. 2008. *Indigenous Diplomacy and the Rights of Peoples: Achieving UN Recognition*. Saskatoon: Purich.

Hong, Keelung, and Stephen O. Murray. 2005. *Looking through Taiwan: American Anthropologists' Collusion with Ethnic Domination*. Lincoln: University of Nebraska Press.

Hoskins, Janet. 1996. "Introduction: Headhunting as Practice and as Trope." In *Headhunting and the Social Imagination in Southeast Asia*, edited by Janet Hoskins, 1–49. Stanford, CA: Stanford University Press.

– 2002. "Predatory Voyeurs: Tourists and 'Tribal Violence' in Remote Indonesia." *American Ethnologist* 29, no. 4 (November): 797–828. https://doi.org/10.1525/ae.2002.29.4.797.

Hsieh, Jolan. 2006. *Collective Rights of Indigenous Peoples: Identity-Based Movement of Plain Indigenous in Taiwan*. New York: Routledge.

Hsieh Shih-Chung 謝世忠. 1992. "偏離群眾的菁英：試論『原住民』象徵與原住民菁英現象的關係" [Elites alienated from the masses: A preliminary discussion of the relationship between "aboriginal" symbolism and the phenomenon of aboriginal elites]. 島嶼邊緣 [*Island Margins*] 2, no. 1: 52–60. http://ntur.lib.ntu.edu.tw/handle/246246/97615.

Huang, Chang-hsing (黃長興, Lowsi Rakaw). 2000. "東賽德克群的狩獵文化" [Hunting culture in eastern Seediq groups]. 民族學研究所資料彙編 [*Field Materials of the Institute of Ethnology*], no. 15, 1–104.

Huang, Lanyin, and Shiang-Fan Chen. 2020. "What Makes Tree Poachers Give Up? A Case Study of Forestry Law Enforcement in Taiwan." *Environmental Conservation* 47, no. 1 (March): 67–73. https://doi.org/10.1017/S0376892919000377.

Huang Ying-Kuei 黃應貴. 1986. "台灣土著族的兩種社會類型及其意義" [Taiwan aborigines' two social types and their meanings]. In 台灣土著社會文化研究論文集 [Anthology of research on Taiwanese aboriginal society and culture], edited by Ying-Kuei Huang, 3–43. Taipei: Lianjing; 台北市：聯經.

Hung, Hsiao-Chun, Yoshiyuki Iizuka, Peter Bellwood, Kim Dung Nguyen, Bérénice Bellina, Praon Siliapanth, Eusebio Dizon, Rey Santiago, Ipoi Datan, and Jonathan H. Manton. 2007. "Ancient Jades Map 3,000 Years of Prehistoric Exchange in Southeast Asia." *Proceedings of the National Academy of Sciences of the United States of America* 104, no. 50 (11 December): 19745–50. https://doi.org/10.1073/pnas.0707304104.

Igung Shiban (田春綢, T'ien Ch'un-Ch'ou). 1997. "Report to the United Nations Working Group on Indigenous Populations: Our Experience of the Incursion of Cement Companies onto the Land of the Taroko People, Hwalien, Taiwan." http://www.nativeweb.org//pages/legal/taroko.html.

Ingold, Tim. 1988. "The Animal in the Study of Humanity." In *What Is an Animal?*, edited by Tim Ingold, 84–99. London: Unwin Hyman.

– 2000. *Perceptions of the Environment*. London: Routledge.

– 2011. *Being Alive: Essays on Movement, Knowledge and Description*. London: Routledge.

– 2013. "Dreaming of Dragons: On the Imagination of Real Life." *Journal of the Royal Anthropological Institute* 19, no. 4 (December): 734–52. https://doi.org/10.1111/1467-9655.12062.

– (1986) 2016. *Evolution and Social Life*. London: Routledge.

Isak Afo 以撒克・阿復. 2016. 原住民族運動・媒體・記憶：後殖民進路 [The Indigenous Peoples' Movement, media, memory: Post-colonial routes]. Taipei: Hanlu; 台北：翰蘆圖書.

Ishii, Shinji. 1916. *The Island of Formosa and Its Primitive Inhabitants*. London: Japan Society.

Jackson, Michael. 2013. *Lifeworlds: Essays in Existential Anthropology*. Chicago: University of Chicago Press.

Kaji Cihung 旮日羿・吉宏. 2011. 太魯閣族部落史與祭儀樂舞傳記 [Truku tribal history and memoir of ritual music and dance]. Taipei: Shan-hai; 台北：山海文化雜誌社.

Kano, Tadao 鹿野・忠雄. 1934. "台湾蕃人の鳥占" [Ornithomancy of the savages of Taiwan]. 野鳥 [*Wild Birds*] 1, no. 6: 615–18.

Kim Kwang-ok. 1980. *The Taruko and Their Belief System*. PhD diss., Institute of Social Anthropology, University of Oxford.

Kojima, Reiitsu 小島麗逸. 2002. "日本帝國主義的台灣山地支配：到霧社蜂起事件為止" [The domination of Taiwan's mountainous areas by Japanese imperialism: Until the Musha Uprising Incident]. In 台灣霧社蜂起事件：研究與資料（上）[The Musha Uprising Incident: Research and materials, vol.

1], edited by Dai Kuo-hui 戴國煇, 62–113. Translated from the Japanese by Wei Ting-chao 魏廷朝. Taipei: Academia Historica; 台北 : 國史館.

Kojima, Yoshimichi 小島由道. (1915) 1996. 番族慣習調查報告書 [第一卷] 泰雅族 [Investigative report on the customs of savage tribes, vol. 1: Atayal]. Translated from the Japanese by the Institute of Ethnology, Academia Sinica. Taipei: Academia Sinica Institute of Ethnology; 台北 : 中央研究院民族所.

Krämer, Augustin. 1926. *Palau, Teilband 3: Stoffliche und geistige Kultur* [Palau, vol. 3: Material culture and intellectual culture]. Hamburg: Friederichsen.

Ku, Kun-hui. 2005. "Rights to Recognition: Minority/Indigenous Politics in the Emerging Taiwanese Nationalism." *Social Analysis* 49, no. 3 (June): 99–121. https://doi.org/10.3167/015597705780886248.

– 2008. "Ethnographic Studies of Voting among the Austronesian Paiwan: The Role of Paiwan Chiefs in the Contemporary State System of Taiwan." *Pacific Affairs* 81, no. 3 (Fall): 383–406. https://doi.org/10.5509/2008813383.

Kuan, Da-wei (Daya Dakasi). 2021. "Indigenous Traditional Territory and Decolonisation of the Settler State: The Taiwan Experience." In *Taiwan's Contemporary Indigenous Peoples*, edited by Chia-yuan Huang, Daniel Davies, and Dafydd Fell, 184–205. London: Routledge.

Kulun Cikal (田貴芳, T'ien Kuei fang). 2010. 太魯閣人耆老百年回憶 ; 都達，德固達雅，德路固，賽德克巴萊女性篇 [A century of Taroko elders' memory: Teuda, Tkedaya, Truku, Seediq Balae women's edition]. Hsiulin: Turuwan Cultural Association; 花蓮秀林鄉 : 都魯彎文教協會.

– 2014. 太魯閣人耆老百年回憶 : 男性篇 [A century of Taroko elders' memory: Men's edition]. Taipei: Hanlu; 台北 : 翰蘆圖書出版社.

Kumar, Mohan B., and Michael Tjepkema. 2019. "Suicide among First Nations People, Métis and Inuit (2011–2016): Findings from the 2011 Canadian Census Health and Environment Cohort (CanCHEC)." *National Household Survey: Aboriginal Peoples*, Statistics Canada, catalogue no. 99-011-X. https://www150.statcan.gc.ca/n1/pub/99-011-x/99-011-x2019001-eng.htm.

Kumu Tapas. 2004a. 霧社事件的口述歷史 (I) [Oral history of the Wushe Incident (I)]. Taipei: Hanlu; 台北 : 翰蘆圖書出版社.

– 2004b. 霧社事件的口述歷史 (II) [Oral history of the Wushe Incident (II)]. Taipei: Hanlu; 台北 : 翰蘆圖書出版社.

Kuo Ming-cheng (郭明正, Dakis Pawan). 2011. 賽德克巴萊 : 真相巴萊 [Real people: Real truth]. Taipei: Yuan-Liou; 台北 : 遠流.

– 2012. 又見真相 : 賽德克族與霧社事件 [Seeing the truth again: The Seediq and the Musha Incident]. Taipei: Yuan-Liou; 台北 : 遠流.

Kuper, Adam. 2003. "The Return of the Native." *Current Anthropology* 44, no. 3 (June): 389–402. https://doi.org/10.1086/368120.

Lambek, Michael. 2010. "Toward an Ethics of the Act." In *Ordinary Ethics: Anthropology, Language, and Action*, edited by Michael Lambek, 39–63. New York: Fordham University Press.

Laplante, Julie, and Marcus Sacrini. 2016. "Présentation : Poétique vivante." In "Phénoménologies en anthropologie/Phenomenologies in Anthropology," ed. Julie Laplante and Marcus Sacrini, special issue, *Anthropologie et Sociétés* 40, no. 3 (January): 9–35. https://doi.org/10.7202/1038632ar.

Lee, Amy Pei-jung. 2015. "Body Part Nomenclature and Categorisation in Seediq." In *New Advances in Formosan Linguistics*, edited by Elizabeth Zeitoun, Stacy Fang-Ching Teng, and Joy J. Wu, 451–83. Canberra, Australia: Asia-Pacific Linguistics.

Lefebvre, Henri. (1974) 1991. *The Production of Space*. Translated by Donald Nicholson-Smith. Oxford: Blackwell.

Lefort, Claude. 1978. "Marx: From One Version of History to Another." *Social Research* 45, no. 4 (Winter): 615–66.

Le Roux, Pierre, and Bernard Sellato. 2006. *Les messagers divins : Aspects esthétiques et symboliques des oiseaux en Asie du Sud-Est*. Paris: Éditions connaissances et savoirs.

Lévi-Strauss, Claude. 1966. *The Savage Mind*. Translated by George Weidenfield and Nicholson, Ltd. Chicago: University of Chicago Press.

Li, Tania Murray. 2000. "Articulating Indigenous Identity in Indonesia: Resource Politics and the Tribal Slot." *Comparative Studies in Society and History* 42, no. 1 (January): 149–79. https://doi.org/10.1017/S0010417 500002632.

– 2014. *Land's End: Capitalist Relations on an Indigenous Frontier*. Durham, NC: Duke University Press.

Lim, Siu-theh 林修澈. 2018. 台灣原住民族部落事典 [Encyclopedia of (Taiwan) Indigenous communities]. Taipei: Council of Indigenous Peoples; 台北：原住民族委員會.

Lin, Chiang-i 林江義. 1996. "談東賽德克群的族群意識" [Discussion of ethnic consciousness of the eastern Seediq group]." In 原住民現代社會適應（二）[The adaption of aborigines to contemporary society, vol. 2], edited by Tsai Chung-han 蔡中涵, 779–93. Taipei: Jiaoyu Guangbodiantai; 臺北市：教育廣播電台.

Lin, Ching-Hsiu. 2011. "The Circulation of Labour and Money: Symbolic Meanings of Monetary Kinship Practices in Contemporary Truku Society, Taiwan." *New Proposals: Journal of Marxism and Interdisciplinary Inquiry* 5, no. 1 (November): 27–44.

Lin, Pei-Hsi. 2016. *Firearms, Technology and Culture: Resistance of Taiwanese Indigenes to Chinese, European and Japanese Encroachment in a Global Context, circa 1860–1914*. PhD diss., Nottingham Trent University.

Linck-Kesting, Gudula. 1978. "Ein Kapitel japanischer Kolonialgeschichte: Die Politik gegenüber der nichtchinesischen Bevölkerung von Taiwan [A chapter of Japanese colonial history: The policy towards the non-

Chinese population of Taiwan]." *Nachrichten der Gesellschaft für Natur- und Völkerkunde Ostasiens/Hamburg* [*News from the Society for Natural History and Ethnology in East Asia/Hamburg*] 123: 61–81.

– 1979. *Ein Kapitel chinesischer Grenzgeschichte: Han und Nicht-Han im Taiwan der Qing-Zeit 1683–1895* [A chapter of Chinese frontier history: Han and non-Han in Qing dynasty Taiwan 1683–1895]. Wiesbaden: Franz Steiner Verlag.

Liu, Gin-Rong 劉振榮, Tang-Huang Lin 林唐煌, and Tsung-Hua Kuo 郭宗華. 2002. "應用NOAA AVHRR植被指數分類資科估算台灣地區森林面積之研究" [Estimation of Taiwan's Forested Areas by Classified NDVI Maps from NOAA AVHRR Data]. 航測及遙測學刊 [*Journal of Photogrammetry and Remote Sensing*] 7, no. 4 (December): 69–76.

Liu, Pi-Chen. 2009. "Animal Head Collecting among the Kavalan of Taiwan: Gender, Masculinity, Male-Female Power and Christian Conversion." In *Religious and Ritual Change: Cosmologies and Histories*, edited by Pamela J. Stewart and Andrew Strathern, 191–213. Durham, NC: Carolina Academic Press.

Liu, Wen. 2021. "From Independence to Interdependence: Taiwan Independence as Critique, Strategy, and Method toward Decoloniality." *American Quarterly* 73, no. 2 (June): 371–7. https://doi.org/10.1353/aq.2021.0018.

Mabuchi, Tōichi. 1974. *Ethnology of the Southwestern Pacific: The Ryukyus-Taiwan-Insular Southeast Asia*. Taipei: Chinese Association for Folklore.

Mackay, George Leslie. (1895) 2005. *From Far Formosa*. Boston: Elibron Classics.

Maier, Charles S. 2016. *Once within Borders: Territories of Power, Wealth, and Belonging since 1500*. Cambridge, MA: Belknap Press of Harvard University Press.

Martin, Jeffrey T. 2019. *Sentiment, Reason, and Law: Policing in the Republic of China on Taiwan*. Ithaca, NY: Cornell University Press.

Marx, Karl. (1852) 2010. *The Eighteenth Brumaire of Louis Bonaparte*. https://www.marxists.org/archive/marx/works/download/pdf/18th-Brumaire.pdf.

Masaw Mowna 廖守臣. 1977. "泰雅族東賽德克群的部落遷徙與分佈 (上)" [The migration and distribution of the eastern Seediq bands of Atayal (part 1)]. 中央研究院民族研究所集刊 [*Journal of the Institute of Ethnology, Academia Sinica*] 44: 61–206.

– 1978. "泰雅族東賽德克群的部落遷徙與分佈 (下)" [The migration and distribution of the eastern Seediq bands of Atayal (part 2)]. 中央研究院民族研究所集刊 [*Journal of the Institute of Ethnology, Academia Sinica*] 45: 81–212.

– 1998. 泰雅族的社會組織 [Atayal social organization]. Hualien: Tzu Chi University Research Center on Aboriginal Health; 花蓮：慈濟醫學院暨人文社會學院原住民健康研究室.

McDermott, Larry, and Peigi Wilson. 2010. "'Ginawaydaganuk': Algonquin Law on Access and Benefit Sharing." *Policy Matters* 17: 205–14.

McKinley, Robert. 1979. "Human and Proud of It! A Structural Treatment of Headhunting Rites and the Social Definition of Enemies." In *Studies in Borneo Societies: Social Process and Anthropological Explanation*, edited by George. N. Appell, 92–126. DeKalb: Northern Illinois University Center for Southeast Asian Studies.

McNaught, Douglas. 2021. "The State of the Nation: Contemporary Issues in Indigenous Language Education in Taiwan." In *Taiwan's Contemporary Indigenous Peoples*, edited by Chia-yuan Huang, Daniel Davies, and Dafydd Fell, 128–46. London: Routledge.

Miller, Bruce. 2003. *Invisible Indigenes: The Politics of Nonrecognition*. Lincoln: University of Nebraska Press.

Montgomery, Janet B. (1922) 1997. *Among the Head-Hunters of Formosa*. Taipei: SMC.

Murray, Stephen O., and Keelung Hong. 1994. *Taiwanese Culture, Taiwanese Society: A Critical Review of Social Science Research Done on Taiwan*. Lanham, MD: University Press of America.

Nadasdy, Paul. 2003. *Hunters and Bureaucrats: Power, Knowledge and Aboriginal-State Relations in the Southwest Yukon*. Vancouver: University of British Columbia Press.

Nakakawa, Kōichi 中川浩一, and Wakamori Tamio 和歌森民男. 1997. 霧社事件：台灣原住民的蜂擁群起 [The Musha Incident: A Taiwan indigenous swarming]. Taipei: Wuling; 台北：武陵出版有限公司.

Namoh Nofu Pacidal and Tzu-Tung Lee. 2016. "Founding a New State: Theory of Taiwan's Indigenous Independence." Conference presentation, North American Association of Taiwan Studies, University of Toronto, 10–11 June.

Narangoa, Li. 2002. "The Power of Imagination: Whose Northeast and Whose Manchuria?" *Inner Asia* 4, no. 1 (January): 3–25. https://doi.org/10.1163/146481702793647524.

Needham, Rodney. 1976. "Skulls and Causality." *Man* 11, no. 1 (March): 71–88. https://doi.org/10.2307/2800389.

Niezen, Ronald. 2003. *The Origins of Indigenism: Human Rights and the Politics of Identity*. Berkeley: University of California Press.

Office of the President, Republic of China (Taiwan). 2019. "President Tsai Ing-wen Issues Statement on China's President Xi's 'Message to Compatriots in Taiwan.'" 2 January. https://english.president.gov.tw/News/5621.

Ortega-Williams, Anna, Ramona Beltrán, Katie Schultz, Zuleka Ru-Glo Henderson, Lisa Colón, and Ciwang Teyra. 2021. "An Integrated Historical Trauma and Posttraumatic Growth Framework: A Cross-Cultural Exploration." *Journal of Trauma & Dissociation* 22, no. 2 (March): 220–40. https://doi.org/10.1080/15299732.2020.1869106.

Pao, Cheng-hao, and Daniel Davies. 2021. "Indigenous Political Participation and Indigenous Voting Behaviour in Taiwan." In *Taiwan's Contemporary Indigenous Peoples*, edited by Chia-yuan Huang, Daniel Davies, and Dafydd Fell, 165–83. London: Routledge.

Pecoraro, Ferdinando. 1977. *Essai de dictionnaire taroko-français*. Paris: EHESS.

Polanyi, Karl. 1967. *The Great Transformation*. Boston: Beacon Press.

Povinelli, Elizabeth A. 2002. *The Cunning of Recognition: Indigenous Alterities and the Making of Australian Multiculturalism*. Durham, NC: Duke University Press.

Presbyterian Church in Taiwan. 1971. "Statement on Our National Fate by the Presbyterian Church in Taiwan." 29 December. http://english.pct.org .tw/Article/enArticle_public_19711229.html.

Presidential Office Indigenous Historical Justice and Transitional Justice Committee. 2019. "Joint Declaration by the Representatives of the Indigenous Peoples of Taiwan Serving on the Indigenous Historical Justice and Transitional Justice Committee." https://www.straight.com/news/1189736/indigenous -peoples-taiwan-tell-xi-jinping-theyve-never-given-their-rightful-claim.

Pusin Tali 布興 · 大立. 2008. 自治是原住民族的唯一活路 [Self-government is the only living road for Indigenous peoples]. Taipei: Avangard: 台北 · 前衛

Quinlan, Marsha. 2005. "Considerations for Collecting Freelists in the Field: Examples from Ethnobotany." *Field Methods* 17, no. 3 (August): 219–34. https://doi.org/10.1177/1525822X05277460.

Rankin, Dominique, and Marie-Josée Tardif. 2020. *They Called Us Savages: A Hereditary Chief's Quest for Truth and Harmony*. Translated by Ben Vrignon. Winnipeg: Vidacom.

Rawski, Evelyn S. 1996. "Presidential Address: Reenvisioning the Qing: The Significance of the Qing Period in Chinese History." *The Journal of Asian Studies* 55, no. 4 (November): 829–50. https://doi.org/10.2307/2646525.

Red Nation. 2021. *The Red Deal: Indigenous Action to Save our Earth*. Brooklyn, NY: Common Notions.

Renan, Ernest. (1882) 1990. "What Is a Nation?" Translated from the French by Martin Thom. In *Nation and Narration*, edited by Homi K. Bhabha, 8–22. London: Routledge.

Rimuy, Aki, ed. 2002. 泰雅族 : 彩虹橋的審判 [The rainbow's judgment: Stories of the Atayal tribe]. With translation from the Chinese by Robin J. Winkler. Taipei: Xin Ziran Zhuyi; 台北 : 新自然主義.

Robbins, Joel. 2004. *Becoming Sinners: Christianity and Moral Torment in a Papua New Guinea Society*. Berkeley: University of California Press.

– 2007. "Continuity Thinking and the Problem of Christian Culture: Belief, Time, and the Anthropology of Christianity." *Current Anthropology* 48, no. 1 (February): 5–38. https://doi.org/10.1086/508690.

Robinson, Cedric J. 2020. *Black Marxism: The Making of the Black Radical Tradition*. 3rd ed. Chapel Hill: University of North Carolina Press.

ROC Council of Indigenous Peoples. 2018a. 106年臺灣原住民族經濟狀況調查 [Economic status survey of Indigenous peoples in Taiwan, 2017]. Taipei: Council of Indigenous Peoples; 台北：原住民族委員會. https://www.cip .gov.tw/zh-tw/news/data-list/C5FBC20BD6C8A9B0/2D9680BFECBE80B 62DD2D2C369C62389-info.html.

– 2018b. 106年度(全年度)原住民就業狀況調查 [Employment status survey of Indigenous peoples, 2017]. Taipei: Council of Indigenous Peoples; 台北： 原住民族委員會. https://www.cip.gov.tw/zh-tw/news/data-list/19F6DD2 5969C101D/2D9680BFECBE80B6A30714374B568F55-info.html.

– 2020. 106年原住民族人口及健康統計年報 [2017 annual report of Indigenous population and health statistics]. Taipei: Council of Indigenous Peoples; 台北：原住民族委員會. https://www.cip.gov.tw/zh-tw/news/data-list/21 7054CAE51A3B1A/2D9680BFECBE80B667E828F57323D819-info.html.

– 2021. 109年原住民 就業狀況調查 [Employment status survey of Indigenous peoples, 2020]. Taipei: Council of Indigenous Peoples; 台北：原住民族委員會. https://www.cip.gov.tw/zh-tw/news/data-list/19F6DD25969C101D/2276 C0E026A83137A4B571F18AE92066-info.html.

– 2022. "原住民人口數統計資料 (每月一次)" [Indigenous population statistics (monthly)]. Accessed 22 January 2023. https://www.cip.gov.tw/zh-tw /news/data-list/812FFAB0BCD92D1A/7F0D9BFE4F791D9CAE9B30328A 2228A5-info.html.

ROC Ministry of Education. 2010. "106年全國語文競賽原住民族語朗讀 【太魯閣語】 高中學生組 編號1號 Sta Duku kuyuh saw sklwiun Truku" [2010 National Language Competition Indigenous Language Reading (Taroko Language), High School Student Group No. 1]. https://alr.alcd .center/article/view/1385?col=2&year=106&no=1.

ROC Ministry of Justice. 2015. "Protection Act for the Traditional Intellectual Creations of Indigenous Peoples." https://law.moj.gov.tw/ENG /LawClass/LawAll.aspx?pcode=D0130021.

– (2005) 2018. "The Indigenous Peoples Basic Law." https://law.moj.gov.tw /ENG/LawClass/LawAll.aspx?pcode=D0130003.

– 2022. "Laws and Regulations Database of the Republic of China (Taiwan)." https://law.moj.gov.tw/ENG/.

Rosaldo, Renato. 1987. "Anthropological Commentary." In *Violent Origins: Ritual Killing and Cultural Formation*, edited by Robert G. Hamerton-Kelly, 239–44. Stanford, CA: Stanford University Press.

Roy, Toulouse-Antonin. 2022. "War in the Camphor Zone: Indigenous Resistance to Colonial Capitalism in Upland Taiwan, 1895–1915." *Japan Forum* 34, no. 3 (May): 333–54. https://doi.org/10.1080/09555803.2020.1794931.

Rudolph, Michael. 1993. *Die Prostitution der Frauen des taiwanesischen Bergminderheiten: Historische, sozio-kulturelle und kultur-psychologische Hintergründe* [The prostitution problem of Taiwan's mountain minorities: Historical, socio-cultural and psycho-cultural factors]. Hamburg: LIT Verlag.

– 2003. *Taiwans multi-ethnische Gesellschaft und die Bewegung der Ureinwohner: Assimilation oder kulturelle Revitalisierung?* [Taiwan's multi-ethnic society and the movement of aborigines: Assimilation or cultural revitalisation?]. Hamburg: LIT Verlag.

– 2004. "The Pan-Ethnic Movement of Taiwanese Aborigines and the Role of Elites in the Process of Ethnicity Formation." In *The Politics of Multiple Belonging: Ethnicity and Nationalism in Europe and East Asia*, edited by Flemming Christiansen and Ulf Hedetoft, 239–54. Burlington, VT: Ashgate.

– 2006. "Nativism, Ethnic Revival, and the Reappearance of Indigenous Religions in the ROC: The Use of the Internet in the Construction of Taiwanese Identities." In "Rituals on the Internet," ed. Kerstin Radde-Antweiler, special issue, *Online – Heidelberg Journal of Religions on the Internet* 2, no. 1 (November): 41–53. https://doi.org/10.11588 /heidok.00006056

– 2008. *Ritual Performances as Authenticating Practices: Cultural Representations of Taiwan's Aborigines in Times of Political Change*. Hamburg: LIT Verlag.

Said, Edward W. 1979. *Orientalism*. New York: Vintage Books.

Sayama, Yūkichi 佐山融吉, ed. (1917) 2011. 台灣總督府臨時台灣舊慣調查會：蕃族調查報告書, 第四冊：賽德克族與太魯閣族 [Taiwan Governor-General Office Provisional Taiwan Committee on the Investigation of Taiwan Old Customs: Investigative report on savage tribes, vol. 4, Sediq and Truku]. Taipei: Academia Sinica: Institute of Ethnology; 台北：中央研究院民族學研究所.

Schröder, Dominik, and Anton Quack. 1979. *Kopfjagdriten der Puyuma von Katipol (Taiwan): eine Textdokumentation* [Headhunting rites of the Puyuma of Katipol (Taiwan): A text documentation]. St. Augustin: Anthropos-Institut.

Scott, James C. 1998. *Seeing Like a State: How Certain Schemes to Improve the Human Condition Have Failed*. New Haven, CT: Yale University Press.

– 2009. *The Art of Not Being Governed: An Anarchist History of Upland Southeast Asia*. New Haven, CT: Yale University Press.

Shah, Alpa. 2010. *In the Shadows of the State: Indigenous Politics, Environmentalism, and Insurgency in Jharkhand, India*. Durham, NC: Duke University Press.

Shen Chün-hsiang 沈俊祥. 2008. 空間與認同：太魯閣人認同建構的歷程 [Space and identity: The historical process of the construction of Truku identity]. Hualien: Dong Hwa University College of Indigenous Studies; 花蓮：東華大學原住民民族學院.

Shen Ming-ren (沈明仁, Pawan Tanah). 1998. 崇信祖靈的民族賽德克人 [A people who believe in ancestral spirits: Sediq people]. Taipei: Haiweng; 台北：海翁.

Shepherd, John. 1993. *Statecraft and Political Economy on the Taiwan Frontier, 1600–1800*. Stanford, CA: Stanford University Press.

– 1995. *Marriage and Mandatory Abortion among the 17th-Century Siraya*. Arlington, VA: American Anthropological Association.

Shih, Fang-long. 2007. "The 'Red Tide' Anti-Corruption Protest: What Does It Mean for Democracy in Taiwan?" *Taiwan in Comparative Perspective* 1 (November): 87–98.

Shimizu, Akitoshi. 1999. "Colonialism and the Development of Modern Anthropology in Japan." In *Anthropology and Colonialism in Asia: Comparative and Historical Colonialism*, edited by Jan van Bremen and Akitoshi Shimizu, 115–71. Richmond, Surrey, UK: Curzon Press.

Sillitoe, Paul. 2002. "Contested Knowledge, Contingent Classification: Animals in the Highlands of Papua New Guinea." *American Anthropologist* 104, no. 4 (December): 1162–71. https://doi.org/10.1525/aa.2002.104.4.1162.

Simon, Scott E. 2002. "The Underside of a Miracle: Industrialization, Land, and Taiwan's Indigenous Peoples." *Cultural Survival Quarterly* 26, no. 2 (10 May): 64–7. https://www.culturalsurvival.org/publications/cultural -survival-quarterly/underside-miracle-industrialization-land-and-taiwans.

– 2003a. "Contesting Formosa: Tragic Remembrance, Urban Space, and National Identity in Taipei." *Identities: Global Studies in Culture and Power* 10, no. 1 (January): 109–31. https://doi.org/10.1080/10702890304338.

– 2003b. *Sweet and Sour: Life-Worlds of Taipei Women Entrepreneurs*. Lanham, MD: Rowman & Littlefield.

– 2004. "Grassroots Education, Identity and Empowerment: The Urban-Rural Mission in Indigenous Taiwan." In *Issues in Aboriginal/Minority Education: Canada, China, Taiwan*, edited by Robert Wesley Heber, 122–41. Regina: Indigenous Studies Research Centre, First Nations University of Canada.

– 2005. *Tanners of Taiwan: Life Strategies and National Culture*. Boulder, CO: Westview Press.

– 2008. "正名賽德克族：國際的觀點" [International perspectives on the name rectification of the Sediq nation]." In 賽德克正名運動 [Seediq name rectification movement], edited by 郭明正 (Dakis Pawan), 141–52. Hualien: Dong Hwa University College of Indigenous Studies; 花蓮：東華大學原住民民族學院.

– 2009. "Writing Indigeneity in Taiwan." In *Re-writing Culture in Taiwan*, edited by Fang-long Shih, Stuart Thompson, and Paul-François Tremlett, 50–68. London: Routledge.

– 2010a. "« Femme économique » ? Circulation et rapports sociaux de sexe dans les communautés seediq et taroko de Taiwan" ["Economic Woman"? Circulation and gender in Seediq and Taroko communities of Taiwan]. *Anthropologie et Sociétés* 34, no. 2 (February): 103–22. https://doi.org/10.7202/045708ar.

- 2010b. "The Hunter's Spirit: Autonomy and Development in Indigenous Taiwan." In *Regional Minorities and Development in Asia*, edited by Huhua Cao and Elizabeth Morell, 59–76. London: Routledge.
- 2010c. "Negotiating Power: Elections and the Constitution of Indigenous Taiwan." *American Ethnologist* 37, no. 4 (November): 726–40. https://doi.org/10.1111/j.1548-1425.2010.01281.x.
- 2012a. "Politics and Headhunting among the Formosan Sejiq: Ethnohistorical Perpectives." *Oceania* 82, no. 2 (July): 164–85. https://doi.org/10.1002/j.1834-4461.2012.tb00127.x.
- 2012b. *Sadyaq Balae ! L'autochtonie formosane dans tous ses états*. Quebec: Presses de l'Université Laval.
- 2013. "Of Boars and Men: Indigenous Knowledge and Co-Management in Taiwan." *Human Organization* 72, no. 3 (Fall): 220–9. https://doi.org/10.17730/humo.72.3.xq24071269xl21j6.
- 2015a. "Émissaires des ancêtres : Les oiseaux dans la vie et dans la cosmologie des Truku de Taïwan" [Emissaries of the ancestors: Birds in the life and cosmology of the Truku of Taiwan]. *Anthropologie et Sociétés* 39, nos. 1–2 (May): 179–99. https://doi.org/10.7202/1030845ar.
- 2015b. "Hunting as an Indigenous Right on Taiwan: A Call to Action." *Savage Minds: Notes and Queries in Anthropology* (blog), 14 December. https://savageminds.org/2015/12/14/hunting-as-an-indigenous-right-on-taiwan-a-call-to-action.
- 2015c. "Real People, Real Dogs, and Pigs for the Ancestors: The Moral Universe of 'Domestication' in Indigenous Taiwan." *American Anthropologist* 117, no. 4 (December): 693–709. https://doi.org/10.1111/aman.12350.
- 2016. "From the Village to the United Nations and Back Again: Aboriginal Taiwan and International Indigenism." *Taiwan Journal of Indigenous Studies* 9, no. 3 (Fall): 49–89.
- 2018. "Penser avec des oiseaux : L'ornithomancie et l'autochtonie à Taïwan" [Thinking with birds: Ornithomancy and indigeneity in Taiwan]. *Anthropologie et Sociétés* 42, nos. 2–3 (October): 151–69. https://doi.org/10.7202/1052641ar.
- 2020a. "A Little Bird Told Me: Changing Human-Bird Relations on a Formosan Indigenous Territory." *Anthropologica* 62, no. 1: 70–84. https://doi.org/10.3138/anth.2018-0089.
- 2020b. "Yearning for Recognition: Indigenous Formosans and the Limits of Indigeneity." *International Journal of Taiwan Studies* 3, no. 2 (August): 191–216. https://doi.org/10.1163/24688800-00302002.
- 2021a. "The Limits of Indigenous Hunting Rights in Taiwan." East Asia Forum, 30 June. https://www.eastasiaforum.org/2021/06/30/the-limits-of-indigenous-hunting-rights-in-taiwan.

– 2021b. "Making God's Country: A Phenomenological Approach to Christianity among the Sediq-Truku of Taiwan." In *Taiwan's Contemporary Indigenous Peoples*, edited by Daffyd Fell, 34–52. London: Routledge Press.

– 2021c. "Wayfaring in Taiwan during COVID-19: Reflections on Political Ontologies of Disease and Geopolitics." *Anthropologica* 63, no. 1: 1–27. https://doi.org/10.18357/anthropologica6312021284.

– 2023. "Hunting Rights, Justice, and Reconciliation: Indigenous Experiences in Taiwan and Canada." In *Indigenous Reconciliation in Contemporary Taiwan: From Stigma to Hope*, edited by Scott E. Simon, Jolan Hsieh, and Peter Kang, 77–95. London: Routledge. https://doi.org/10.4324/9781003183136.

Simon, Scott, and Awi Mona. 2013. "L'autonomie autochtone à Taiwan : Un cadre légal en construction." In *Peuples autochtones dans la mondialisation : Les avancées du droit*, edited by Irène Bellier, 147–64. Paris: L'Harmattan.

Simpson, Audra. 2014. *Mohawk Interruptus: Political Life Across the Borders of Settler States*. Durham, NC: Duke University Press.

Simpson, Leanne Betasamosake. 2011. *Dancing on Our Turtle's Back: Stories of Nishnnabeg Re-creation, Resurgence, and a New Emergence*. Winnipeg: ARP Books.

Siragusa, Laura, Clinton N. Westman, and Sarah C. Moritz. 2020. "Shared Breath: Human and Nonhuman Copresence through Ritualized Words and Beyond." *Current Anthropology* 61, no. 4 (August): 471–94. https://doi.org/10.1086/710139.

Siyat Ulon 劉韶偉. 2004. *Gimi Ka Truku Zhaohui Tailuge* 找回太魯閣 [Recovering the Truku]. Taipei: Hanlu Tushu Chubanshe; 臺北市：翰蘆圖書出版公司.

Stafford, Charles, ed. 2013. *Ordinary Ethics in China*. London: Bloomsbury.

Stainton, Michael. 1995. *Return Our Land: Counterhegemonic Presbyterian Aboriginality in Taiwan*. Master's thesis, York University, Toronto.

– 2006 "Houshan, Qianshan, Mugan: Categories of Self and Other in a Tayal Village." In *History, Culture and Ethnicity: Selected Papers from the International Conference on the Formosan Indigenous Peoples*, edited by Yeh Chuen-rong, 393–426. Taipei: Shung Ye Museum of Formosan Aborigines.

Statistics Canada. 2017. "Life Expectancy." *Aboriginal Statistics at a Glance*, catalogue no. 89-645-X. https://www150.statcan.gc.ca/n1/pub/89-645-x/2010001/life-expectancy-esperance-vie-eng.htm.

– 2021a. "Table 11-10-0134-01: Gini Coefficients of Adjusted Market, Total and After-Tax Income." https://doi.org/10.25318/1110013401-eng.

– 2021b. "Table 14-10-0365-01: Labour Force Characteristics by Region and Detailed Indigenous Group." https://doi.org/10.25318/1410036501-eng.

Stefano, Varese. 1997. "Memories of Solidarity: Anthropology and the Indigenous Movement in Latin America." *Cultural Survival Quarterly*, 25 March. https://www.culturalsurvival.org/publications/cultural-survival-quarterly/memories-solidarity-anthropology-and-indigenous-movement.

Sterk, Darryl. 2019. "Translating Sovereignty into Seediq." Paper presented at the Association of Asian Studies, Denver, 22 March.

– 2020. *Indigenous Cultural Translation: A Thick Description of Seediq Bale*. London: Routledge.

– 2021. "Ecologising Seediq: Towards an Ecology of an Endangered Indigenous Language from Taiwan." *International Journal of Taiwan Studies* 4, no. 1 (March): 54–71. http://doi.org/10.1163/24688800-20201153.

Sugimoto, Tomonori. 2018. "Settler Colonial Incorporation and Inheritance: Historical Sciences, Indigeneity, and Settler Narratives in Post-WWII Taiwan." *Settler Colonial Studies* 8, no. 3 (July): 283–97. https://doi.org/10.1080/2201473X.2017.1303596.

– 2019. "Urban Settler Colonialism: Policing and Displacing Indigeneity in Taipei, Taiwan." *City & Society* 31, no. 2 (August): 227–50. https://doi.org/10.1111/ciso.12210.

Suzuki, Tadasu 鈴木質. 1932. *Taiwan Banjin fūzokushi* 台湾蕃人風俗誌 [Gazetteer of Taiwan savage customs]. Taihoku: Riban no tomo Hakkōjo; 台北：理蕃の友發行所.

Taintor, Edward C. 1874. *The Aborigines of Northern Formosa: A Paper Read before the North China Branch of the Royal Asiatic Society, Shanghai, 18th June 1874.* Shanghai: Customs Press.

Taiwan Affairs Office of the State Council. 2019. "Working Together to Realize Rejuvenation of the Chinese Nation and Advance China's Peaceful Reunification." Speech at the Meeting Marking the 40th Anniversary of the Issuance of the "Message to Compatriots in Taiwan," 2 January. http://www.gwytb.gov.cn/wyly/201904/t20190412_12155687.htm.

Takekoshi, Yosaburo. (1907) 1996. *Japanese Rule in Formosa*. Translated from the Japanese by George Braithwaite. Taipei: SMC.

Takoshima, Sunao 蛸島直. 2015. "台湾原住民の鳥占の多様性をめぐって" [About the diversity of ornithomancy among the aborigines of Taiwan]. 台湾原住民研究 [*Taiwan Indigenous Research*] 19 (November): 3–21.

Takun Walis 邱建堂. 2002. Kari Berah Rwahan Patis 序 [Preface]. In Chien, Iwan, and Kuo 2002, 5–6.

– 2012. 臺灣原住民餘生後裔眼中的霧社事件 [The Musha Incident in the eyes of the Taiwan Indigenous survivors]. Appendix 1 in Kuo 2012, 276–89.

Teng, Emma. 2004. *Taiwan's Imagined Geography: Chinese Colonial Travel Writing and Pictures, 1683–1895*. Cambridge, MA: Harvard University Asia Center.

Tera Yudaw 李季順. 2003. *Muda Hakaw Utux Zouguo caihong* 走過彩虹 [Crossing the Rainbow Bridge]. Hualien: Tailugezu Wenhua Gongzuofang; 花蓮：太魯閣族文化工作坊出版.

Thomas, Julia Adeney. 2001. *Reconfiguring Modernity: Concepts of Nature in Japanese Political Ideology*. Berkeley: University of California Press.

Tierney, Robert Thomas. 2010. *Tropics of Savagery: The Culture of Japanese Empire in Comparative Frame*. Berkeley: University of California Press.

Todd, Zoe. 2016. "An Indigenous Feminist's Take on the Ontological Turn: 'Ontology' Is Just Another Word for Colonialism." *Journal of Historical Sociology* 29, no. 1 (March): 4–22. https://doi.org10.1111/johs.12124.

Trouillot, Michel-Rolph. 2003. *Global Transformations: Anthropology and the Modern World*. New York: Palgrave Macmillan.

Tseng, Li-nan. 2006. "仁愛鄉長陳世光涉賄選案：一審判處一年徒刑" [Ren'ai Township Magistrate Chen Shih-kuang's election fraud case: Sentenced for one year]. 大紀元 [*Epoch Times*], 8 November. https://www.epochtimes.com/b5/6/11/8/n1514725.htm.

Tsing, Anna Lowenhaupt. 2005. *Friction: An Ethnography of Global Connection*. Princeton, NJ: Princeton University Press.

Tweed, Thomas A. 2006. *Crossing and Dwelling: A Theory of Religion*. Cambridge, MA: Harvard University Press.

Uno Toshiharu 宇野利玄. 2002. "台灣的「蕃人」教育" [Taiwan "savage" education]. In 台灣霧社蜂起事件研究與資料(上) [The aboriginal uprising of Musha, 1930: Studies and references, vol. 1], edited by Tai Kokoki 戴國煇, 114–56. Translated from the Japanese by Wei Ting-chao 魏廷朝. Taipei: Academia Historica; 台北：國史館.

Upton, John Christopher. 2020. *Culture on Trial: Law, Custom, and Justice in a Taiwan Indigenous Court*. PhD diss., Indiana University.

– 2021. "From Thin to Thick Justice and Beyond: Access to Justice and Legal Pluralism in Indigenous Taiwan." *Law & Social Inquiry* 47, no. 3 (August): 996–1025. https://doi.org/10.1017/lsi.2021.55.

Utsurikawa Nenozō, Mabuchi Tōichi, and Miyamoto Nobuhiro 移川子之蔵・馬淵東一・宮本延人. 1935. 台湾高砂族系統所属の研究 [Formosan native tribes: A genealogical and classificatory study]. Taihoku: Taihoku Imperial University Institute of Ethnology; 台北：台北帝国大学土俗人種学研究室.

Van Bekhoven, Jeroen. 2016. "Identity Crisis: Taiwan's Laws and Regulations on the Status of Indigenous Peoples." *Asia Pacific Law Review* 24, no. 2 (December): 202–32. https://doi.org/10.1080/10192557.2016.1245399.

– 2019. "Reforming the Constitution; Reforming the Postcolonial State? Indigenous Peoples and Constitutional Reforms in Taiwan." *Asian Journal of Comparative Law* 14, no. 2 (December): 245–78. https://doi.org/10.1017/asjcl.2019.28.

Van Gennep, Arnold. 1969. *The Rites of Passage*. Chicago: University of Chicago Press.

Walis Beilin 瓦歷斯・貝林. 2009. *Seediq Tgdaya* 的傳統領域與文化場域 [Seediq Tgdaya traditional territories and cultural fields]. Puli: Chi Nan University Institute of Anthropology; 埔里：暨大人類所.

Walis Nogan 瓦曆斯・諾杆 and Yu Guang-hong 余弘光. 2002. 臺灣原住民史 ：泰雅族史篇 [Taiwan's indigenous history: The Atayal]. Nantou: Taiwan Wenxian guan; 南投: 臺灣文獻館.

Wang, Fu-chang 王甫昌. 2002. "族群接觸機會？還是族群競爭？本省閩南人族群意識內涵與地區差異模式之解釋" [Opportunities for ethnic contact? Or ethnic competition? Explanations of the content of Native Taiwanese Minnan ethnic identity and modes of regional difference]. 台灣社會學 [*Taiwanese Sociology*] 4 (December): 11–74.

– 2004–5. "Why Did the DPP Win Taiwan's 2004 Presidential Election? An Ethnic Politics Interpretation." In "Domestic and International Considerations of Taiwan's 2004 Presidential Election: An Interdisciplinary Roundtable." *Pacific Affairs* 77, no. 4: (Winter): 691–6.

Wang, Mei-hsia 王梅霞. 2006. 泰雅族 [The Atayal]. Taipei: Sanmin; 台北 ：三民書局.

– 2008. "The Reinvention of Ethnicity and Culture: A Comparative Study on the Atayal and the Truku in Taiwan." *Journal of Archaeology and Anthropology* 68 (June): 1–44. https://doi.org/10.6152/jaa.2008.06.0001.

Wang, Ting-jieh. 2021. "Indigenous Peoples and the Politics of the Environment in Taiwan." In *Taiwan's Contemporary Indigenous Peoples*, edited by Chia-yuan Huang, Daniel Davies, and Dafydd Fell, 223–38. London: Routledge.

Wei Hwei-lin 衛惠林. 1965. 臺灣土著社會的部落組織與權威制度 [Tribal organization and authority systems of Taiwanese aboriginal society]. 考古人類學刊 [*Journal of Archaeology and Anthropology*] 25–26 (November): 71–92.

Wu Si-wei 吳思瑋. 2006. 賽德克族正式提復名 再起族群認同爭議 [The Seediq demand formally the return of their name: More debates on ethnic identity]. 大紀元 [*Epoch Times*], 7 April. https://www.epochtimes.com/b5/6/4/7/n1280419.htm.

Wu He. 2011. *Les survivants*. Translated from the Chinese by Esther Lin-Rosolato and Emmanuelle Péchenart. Arles: Actes Sud.

– 2017. *Remains of Life: A Novel*. Translated from the Chinese by Michael Berry. New York: Columbia University Press.

Xianfa Yuanzhuminzu Zhengce Zhixian Tuidong Xiaozu 憲法原住民族政策制憲推動小組 [Constitutional Indigenous Peoples Policy Constitution Promotion Group]. 2005. 原住民族憲法專章會議實錄 [Minutes of the meetings about a special section for Indigenous peoples in the Constitution]. Taipei: Council of Indigenous Peoples; 台北 ：原住民族委員會.

Yamada, Hitoshi 山田仁史. 2014. "夢占と鳥占：台湾原住民と東南アジアを中心に" [Oniromancy and ornithomancy: Centred on the aborigines of Taiwan and south-east Asia]. 台湾原住民研究 [*Taiwan Indigenous Research*] 18 (November): 3–26.

– 2015. *Religions ethnologie der Kopfjagd* 首狩の宗教民族学. Tokyo: Chikuma Shobō; 東京都 ：筑摩書房.

Yamaguchi, Masaji 山口政治. 1999. 東台湾開発史：花蓮港とタロコ [Development history of eastern Taiwan: Hualien Port and Taroko]. Tokyo: Chūnichi Sankei shijin; 東京：中日産経資訊.

Yan, Ai-ching 顔愛竟 and Kuo-chu Yang 楊國柱. 2004. 原住民族土地制度與經濟發展 [Indigenous peoples' land system and economic development]. Banqiao: Daoxiang Publishers; 板橋市：稻鄉.

Yang, Mayfair Mei-hui. 1994. *Gifts, Favors and Banquets: The Art of Social Relations in China*. Ithaca, NY: Cornell University Press.

Yang, Nan-chün. 2012. 台灣原住民族系統所屬之研究 [The Formosan native tribes: A genealogical and classificatory study]. Taipei: Council of Indigenous Peoples; 台北：原住民族委員會.

Yang, Pi-chuan. 2019. "The 228 Massacre in Alishan: 'All We Have Left Are Ashes and Bones.'" *The Taiwan Gazette*, 8 March. https://www .taiwangazette.org/news/2019/3/8/the-228-massacre-and-the-indigenous -people-of-alishan-all-we-have-left-are-ashes-and-bones.

Yang, Shu-Yuan. 2005. "Imagining the State: An Ethnographic Study." *Ethnography* 6, no. 4 (December): 487–516. https://doi.org/10.1177/1466138105062474.

– 2015. "The Indigenous Land Rights Movement and Embodied Knowledge in Taiwan." In "Social Movements and the Production of Knowledge: Body, Practice, and Society in East Asia," ed. Kyonosuke Hirai, special issue, *Senri Ethnological Studies* 91 (July): 25–43. http://doi.org/10.15021/00002338.

Young, Iris M. (1990) 2011. *Justice and the Politics of Difference*. Princeton, NJ: Princeton University Press.

Zelenietz, Martin. 1979. "The End of Headhunting in New Georgia." In *The Pacification of Melanesia*, edited by Margaret Rodman and Matthew Cooper, 91–108. Ann Arbor: University of Michigan Press.

Index

Notes: Following Formosan Indigenous convention, Indigenous names are not inverted in this index. Communities (Alang) are sorted under their respective names. For example, Alang Bsngan can be found under Bsngan. The letter *f* following a page number denotes a figure; the letter *t*, a table; the letter *m*, a map.

Formosan striped squirrel (*Tamiops maritinus*, tuku), 116
Frank, Andre Gunder, 22
free-listing exercise, 109
Freud, Sigmund, 161
Fried, Morton, 222
Friedman, Kerim, 63
Furuno Kiyoto, 136, 164–5, 189
Fushih Village, 74–5, 181–2, 183. *See also* Bsngan

gall bladder, 98, 309n6
ganqing 感情 (affection), 222, 223, 228
Gao Cai-yun (Obin Tadaw), 267–8, 315n7
Gaoshan Qing 高山青 (Green of the High Mountains; magazine), 207
Gao Yong-qing (Pihu Walis), 255, 260, 261, 267–8
garbage trucks, 15
Gaya (ancestral law, culture, political ontology): about, 4, 30–1, 32, 63, 94, 277, 281, 286, 289; alang (community) and, 16, 63, 274; author's engagement with, 277, 279; Christianity and, 177–9, 188–9, 190, 191; as culture, 93; vs. everyday ethics, 201–2; headhunting and, 125–8; human rights and, 286; hunting and, 81, 88, 97, 99–100, 117; land administration and, 16, 286; money and, 198; morality and, 31, 94; non-interference and, 61; as pathway to the future, 278–9, 295–6; rmuba (misfortune due to violating Gaya), 177–8, 288; sharing and, 100, 198, 286; sisil and, 106–7, 278; sovereignty and, 54, 63. *See also* lnglungan (heart); maduk (hunting); mgaya

(headhunting); samat (forest animals); tminun (weaving); utux (ancestors, spirits)
Gazetteer of Zhuluo County (1717), 39
geckos, 92
gender, 90, 91, 132, 171–2. *See also* men; women
generosity (mhuway), 200–1
geography, as lived experience, 29. *See also* maps
ghosts, 166, 175–6, 189, 269, 273
Ginawaydaganuk (Algonquin law, interconnectedness of all things), 4–5, 277
Gluban, Nantou (Alang Gluban): about, 73; author at, 65; Catholic church near, 182, 182f, 184; on colonialism, 260; establishment, 268; Musha Incident and, 254, 255, 258; reconciliation and, 276; rice harvest celebration, 74f; Sisters' Incident and, 258; 2:28 Incident and, 264–5
Gotō Shinpei, 66
Graeber, David, 312n9
grey-cheeked fulvetta (*Alcippe morrisonia*, sisil). *See* sisil
guanxi 關係 (relations), 222–3
Gungu (Alang Gungu), 72, 256, 259t, 260, 261, 268–9. *See also* Snuwil
guo 國 (country), 14, 308n8

Hakaw Utux (Rainbow Bridge), 99, 163, 165, 184, 238
Hakka, 103, 202, 204, 207. *See also* Han Taiwanese
Hanaoka Ichirō (Dakis Nobing), 255, 262
Hanaoka Jirō (Dakis Nawi), 255, 262, 267
Han Kuo-yu, Daniel, 214, 293

peoples; Formosan Indigenous peoples; indigeneity; Indigenous resurgence; Indigenous rights movements

Indigenous Peoples Basic Law (2005): basis in Indigenous sovereignty and rights, 26, 87, 226; critique of, 282; hunting and, 85; implementation of, 17, 87; as indigeneity, 283; legal definitions in, 13–14; Taiwanese state-led indigeneity and, 198; Talum Suqluman case and, 118

Indigenous resurgence: culture and, 24; decolonization of anthropology and, 286–9; hunting and, 82, 117, 310n10; indigeneity and, 25, 283–5; as pathway to future, 296; in Taiwan, 62–3, 191, 278; Western understandings and, 61–2

Indigenous rights movements: anthropology and, 24–5; beginnings of in Taiwan, 45, 207–8; politics and, 198–9, 208; Presbyterian Church and, 45, 62, 151, 156, 208, 209–10, 284; Wu Feng headhunting myth and, 123

influenza, Spanish, 262

Ingold, Tim: on Cartesian space, 35; on common stream of consciousness, 239; on ecological crisis, 288; on getting to know nature, 116; on hunting, 99; on indigeneity, 25–6; on intergenerational transmission of perceptual skills, 95; on knots in the meshwork of life, 30, 161; on religion, 176

ini klgug (plants, things that don't move), 92

insects (kuwi), 92

Iroquois, 8, 21–2, 38, 315n4
Isak Afo, 53
Ishii, Shinji, 154

jade, nephrite, 37
James, William, 162
Japan, 40, 56, 94
Japanese colonialism, in Taiwan: ethnographic literature from, 66, 89, 164–5; Formosan Indigenous peoples and, 12, 14–15, 16, 40–3, 47, 208–9, 223, 237, 241, 244, 256, 289; headhunting and, 135–6, 145–6; Hsincheng Incident (1896), 241; intermarriage with locals, 314n5; Japanese policemen, 260–1; religious change under, 173–4, 189–90; Sisters' Incident (1903), 258, 265; tattoo prohibition, 126–7; violence by, 273; Weili Incident (1906), 241

Japanese white-eye (*Zosterops japonicus*, psima), 113
Jingying Village, 72. *See also* Buarung

kaalang (foreigners), 133, 134, 266
Kado Kimi (Ai Chung-Chih), 125–6, 131, 246, 312nn12–13
Kaji Cihung, 4, 31, 107, 166, 195, 311n2
Kanakanavu, 46t, 48t
Kangxi (Qing emperor), 35
Kano, Tadao, 106
Kavalan, 28m, 46t, 48t
Kbayan (Alang Kbayan), 245
Kele, Hualien (Alang Qlgi), 75–6
Ke Shih-mei, 223, 224f, 225–6, 315n9
Khilan (Hakka), 204. *See also* Hakka
Kimi Sibal, 7, 57–9, 60, 61, 127

Anthropological Horizons

Editor: Michael Lambek, University of Toronto

Of Property and Propriety: The Role of Gender and Class in Imperialism and Nationalism/Edited by Himani Bannerji, Shahrzad Mojab, and Judith Whitehead (2001)

An Irish Working Class: Explorations in Political Economy and Hegemony, 1800–1950/Marilyn Silverman (2001)

The Double Twist: From Ethnography to Morphodynamics/Edited by Pierre Maranda (2001)

The House of Difference: Cultural Politics and National Identity in Canada/Eva Mackey (2002)

Writing and Colonialism in Northern Ghana: The Encounter between the LoDagaa and "the World on Paper," 1892–1991/Sean Hawkins (2002)

Guardians of the Transcendent: An Ethnography of a Jain Ascetic Community/Anne Vallely (2002)

The Hot and the Cold: Ills of Humans and Maize in Native Mexico/Jacques M. Chevalier and Andrés Sánchez Bain (2003)

Figured Worlds: Ontological Obstacles in Intercultural Relations/Edited by John Clammer, Sylvie Poirier, and Eric Schwimmer (2004)

Revenge of the Windigo: The Construction of the Mind and Mental Health of North American Aboriginal Peoples/James B. Waldram (2004)

The Cultural Politics of Markets: Economic Liberalization and Social Change in Nepal/Katharine Neilson Rankin (2004)

A World of Relationships: Itineraries, Dreams, and Events in the Australian Western Desert/Sylvie Poirier (2005)

The Politics of the Past in an Argentine Working-Class Neighbourhood/Lindsay DuBois (2005)

Youth and Identity Politics in South Africa, 1990–1994/Sibusisiwe Nombuso Dlamini (2005)

Maps of Experience: The Anchoring of Land to Story in Secwepemc Discourse/Andie Diane Palmer (2005)

We Are Now a Nation: Croats between "Home" and "Homeland"/Daphne N. Winland (2007)

Beyond Bodies: Rainmaking and Sense Making in Tanzania/Todd Sanders (2008)

Kaleidoscopic Odessa: History and Place in Contemporary Ukraine/Tanya Richardson (2008)

Invaders as Ancestors: On the Intercultural Making and Unmaking of Spanish Colonialism in the Andes/Peter Gose (2008)

From Equality to Inequality: Social Change among Newly Sedentary Lanoh Hunter-Gatherer Traders of Peninsular Malaysia/Csilla Dallos (2011)

Rural Nostalgias and Transnational Dreams: Identity and Modernity among Jat Sikhs/Nicola Mooney (2011)

Dimensions of Development: History, Community, and Change in Allpachico, Peru/Susan Vincent (2012)

Printed and bound by CPI Group (UK) Ltd, Croydon, CR0 4YY

09/06/2025

14685790-0001